This is the second of three volumes containing papers presented in the invited symposium of the Seventh World Congress of the Econometric Society. The papers summarize and interpret key recent developments and discuss current and future directions in a wide range of topics in economics and econometrics. They cover both theory and applications. Authored by leading specialists in their fields, these volumes provide a unique survey of progress in the discipline

Econometric Society Monographs No. 27

Advances in economics and econometrics: theory and applications

Volume II

Advances in economics and econometrics: theory and applications

Seventh World Congress

Volume II

Edited by

DAVID M. KREPS

and

KENNETH F. WALLIS

CAMBRIDGE
UNIVERSITY PRESS

Published by the Press Syndicate of the University of Cambridge
The Pitt Building, Trumpington Street, Cambridge CB2 1RP
40 West 20th Street, New York, NY 10011-4211, USA
10 Stamford Road, Oakleigh, Melbourne 3166, Australia

First published 1997

Printed in Great Britain at the University Press, Cambridge

A catalogue record for this book is available from the British Library

A catalogue record for this book is available from the Library of Congress

ISBN 0 521 58012 9 hardback
ISBN 0 521 58982 7 paperback

VN

Contents

Contributors

Robert Gibbons
Cornell University

N. F. R. Crafts
London School of Economics

Avner Greif
Stanford University

Partha Dasgupta
University of Cambridge

Robert M. Townsend
University of Chicago

John McMillan
University of California, San Diego

Mathias Dewatripont
Université Libre de Bruxelles

Gérard Roland
Université Libre de Bruxelles

Philippe Aghion
Nuffield College, Oxford

Peter Howitt
Université des Sciences Sociales de Toulouse

Boyan Jovanovic
New York University

Preface

This book contains papers presented in the invited symposium sessions of the Seventh World Congress of the Econometric Society, held at Keio University, Tokyo in August 1995, for which we were Program Co-Chairs. The papers summarize and interpret key recent developments and discuss current and future directions in a wide range of topics in economics and econometrics. These were chosen on the basis of their broad interest to members of the Society, and so cover both theory and applications, and to demonstrate the progress made in the period since the previous World Congress. The program also reflected the fact that this was the first World Congress held outside Europe and North America. The authors are leading specialists in their fields, yet do not overemphasize their own reseach contributions. In one case, the two speakers in the session have combined their papers into a single chapter for this book – a long one, needless to say.

The more general objectives are reflected in the presentation of all the papers in a single book under a general title, with joint editorship, thus departing from the previous practice of separate "economic theory" and "econometrics" books. The size of the book has necessitated its division into three volumes, and thematic connections have suggested the contents of each volume. Within each volume the papers appear in the order of their presentation in Toyko, which we hope will help readers who were there to remember what a marvellous occasion the Congress was.

We are grateful to the members of our Program Committee for much valuable advice, to the Chairs and discussants of the invited symposium sessions for their contributions, and to Patrick McCartan at Cambridge University Press for his guidance during the preparation and production of this book. More generally we wish to acknowledge the steadfast support we received in our task from Robert and Julie Gordon, respectively Treasurer and Secretary of the Society, and from Masahiro Okuno-Fujiwara, Chair of the Local Organizing Committee for the Congress.

David M. Kreps
Kenneth F. Wallis

CHAPTER 1

Incentives and careers in organizations

Robert Gibbons

An outsider might be surprised to learn that modern labor economics has little to say about activities inside firms. After all, is not work (i.e., what workers do once they go through a firm's doors) one of the field's most natural areas of inquiry?

Let's take stock. Several research areas in labor economics end precisely when an employment relationship begins: unemployment duration and labor-force participation are examples, and even labor demand typically focuses on how many workers should be hired rather than on what the firm should then do with them. Other research areas in labor economics reduce the employment relationship to a wage, or at most a wage profile: on-the-job search, labor supply, and human-capital models of earnings, for example. Even research on the return to seniority more often focuses on econometric issues than on what actually happens during an employment relationship; similarly, research on training more often focuses on pre-employment government-sponsored programs than on skill development in firms. Simply put, modern labor economics contains little work on work.

The situation may be changing. In this chapter I describe theory and evidence on two aspects of some employment relationships: incentive pay and careers in organizations.[1] Most of the theory I describe is recent, emphasizing games and contracts rather than the workhorse theories of labor economics in the 1970s and 1980s, human capital and search. Much of the evidence is also new, at least in the sense of not having been part of the published discourse in labor economics over the last few decades. This same evidence is also old, however, both in the sense of sometimes referring to events long past (sharecropping in 1910 or a machine shop in Chicago around 1950, for example) and in the sense of sometimes being fairly well-known outside labor economics.

Because there is not much empirical work on employment relationships in labor economics, I draw on other fields – including accounting, human resource management, industrial relations, and organizational sociology – whenever my exposure allows. Unfortunately, data on employment relationships often must be collected virtually by hand. Doing the hard work of data collection and utilizing the microeconometric expertise that has become the hallmark of labor economics are crucial next steps for this emerging literature. In the meantime, I limit discussion of theory to classes of models that seem likely to deliver empirical implications (or, better still, have already done so).

1 INCENTIVE PAY

There are many senses in which pay may be linked to performance. Perhaps the simplest case is where workers' productivities differ and wages equal marginal products. More often, however, the phrase "pay for performance" connotes the provision of incentives. In this section I discuss the dominant model of incentive contracting, the principal-agent model.[2]

Several of the main issues can be illustrated quite simply in the context of sharecropping. Three standard sharecropping contracts are: wage labor, which imposes no risk on the agent; crop sharing, which shares risk between the principal and the agent; and fixed-payment land rental, which leaves the agent with all the crop risk. The classic agency model, which emphasizes the tradeoff between incentives and insurance, implies that where there is greater crop risk there should also be more risk sharing – more used of fixed wages and crop sharing rather than land rental. Higgs (1973) presents evidence consistent with this prediction: for both cotton and corn, and for two empirical measures of risk, a cross-sectional analysis of the southern states of the US for 1910 finds more risk sharing in states with greater crop risk. But Alston and Higgs (1982) document that Higgs's comforting finding obscures both (1) enormous variation within each of these main classes of contracts and (2) significant variation across the three classes of contracts even after controlling for risk.

Both the organization and the spirit of this section parallel this research on sharecropping. Parallel to Higgs's paper, I begin by summarizing the theory and evidence on the classic agency model. Parallel to Alston and Higgs's paper, I then explore five new issues, in the hope of accounting for some of the enormous richness in incentive contracting that the classic agency model simply chalks up as unexplained variation. I conclude that risk is a significant issue in incentive contracting, but that the principal-agent literature's initial obsession with its consequences distracted us from a host of equally important issues.

1.1 The much-studied tradeoff between incentives and insurance

The classic model in agency theory involves an agent who takes an action a to produce output of value y. The principal owns the output but contracts to share it with the agent by paying a wage contingent on output, $w(y)$. There is noise in the production function, so the agent's output is uncertain. Furthermore, the agent is risk averse. Paying a constant wage, independent of y, would provide the agent with full insurance but no incentive; selling the agent the firm for a fee of F (or, equivalently, paying the agent $w(y) = y - F$) would provide the agent with full incentives but no insurance.

An intuitive closed-form solution can be derived in the linear-normal-exponential case. The production function is linear, $y = a + \varepsilon$, where ε is a normally distributed noise term with zero mean and variance σ^2. The incentive contract is linear, $w(y) = s + by$, where the intercept s is the salary and the slope b is the bonus rate. The agent's utility function is $U(x) = -e^{-rx}$, where $r > 0$ is the agent's coefficient of absolute risk aversion and $x = w - c(a)$ is the agent's net payoff – the realized wage minus the convex disutility of action $c(a)$. The principal is risk neutral and so seeks to maximize the expected value of profit, $y - w$.

Given a contract $w(y) = s + by$, the agent's problem is to choose an action to maximize the expected utility

$$\int_\varepsilon e^{-r[s+b(a+\varepsilon)-c(a)]}\phi(\varepsilon)d\varepsilon = -e^{-r[s+ba-c(a)]}\int_\varepsilon e^{-rb\varepsilon}\phi(\varepsilon)d\varepsilon,$$

where $\phi(\varepsilon)$ denotes the normal density function. The agent's optimal action, denoted $a^*(b)$, solves $c'(a) = b$. The agent's maximized expected utility is therefore

$$-e^{-r\{s+ba^*(b)-c[a^*(b)]\}}\int_\varepsilon e^{-rb\varepsilon}\phi(\varepsilon)d\varepsilon$$
$$= -e^{-r\{s+ba^*(b)-c[a^*(b)]-(\frac{1}{2})rb^2\sigma^2\}},$$

so the agent's equivalent is

$$CE(s,b) = s + ba^*(b) - c[a^*(b)] - \tfrac{1}{2}rb^2\sigma^2.$$

That is, the agent's certainty equivalent from the contract $w(y) = s + by$ is the expected wage minus the cost of effort minus the cost of bearing risk. The principal's expected profit is

$$E^\pi(s,b) = (1-b)a^*(b) - s,$$

so the total surplus (i.e., the sum of the principal's expected profit and the agent's certainty equivalent) depends on b but not on s

$$CE(s, b) + E\Pi(s, b) = a^*(b) - c[a^*(b)] - \tfrac{1}{2}rb^2\sigma^2 = TS(b).$$

We can now determine the efficient contract slope, denoted b^*: it is the slope that maximizes the total surplus $TS(b)$. If the parties agreed to a contract with some other slope then both parties could be made better off by switching to a contract with slope b^* and choosing an appropriate value of s to distribute the increased total surplus. The first-order condition for b^* is $a^{*\prime} - c'a^{*\prime} - rb\sigma^2 = 0$. Because $c'[a^*(b)] = b$, we have $a^{*\prime} = 1/c''$ and hence

$$b^* = \frac{1}{1 + r\sigma^2 c''}.$$

This result makes sense. Since r, σ^2, and c'' are positive, b^* is between zero (full insurance) and one (full incentives). Furthermore, b^* is smaller if the agent is more risk averse (r is higher) or there is more uncertainty in production (σ^2 is higher) or marginal disutility increases more quickly (c'' is higher).

This solution to the classic model is tidy but flawed: Mirrlees (1974) showed that the best linear contract, $w = s + b^*y$, is inferior to various non-linear contracts. In particular, a step-function contract (where the agent earns w_H if $y \geq y_0$ but $w_L < w_H$ if $y < y_0$) can perform very well, approaching the twin goals of full incentives and full insurance in the limit (as y_0 and w_L decrease in appropriate fashion, so that the agent almost surely receives w_H and yet has incentives from fear of w_L). Mirrlees's result prompted a decade of research on how the optimal contract depends on the details of the utility function and the conditional distribution of output given the agent's action. In brief, this work showed that the optimal contract in the classic agency model is extremely sensitive to these details. In particular, the optimal contract is linear only under very special assumptions about the utility function and the conditional distribution of output.

Holmstrom and Milgrom (1987) reinterpreted the classic agency model so as to rescue linear contracts. Rather than a single action (a) that influences a single outcome (y), Holmstrom and Milgrom envision a sequence of actions (say, one per day, over the course of a year) influencing a corresponding sequence of outcomes. There are no connections across days (i.e., the action a_t on day t affects that day's outcome, y_t, but has no influence on any other day's outcome) and all past outcomes are observed before the next day's action is chosen. The output y from the classic model is interpreted as the aggregate output for the year in the sequential-action model: $y = \Sigma y_t$.

Suppose that each day's outcome takes one of two values – say L or H. Then a *one-day* incentive contract is simply a pair of wages: w_H is paid if the outcome is H; w_L if L. Suppose that the agent labors under the same one-day contract for all the days of the year. If there are T days in the year and the agent produces H on N of these days then the aggregate output for the year is $y = TL + N(H - L)$ and the aggregate wage for the year is $w = Tw_L + N(w_H - w_L)$. Thus, $N = (y - TL)/(H - L)$ and

$$w = \frac{T(Hw_L - Lw_H)}{H - L} + \frac{w_H - w_L}{H - L} y = s + by.$$

That is, if the agent labors under the same one-day contract throughout the year then the aggregate wage is a linear function of the aggregate output. Given several other assumptions, Holmstrom and Milgrom show not only that it is optimal for the agent to labor under a constant one-day contract but also that the optimal slope in the aggregate representation of this contract (i.e., $w = s + by$) is b^*, just as in the classic agency model.

In my view, the main contribution of this Holmstrom–Milgrom model is not that it justifies linear contracts (by imposing quite strong assumptions), but rather that it alerts us to gaming as a natural consequence of non-linearity. For example, a step-function contract of the kind studied by Mirrlees (in the classic one-action model) induces no effort once the agent's aggregate output to date passes the hurdle y_0 (in the daily-action model). More generally, if the incentive contract for the year is a non-linear function of year-end aggregate output then the worker's incentives change from day to day, depending on the aggregate output to date. A growing body of evidence is consistent with this prediction: see Healy (1985) on bonus plans with ceilings and floors, Asch (1990) and Oyer (1995) on bonuses tied to quotas, Chevalier and Ellison (1995) on the effects of even modest convexities in smooth pay plans, and Ehrenberg and Bognanno (1990) on performance across rounds in professional golf tournaments.[3]

There is other evidence more closely related to the classic agency model. One basic question is "Does pay vary with performance?" For example, by the early 1980s, the received wisdom was that the compensation of chief executive officers (CEOs) in large US firms was closely related to the firm's size but unrelated (or even negatively related!) to its stock-market performance. Murphy (1985) noted, however, that if big firms pay higher salaries but small firms have superior stock-market performance (the "small-firm effect" from finance) then a cross-section regression of cash compensation (salary plus bonus) on stock-market performance will be biased downwards, unless there are adequate controls for firm heterogeneity. Murphy found that including fixed effects in a panel-data model produces a strong statistical relationship between CEO pay and stock-market performance.[4]

A second basic question is "Do incentives matter?" In brief, the answer is "Yes." For example, the evidence summarized above on the effects of non-linear incentive plans motivates this conclusion. Others have studied the proposition that steeper slopes create stronger incentives: $a^*(b)$ increases with b. Lazear (1996), for example, finds that the output of workers installing automobile windshields increased after a switch from hourly wages to piece rates.[5] Abowd (1990) and Kahn and Sherer (1990) estimate the sensitivity of managerial pay to current performance and then estimate the effect of this sensitivity on subsequent performance.[6] The results are generally consistent with the theory but are somewhat noisy, in keeping with having to estimate rather than observe the relation between pay and performance. Gaynor and Gertler (1995) use data on medical partnerships, where the sharing rule is included in the data but was chosen by the partners. Their instrumental-variable estimates again are consistent with the simple proposition that incentives matter. Finally, there is evidence that investors believe that incentives matter. Brickley, Bhagat, and Lease (1985) find that there is a significant increase in a firm's stock price (net of any movement in the market as a whole) when the firm announces a stock-based compensation plan; Tehranian and Waegelein (1985) present analogous evidence for announcements of accounting-based bonus contracts.

There is also evidence related to the main idea behind the classic agency model – the tradeoff between incentives and insurance. For example, there is evidence that the slope falls as risk or risk aversion increases. As noted earlier, Higgs (1973) presents evidence from sharecropping in 1910 that the slope falls as risk increases; Garen (1994) offers similar evidence for CEOs of large US firms. Gaynor and Gertler (1995) find that the slope of the sharing rule in medical partnership falls as the partners' risk aversion increases.

The tradeoff between insurance and incentives produces further predictions in a richer model with multiple performance measures, as follows. Suppose there is a second performance measure, $z = a + \mu$, where μ is a normally distributed noise term possibly correlated with ε. (Theoretical and empirical work in accounting often interprets y as the change in the firm's stock-market value and z as the firm's accounting earnings, but many other interpretations are possible.) Consider the contract $w = s + by + dz$. Holmstrom (1979) shows that the optimal contract uses both performance measures (i.e., $b^* \neq 0$ and $d^* \neq 0$) unless one is a sufficient statistic for the other. That is, $d^* = 0$ only if z contains no additional information about the agent's action beyond what is contained in y (i.e., $z = y + \phi$, or $\mu = \varepsilon + \phi$, where ϕ is independent of ε); likewise, $b^* = 0$ only if y contains no additional information beyond z (i.e., $y = z + \phi$, or $\varepsilon = \mu + \phi$, where ϕ is independent of μ). In Holmstrom's model, therefore, performance measures are simply signals about the agent's action, and a signal is not useful if it conveys no incremental information.

Some performance measures come from outside the firm, such as from other firms in the same industry. Consider n firms, each subject to a common shock (θ) and an idiosyncratic shock (ε_i). Suppose $y_i = a_i + \theta + \varepsilon_i$, where θ and $(\varepsilon_1, \ldots, \varepsilon_n)$ are independent normal noise terms. Let z_i denote the average of the $n - 1$ other firms' outputs (y_j). Then the pure own-performance contract $w_i = s + by_i$ subjects the agent to two noise terms, θ and ε_i, whereas the pure relative-performance contract $w_i = s + b(y_i - z_i)$ eliminates θ but subjects the agent to ε_i and to the average of the $n - 1$ other idiosyncratic error terms (ε_j). Holmstrom (1982a) shows that the efficient contract is $w_i = s + by_i - dz_i$, where $b^* > d^* > 0$. That is, the efficient contract reflects a tradeoff between eliminating the risk from θ (through the pure relative-performance contract) and avoiding the risk from the average of the $n - 1$ other error terms (through a pure own-performance contract). If the variance of θ is small then it is not worth introducing the risk from the $n - 1$ other error terms so d^* is close to zero; if the variance of θ is large then it is important that the contract filter out θ, even at the cost of introducing risk from the other error terms, so d^* is close to b^*.

Antle and Smith (1986) look for evidence of relative performance evaluation in CEO pay. Using data on 39 firms in three two-digit industries, they find weak support for the theory, even though they carefully compute the correlation in "output" for each pair of firms. Gibbons and Murphy (1990) use a less-sophisticated approach but a much larger dataset, including data on pay and performance from 1,000 firms, with performance comparisons computed from data on 11,000 firms. Gibbons and Murphy find stronger support for the theory: CEO pay depends on the firm's stock-market performance relative to the market as a whole and (additionally) on the firm's stock-market performance relative to its one-digit industry. Janakiraman, Lambert, and Larcker (1992) estimate separate regressions for each of 554 firms (as opposed to the pooled regression in Gibbons and Murphy). The mean of the firm-specific estimates in Janakiraman, Lambert, and Larcker is similar to the pooled coefficient in Gibbons and Murphy.[7]

In sum, there is a large body of theory and evidence related to the classic agency model. The theory has developed several insights, such as the role of linear contracts in deterring gaming and the interpretation of performance measures as signals of the agent's action. The evidence is broadly consistent with both the basic theory and its extension to multiple performance measures. But the literature does not explain (or even hint at) why paying for performance is so problematic for many firms.

1.2 Complications in real incentive contracts

The main idea behind the classic agency model is that there is a tradeoff between incentives and insurance, but the most striking single fact about real attempts to tie pay to performance is that it is a tricky business. The following examples are all too typical:

> At the H.J. Heinz Company, division managers received bonuses only if earnings increased from the prior year. The managers delivered consistent earnings growth by manipulating the timing of shipments to customers and by prepaying for services not yet received, both at some cost to the firm (Post and Goodpaster 1981). At Bausch & Lomb, the hurdle for a bonus was higher, often entailing double-digit earnings growth. Again, managers met their targets in ways that were not obviously in the best long-run interest of the firm (e.g., over half a million pairs of "sold" sunglasses were discovered in a warehouse in Hong Kong; Maremont 1995). At Dun & Bradstreet, salespeople earned no commission unless the customer bought a larger subscription to the firm's credit-report services than in the previous year. In 1989, the company faced millions of dollars in lawsuits following charges that its salespeople deceived customers into buying larger subscriptions by fraudulently overstating their historical usage (Roberts 1989). In 1992, Sears abolished the commission plan in its auto-repair shops, which paid mechanics based on the profits from repairs authorized by customers. Mechanics misled customers into authorizing unnecessary repairs, leading California officials to prepare to close Sears' auto-repair business statewide. (Patterson (1992))

In brief, "business history is littered with firms that got what they paid for" (Baker, Gibbons, and Murphy (1994, p. 1125)).[8]

I find it hard to relate the classic agency model to this evidence (and the larger body of evidence it represents). First, much of the evidence concerns non-linear contracts, whereas the classic model began with (and has recently returned to) linear contracts. Second, I see no necessary role for risk aversion in this evidence, whereas in the classic model the only reason to limit incentives is to provide insurance. Third, and most important, the performance measures used in these real incentive contracts differ from those envisioned in the classic model, as I describe below. In this subsection, therefore, I abandon the classic model, turning instead to five other issues in incentive contracting – performance measurement, implicit contracts, labor mobility, the ratchet effect, and career concerns. To emphasize that these five issues are departures from the classic model, I assume throughout this subsection that the agent is risk neutral. For lack of space, I give only brief attention to labor mobility, the ratchet effect, and career concerns; I focus on performance measurement and implicit contracts because I believe that together they offer an important complement to the classic agency model.

1 *Performance measurement* I lack the information to assess whether the incentive plans at Heinz, Bausch & Lomb, Dun & Bradstreet, and Sears were mistakes (as opposed to best responses to tough environments), but some of my colleagues in organizational behavior (OB) are less reticent. Kerr's (1975) classic title conveys his field's judgment: "On the folly of rewarding A, while hoping for B." Kerr's paper is so well known in OB that it has earned a place in the canonical MBA core course on organizations; in economics, in contrast, until recently there was no model that could even express Kerr's idea, not to mention evaluate or extend it.

Fortunately, Holmstrom and Milgrom (1991) and Baker (1992) now offer simple models of such distortionary performance measurement. Both emphasize the distinction between the agent's total contribution to firm value (henceforth denoted y) and the agent's measured performance (henceforth p). Even well-informed insiders may find it extremely difficult to assess an agent's total contribution to firm value, because total contribution includes aspects of performance such as the effects of the agent's actions on co-workers and the long-run effects of the agent's current actions. Furthermore, to enforce a contract contingent on the agent's total contribution, the parties would have to specify *ex ante* how y is to be measured *ex post* (so that a court would know what to measure if called in to enforce the contract).

These difficulties are assumed away in the classic agency model: the agent's total contribution is called "output," as though it could simply be counted at the end of the contract period, and contracts such as $w = s + by$ are assumed to be simple to write and enforce. The classic model may capture some employment relationships, where there are few interactions among co-workers and few long-run effects of current actions. Lazear's (1996) study of piece rates paid to workers installing auto windshields may be one example; more generally, Brown (1990) finds that piece rates are more likely to be used in jobs with a narrow set of routines than in jobs with a variety of duties.

In a vast array of jobs, however, the Holmstrom–Milgrom and Baker distinction between total contribution and measured performance seems crucially important. For example, Eccles and Crane (1988) describe how investment banks deliver a substantial fraction of a trader's compensation through a subjectively determined bonus, even though many objective aspects of the individual's performance are easily measured on a daily basis.

Similarly, Burtis and Gabarro (1995) offer a fictitious but persuasive account of the difficulties of performance evaluation in a law firm: nine objective measures paint a narrow and distorted picture (even when combined with four subjective assessments). Evaluating the performance of almost any manager or professional worker seems likely to involve similar issues – for example, see Greene and Schlesinger (1992) on incentive pay in a cable television firm. Finally, the recent enthusiasm for empowerment, participation, and self-managed teams suggests that difficulties in performance evaluation may become increasingly important for non-managerial workers as well.

Baker models the worker's contribution to firm value as $y = \theta a + \varepsilon$, whereas measured performance is $p = \mu a + v$. As in the classic model, ε and v are noise terms (independent of θ, μ, and each other), but θ and μ are features of the environment that are privately observed by the worker before choosing an action. As motivated above, Baker assumes that a contract contingent on y cannot be enforced, so the firm is reduced to contracting on p, through the linear contract $w = s + bp$. Because the agent's utility, $w - c(a)$, depends on p, the agent will be induced to take large actions when dp/da (i.e., μ) is large; because the firm's profit, $y - w$, depends importantly on y, the firm will value large actions when dy/da (i.e., θ) is large. Hence Baker's central insight: a good performance measure induces the agent to do the right thing at the right time (i.e., to work hard when doing so is valuable to the firm), so the quality of a performance measure depends on the correlation between dp/da and dy/da. Thus, whereas the classic model views a performance measure as a signal of the agent's action, Baker focuses on the value of the actions that a contract based on the performance measure will induce.

When measured performance omits important dimensions of total contribution, firms understand that they will "get what they pay for," and so may choose weak incentives in preference to strong but frequently dysfunctional incentives. In Kerr's terms, the Holmstrom–Milgrom and Baker models explore environments in which it might be necessary to reward A while hoping for B, but these models caution against over rewarding A.[9]

2 *Implicit contracts* A worker's total contribution to firm value may be impossible for a court to measure using a method specified *ex ante*, but well-informed insiders may nonetheless agree *ex post* on a particular worker's contribution (or at least on an estimate of this contribution). The great advantage of such *ex post* settling up is that the parties can take into account events that occurred during the contract period that were not foreseen (or were not articulated) *ex ante*. Thus, it might be possible for the

worker and the firm to use an "implicit" contract (i.e., an understanding backed by the parties' reputations instead of law) based on total contribution (y) rather than an "explicit" contract backed by a court but based on distortionary performance measures (p). For example, the firm might promise to pay a bonus if the worker's total contribution exceeds a critical level. The problem is that the firm will be tempted to renege, pocketing the worker's contribution and saving the bonus.

Bull (1987) and MacLeod and Malcomson (1989) model such implicit contracts as repeated-game equilibria. In these models, the firm chooses not to renege only if the present value of the ongoing relationship outweighs the immediate gain from reneging. For example, suppose that y can be either L or H, and suppose that the firm pays a salary of S at the beginning of the period and promises to pay a bonus of B at the end of the period if $y = H$. If the worker believes that the firm will keep its promise then the prospect of the bonus induces an optimal action $a^*(B)$ from the worker, which in turn determines the firm's expected profit per period from keeping its promise, $E\pi(S,B)$.

Suppose that the worker will leave the firm if the firm reneges on a bonus. (Stewart's (1993) account of the rupture of the subjective bonus plan at the investment bank First Boston suggests how difficult it is for a firm to regain its workers' trust after it is perceived to have reneged on an implicit contract.) If the worker produces $y = H$ then the firm can either pay the bonus, resulting in a payoff of $H - S - B$ this period and a payoff of $E\pi(S,B)$ in all future periods, or renege on the bonus, resulting in a payoff of $H - S$ this period but the loss of the worker thereafter. For simplicity, normalize the firm's payoff after reneging to zero, perhaps from employing a new worker at a wage equal to productivity. Then, given an interest rate r, the present value from paying the bonus exceeds the present value from reneging if

$$H - S - B + \frac{1}{r} E\pi(S,B) \geq H - S + \frac{1}{r} \cdot 0,$$

or $E\pi(S,B) \geq rB$. Thus, a decrease in the profitability of the ongoing relationship may wreck an implicit contract; the collapse of the junk bond market may have been just such a precipitating event at First Boston.

Some firms use both explicit and implicit contracts. Lincoln Electric, for example, is well-known for its use of piece rates, but about half of a worker's compensation rides on a subjectively determined bonus (Fast and Berg (1975)). Baker, Gibbons, and Murphy (1994) explore the simultaneous use of explicit contracts based on distortionary performance measures (e.g., $w = s + bp$) and implicit contracts based on total contribution (e.g., $W = S + By$, so that total compensation is $w + W$). One role of the explicit contract is to reduce the size of the implicit-contract bonus that the firm could save by reneging; one role of the implicit contract is to reduce the distortionary incentives created by the explicit contract. Baker, Gibbons, and Murphy show that, under one set of circumstances, the two types of contract are complementary: if the performance measure (p) becomes less distortionary (i.e., if the correlation between dp/da and dy/da increases) then the explicit contract increases the profitability of the ongoing relationship, thereby making it credible for the firm to promise a larger bonus in the implicit contract. Under the opposite circumstances, explicit contracts hinder implicit contracts: if the explicit contract alone is sufficiently effective then the firm's payoff after reneging is not zero but rather the payoff from using the optimal explicit contract alone; as this payoff increases, it becomes more tempting for the firm to renege on an implicit contract, reducing the bonus the firm can credibly promise.

3 *Labor mobility* One of the fundamental assumptions in labor economics is that workers cannot be bound to firms. That is, firms may provide financial inducements for workers to stay, but a contract stipulating that a worker must stay would not be upheld by a court (as least in the US and similar settings). This assumption pervades the literature on wage determination, from Becker's (1962) analysis of general-purpose human capital to Harris and Holmstrom's (1982) and Beaudry and DiNardo's (1991) analyses of incomplete insurance. The classic agency model, on the other hand, makes the opposite assumption: once the worker has been induced to sign the incentive contract, its eventual consequences can be enforced on the worker. The following evidence from sharecropping suggests that labor mobility may be quite important in incentive contracting, especially if one adopts the Holmstrom–Milgrom sequential-action reinterpretation of the classic agency model.

Recall that Higgs (1973) found that states with higher crop risk have less risk sharing in their sharecropping contracts (i.e., more wage labor and less crop sharing and fixed-payment land rental), but that Alston and Higgs (1982) found significant variation across the three classes of contract even after controlling for risk. Alston and Higgs argue that one important source of this variation is the prospect of labor mobility. For example, during harvests when the price of cotton was high, bidding wars for labor ensued. Hands paid as wage laborers had no incentive to ignore tempting offers to move, whereas hands paid with crop sharing and hands renting the land would forgo their crop if they moved. Thus, in settings where risk considerations alone would imply that wage labor is optimal, the addition of enforcement considerations might make crop sharing efficient. (Crop sharing thus functions like a "hostage" in Williamson's (1983) analysis.) Consistent with this argument, Alston (1981) finds that, holding risk and other factors constant, farmers closer to urban areas (i.e., sources of temporary labor that reduce the likelihood and the effect of bidding wars) use wage labor more than either form of risk sharing.

4 *The ratchet effect* Lincoln Electric is well-known for its piece rates because it has avoided both the infamous ratchet effect (where the firm reduces the piece rate if it learns that the job can be done more easily than was at first thought) and its repercussion, output restriction (where workers anticipate that the firm will ratchet the rate and so work slowly to prevent the firm from discerning the true pace at which the job could be done). A large body of evidence suggests that Lincoln is a rare exception. Clawson (1980, p. 170) summarizes many case studies and concludes that "employers insisted that they would never cut a price once it was set, yet every employer did cut prices," Mathewson (1931) offers a huge collection of vignettes concerning output restriction, and Roy (1952) gives detailed evidence of carefully restricted productivity in a machine shop.

To explore these qualitative accounts analytically, it seems natural to consider an environment in which the workers have private information about the job's difficulty and a worker's effort cannot be monitored. In a two-period model of such an environment, Gibbons (1987) shows that if neither the firm nor the worker can commit across periods (i.e., the firm cannot commit in the first period to the second-period piece rate and the worker cannot commit in the first period to remain with the firm for the second period) then both the ratchet effect and output restriction are unavoidable: there is no equilibrium compensation scheme that induces efficient effort.

Kanemoto and MacLeod (1991) and Carmichael and MacLeod (1993) study environments that allow firms to avoid the ratchet effect (and so avoid output restriction as well). Kanemoto and MacLeod analyze a two-period model where the worker's output conveys information about the worker's ability, rather than about the job's difficulty as in Gibbons. In the Kanemoto–MacLeod model, competition for the worker's services from the market of prospective employers gives the worker confidence that the firm will match the market in the second period. Carmichael and MacLeod explore a repeated-game (rather than a two-period) model in which the future value of the ongoing relationship may allow the firm to commit. For example, they describe mutual-monitoring arrangements among British cotton spinners in the nineteenth century in which piece rates were publicly posted and sanctions were administered (by other firms!) against firms that cut rates.

5 *Career concerns* When a worker's current performance affects the market's belief about the worker's ability, and hence the worker's future compensation, we say that the worker has current incentives from "career concerns." Fama (1980) suggested that career concerns could eliminate the need for managerial incentive contracts, but Holmstrom (1982b) showed that, in the absence of contracts, career concerns produce an inefficient (but intuitive) pattern of effort over time: managers typically work too hard in early years (while the market is still assessing the manager's ability and the manager has a long time to reap the rewards of improving the market's belief) and not hard enough in later years (when the market's belief is hard to budge and the manager has little time to go).

Gibbons and Murphy (1992) add incentive contracts (like those in the classic agency model) to the Fama–Holmstrom model. Because career-concern incentives decline as the manager approaches retirement, the slope of the optimal incentive contract increases, keeping total incentives (roughly) constant. Gibbons and Murphy present evidence on CEO compensation consistent with this prediction. Gompers and Lerner (1994) offer similar evidence for venture capitalists.

1.3 New dimensions

I have so far tried to make two points. First, risk matters in incentive contracting, but focusing on risk alone yields a sterile perspective. Second, several promising new classes of models have been developed recently, emphasizing aspects of real incentive contracting that are orthogonal to the tradeoff between insurance and incentives. To conclude this section I briefly consider three new issues: motivation, social comparison, and groups.

Baron (1988, p. 494) describes the imagery of workers in economic models of pay for performance as "somewhat akin to Newton's first law of motion: employees remain in a state of rest unless compelled to change the state by a stronger force impressed upon them – namely, an optimal labor contract." Many psychologists subscribe to another view, based on the distinction (and interaction) between intrinsic and extrinsic motivation. Staw (1977) considers two extreme cases: insufficient justification (i.e., low intrinsic rewards, say from a dull task, and no extrinsic rewards) and oversufficient justification (i.e., high intrinsic rewards, say from an interesting task, and high extrinsic rewards). Staw argues that those who choose to perform a task in the insufficient-justification condition may come to believe that the task is interesting, in order to justify their behavior to themselves, whereas those in the oversufficient-justification condition may mistakenly infer that continued participation is motivated by high extrinsic rewards and so come to believe that the task is not interesting.

As a test of the *insufficient*-justification hypothesis, Staw (1974) measured the attitudes and the performance of Reserve Officer Training Corps (ROTC) cadets both before and after they learned their draft numbers. As predicted, those with draft numbers such that there was no risk of being drafted (who therefore were engaged in dull tasks with no extrinsic rewards) showed improved attitudes about ROTC and even slightly enhanced performance. Staw (1977) summarizes several experiments that suggest limits to the applicability of the *oversufficient*-justification hypothesis, such as that there should be no pre-existing norm for payment. These limits suggest that the oversufficient-justification effect will be unlikely to be central in employment relationships, but might be important in voluntary organizations or with reference to tasks in an employment relationship that are usually performed voluntarily.

Another prominent aspect of social psychology that bears on employment relationships is social comparison theory (Vroom (1968), Goodman (1977)). O'Reilly, Main, and Crystal (1988) apply this theory CEO pay; Frank (1985) studies other economic applications. After controlling for firm performance, sales, size, and industry effects (at something between the one- and two-digit level), O'Reilly, Main, and Crystal find that CEO pay is significantly related to the average salary of the outside directors (in their main jobs) and even more strongly related to the average salary of the outside directors on the compensation committee. I would like to see this finding replicated on richer cross-section data with finer industry controls, and on panel data with changes in board composition. More generally, I think such findings from other fields should be pursued rather than dismissed.[10]

The issue of social comparison leads naturally to the issue of groups – another arena in which economic thinking often diverges from social-psychological and sociological views. Recent economic research on the effects of group incentive plans documents non-trivial productivity increases, such as Kruse (1993) on profit sharing and Jones and Kato (1995) on employee stock-ownership plans. To an economist, these results raise the question of free-riding: how do group incentive plans solve the so-called $1/N$ problem (Alchian and Demsetz (1972), Holmstrom (1982a))? Social psychologists and sociologists, however, have long emphasized the importance of informal norms in influencing behavior in groups.

Some arguments involving norms have the "oversocialized" character (i.e., norms so strong that no room remains for individual choice) that economists have found troubling, but subtler arguments are also available. Granovetter (1985, p. 486), for example, argues that "culture is not a one-for-all influence but an ongoing process, continuously constructed and reconstructed during interaction. It not only shapes its members but also is shaped by them, in part for their own strategic reasons." Tirole's (1996) analysis of corruption has something of this flavor; similar analyses of useful rather than destructive cultures should also be possible.

Economists have just begun to think about groups in organizations, but even the seemingly small step of adding a third actor to the classic agency model (i.e., a supervisor, as well as a principal and an agent) opens new horizons, as Tirole (1986) showed in his seminal analysis of collusion. All three actors in Tirole's model have the conventional preferences for actors in an economic model. More recently, other theorists have begun to explore preferences drawn from the social psychology and sociology literatures: see Kandel and Lazear (1992) and Barron and Gjerde (forthcoming) on peer pressure and Rotemberg (1994) on altruism in the workplace. Gaynor and Rebitzer (1995) deserve special recognition not only for developing a model involving group norms but also trying to test it!

2 CAREERS IN ORGANIZATIONS

Virtually all of the foregoing theory and evidence on incentive pay was cast as occurring within a firm, but much of it could just as well have been cast as between firms. In this section I step more resolutely inside the firm, by focusing on careers in organizations. Most of the evidence I report concerns white-collar workers, especially managerial and professional workers. Most of the work settings that generated the data are similar to the idealized employment system Osterman (1987) calls "salaried" (as opposed to "industrial," "craft," or "secondary").

I will treat jobs as defined in advance, independent of the people who fill them. This assumption may seem unremarkable, but some firms have no jobs of this kind (Kaftan and Barnes (1991)) and some firms with many highly formalized jobs nonetheless have an important minority of jobs that do not fit this description (Miner (1987)). I will also largely treat jobs as defined for individuals, rather than for teams, in spite of the recent surge of interest in the latter (e.g., Katzenbach and Smith (1993)).

One might think that, having sidestepped these fashionable issues in job design, I would be reduced to discussing a mature body of theory and evidence focused on a somewhat outdated definition of a job. Unfortunately, the situation is not that good. Instead, I see this section, like the second half of the first section, as an attempt to survey an emerging literature – this time on jobs, and how they are strung into careers in organizations. I begin with evidence, then turn to theory, and finally suggest some new dimensions.

2.1 Evidence

In this subsection I describe a wide range of findings concerning wages, promotions, and performance evaluations inside firms. I attempt to assess which findings are true in a variety of environments and which may be limited to narrower settings such as a particular firm, industry, or occupation. Most of the evidence I present concerns white-collar, salaried workers employed by large US firms. Nonetheless, the literature is large and varied. I therefore consider only four categories of evidence: positions, wages, the interplay between positions and wages, and performance evaluation. Even in a fairly narrow category such as positions, however, it is difficult to compare and evaluate some of the findings. Different authors have asked different questions of seemingly comparable datasets. It would be very helpful if authors of future studies would address a common core of questions before turning to specific issues of their own interest. Indeed, the same could be said of the existing studies: it would be very helpful if these authors would return to their data to address remaining core questions. To prompt discussion, I propose a set of such core questions at the end of this subsection.

1 *Positions* The first, simple finding is that demotions are rare. This is intuitive but rarely documented, in part because defining a demotion requires that jobs be ordered. One way to order jobs is by ranking their wages (Lazear (1992)); another is via patterns in observed job transitions (Baker, Gibbs, and Holmstrom (1994a)); a third is to ask whether formal job ladders exist (Baron, Davis-Blake, and Bielby (1986) and are used (DiPrete (1987)). Relatively few studies produce job orderings; as far as I know, only Baker, Gibbs, and Holmstrom (hereafter BGH) document the unsurprising fact that demotions are rare.

Much more attention has been paid to promotions (which again require jobs to be ordered by some method). In particular, serial correlation in promotion rates (i.e., a "fast track") has been studied extensively (Rosenbaum (1984), Brüderl, Diekmann, and Preisendörfer (1991), Baker, Gibbs, and Holmstrom (1994a), Spilerman and Petersen (1993), Spilerman and Ishida (1994), and Podolny and Baron (1995)). There has also been some analysis of the hazard rate for job-to-job transitions within a firm (Felmlee (1982), Althauser and Kalleberg (1990), and Lazear (1992)). This work varies in its sensitivity to issues such as competing risks (e.g., promotion versus exit, or up versus across job ladders) and unobserved heterogeneity. It also varies in its conclusions: Felmlee and Althauser–Kalleberg find positive duration dependence (i.e., an increasing escape rate to another job in the firm as time on the current job increases), whereas Lazear finds negative.

The natural extension of work on fast tracks and hazard rates is to analyze more detailed information from the history of a worker's job assignments within a firm, such as the following analysis by Chiappori,

Salanié, and Valentin (1996). Consider two workers who begin in level 1 at date 1 and are both in level 2 at date 3. Suppose worker A was promoted between dates 1 and 2, whereas worker B was promoted between dates 2 and 3. One can ask which worker fares better after date 3. As predicted by a learning model akin to Harris and Holmstrom (1982), Chiappori *et al.* find that worker B fares better after date 3.[11]

2 *Wages* Using administrative records to study salaried managers during their careers at a single firm, Baker, Gibbs, and Holmstrom (1994b) find that nominal wage cuts are extremely rare (200 observations out of more than 60,000), but that zero nominal increases are not. It would be interesting to use large panel datasets to study the generality of these findings across firms, but such efforts must confront several issues. First, for non-salaried workers, fluctuations in hours (e.g., via overtime) would change earnings even if wages were constant. Second, there may be substantial measurement error in earnings or wages. Third, there may be measurement error in firm affiliation, clouding the question of who stayed with the firm.

Card and Hyslop (1995) confront these issues using data from the Current Population Survey (CPS) and the Panel Study of Income Dynamics (PSID) covering hourly workers who stayed with their employer for two consecutive interview dates. Card and Hyslop's findings are qualitatively similar to BGH's: nominal wage cuts are rare (but not as rare as in Baker, Gibbs, and Holmstrom), but zero nominal increases are not (indeed, they form a prominent spike in the distribution). Kahn (1994) presents similar evidence. Card and Hyslop (1995), Kahn (1994), Baker, Gibbs, and Holmstrom (1994b), and McLaughlin (1994) all find that real wage cuts are not rare.

Taking a cue from the large literature on fast tracks, Baker, Gibbs, and Holmstrom (1994b) ask the analogous question about wages: is there serial correlation in wage changes? They find that the correlation between $\Delta w_t (= w_t - w_{t-1})$ and Δw_{t-1} is 0.30, and between Δw_t and Δw_{t-2} is 0.25. Of course, this finding could reflect concave effects of experience and/or tenure, so BGH compute the analogous correlations for changes in wage residuals rather than in wages. These correlations are indeed smaller: 0.17 and 0.12, respectively.

As with wage cuts, there has been some analysis of the serial correlation of wage changes (and changes in wage residuals) using large panel datasets. Using data on American scientists, Lillard and Weiss (1979) find statistically significant person effects in both the level and the growth of earnings residuals, as well as a significant correlation between the two. Similarly, Hause (1980) finds significant person effects in the growth of earnings among young Swedish males. Abowd and Card (1989), however, analyze three larger and more heterogeneous datasets (the PSID, the National Longitudinal Survey, and the Seattle/Denver Income Maintenance Experiment) and cannot reject a statistical model that has no person effect in the growth rate of (experience-adjusted) earnings.

Workers in the Lillard–Weiss, Hause, and Abowd–Card samples did not necessarily remain with a single employer, as was the case in Baker, Gibbs, and Holmstrom, but Topel (1991) and Topel and Ward (1992) study within-firm wage growth. Both papers find that within-firm changes in wage residuals are serially uncorrelated, using data from the PSID and Social Security earnings records, respectively. Topel and Ward also find, however, that prior wage growth affects job mobility, even after controlling for the current wage – a finding that would be easily explained by person effects in wage growth.

In sum, three small, relatively homogeneous samples (Baker–Gibbs–Holmstrom, Lillard–Weiss, and Hause) find evidence of a person effect in the growth rate of earnings, whereas five large, heterogeneous samples (three from Abowd–Card, one (related) from Topel, and one from Topel–Ward) do not. This welter of findings deserves further attention. One possible explanation is that only certain small groups of workers (such as the managerial and professional workers in Baker–Gibbs–Holmstrom and Lillard–Weiss) exhibit such a person effect. If most groups of workers do not exhibit this effect then the representative cross-sections in Abowd–Card, Topel, and Topel–Ward would not either.

Finally, Baker, Gibbs, and Holmstrom (1994b) find that a difference in the starting wages of two cohorts persists as the cohorts age. Put differently, raises for workers already in the firm are highly correlated, regardless of cohort, so much of the wage difference between two cohorts comes from the difference in their starting wages. This finding is reminiscent of Doeringer and Piore's (1971) description of how an internal labor market buffers workers from the vagaries of the external market, and of Beaudry and DiNardo's (1991) evidence on the effect of previous unemployment rates on current wages (although Beaudry and DiNardo find that the lowest unemployment rate since being hired has the largest effect, rather than the unemployment rate at the date hired).

3 *Positions and wages* Just as the first, simple finding on positions was that demotions are rare, the first, simple finding on wages and positions is that the wage increase upon promotion is larger than for those not promoted. For example, in a study of 461 top executives in 72 large US manufacturing firms from 1964 to 1981, Murphy (1985) found that the average real increase in salary plus bonus for the whole sample was 3.7 percent but the average

increase for a Vice President promoted to President was 20.9 percent, and for a President promoted to CEO 14.3 percent. On the other hand, the wage change at promotion can be small compared with the difference in average wages between the two levels. For example, Murphy found that the average salary plus bonus for Presidents was 60 percent higher than for Vice Presidents (but only 13 percent higher for CEOs than for Presidents). Baker, Gibbs, and Holmstrom (1994b) replicate these results for lower-level managers in one firm: wage increases upon promotion are larger than for those not promoted, but smaller than the difference in average wages between the two levels.

In keeping with the findings of serial correlation in promotion rates and in wage changes, Baker, Gibbs, and Holmstrom (1994b) find that wage increases forecast promotions. That is, among all the workers just promoted to level n, the next raise is lower for those who subsequently wait longer to be promoted to level $n + 1$.

Baker, Gibbs, and Holmstrom (1994a) find that promotions come disproportionately from the upper deciles of the wage distribution for the lower job, but not exclusively: some promotions come from each decile. Similarly, some promotions go into each decile of the wage distribution for the upper job, although most go into the lower deciles. At higher job levels, a larger fraction of promotions come from the upper deciles of the lower job and go into the lower deciles of the upper job.

Murphy (1991) describes the official schedule of wage-increase ranges at Merck & Co.: controlling for performance evaluation, wage increases are smaller for those who begin in higher quartiles of the wage distribution of a given job level. Baker, Gibbs, and Holmstrom (1994a) replicate and extend this finding: in the firm they study, the fact holds for those who are not promoted, for those who are, and for the sample as a whole.

4 *Performance evaluations* Much of what we know about the relationship between wages and performance evaluations is drawn from two influential papers by Medoff and Abraham (1980, 1981). They study managerial and professional workers in three firms and report three basic facts: wages increase with seniority; wages increase with performance evaluation; and the effect of seniority on wages is essentially independent of the presence of controls for performance evaluation. An implication of these three facts (borne out in their data) is that performance evaluation is essentially independent of seniority. All of this might cause one to question the role of performance evaluation, but Medoff and Abraham find that increases in performance evaluation predict raises and promotions. Gibbs (1995) presents similar evidence on the effects of performance evaluations in the firm studied by Baker, Gibbs, and Holmstrom (1994a and b).

Waldman and Avolio (1986) conduct a meta-analysis of 40 samples, largely from the literature in industrial psychology. Waldman and Avolio find that productivity increases with age but performance evaluation is essentially flat with age. Replacing "productivity" with "wage" and "age" with "seniority" makes the two Waldman–Avolio findings identical to two of the Medoff–Abraham findings.

5 *Summary* There is a large and diverse set of findings concerning wage and promotion dynamics within firms. Some of the findings have so far been documented only in individual firms, but I have attempted to report evidence from large panel datasets whenever possible. It would be a great service if empirical researchers would provide evidence on a core set of questions before studying specific issues of their own. Among these core questions might be: (1) is there a fast track?, (2) are nominal wage cuts rare?, (3) are changes in wage residuals serially correlated?, (4) are there cohort effects in wages?, (5) are wage increases upon promotion large compared to normal wage changes but small compared with the difference in average wages between the two levels?, (6) do wage increases forecast promotions?, (7) do promotions come from and go to all the deciles of the wage distributions for the lower and upper levels?, (8) are wage increases smaller for those who begin in higher quartiles of the wage distribution for that level?, (9) do wages increase and are promotions more likely with higher performance evaluations (both in cross-section and in time series)?, and (10) is the effect of seniority on wages independent of the presence of controls for performance evaluation? Theoretical researchers, for their part, could advance the literature by developing models that address broad patterns of facts, abandoning the more common strategy of developing a model to explain one or a few findings in isolation.

2.2 Towards a theory

There are at least four potential building blocks for a theory of wage and promotion dynamics within firms: task assignment, tournaments, on-the-job human-capital acquisition, and learning. Each of these building blocks has received some development in the literature, but many of the resulting models were designed to explain at most a few stylized facts. I will therefore briefly describe some of the major contributions to these four literatures, indicating some of the facts each was designed to explain. I will then argue, however, that future theorizing should aim at explaining broad patterns of evidence rather than a fact or two, and I will give examples of recent theorizing in this vein.

1 *Task assignment* The task-assignment literature begins with static, full-information models (Sattinger (1975), Rosen (1982), Waldman (1984a)) that offer an explanation for skewness in the wage distribution; see Sattinger (1993) for a review. A new line of research emphasizes that the firm's decision to assign a worker to a new task signals information to prospective employers about the worker's productive ability (Waldman (1984b), Ricart i Costa (1988), Bernhardt and Scoones (1993)). This signaling effect offers an explanation for the large wage increase upon promotion. Because prospective employers bid up the wage of promoted workers, however, the current employer chooses an inefficiently tough promotion criterion: workers who would be marginally more productive in the new job are not more productive enough to compensate for the wage increase.

2 *Tournaments* The tournaments literature begins with the classic analysis by Lazear and Rosen (1981) that offers an explanation for large wage increases upon promotion. Rosen's (1986) sequential-elimination model shows that a big prize at the end (such as promotion to CEO) has important effects on incentives in the early rounds, so the distribution of prizes can be quite convex and yet create constant incentives across rounds. Meyer (1992) shows that in a sequence of (non-elimination) tournaments it is efficient to introduce second-round bias in favor of the first-round winner. (A small second-round bias causes a second-order reduction in second-round effort but a first-order increase in first-round effort.) Thus, a fast track can emerge from an optimal incentive scheme.

3 *Human capital* From the perspective of careers in organizations, the human-capital literature moves from Becker (1962) to Hashimoto (1981) to Carmichael (1983). Becker suggested that the firm and the worker will share both the costs and the benefits of investments in specific capital. Hashimoto emphasized that such sharing would not be necessary if the firm and the worker did not have private information about post-investment match quality. In the presence of such private information, however, the optimal sharing rule produces inefficient turnover. Carmichael made the first explicit reference to careers in organizations by showing that a promotion ladder (i.e., wages attached to jobs, with jobs assigned by seniority) can induce investment and produce efficient turnover.

More recently, Kahn and Huberman (1988), Waldman (1990), and Prendergast (1993) built on Carmichael's insight to analyze promotion and up-or-out rules. Others have reinvestigated the Becker–Hashimoto sharing model. Chang and Wang (1996), for example, derive a host of new results, including underinvestment in general human capital, in the (plausible) case in which human-capital investments cannot be observed by prospective employers. And Prendergast (1989), Acemoglu and Pischke (1996), and Chang and Wang (1995) show that the interaction of investment and turnover can create multiple equilibria: if almost no one will be laid off then it is efficient to invest, so almost no one is laid off, and vice versa.

4 *Learning* I organize the literature on learning about workers into four categories: passive response, active experimentation, commitment problems, and strategic information transmission. Jovanovic (1979) and MacDonald (1982) are classic examples from the passive-response category – information (say, about a worker's productivity) arrives and the firm responds optimally (say, by changing the worker's wage). Murphy (1986) develops two models – one emphasizing passive learning, the other incentives – and tests their distinctive predictions. Murphy's evidence is inconclusive, perhaps because both models are actually at work in the data, but his paper is noteworthy for its attempt to distinguish between competing reasons why pay might be linked to performance. O'Flaherty and Siow (1992, 1995) use a passive-learning model to study up-or-out rules.

Meyer (1991) falls in the active-experimentation category: in a sequence of contests (similar to Meyer (1992), described above, but with learning about worker ability rather than moral hazard), the firm finds it optimal to bias the second round in favor of the first-round winner. (Without a second-round bias either the first-round winner wins the second round, merely confirming the first-round information, or the first-round loser wins, canceling out the first-round information.) Thus, as in Meyer (1992), a firm may find it optimal to create a fast track.

Harris and Holmstrom (1982) show how learning can cause commitment problems. A risk-neutral firm would like to guarantee a risk-averse worker a constant wage, but information about the worker's performance may cause prospective employers to bid up the worker's wage. If the current employer cannot bind the worker to the firm then only those workers with poor performance will be left working at the guaranteed wage. Consequently, the firm can offer only limited insurance (in the form of a guaranteed wage) and must collect a premium for it up front (in the form of a wage below expected productivity during the time before performance information arrives).

Finally, Greenwald (1986), Lazear (1986b), and the signaling papers noted above in the task-assignment literature analyze strategic information transmission. Greenwald studies the winner's curse that afflicts a prospective employer when making an offer; Lazear considers the possibility that the prospective employer may have superior information, in which case workers who never get offers are stigmatized. Gibbons and Katz (1991) develop a similar model of layoffs and present evidence consistent with the model: for white-collar workers (who are less likely to be subject to inverse-seniority layoff rules), the re-employment wages of laid-off workers are lower than those of observationally equivalent workers displaced in plant closings, consistent with a layoff being a bad signal about the worker's ability.

5 *Beyond building blocks* These four literatures – task assignment, tournaments, human capital, and learning – have developed some important theory and met with some empirical success. In the last few years, however, a new style of theory on career dynamics has begun to emerge, in which models speak to broad patterns of facts rather than one or a few in isolation. Harris and Holmstrom (1982), MacLeod and Malcomson (1988), Demougin and Siow (1994) and Bernhardt (1995) are contributions in this vein. I will briefly describe Gibbons and Waldman (1996), because it makes the broadest attempt to relate to a detailed pattern of facts about careers in organizations.

Waldman and I develop a model that blends task assignment, on-the-job human capital acquisition, and learning. The predictions of the model are consistent with much of the evidence on positions, wages, and positions and wages described in the previous subsection, including: (1) both demotions and (real) wage decreases will be rare, although demotions will be much more rare; (2) on average, workers who receive large wage increases early in their stay at one level of a job ladder will be promoted more quickly to the next level; (3) promotions will be associated with large wage increases, but these wage increases will be small relative to the difference between average wages across the relevant job levels; (4) there will be significant serial correlation in both wage increases and promotion rates; and (5) individuals promoted from one job level to the next will come disproportionately (but not exclusively) from the top of the lower job's wage distribution and will arrive disproportionately (but not exclusively) towards the bottom of the higher job's wage distribution. Furthermore, the model is also consistent with the fourth category of evidence, on performance evaluations.

The main elements of the model are simple. A worker with innate ability θ and labor-market experience x has productive ability $\eta(\theta, x)$. A worker's innate ability can be either high or low; experience improves a worker's productivity through learning by doing. There are three jobs, which differ in their sensitivity to productive ability. Under full information, workers with high values of η would be assigned to the top job, workers with intermediate values of η to the middle job, and workers with low values of η to the bottom job. With imperfect information about innate ability, workers are assigned to jobs based on their expected productive abilities and paid their expected outputs in their assigned jobs.

In each period, a worker's output provides a noisy signal about his or her productive ability. Because labor-market experience is observable, the signal about productive ability can be translated into a signal about innate ability. Growth in productive ability with experience implies that, on average, workers progress up the job ladder, receiving wage increases every period and promotions every so often. But learning about innate ability implies that wage cuts sometimes occur; indeed, demotions, while rare, are possible. Serial correlation in promotion rates and wage increases follow from the differences in innate ability, as does the finding that wage increases forecast promotion. Large wage increases at promotion follow in part from a selection effect: those who get promoted in a given period are disproportionately those who received good news about their abilities. Finally, the findings on performance evaluations follow if it is innate ability (θ) rather than productive ability (η) or realized output that is evaluated; that is, evaluators adjust realized output for the skill acquired with experience.

The Gibbons–Waldman model (and others like it) address broad patterns of facts about careers in organizations. Nonetheless, each existing model fails to produce some of the existing facts. There are four main facts that do not emerge from the Gibbons–Waldman model: nominal wage cuts are rare (but see MacLeod and Malcomson (1993) for a theory of nominal rigidity), wage differences between cohorts are primarily a function of differences in their starting wages, wage increases are smaller for those who begin in higher quartiles, and wage distributions for different job levels overlap (although this last fact could be due to excessively coarse job definitions in some datasets). Of course, some of these existing "facts" have not yet been established beyond a single firm, hence my appeal for systematic empirical analysis of core questions.

2.3 New dimensions

Sociologists have long explored the effects of aggregate-level variables such as vacancy chains, social networks, and organizational demography on individual-level outcomes such as attainment and turnover. It would be interesting to consider whether the theoretical or econometric tools of labor economics can shed any new light on the sociologists' preferred interpretations of these effects.

White (1970), for example, introduced and explored the consequences of vacancy chains: if worker A gets promoted from job 2 to job 3, it creates an opportunity for worker B to be promoted from job 1 to job 2. The basic idea is not startling, but it is sensible; see Stewman (1986) for elaborations.

Demougin and Siow (1994) and Rebitzer and Taylor (1995) have made nice starts towards incorporating such demand-side effects into theoretical models in labor economics.

Granovetter (1974) analyzed the importance of friends and relatives as sources of information for job seekers. More recently, Burt (1992) and Podolny and Baron (1995) have studied analogous networks within firms, asking how the size and interconnectedness of an individual's network influences the individual's promotion prospects. Burt gives special prominence to the idea of a "structural hole," where worker A knows several workers of type B and several of type C, but no B worker knows a C worker. The existing sociological research largely treats networks as exogenous and asks what they do. This approach has already migrated into the economics literature; see Montgomery (1991), for example. But if certain network forms are advantageous, such as Burt's structural hole, then it would be interesting to consider under what circumstances such networks might be formed or modified endogenously.

Finally, Pfeffer (1983) pioneered the study of "organizational demography" by suggesting how the *distributions* of individual attributes (such as age, sex, race, education level, and seniority) within an organization or work group might influence outcomes such as innovation, productivity, satisfaction, and turnover. A large empirical literature now exists. Wagner, Pfeffer, and O'Reilly (1984), for example, study turnover in 599 top-management groups in 31 *Fortune* 500 firms. In a logistic regression on individual turnover, including controls for the individual's age and the firm's performance, the extent to which the individual is similar in age to other group members decreases the chance of turnover.

3 CONCLUSION

I hope to have shown that labor economics has made some progress towards understanding two limited aspects of employment relationships: incentive pay and careers in organizations. Several other concrete questions also deserve attention, including job design, skill development, and participative decision making. A more fundamental and abstract question also needs work: what is an employment relationship? The classic papers by Simon (1951) and Williamson, Wachter, and Harris (1975) provide good starts. An ideal answer to this fundamental question would also shed light on some of the concrete issues – incentives, job design, and the like.

Much of the theory and evidence I have described is geared towards white-collar workers (especially managers and professionals) in large US firms. That is, I have focused on Osterman's (1987) "salaried" employment system, rather then the "industrial," "craft," or "secondary" employment systems. All four systems deserve more attention, as do systems (and their institutions) in other countries and from other eras.

One view is that economics is about markets, so labor economics should focus on the labor market, leaving the study of what goes on inside firms to fields such as human resource management, industrial relations, organizational psychology, and organizational sociology. Obviously, I disagree: I think labor economics has too many theoretical and empirical tools at its disposal to make such an allocation of attention socially optimal. At the same time, I hope to have suggested several areas in which labor economics could benefit from an exchange of theory and evidence with the many other fields that study employment relationships.

Notes

I thank John Abowd, George Baker, James Baron, Henry Farber, Bengt Holmstrom, Lawrence Katz, David Kreps, Edward Lazear, Bentley MacLeod, Margaret Meyer, Kevin J. Murphy, Canice Prendergast, and Michael Waldman for years of discussions on these topics. The Center for Advanced Study in the Behavioral Sciences provided an ideal setting and financial support (through a Fellowship funded in part by NSF grant SBR-9022192).

1 Other aspects of employment relationships also deserve attention, such as job design, skill development, and participative decision making. Research on these issues seems less ready for summary and assessment, but intriguing theory and evidence has begun to emerge: see Milgrom and Roberts (1988), Holmstrom and Milgrom (1991), Itoh (1992), Prendergast (1995), and Meyer, Olsen, and Torsvik (forthcoming) for theory and Osterman (1994, 1995), Pencavel and Craig (1994), and Ichniowski, Shaw, and Prennushi (1995) for evidence.

2 For lack of space, I ignore two smaller literatures on incentives: efficiency-wage and deferred-payment models, which differ from the principal-agent model in that wages do not vary with performance. In an efficiency-wage model, a firm pays a high wage to all workers but subsequently fires those whose performance is too low; see Shapiro and Stiglitz (1984) for theory and Capelli and Chauvin (1991), Krueger (1991), and Abowd, Kramarz, and Margolis (1994) for evidence. In a deferred-payment model, workers are again fired for poor performance, but now forfeit higher wages later in their career (or after retirement, through a pension); see Lazear (1979) for theory and Goldin (1986), Hutchens (1987), and Margolis (1995) for evidence.

3 Incentive contracts obviously exist outside as well as inside employment relationships, golf tournaments being just one example. In trying to understand incentive contracts inside firms, I will sometimes draw on examples from outside. Much work remains to be done on how incentive contracts differ (by choice or by constraint) depending on whether they are inside or outside firms; see Holmstrom and Milgrom (1991) and Baker, Gibbons, and Murphy (1996) for initial exploration of this issue.

4 Jensen and Murphy (1990) estimate that the pay-for-performance slope for the CEO of a typical large US firm is at most $b = 0.003$. Jensen and Murphy argue that such a pay-for-performance relation is statistically but not economically significant, whereas Haubrich (1994) argues that plausible parameter values in the classic agency model can yield an efficient slope of this magnitude.

5 Even this seemingly simple comparison raises several issues. First, output was not zero before the imposition of piece rates, suggesting that monitoring and/or efficiency wages should be included in the theoretical and empirical analyses. Second, as Lazear (1986a) and Brown (1992) analyze, high-productivity workers may prefer piece rates to salaries, so the switch to piece rates may change the composition of the workforce; fortunately, Lazear (1996) has data on individual workers over time. Third, and perhaps most important, many piece-rate plans eventually run afoul of the "ratchet effect" described in the next subsection.

6 Because the agent's action is unobservable, empirical work cannot directly test whether $a^*(b)$ increases with b, and so relies on either performance (y) or profit ($\pi = y - w$) as a proxy for the agent's action. Lazear uses performance; Abowd uses various forms of profit; and Kahn and Sherer use numerical performance ratings awarded by supervisors (which are more like y than like π, provided that supervisors are not judging performance relative to wages). The distinction between performance and profit affects the interpretation of the evidence. If observations on b were randomly sprinkled near b^* (say, due to small mistakes) then $a^*(b)$ would increase with b, so $E(y)$ would increase with b, but $E(\pi)$ would be locally constant, because TS(b) is maximized at b^*. On the other hand, if variations in b were due to (say) unmeasured variation in risk aversion then both $E(y)$ and $E(\pi)$ would increase in b.

7 Antle–Smith, Gibbons–Murphy, and Janakiraman–Lambert–Larcker also examine the effect of accounting earnings on CEO pay, again relative to the market as a whole and the firm's industry. They all find little evidence of relative performance evaluation involving accounting earnings. Sloan (1993) suggest why, by showing that market-wide movements in earnings are not a major source of noise in earnings. Sloan also finds that earnings are closely correlated with the firm's stock-market performance relative to the market as a whole. That is, an own-performance contract based on the firm's earnings could have the effect of a relative-performance contract based on own and market stock movements.

8 Firms are not the only ones who get what they pay for – governments do, too. Anderson, Burkhauser, and Raymond (1993) offer evidence of cream-skimming in the Job Training Partnership Act (JTPA): the program's goals are to reduce an individual's unemployment and increase the individual's earnings, but program operators are paid based on the measured unemployment and earnings of program participants, so operators have an incentive to enroll participants who would have had short unemployment and high earnings without training. Using cross-state variation in incentive intensity, Cragg (1995) finds that cream-skimming increases when incentives are stronger, but so do the outcomes that the program is intended to induce – reduced unemployment and increased earnings conditional on the characteristics of those enrolled.

9 Lazear (1989), Gibbons and Murphy (1990), and Dye (1992) issue similar cautions regarding unbridled use of relative performance evaluation: managers have incentives to choose a reference group they can beat, rather than one that offers high returns; similarly, within a firm, managers have incentives to sabotage the performances of co-workers as well as to improve their own performances.

10 Hallock (1995) studies a related issue: reciprocity via interlocking directorates (i.e., the CEO of firm A is a director of firm B, and vice versa). Hallock finds that, after controlling for firm characteristics, interlocking directorates are associated with no more than 10 percent higher pay.

11 At first blush, this finding may seem inconsistent with the existence of a fast track. The Chiappori *et al.* finding could be compatible with a fast track, however, because some fast-trackers may not be eligible for the sample constructed by Chiappori *et al.*: workers A and B are at level 2 at date 3, but a true fast-tracker may already have been promoted to level 3 by this date. This is one example of how it would be useful for past, present, and future authors to address a core set of questions before turning to issues specific to their paper.

References

Abowd, John (1990). "Does performance-based managerial compensation affect corporate performance?" *Industrial and Labor Relations Review*, 43: 52S–73S.

Abowd, John and Card, David (1989). "On the covariance structure of earnings and hours changes." *Econometrica*, 57: 411–45.

Abowd, John, Kramarz, Francis, and Margolis, David (1994). "High wage workers and high wage firms." National Bureau of Economic Research Working Paper No. 4917.

Acemoglu, Daron and Pischke, Jörn-Steffen (1996). "Why do firms train? Theory and evidence." National Bureau of Economic Research Working Paper No. 5605.

Alchian, Armen and Demsetz, Harold (1972). "Production, information costs, and economic organization." *American Economic Review*, 62: 777–95.

Alston, Lee (1981). "Tenure choice in southern agriculture, 1930–1960." *Explorations in Economic History*, 18: 211–32.

Alston, Lee and Higgs, Robert (1982). "Contractual mix in southern agriculture since the Civil War: facts, hypotheses, and test." *Journal of Economic History*, 42: 327–53.

Althauser, Robert and Kalleberg, Arne (1990). "Identifying career lines and internal labor markets within firms: a study in the interrelationships of theory and methods." In Breiger, R. (ed.), *Social Mobility and Social Structure*. Cambridge: Cambridge University Press.

Anderson, Kathryn, Burkhauser, Richard, and Raymond, Jennie (1993). "The effect of creaming on placement rates under the job training partnership act." *Industrial and Labor Relations Review*, 46: 613–24.

Antle, Rick and Smith, Abbie (1986). "An empirical investigation of the relative performance evaluation of corporate executives." *Journal of Accounting Research*, 24: 1–39.

Asch, Beth (1990). "Do incentives matter? The case of navy recruiters." *Industrial and Labor Relations Review*, 43: 89–106.

Baker, George (1992). "Incentive contracts and performance measurement." *Journal of Political Economy*, 100: 598–614.

Baker, George, Gibbons, Robert, and Murphy, Kevin J. (1994). 'Subjective performance measures in optimal incentive contracts." *Quarterly Journal of Economics*, 109: 1125–56.

(1996). "Implicit contracts and the theory of the firm." Unpublished manuscript, Cornell University.

Baker, George, Gibbs, Michael, and Holmstrom, Bengt (1994a). "The internal economics of the firm: evidence from personnel data." *Quarterly Journal of Economics*, 109: 881–919.

(1994b). "The wage policy of a firm." *Quarterly Journal of Economics*, 109: 921–55.

Baron, James (1988). "The employment relation as a social relation." *Journal of the Japanese and International Economies*, 2: 492–525.

Baron, James, Davis-Blake, Alison, and Bielby, William (1986). "The structure of opportunity: how promotion ladders vary within and among organizations." *Administrative Science Quarterly*, 31: 248–73.

Barron, John and Gjerde, Kathy Paulson (forthcoming). "Peer pressure in an agency relationship." *Journal of Labor Economics.*

Beaudry, Paul and DiNardo, John (1991). "The effect of implicit contracts on the movement of wages over the business cycle: evidence from microdata." *Journal of Political Economy*, 99: 665–88.

Becker, Gary (1962). *Human Capital.* New York: Columbia University Press.

Bernhardt, Dan (1995). "Strategic promotion and compensation." *Review of Economic Studies*, 62: 315–39.

Bernhardt, Dan and Scoones, David (1993). "Promotion, turnover, and preemptive wage offers." *American Economic Review*, 84: 771–91.

Brickley, James, Bhagat, Sanjai, and Lease, Ronald (1985). "The impact of long-range managerial compensation plans on shareholder wealth." *Journal of Accounting and Economics*, 7: 115–30.

Brown, Charles (1990). "Firm's choice of method of pay." *Industrial and Labor Relations Review*, 43: 165S–182S.

(1992). "Wage levels and methods of pay." *Rand Journal of Economics*, 23: 366–75.

Brüderl, Josef, Diekmann, Andreas, and Preisendörfer, Peter (1991). "Patterns of intraorganizational mobility: tournament models, path dependency, and early promotion effects." *Social Science Research*, 20: 197–216.

Bull, Clive (1987). "The existence of self-enforcing implicit contracts." *Quarterly Journal of Economics*, 102: 147–59.

Burt, Ronald (1992). *Structural Holes: The Social Structure of Competition.* Cambridge, MA: Harvard University Press.

Burtis, Andrew and Gabarro, John (1995). "Brainard, Bennis & Farrell." Harvard Business School Case No. 9-485-037.

Card, David and Hyslop, Dean (1995). "Does inflation 'Grease the Wheels of the Labor Market'?" Princeton University Industrial Relations Section Working Paper No. 356, December.

Cappelli, Peter and Chauvin, Keith (1991). "An interplant test of the efficiency wage hypothesis." *Quarterly Journal of Economics*, 106: 769–87.

Carmichael, Lorne (1983). "Firm-specific human capital and promotion ladders." *Bell Journal of Economics*, 14: 251–8.

Carmichael, Lorne and MacLeod, Bentley (1993). "Worker cooperation and the ratchet effect." Unpublished Manuscript, Queen's University.

Chang, Chun and Wang, Yijiang (1996). "Human capital investment under asymmetric information: the Pigovian conjecture revisited." *Journal of Labor Economics*, 14: 505–19.

(1995). "A framework for understanding differences in labor turnover and human capital investment." *Journal of Economic Behavior and Organization*, 28: 91–105.

Chiappori, Pierre-André, Salanié, Bernard, and Valentin, J. (1996). "Insurance, learning, and career profiles: an empirical test." Unpublished manuscript, INSEE (CREST) Working Paper No. 9623.

Chevalier, Judith and Ellison, Glen (1995). "Risk taking by mutual funds as a response to incentives." NBER Working Paper No. 5234 (August).

Clawson, Daniel (1980). *Bureaucracy and the Labor Process*. New York: Monthly Review Press.

Cragg, Michael (1995). "Performance incentives in government subcontracting: evidence from the job training partnership act (JTPA)." Unpublished manuscript, Columbia University.

Demougin, Dominique and Siow, Aloysius (1994). "Careers in ongoing hierarchies." *American Economic Review*, 84: 1261–77.

DiPrete, Thomas (1987). "Horizontal and vertical mobility in organizations." *Administrative Science Quarterly*, 32: 422–44.

Doeringer, Peter and Piore, Michael (1971). *Internal Labor Markets and Manpower Analysis*. Lexington, MA: Heath Lexington Books.

Dye, Ronald (1992). "Relative performance evaluation and project selection." *Journal of Accounting Research*, 30: 27–52.

Eccles, Robert and Crane, Dwight (1988). *Doing Deals: Investment Banks at Work*. Boston: Harvard Business School Press.

Ehrenberg, Ronald and Bognanno, Michael (1990). "Do tournaments have incentive effects?" *Journal of Political Economy*, 98: 1307–24.

Fama, Eugene (1980). "Agency problems and the theory of the firm." *Journal of Political Economy*, 88: 288–307.

Fast, Norman and Berg, Norman (1975). "The Lincoln Electric Company." Harvard Business School Case No. 376-028.

Felmlee, Diane (1982). "Women's job mobility processes." *American Sociological Review*, 47: 142–51.

Frank, Robert (1985). *Choosing the Right Pond: Human Behavior and the Quest for Status*. New York: Oxford University Press.

Garen, John (1994). "Executive compensation and principal-agent theory." *Journal of Political Economy*, 102: 1175–99.

Gaynor, Martin and Gertler, Paul (1995). "Moral hazard and risk spreading in partnerships." *Rand Journal of Economics*, 26: 591–613.

Gaynor, Martin and Rebitzer, James (1995). "Equity and effort: a study of group norms and incentives in pay systems." Unpublished manuscript, Carnegie Mellon University.

Gibbons, Robert (1987). "Piece-rate incentive schemes." *Journal of Labor Economics*, 5: 413–29.

Gibbons, Robert and Katz, Lawrence (1991). "Layoffs and lemons." *Journal of Labor Economics*, 9: 351–80.

Gibbons, Robert and Murphy, Kevin J. (1990). "Relative performance evaluation for chief executive officers." *Industrial and Labor Relations Review*, 43: 30S–51S.

(1992). "Optimal incentive contracts in the presence of career concerns: theory and evidence." *Journal of Political Economy*, 100: 468–505.

Gibbons, Robert and Waldman, Michael (1996). "A theory of wage and promotion dynamics inside a firm." Unpublished manuscript, Cornell University.

Gibbs, Michael (1995). "Incentive compensation in a corporate hierarchy." *Journal of Accounting and Economics*, 19: 247–77.

Goldin, Claudia (1986). "Monitoring costs and occupational segregation by sex: a historical analysis." *Journal of Labor Economics*, 4: 1–27.

Gompers, Paul and Lerner, Josh (1994). "An analysis of compensation in the U.S. venture capital partnership." Unpublished manuscript, Harvard Business School.

Goodman, Paul (1977). "Social comparison processes in organizations." In Staw, B. and Salancik, G. (eds.), *New Directions in Organizational Behavior*. Chicago: St Clair Press.

Granovetter, Mark (1974). *Getting a Job: A Study of Contacts and Careers.* Cambridge, MA: Harvard University Press.

(1985). "Economic action and social structure: the problem of embeddedness." *American Journal of Sociology*, 91: 481–510.

Greene, Sarah and Schlesinger Leonard (1992). "Gain sharing at star cablevision group." Harvard Business School Case No. 9-692-012.

Greenwald, Bruce (1986). "Adverse selection in the labor market." *Review of Economic Studies*, 53: 325–47.

Hallock, Kevin (1995). "Executive pay and reciprocally interlocking boards of directors." Princeton University Industrial Relations Section Working Paper No. 340.

Harris, Milton and Holmstrom, Bengt (1982). "A theory of wage dynamics." *Review of Economic Studies*, 49: 315–33.

Hashimoto, Masanori (1981). "Firm-specific human capital as a shared investment." *American Economic Review*, 71: 475–81.

Haubrich, Joseph (1994). "Risk aversion, performance pay, and the principal-agent problem." *Journal of Political Economy*, 102: 258–76.

Hause, John (1980). "The fine structure of earnings and the on-the-job training hypothesis." *Econometrica*, 48: 1013–30.

Healy, Paul (1985). "The effect of bonus schemes on accounting decisions." *Journal of Accounting and Economics*, 7: 85–107.

Higgs, Robert (1973). "Race, tenure, and resource allocation in southern agriculture, 1910." *Journal of Economic History*, 33: 149–69.

Holmstrom, Bengt (1979). "Moral hazard and observability." *Bell Journal of Economics*, 10: 7–91.

(1982a). "Moral hazard in teams." *Bell Journal of Economics*, 13: 324–40.

(1982b). "Managerial incentive problems – a dynamic perspective." *Essays in Economics and Management in Honor of Lars Wahlbeck*. Helsinki: Swedish School of Economics.

Holmstrom, Bengt and Milgrom, Paul (1987). "Aggregation and linearity in the provision of intertemporal incentives." *Econometrica*, 55: 303–28.

(1991). "Multitask principal-agent analyses: incentive contracts, asset ownership, and job design." *Journal of Law, Economics, and Organization*, 7: 24–52.

Hutchens, Robert (1987). "A test of Lazear's theory of delayed payment contracts." *Journal of Labor Economics*, 5: S153–S170.

Ichniowski, Casey, Shaw, Kathryn, and Prennushi, Giovanna (1995). "The effects of human resource management practices on productivity." National Bureau of Economic Research Working Paper No. 5333.

Itoh, Hideshi (1992). "Cooperation in hierarchical organizations: an incentive perspective." *Journal of Law, Economics, and Organization*, 8: 321–45.

Janakiraman, Surya, Lambert, Richard, and Larcker, David (1992). "An empirical investigation of the relative performance evaluation hypothesis." *Journal of Accounting Research*, 30: 53–69.

Jensen, Michael and Murphy, Kevin J. (1990). "Performance pay and top-management incentives." *Journal of Political Economy*, 98: 225–64.

Jones, Derek and Kato, Takao (1995). "The productivity effects of employee stock-ownership plans and bonuses: evidence from Japanese panel data." *American Economic Review*, 85: 391–414.

Jovanovic, Boyan (1979). "Job matching and the theory of turnover." *Journal of Political Economy*, 87: 972–90.

Kaftan, Colleen and Barnes, Louis (1991). "Sun hydraulics corporation." Harvard Business School Case No. 491-119.

Kahn, Charles and Huberman, Gur (1988). "Two-sided uncertainty and 'up-or-out' contracts." *Journal of Labor Economics*, 6: 423–44.

Kahn, Lawrence and Sherer, Peter (1990). "Contingent pay and managerial performance." *Industrial and Labor Relations Review*, 43: 107S–120S.

Kahn, Shulamit (1994). "Evidence of nominal wage stickiness from microdata." Unpublished manuscript, Boston University.

Kandel, Eugene and Lazear, Edward (1992). "Peer pressure and partnership." *Journal of Political Economy*, 100: 801–17.

Kanemoto, Yoshitsugu and MacLeod, Bentley (1991). "The ratchet effect and the market for secondhand workers." *Journal of Labor Economics*, 10: 85–98.

Katzenbach, Jon and Smith, Douglas (1993). *The Wisdom of Teams: Creating the High-Performance Organization.* Boston: Harvard Business School Press.

Kerr, Steven (1975). "On the folly of rewarding A, while hoping for B." *Academy of Management Journal*, 18: 769–83.

Krueger, Alan (1991). "Ownership, agency, and wages: an examination of franchising in the fast food industry." *Quarterly Journal of Economics*, 106: 75–101.

Kruse, Douglas (1993). *Profit Sharing: Does It Make a Difference?* Kalamazoo, MI: W.E. Upjohn Institute for Employment Research.

Lazear, Edward (1979). "Why is there mandatory retirement?" *Journal of Political Economy*, 87: 1261–84.

(1986a). "Salaries and piece rates." *Journal of Business*, 59: 405–31.

(1986b). "Raids and offer matching." *Research in Labor Economics*, 8: 141–56.

(1989). "Pay equality and industrial politics." *Journal of Political Economy*, 97: 561–80.

(1992). "The job as a concept." In Bruns, W. (ed.), *Performance Measurement, Evaluations, and Incentives.* Boston: Harvard Business School Press.

(1996). "Performance pay and productivity." Unpublished manuscript, Stanford University.

Lazear, Edward and Rosen, Sherwin (1981). "Rank-order tournaments as optimum labor contracts." *Journal of Political Economy*, 89 (October): 841–64.

Lillard, Lee and Weiss, Yoram (1979). "Components of variation in panel data: American scientists 1960–1970." *Econometrica*, 47: 437–54.

MacDonald, Glenn (1982). "A market equilibrium theory of job assignment and sequential accumulation of information." *American Economic Review*, 72: 1038–55.

MacLeod, W. Bentley and Malcomson, James (1988). "Reputation and hierarchy in dynamic models of employment." *Journal of Political Economy*, 96: 832–54.

(1989). "Implicit contracts, incentive compatibility, and involuntary unemployment." *Econometrica*, 57: 447–80.

(1993). "Investments, holdup, and the form of market contracts." *American Economic Review*, 83: 811–37.

Maremont, Mark (1995). "Blind ambition: how the pursuit of results got out of hand at Bausch & Lomb." *Business Week*, October 23.

Margolis, David (1995). "Firm heterogeneity and worker self-selection bias estimated returns to seniority." CIRANO, University of Montreal, Working Paper No. 95s-4.

Mathewson, Stanley ([1931] 1969). *Restriction of Output Among Unorganized Workers.* Carbondale, IL: Southern Illinois University Press.

McLaughlin, Kenneth (1994). "Rigid Wages?" *Journal of Monetary Economics*, 34: 383–414.

Medoff, James and Abraham, Katharine (1980). "Experience, performance, and earnings." *Quarterly Journal of Economics*, 95: 703–36.

(1981). "Are those paid more really more productive?" *Journal of Human Resources*, 16: 186–216.

Meyer, Margaret (1991). "Learning from coarse information: biased contests and career profiles." *Review of Economic Studies*, 58: 15–42.
(1992). "Biased contests and moral hazard: implications for career profiles." *Annales d'Economie et de Statistique*, 25/26: 165–87.
Meyer, Margaret, Olsen, Trond, and Torsvik, Gaute (forthcoming). "Limited intertemporal commitment and job design." *Journal of Economic Behavior and Organization.*
Milgrom, Paul and Roberts, John (1988). "An economic approach to influence activities in organizations." *American Journal of Sociology*, 94: S154–79.
Miner, Anne (1987). "Idiosyncratic jobs in formalized organizations." *Administrative Science Quarterly*, 32: 327–51.
Mirrlees, James (1974). "Notes on welfare economics, information, and uncertainty." In Balch, M., McFadden, D., and Wu, S. (eds.), *Essays on Economic Behavior Under Uncertainty*. Amsterdam: North-Holland.
Montgomery, James (1991). "Social networks and labor-market outcomes: toward an economic analysis." *American Economic Review*, 81: 1408–18.
Murphy, Kevin J. (1985). "Corporate performance and managerial remuneration: an empirical analysis." *Journal of Accounting and Economics*, 7: 11–42.
(1986). "Incentives, learning, and compensation: a theoretical and empirical investigation of managerial labor contracts." *Rand Journal of Economics*, 17: 59–76.
(1991). "Merck & Co., Inc. (A)." Harvard Business School Case No. 9-491-005.
O'Flaherty, Brendan and Siow, Aloysius (1992). "On the job screening, up or out rules, and firm growth." *Canadian Journal of Economics*, 25: 346–68.
(1995). "Up-or-out rules in the market for lawyers." *Journal of Labor Economics*, 13: 709–35.
O'Reilly, Charles, Main, Brian, and Crystal, Graef (1988). "CEO compensation as tournament and social comparison: a tale of two theories." *Administrative Science Quarterly*, 33: 257–74.
Osterman, Paul (1987). "Choice of employment systems in internal labor markets." *Industrial Relations*, 26: 46–67.
(1994). "How common is workplace transformation and who adopts it?" *Industrial and Labor Relations Review*, 47: 173–88.
(1995). "Skill, training, and work organization in American establishments." *Industrial Relations*, 34: 125–46.
Oyer, Paul (1995). "The effect of sales incentives on business seasonality." Princeton University Industrial Relations Section Working Paper No. 354.
Patterson, Gregory (1992). "Distressed shoppers, disaffected workers prompt stores to alter sales commission." *Wall Street Journal*, July 1.
Pencavel, John and Craig, Ben (1994). "The empirical performance of orthodox models of the firm: conventional firms and worker cooperatives." *Journal of Political Economy*, 102: 718–44.
Pfeffer, Jeffrey (1983). "Organizational demography." In Cummings, L. and Staw, B. (eds.), *Research in Organizational Behavior*. Greenwich, CT: JAI Press.
Podolny, Joel and Baron, James (1995). "Resources and relationships: social

networks, mobility, and satisfaction in the workplace." Unpublished manuscript, Stanford University.

Post, Richard J. and Goodpaster, Kenneth E. (1981). "H.J. Heinz Company: the administration of policy." Harvard Business School Case No. 382-034.

Prendergast, Canice (1989). *Theories of Internal Labor Markets.* Unpublished doctoral dissertation. Yale University.

(1992). "Career development and specific human capital collection." *Journal of the Japanese and International Economies*, 6: 207–27.

(1993). "The role of promotion in inducing specific human capital acquisition." *Quarterly Journal of Economics*, 108: 523–34.

(1995). "A theory of responsibility in organizations." *Journal of Labor Economics*, 13: 387–400.

Rebitzer, James and Taylor, Lowell (1995). "When knowledge is an asset: explaining the organizational structure of large law firms." Unpublished manuscript, Carnegie-Mellon University.

Ricart i Costa, Joan (1988). "Managerial task assignment and promotions." *Econometrica*, 56: 449–66.

Roberts, Johnnie L. (1989). "Credit squeeze: Dun & Bradstreet faces flap over how it sells reports on businesses." *Wall Street Journal*, March 2.

Rosen, Sherwin (1982). "Authority, control, and the distribution of earnings." *Bell Journal of Economics*, 13: 311–23.

(1986). "Prizes and incentives in elimination tournaments." *American Economic Review*, 76: 701–15.

Rosenbaum, James (1984). *Career Mobility in a Corporate Hierarchy.* New York: Academic Press.

Rotemberg, Julio (1994). "Human relations in the workplace." *Journal of Political Economy*, 102: 684–717.

Roy, Donald (1952). "Quota restriction and goldbricking in a machine shop." *American Journal of Sociology*, 57: 427–42.

Sattinger, Michael (1975). "Comparative advantage and the distributions of earnings and abilities." *Econometrica*, 43: 455–68.

(1993). "Assignment models of the distribution of earnings." *Journal of Economic Literature*, 31: 831–80.

Shapiro, Carl and Stiglitz, Joseph (1984). "Equilibrium unemployment as a discipline device." *American Economic Review*, 74: 433–44.

Simon, Herbert (1951). "A formal model of the employment relationship." *Econometrica*, 19: 293–305.

Sloan, Richard (1993). "Accounting earnings and top executive compensation." *Journal of Accounting and Economics*, 16: 55–100.

Spilerman, Seymour and Ishida, Hiroshi (1994). "Stratification and attainment in large Japanese firms." Unpublished manuscript, Columbia University.

Spilerman, Seymour and Petersen, Trond (1993). "Organizational structure, determinants of promotion, and gender differences in attainment." Unpublished manuscript, Columbia University.

Staw, Barry (1974). "Attitudinal and behavioral consequences of changing a major organizational reward: a natural field experiment." *Journal of Personality and Social Psychology*, 6: 742–51.

(1977). "Motivation in organizations: towards synthesis and redirection." In Staw, B. and Salancik, G. (eds.), *New Directions in Organizational Behavior*. Chicago: St. Clair Press.

Stewart, James (1993). "Taking the dare." *The New Yorker*, July 26, pp. 34–9.

Stewman, Shelby (1986). "Demographic models of internal labor markets." *Administrative Science Quarterly*, 31: 212–47.

Tehranian, Hassan and Waegelein, James (1985). "Market reaction to short-term executive compensation plan adoption." *Journal of Accounting and Economics*, 7: 131–44.

Tirole, Jean (1986). "Hierarchies and bureaucracies: on the role of collusion in organizations." *Journal of Law, Economics, and Organization*, 2: 181–214.

(1996). "A theory of collective reputations (with applications to the persistence of corruption and firm quality)." *Review of Economic Studies*, 63: 1–22.

Topel, Robert (1991). "Specific capital, mobility, and wages: wages rise with job seniority." *Journal of Political Economy*, 99: 145–76.

Topel, Robert and Ward, Michael (1992). "Job mobility and the careers of young men." *Quarterly Journal of Economics*, 107: 439–79.

Wagner, W. Gary, Pfeffer, Jeffrey, and O'Reilly, Charles (1984). "Organizational demography and turnover in top-management groups." *Administrative Science Quarterly*, 29: 74–92.

Waldman, David and Avolio, Bruce (1986). "A meta-analysis of age differences in job performance." *Journal of Applied Psychology*, 71: 33–8.

Waldman, Michael (1984a). "Worker allocation, hierarchies, and the wage distribution." *Review of Economic Studies*, 51: 95–109.

(1984b). "Job assignment, signaling, and efficiency." *RAND Journal of Economics*, 15: 255–87.

(1990). "Up-or-out contracts: a signaling perspective." *Journal of Labor Economics*, 8: 230–50.

White, Harrison (1970). *Chains of Opportunity: System Models of Mobility in Organizations*. Cambridge, MA: Harvard University Press.

Williamson, Oliver (1983). "Credible commitments: using hostages to support exchange." *American Economic Review*, 83: 519–40.

Williamson, Oliver, Wachter, Michael, and Harris, Jeffrey (1975). "Understanding the employment relation: the analysis of idiosyncratic exchange." *Bell Journal of Economics*, 6: 250–78.

Vroom, Victor (1968). "Industrial social psychology." In Lindzey, G. and Aronson, E. (eds.), *The Handbook of Social Psychology*.

CHAPTER 2

Endogenous growth: lessons for and from economic history

N. F. R. Crafts

1 INTRODUCTION

In a survey of economic history written in the mid 1980s, I wrote that "economic history has had little influence upon and has been relatively little affected by growth theory of the postwar variety" (Crafts (1987, p. 40)). Clearly, growth accounting had been highly influential for measurement purposes but, at that point, for economic historians keen to understand productivity growth in terms of induced innovation or endogenous technological change, economic theory had little to offer, as the review of the well-known Habakkuk debate in David (1975) had made painfully obvious.

Since the mid 1980s, endogenous growth theory has developed very rapidly and has produced a large volume of theoretical research. At the core of these models is the proposition that investment in a broad sense, including human as well as physical capital and the production of new processes and products through research, is central to growth which can be driven on without being halted by diminishing returns.

One branch of endogenous growth theory obtains results by arguing for constant returns to routine investment in broad capital with the production function, $Y = A\tilde{K}$, as in Rebelo (1991). The key to rapid long-run growth is to be found in cultures, institutions, and tax policies which make a high rate of saving optimal. In this "capital-fundamentalist" approach there is no explicit role for total factor productivity (TFP), growth, or technological change. Despite the initial appeal of ideas of this kind, they are not persuasive as models of long-run growth. For example, cross-sectional regression evidence on the growth of GDP across countries (Mankiw, Romer and Weil (1992), Islam (1995)) and on output across British manufacturing sectors (Oulton and O'Mahony (1994)) suggests that the sum of the exponents on physical and human capital in the production function is less than one and that there are diminishing returns to routine investment in the long run.

Perhaps more importantly, as Romer has recently written, "our knowledge of economic history, of what production looked like 100 years ago, and of current events convinces us beyond any doubt that discovery, invention and innovation are of overwhelming importance in economic growth and that the economic goods that come from these activities are different in a fundamental way from ordinary objects. We could produce statistical evidence suggesting that all growth came from capital accumulation with no room for anything called technological change. But we would not believe it" (Romer (1993, p. 562)).

The second strand of modern growth theory seeks to explain rather than to abolish TFP growth. In doing so it emphasizes the role of profit-motivated investments in discovering new products and/or processes. This has involved the development of growth models of an aggregate economy in which at the microlevel production takes place under conditions of imperfect competition which allows the appropriation of profits to cover the fixed costs of research and development (R&D). The key feature of these models is that growth depends on the incentives to invest in improving technology. This can be seen to some extent as formalizing ideas long familiar in economic history and is likely to be found much more congenial by economic historians than capital fundamentalism.

Grossman and Helpman (1991) developed the paradigmatic model of this kind. Production is assumed to be a function of capital, labor and differentiated products used as intermediate inputs, and growth of output is proportional to the rate of innovation. The endogenous steady improvement in intermediate inputs is analogous to growth in TFP in the traditional neoclassical model and, as might be expected, the rate of capital formation adjusts to the rate of innovation rather than vice versa. Growth depends on the allocation of resources to innovation and is promoted by larger markets, more productive labor in research, and greater market power in exploiting discoveries.

A central concern of this chapter is to assess both the potential of this approach for research in economic history and the implications of historical experience for further development of endogenous innovation models of growth. Here there seems to be an important opportunity for the two-way flow of ideas and information which ought to characterize the relationship between economics and economic history.

Thus the new growth economics offers new and/or better specified models with which to investigate why growth rates have differed while economic history provides a much richer array of experience with which to test and refine growth models than is comprised in the much used Heston–Summers data set relating to the world since 1960. Beyond this, however, endogenous growth theory allows institutions and government policy to play a cental role in long-run growth outcomes. This may open the door to a deeper understanding of the growth process and connects with central concerns of the historical growth and development literature. Here the intellectual arbitrage possibilities may be particularly promising.

2 OVERVIEW OF THE HISTORICAL EXPERIENCE OF ECONOMIC GROWTH

A major part of the quantitative economic historian's task is the construction of datasets. Over the last 40 years a massive effort has gone into historical national accounting together with the collection of information on prices to permit the calculation of purchasing power parity adjusted estimates of income levels. The 16 rich countries dataset compiled by Maddison (1991) which contains annual data on real GDP since 1860 in most cases is well known and has already been widely used in econometric exercises. Maddison (1995) gives information on a much larger sample of countries and will permit further testing. Table 2.1 presents some of Maddison's most recent estimates.

Several features of table 2.1 stand out. First, given the (conventional) periodization of the table, the difference in average growth rates across phases is apparent – in particular the 3.3 percent of the 1950–73 "Golden Age" is more than double the mean of any other period. Second, "catching-up" in the sense of an inverse correlation between the initial income level and subsequent growth is stronger after 1950, with the highest rank correlation coefficient of 0.54 in 1950–73. Third, there are still large discrepancies in real income levels in 1992 even in this sample of countries although the coefficient of variation among the original 20 listed for 1870 falls from 0.36 in 1870 to 0.31 in 1900, and from 0.37 in 1950 to 0.23 in 1973 and 0.21 in 1992. In Barro and Sala-i-Martin's (1991) terminology the 1950–73 period emerges as a period of unusually strong β- and σ-convergence; this remark applies even more strongly to the European subset (Crafts and Toniolo (1996)).

Economic historians tend generally to believe quite strongly in the notion of different phases in economic growth. Thus the interwar period is taken to be an era when the breakdown of international commodity and factor markets tended to impede economic growth and convergence tendencies (Williamson (1995)), the possibilities for and extent of technology transfer are argued to have been much greater after World War II than previously (Nelson and Wright (1992)), the pace and nature of technological

Table 2.1. *International cross-sections of real output levels and growth rates per capita, 1870–1992*

	Y/P 1870	Y/P 1913	Growth rate	(Rank)
1 Portugal	1,085	1,354	0.53	(20)
2 Finland	1,107	2,050	1.45	(9 =)
3 Norway	1,303	2,275	1.31	(11)
4 Argentina	1,311	3,797	2.50	(2)
5 Spain	1,376	2,255	1.16	(14)
6 Italy	1,467	2,507	1.26	(12)
7 Canada	1,620	4,213	3.28	(1)
8 Sweden	1,664	3,096	1.46	(7 =)
9 Ireland	1,773	2,733	1.10	(16 =)
10 France	1,858	3,452	1.45	(9 =)
11 Austria	1,875	3,488	1.46	(7 =)
12 Germany	1,913	3,833	1.64	(4)
13 Denmark	1,927	3,764	1.58	(5)
14 Switzerland	2,172	4,207	1.56	(6)
15 USA	2,457	5,307	1.82	(3)
16 Belgium	2,640	4,130	1.05	(15)
17 Netherlands	2,640	3,950	0.95	(18)
18 New Zealand	3,115	5,178	1.19	(13)
19 UK	3,263	5,032	1.01	(16 =)
20 Australia	3,801	5,505	0.88	(19)
	Y/P 1900	Y/P 1950		
1 Portugal	1,408	2,132	0.85	(15)
2 Finland	1,620	4,131	1.90	(3 =)
3 Italy	1,746	3,425	1.36	(9 =)
4 Norway	1,762	4,969	2.10	(1)
5 Chile	1,949	3,827	1.36	(9 =)
6 Spain	2,040	2,397	0.33	(21)
7 Ireland	2,495	3,518	0.70	(18)
8 Sweden	2,561	6,738	1.95	(2)
9 Argentina	2,756	4,987	1.20	(12)
10 Canada	2,758	7,047	1.90	(3 =)
11 France	2,849	5,221	1.22	(11)
12 Austria	2,901	3,731	0.52	(20)
13 Denmark	2,902	6,683	1.69	(7)
14 Germany	3,134	4,281	0.64	(19)
15 Switzerland	3,531	8,939	1.88	(5)
16 Netherlands	3,533	5,850	1.01	(14)

Table 2.1. *continued*

	Y/P 1900	Y/P 1950	Growth rate	(Rank)
17 Belgium	3,652	5,346	0.78	(17)
18 USA	4,096	9,573	1.72	(6)
19 Australia	4,299	7,218	1.04	(13)
20 New Zealand	4,320	8,495	1.37	(8)
21 UK	4,593	6,847	0.82	(16)
	Y/P 1950	Y/P 1973		
1 Portugal	2,132	7,568	5.68	(2)
2 Peru	2,263	3,953	2.46	(17)
3 Spain	2,397	8,739	5.80	(1)
4 Italy	3,425	10,409	4.93	(4)
5 Ireland	3,518	7,023	3.05	(14)
6 Austria	3,731	11,308	4.92	(5)
7 Chile	3,827	5,028	1.20	(23)
8 Finland	4,131	10,768	4.25	(6)
9 Germany	4,281	13,152	5.00	(3)
10 Norway	4,969	10,229	3.19	(10)
11 Argentina	4,987	7,970	2.06	(20)
12 France	5,221	12,940	4.03	(7)
13 Belgium	5,346	11,905	3.54	(8)
14 Netherlands	5,850	12,763	3.45	(9)
15 Denmark	6,683	13,416	3.08	(11 =)
16 Sweden	6,738	13,494	3.07	(13)
17 UK	6,847	11,992	2.47	(16)
18 Canada	7,047	13,644	2.91	(15)
19 Australia	7,218	12,485	2.41	(19)
20 Venezuela	7,424	10,717	1.62	(22)
21 New Zealand	8,495	12,575	1.73	(21)
22 Switzerland	8,939	17,953	3.08	(11 =)
23 USA	9,573	16,607	2.42	(18)
	Y/P 1973	Y/P 1992		
1 Ireland	7,023	11,711	2.73	(3)
2 Portugal	7,568	11,130	2.05	(6 =)
3 Argentina	7,970	7,616	−0.23	(21)
4 Spain	8,739	12,498	1.91	(9)
5 Norway	10,229	17,543	2.88	(2)

Table 2.1. *continued*

	Y/P 1973	Y/P 1992	Growth rate	(Rank)
6 Italy	10,409	16,229	2.37	(4)
7 Venezuela	10,717	9,163	−0.73	(22)
8 Finland	10,768	14,646	1.64	(12)
9 Japan	11,017	19,425	3.03	(1)
10 Austria	11,308	17,160	2.22	(5)
11 Belgium	11,905	17,165	1.95	(8)
12 UK	11,992	15,738	1.45	(15)
13 Australia	12,485	16,237	1.40	(16)
14 New Zealand	12,575	13,947	0.56	(20)
15 Netherlands	12,763	16,898	1.49	(14)
16 France	12,940	17,959	1.75	(10)
17 Germany	13,152	19,351	2.05	(6 =)
18 Denmark	13,416	18,293	1.65	(11)
19 Sweden	13,494	16,927	1.20	(18)
20 Canada	13,644	18,159	1.52	(13)
21 USA	16,607	21,558	1.39	(17)
22 Switzerland	17,953	21,036	0.86	(19)

Notes: All income levels are measured in 1990 International dollars and all growth rates are endpoint calculations measured per annum. The sample of countries in each period is based on a threshold income level of \$1,000 in 1870, \$1,400 in 1900, \$2,100 in 1950 and \$7,000 in 1973.
Source: Derived from Maddison (1995).

change are held to have been transformed in the early twentieth century (Abramovitz (1993)), and so on.

In a European context, there may be strong reasons for seeing both the world wars as exogenous shocks which led to a changed economic environment which impinged on growth performance (Maddison (1991)). The early post-World War II years have generally been seen as providing an unusually favorable climate for growth and for catching-up by follower countries in terms of a reconstruction stimulus, technological opportunities, macroeconomic stability, and a policy framework of international liberalization and domestic post-war settlements conducive to wage moderation and high investment (Abramovitz (1986), Boltho (1982), Dumke (1990), Eichengreen (1996)).

Table 2.2 reports the results of estimating a segmented trend model for seventeen countries using predetermined break points which match

Table 2.2. *Estimated trend rates of growth of output per person: predetermined breaks, unrestricted model*

% p.a. segment k	T_1–1914 1	15–19 2	20–39 3	40–50 4	51–73 5	74–89 6
Australia	0.36	0.31	0.62	2.08	2.32	1.90
Austria	1.31**	−4.44**	1.29**	−0.32	5.50**	1.83**
Belgium	0.90**	−0.63	1.01	−0.17	3.90**	2.09*
Canada	2.46**	−0.05	0.89	3.98*	2.47	2.91
Denmark	1.77**	−0.39*	1.58	0.91	3.46**	1.59**
Finland	1.45**	−1.71**	3.25**	1.56**	4.12**	2.83**
France	0.96**	0.85	0.78	0.70	4.92**	1.42**
Germany	1.47**	−2.19*	2.91	3.28	5.11**	1.26**
Italy	1.47**	3.16	0.21	1.01	5.31**	2.05**
Japan	1.48**	3.35	1.95	−2.76**	8.03**	2.70**
Netherlands	−0.42	6.01	−0.08	0.84	4.16*	0.96*
Norway	1.13**	2.45	2.28	1.96	3.49**	3.48
Spain	0.87**	2.22	−0.15	−0.66	4.95**	1.56**
Sweden	1.52**	−3.04**	3.03**	2.63	3.42*	1.62**
Switzerland	0.57	2.02	1.69	3.28	2.91	0.84**
UK	1.04**	−1.47**	1.56**	1.20	2.24*	1.83
USA	1.70**	1.58	0.86	3.76*	1.54*	1.89

Notes: T_1 is the series starting date; * and ** denote that a change in trend growth at the break T_k is significant at the 5 percent and 1 percent levels.
Source: Crafts and Mills (1996).

Maddison's epochal account based on Crafts and Mills (1996). The model is

$$x_t = \gamma_0 + \gamma_1 t + \Sigma_i = {}_6^2\gamma_i D_{it} + u_t \qquad (1)$$

where x is the logarithm of output per person and $D_{it} = (t - T_i).1(t > T_i)$, 1(.) is the indicator function and $T_i = 2, \ldots, 6$ correspond to the break years 1914, 1919, 1939, 1950, and 1973. This segmented trend stationary process was treated as the alternative to the unit root null. The test statistics reported in appendix 1 provide convincing evidence that all output per person series are stationary around a segmented trend, a finding which remains when the final breakpoint is allowed to be determined endogenously. The error u_t was then modeled by an autoregressive process

$$u_t = \rho u_{t-1} + \Sigma_i \delta_i \Delta u_{t-i} + a_t \qquad (2)$$

and equations (1) and (2) were jointly estimated.

The analysis underlying table 2.2 reveals a number of interesting features of the long-run growth process. First, the hypothesis of a "Golden Age" of growth for European countries in the early post-war period is not rejected. Second, the hypotheses that after the Golden Age European countries were either back to the pre-depression and war trend path or a parallel path with higher productivity are rejected for all countries except Denmark. Third, in all European countries GDP/hours worked relative to the USA is higher in 1989 than in 1913.

Regression analysis of international cross-sections for the recent past is favorable to the hypothesis of conditional (β) convergence in the Barro and Sala-i-Martin sense that growth is inversely related to initial productivity relative to the leading economy (Dowrick and Nguyen (1989), Levine and Renelt (1992)). Two points should be noted about this finding, neither of which should be too surprising given tables 2.1 and 2.2.

First, regression analysis of the long-run Maddison dataset suggests that the null hypothesis of no catching-up cannot be rejected outside of the unusual 1950–73 period (van de Klundert and van Schaik (1996)). Second, conditional convergence in the post-war cross-sections does not imply ultimate convergence in the strong sense that the long-term forecasts of output per person are equal. Bernard and Durlauf (1995) reject this hypothesis using cointegration techniques on the Maddison dataset.

Research in economic history has for many years made extensive use of growth accounting and much attention has been paid to the behavior of the Solow residual. Obviously, the advent of the new growth economics potentially undermines the assumptions on which this work has been based. Current research does, however, suggest that profits share may be a reasonable approximation for the elasticity of output with respect to physical capital investment where externalities are probably small (King and Levine (1994), Oulton and O'Mahony (1994)). In this event, it is interesting to consider traditional estimates of Solow's residual which can be thought of as the explicandum of the new growth economics, either to be explained by an endogenous innovation model or to be explained away by better measurement of broad capital formation.

The estimates in table 2.3 are based on traditional growth accounting, are necessarily crude for earlier periods, and are not strictly comparable over time or between the two countries in the sense that the precise details of the methods used to produce them are not exactly the same. Nevertheless, the broad outline shown by the table is useful and deserves to be addressed by the new growth economics. Three points might be noted about table 2.3. First, for the United States, there has been much greater TFP growth during most of the twentieth than in the nineteenth century. Second, the American acceleration in TFP growth in the early twentieth century was

Table 2.3. *Total factor productivity growth in the long run (% per annum)*

	USA		UK
1800–55	0.2	1780–1831	0.3
1855–1905	0.5	1831–73	0.8
1905–27	1.7	1873–1913	0.5
1929–48	1.8	1924–37	0.6
1948–66	2.2	1951–73	2.1
1966–89	0.8	1973–92	0.6

Sources: Abramovitz (1993), Crafts (1995b), Maddison (1996), Matthews *et al.* (1982).

not matched by the UK. Third, there may also have been a change in the factor-saving bias of technological change between the nineteenth and the twentieth centuries from physical capital-using to intangible (human and knowledge) capital-using (Abramovitz (1993, p. 224)).

The most ambitious growth accounting exercises by an economic historian are those of Maddison whose latest estimates are reported in table 2.4. An intriguing feature of his work is the attempt to attribute TFP growth to specific sources. This represents essentially a set of hypotheses based on a reading of the historical experience rather than a series of estimated results and requires strong assumptions, for example on the counterfactual productivity performance had there been a different pattern of structural change in employment. The unusually rapid European growth in the Golden Age is seen as resulting to a large extent from high TFP growth which in turn derives from several sources, although the related factors of trade liberalization and technology transfer clearly underwrite this episode.

Four aspects of the estimates in table 2.4 require comment. First, it is striking how little part human capital formation appears to play in why growth rates differed. In the table years of education impact through the contribution of the labor force. This raises issues both of weighting and of measurement, i.e., the use of schooling as a proxy variable. Second, a good deal of the variation over time and across countries in TFP growth is regarded even by Maddison as unexplained. Third, no explicit role for R&D expenditure is identified. Fourth, even so, it is apparent that this approach would stress that it is quite wrong to equate TFP growth with technological progress or a fortiori with the effects of R&D according to the historical evidence. Table 2.4 both indicates the size of the challenge to endogenous growth theory in terms of what needs to be accounted for and also explains why both economic historians and growth economists became so frustrated with traditional growth economics.

Table 2.4. *Maddison on the sources of growth (% per annum)*

	1913–50	1950–73	1973–92
France			
GDP	1.15	5.02	2.26
Total factor input	0.48	1.96	1.61
Non-residential capital	0.63	1.59	1.26
Education	0.36	0.36	0.67
Total factor productivity	0.67	3.06	0.65
Foreign trade effect	0.03	0.37	0.12
Catch-up effect	0.00	0.46	0.31
Structural effect	0.04	0.36	0.15
Scale effect	0.03	0.15	0.07
Unexplained	0.57	1.72	0.00
Germany			
GDP	1.28	5.99	2.30
Total factor input	1.00	2.71	0.77
Non-residential capital	0.59	2.20	0.93
Education	0.24	0.19	0.11
Total factor productivity	0.28	3.28	1.53
Foreign trade effect	−0.13	0.48	0.15
Catch-up effect	0.00	0.62	0.31
Structural effect	0.20	0.36	0.17
Scale effect	0.04	0.18	0.07
Unexplained	0.17	1.64	0.83
United Kingdom			
GDP	1.29	2.96	1.59
Total factor input	0.94	1.71	0.96
Non-residential capital	0.72	1.64	0.93
Education	0.33	0.18	0.43
Total factor productivity	0.35	1.25	0.63
Foreign trade effect	0.01	0.32	0.15
Catch-up effect	0.00	0.08	0.20
Structural effect	−0.04	0.10	−0.09
Scale effect	0.04	0.09	0.05
Unexplained	0.34	0.66	0.32
United States			
GDP	2.79	3.91	2.39
Total factor input	1.53	2.34	2.22
Non-residential capital	0.81	1.05	0.90
Education	0.41	0.48	0.46
Total factor productivity	1.26	1.57	0.17
Foreign trade effect	0.04	0.11	0.05
Catch-up effect	0.00	0.00	0.00
Structural effect	0.29	0.10	−0.17
Scale effect	0.08	0.12	0.07
Unexplained	0.85	1.24	0.22

Note: Some factor inputs not listed separately in this table.
Sources: Derived from Maddison (1991) (1996).

It should also be remembered that there is a substantial literature of empirical studies of technological change contributed by economic historians and other researchers in the field of technology economics which has gone, so far, largely unconsulted by growth economists. While in many ways this is broadly supportive of the endogenous innovation models of growth, this research suggests the need for further refinement of the early work in new growth theory.

First, in judging the performance of the endogenous innovation models over time it is important to allow for the notion of phases in growth discussed earlier. More importantly, work by economic historians of technology suggests that it is important to take into account "technological opportunity" when seeking to explain either the inputs into or the outputs from R&D. A fully Schumpeterian vision would embrace not only creative destruction but also technologically based long waves in economic growth (von Tunzelmann (1995)). Empirical research on the determinants of R&D and patenting underlines the importance of technological opportunity in research based on experience since 1950 in both Europe and America (Pakes and Schankerman (1984), Stoneman (1979)). At the same time these studies tend to be consistent with the endogenous innovation growth models in that they also find that appropriability conditions matter, as does market size and demand growth. Perhaps the most comprehensive paper which confirms all these points is that of Jaffé (1988).

Second, in considering the rise of the American technological lead from the late nineteenth to the mid twentieth century, the historical literature anticipates and confirms the broad outlines of an explanation along the lines of the endogenous innovation branch of new growth theory. Thus the American research effort is seen as having been stimulated by the scale effects of a better integrated and ever larger domestic market well beyond that of any European country (Chandler (1990), Nelson and Wright (1992)). By the 1930s the volume of R&D in the US was about ten times that of the UK (Edgerton and Horrocks (1994, p. 233)) while American population and GDP which had been similar to that of the UK in the 1860s were now three times and four times larger respectively (Maddison (1995)). Detailed research on the motivation for the development of American industrial research also stresses the rapid growth of educational programs which increased the supply of chemists and engineers, the strengthening of protection for intellectual property, and the growing realization that ongoing research acted to increase market power (Mowery and Rosenberg (1989), Reich (1985)).

It would not, however, be plausible to attribute all the increase in TFP growth since the mid nineteenth century to R&D. It seems plausible that R&D spending was between 2.5 and 3 percentage points of GDP higher in

1948–66 than in 1855–1905. Using the 40 percent social rate of return to R&D suggested by Griliches (1995, p. 60) would imply that TFP growth would have been raised by between 1.0 and 1.2 percentage points, whereas the total change is of the order of 1.7 percentage points.

Third, in assessing the predictions of the (neo-Schumpeterian) endogenous innovation growth models, it is important to distinguish between the importance of the appropriability of returns and monopoly or concentration as factors promoting innovative activity. Empirical evidence suggests that appropriability is related in particular to lead times over rivals rather than patents (Levin *et al.* (1987)) and that large business units may have an advantage in exploiting learning curves and spreading fixed costs (Cohen (1995)), but that rivalry among big firms is advantageous in promoting R&D (Patel and Pavitt (1992)). Collusion among British manufacturing firms in the post-war period seems to have retarded productivity growth (Broadberry and Crafts (1996)) and in properly specified regression studies there is no relation between concentration and R&D (Cohen (1995)). As theorists have begun to recognize (Aghion and Howitt (1995)), history suggests that the implication in many current new growth models that market power is good for growth needs to be handled with care.

3 ENDOGENOUS INNOVATION MODELS OF GROWTH: HOW WELL DO THEY WORK IN ECONOMIC HISTORY?

In this section I wish to explore the value added from approaching economic history from the perspective of endogenous growth theory. To do so, I shall consider three highly controversial phases of British economic growth with the aim of asking both whether the new growth models improve our understanding and/or help to resolve old debates and also whether existing historical accounts suggest ways in which work in growth economics could be strengthened. Each of these episodes will be treated in a highly selective fashion with no pretension to providing a balanced or comprehensive survey of the literature.

3.1 The Industrial Revolution reconsidered[1]

Trying to explain why the First Industrial Revolution happened in Britain over several decades in the late eighteenth and early nineteenth century is one of the classic historical questions. The current state of the ongoing debate is well summarized in the contributions to Floud and McCloskey (1994). Recent research has also devoted considerable effort to better estimates of growth rate at this time, an exercise which is fraught with index number problems and hampered by data imperfections (Crafts and Harley (1992)). It is now widely believed that the overall acceleration of economic growth was fairly modest but argument lingers on (Cuenca Esteban (1994, 1995), Harley and Crafts (1995)).

Table 2.5 displays what seem to be the most plausible growth estimates, set out in a fairly conventional periodization, together with data on factor accumulation and TFP growth estimates using basic growth accounting assumptions, as in table 2.3. It is noticeable that by modern standards investment in both physical and human capital was sparse and rose only slowly. The correlation between changes in TFP growth and broad capital accumulation as measured is clearly quite small. In fact, looking at this table from a factor accumulation perspective, it is not at all obvious that we can fully explain the speeding up of economic growth during the Industrial Revolution and our *ex ante* expectations of growth would probably have been low, as were Adam Smith's (Wrigley (1987, p. 21)).[2]

The central themes of the endogenous innovation growth models have a strong echo in the classic debate on the causes of the Industrial Revolution. Writings in the property rights tradition have stressed the importance of the early development of the patent system in England (Dutton (1984), North and Thomas (1973)) and the old theme of transport improvements and integration of the market as a stimulus to innovation has recently been reasserted by Szostak (1991). Examples of careful calculation and profit-maximizing behavior in weighing alternative strategies to exploit the value of discoveries once invented abound in recent work on technical change in the eighteenth and early nineteenth centuries (Macleod (1992)).

Nevertheless, the most authoritative recent discussion of technological change in this period by Mokyr (1990) stresses other aspects which are not part of the basic endogenous innovation growth model. Mokyr suggests that "A technological definition of the Industrial Revolution is a cluster of macroinventions leading to an acceleration in microinventions" (1993, p. 22). "Macroinventions" are radical new ideas which are unpredictable and should be seen as exogenous technological shocks. "Microinventions" come through improvement, adaptation and diffusion of a technology, and learning by doing. They are conditioned by economic factors and account for the majority of productivity improvement but within any particular technology are subject to diminishing returns.

It is a central feature of research on the Industrial Revolution that the full impact of technological changes often took many decades to be realized – for example, the steam engine (Kanefsky (1979), von Tunzelmann (1978)) – and often involved extensive learning – for example, in the iron industry (Allen (1983), Hyde (1977)). A recent econometric analysis of the renewal of patent rights in the period 1852–76 obtained three important results. First,

Table 2.5. *Broad capital accumulation and growth in Britain, 1760–1913* (All data in percent except years of schooling)

	1760–80	1780–1801	1801–31	1831–73	1873–99	1899–1913
Investment/GDP	5.7	6.3	8.3	8.7	8.3	8.7
Equipment investment/GDP	1.1	1.3	1.6	1.9	2.0	2.2
Male literacy	62	62	65	70	86	98
School enrollment						
Primary[a]			36	76	94	100
Secondary[b]				17	30	55
Years of schooling[c]			2.30	4.21	5.32	6.75
GDP growth	0.6	1.3	1.9	2.4	2.1	1.4
TFP growth	0.0	0.1	0.4	0.75	0.75	0.05

Notes:
[a]Estimates refer to 1818, 1851, 1881, 1906.
[b]Estimates refer to 1867, 1895, 1913.
[c]Estimates refer to cohort of workers born before 1805, to 1871, 1891 and 1911.
Sources: Investment estimates are from Feinstein (1988, pp. 431–2); literacy is based on Schofield (1973, pp. 441–6); primary school enrollment derived from Mitch (1982, p. 10) and Mitchell (1988, pp. 15, 799); secondary school enrolment derived from Great Britain (1867/8, p. 815) (1895, p. 424) and Mitchell (1988, p. 863); GDP growth and TFP growth based on Crafts and Harley (1992) and Matthews *et al.* (1982).

the value of patent rights was much smaller relative to physical investment and GDP and, second, the positive influence of a larger market on renewals was much smaller than in modern times. Third, in contrast to the modern period, the stock of patents already extant has a positive effect on expected returns to further invention (Sullivan (1994)). The plausible interpretation given by the author is that R&D mattered much less 150 years ago, that exogenous discovery mattered much more, and that it tended to trigger further innovation through microinvention.

In terms of trend growth this account suggests that the technological changes associated with the classic Industrial Revolution would tend to promote a period of steadily increasing output and productivity growth as learning and diffusion took place followed by decreasing output and productivity growth as microinvention ran into diminishing returns. The increases in factor accumulation during the period would neither fully explain growth nor be sufficient to sustain growth at the peak rate. This would be consistent with the findings of Crafts and Mills (1994) that trend growth of industrial output varied significantly between periods and that the most satisfactory model is a segmented quadratic trend with endogenous break points found at 1776, 1834, and 1874.[3]

During the classic Industrial Revolution years exogenous technological change was a central element in the acceleration of economic growth. Furthermore, productivity improvement through learning was far more important than that obtained through high fixed cost investment in R&D. This offers further support for the view that changes in technological opportunity over time may need to be allowed for in applying endogenous growth models to the long run. While the basic endogenous innovation growth models cannot encompass this experience, a stochastic version of the expanded model, proposed by Young (1993), which embraces learning effects, may be more appropriate.

Young's model has two important features. First, there is a stagnation equilibrium in which, if market size is too small relative to the expected costs of invention, there will be no discoveries and also no learning. Second, in general, the steady-state rate of growth depends not only on incentives to inventive activity but also on the rate of learning, which for any particular technology is bounded (Young (1993), pp. 444–8)). Economic historians of the Industrial Revolution should particularly applaud this last formulation and hope for further exploration of learning in endogenous innovation growth models.

Young sees the eighteenth-century British experience basically as an escape from the stagnation equilibrium and emphasizes that, once this breakthrough had occurred, learning by doing was crucial to the success of inventions like James Watt's engine (1993, pp. 446 and 465). However, while Young anticipates that differences in market size may be more important than differences in learning capabilities in determining growth rates, Mokyr argues that in explaining British pre-eminence in the early nineteenth century the opposite is probably the case. He interprets the historical evidence relating to skills and experience to be that "The key to British technological success was that it had a comparative advantage in microinventions" (1993, p. 33).

It must also be stressed that Young (1993) does not account for the timing of the Industrial Revolution and it may well be too much to expect of an endogenous innovation growth model that it could convincingly do this. The important contributions of these models may lie rather in terms of explaining why TFP growth was so low even in Britain in the early nineteenth century and in terms of comparing the expected growth potential of different countries at this time.

Five characteristics of the economic environment of 200 years ago might lead to predictions of modest TFP growth using endogenous innovation models and would explain the lack of research laboratories. First, the size of markets was very small by today's standards. For example, using the estimates in Maddison (1995), in 1820 real GDP in the UK was about 10 percent of its 1950 level. Second, the costs of invention were high insofar as the contributions that science and formal education made to technological progress were modest (Mokyr (1990)). Third, the protection offered by the patent system was less secure and the costs of taking a patent out were still very high relative to the later nineteenth century (Dutton (1984)). Fourth, in the years of "Old Corruption" rent-seeking in the law, the bureaucracy, the Church and the military remained a very attractive alternative to entrepreneurship and led to an adverse allocation of talent (Rubinstein (1983)).[4] Fifth, realization of the profits from invention was made difficult by the need also to ensure that workers did not *ex-post* misappropriate them and this required further ingenuity of the pioneers.[5]

Similarly, five aspects of the British economy might be seen as making for generally higher TFP growth potential than in France without, however, explaining the location of (exogenous) macroinventions. First, despite a higher GDP in the larger French economy, better integration of markets and a large empire made for a larger effective market size (Szostak (1991)). Second, the percentage of the population urbanized, which reduced the costs of acquiring and developing knowledge, was twice the French level (Bairoch (1991)). Third, the superior skill base of the British labor force and, especially, expertise in using coal-based technologies, enhanced learning in Britain and limited technology transfer to France (Harris (1976)). Fourth, there is little doubt that rent-seeking was much more prevalent in eighteenth-century France (Root (1991)). Fifth, a lower direct tax rate may have been favorable to Britain.[6]

3.2 Did late Victorian Britain really fail?

The late nineteenth and early twentieth century is generally recognized as the period when economic and technological leadership passed from the UK to the United States. Table 2.1 shows the USA moving ahead in terms of real GDP/person and the growth accounting of table 2.3 indicates that in the early twentieth century, American TFP growth accelerated to a new higher rate while British TFP growth failed to do so. Table 2.5 highlights the "climacteric" that Matthews, Feinstein, and Odling-Smee (1982) claim occurred during 1899–1913 when weak growth of GDP was associated with a dramatic slowdown in TFP growth.

Not surprisingly, this episode has provoked much criticism of British performance with suggestions that there was an avoidable growth failure, associated with alleged weakness in institutions and policy, reflected in inadequate investment and company management. In the terminology of Abramovitz (1986) this might be seen as a weakening of "social capability." This alleged failure became a focus of attention for the vanguard of the new economic historians who attempted an exoneration of British entrepreneurs and capital markets, arguing that resources were allocated efficiently and technical choices were made rationally according to profit-maximizing criteria. The answer given to the question: "Did Victorian Britain fail?" was a resounding "No!"; McCloskey summed up, as follows: "There is, indeed, little left of the dismal picture of British failure painted by historians. The alternative is a picture of an economy not stagnating but growing as rapidly as permitted by the growth of its resources and the effective exploitation of the available technology" (1970, p. 451). The controversy is well covered by the material in Floud and McCloskey (1994).

Two points should be noted about the growth economics which was used either implicitly or explicitly by the new economic historians 25 years ago. First, the traditional Solow model was an important underpinning of arguments that denied that a higher domestic investment rate could have produced faster growth and which examined choices of technique with existing technology but did not take seriously the question of what determined the steady-state TFP growth rate. Second, the world was not seen as one of unconditional convergence. In particular, the stress placed on different factor endowments in a world of imperfect factor mobility implied that steady-state income and productivity would differ and that, given its advantages in terms of natural resources, it might be expected that American income per head and labor productivity would exceed British levels.

Subsequent research in this tradition has strengthened these arguments about convergence. Two particular themes stand out. First, research in the history of technology has stressed the importance of learning effects in nineteenth-century productivity improvement while recognizing that international transfer of such tacit knowledge was often difficult (Nelson and Wright (1992)). Second, it has been strongly argued that British firms were generally rational to regard the new American mass production technologies as inappropriate to British conditions and to continue with craft production methods both because of the absence of a large standardized domestic demand and because of the greater availability of skilled labor together with the entrenched tradition of craft unions' organization of the shopfloor (Broadberry (1994)).

How might the debate over British economic performance in the pre-1914 period be modified by the advent of endogenous growth theory? Clearly, this can be used to compare TFP growth in the UK and the USA and to add a further dimension to the analysis of business investment decisions. The straightforward prediction of the basic Grossman–Helpman

Table 2.6. *The economic environment of R&D in early twentieth-century UK and USA*

	UK	USA
Factors influencing size of R&D effort		
Population (millions, 1913)	45.6	97.6
Real GDP ($int 1990 bn, 1913)	230	518
University students (thousands, 1910)	27.7	355
Science/technology	3.0	65
Engineers/unskilled pay ratio 1913/14	4.63	3.71

	UK		USA	
	1913	1937	1913	1937
Revealed comparative advantage rankings				
Agricultural equipment	10	16	2	1
Cars and aircraft	12	11	4	2
Industrial equipment	5	7	3	3
Electricals	8	5	5	4
Iron and steel	3	9	9	5
Non-ferrous metals	16	15	1	6
Books and films	13	8	10	7
Chemicals	11	12	12	8
Metal manufactures	7	13	6	9
Brick and glass	14	10	11	10
Wood and leather	15	14	7	11
Rail and shipping	1	3	8	12
Fancy goods	9	4	13	13
Apparel	6	6	14	14
Alcohol and tobacco	4	1	15	15
Textiles	2	2	16	16

Sources: Population and real GDP: Maddison (1995). University students: Mitchell (1988, 1993) with science and technology component from Pollard (1989, p. 196) and Blank and Stigler (1957, pp. 6, 75). Pay ratio: Routh (1980, pp. 63, 120) for UK; for USA calculated using Blank and Stigler (1957, p. 124) and Melman (1956, p. 206). Revealed comparative advantage is based on relative export market shares by sectors and is derived from Crafts (1989, table 1).

model is that in the late nineteenth and early twentieth centuries not only would economic circumstances favor an upsurge of innovative activity in the United States but that this would be much less the case in Britain. Table 2.6 reveals the reasons.

On the eve of World War I the United States was much the larger economy, was producing substantially more college graduates in key disciplines, and had relatively cheaper technical personnel. In the light of the evidence on induced innovation, both cost and demand conditions might explain the relatively low R&D spending in the UK without implying entrepreneurial failure. By the 1930s, when relatively reliable data are available, the United States was spending at least twice as high a share of its GDP on R&D as either Britain or Germany, leading European countries (Edgerton and Horrocks (1994)). The rank correlation of revealed comparative advantage in 1937 with R&D intensity is + 0.72 for the USA but − 0.33 for the UK (Crafts (1989, pp. 132, 134)).

The importance of this for differences in TFP growth must not be exaggerated, however. On the basis of the modern rate of return evidence, the discrepancy might be expected to have raised the growth rate of TFP in the USA by, say, 0.4 percentage points relative to the UK – less than half the gap shown in table 2.4 for the interwar years. Table 2.4 suggests that a fairly similar impact may have resulted from structural change. It would also be anachronistic to attribute much of the 0.4 percent TFP growth gap which seems to have existed throughout the 40 years or so before 1914 to a gap in R&D while the so-called climacteric coincides with the beginnings of serious industrial research in Britain.[7]

Indeed, while the historical literature certainly recognizes the greater incentives to purposive investment in R&D which were emerging in the United States, the major stress in economic historians' accounts of nineteenth-century British and American technical progress, since the pioneering work of Rosenberg (1972) and David (1975), has been that American advantages derived mostly from relatively strong learning effects, particularly with natural resource-intensive technologies favored by American factor endowments. It has also been shown that late nineteenth/early twentieth-century American comparative advantage in manufacturing increasingly lay in natural resource-intensive exports (Wright (1990)). Table 2.8 confirms that the two economies were quite dissimilar in terms of revealed comparative advantage in exporting.

All this suggests that the growth model most relevant for pre-1914 Anglo-American comparisons may be that of Krugman–Lucas (Krugman (1987), Lucas (1988)) rather than Grossman–Helpman. In the original Krugman–Lucas model, specialization according to comparative advantage delivers persistently different growth rates where human capital is augmented by learning at sectorally different rates. Kennedy (1987) stressed that the sectors associated with strong productivity advance were smaller in the UK and, in a highly controversial counterfactual simulation, claimed that the growth rate during 1873–1913 could have been raised very substantially by structural shifts toward sectors with more growth potential. He attributed the failure to achieve this transformation largely to imperfections in the capital market, an argument which is also much disputed (Michie (1988)).

Two points deserve discussion. First, Lucas (1993) has proposed a more realistic version of his 1988 model in which learning in any particular sector is bounded, as with the Young (1993) model considered earlier. In the long run, persistently faster growth will then depend on continually renewing comparative advantage and respecializing in new fast-learning sectors; in the Lucas model this can be achieved through learning spillovers. What is clear about the UK in the long nineteenth century is that this did not happen. What remains for further research is to explore more deeply the reasons for this – were learning spillovers generally very weak, did natural resource endowments dominate the outcome, or were there institutional obstacles to the necessary restructuring?

Second, models of the Krugman–Lucas kind are more intuitively appealing when applied to the past both because spontaneous learning rather than R&D mattered more and because international spillovers of learning were smaller. At the same time, it is important to remember that issues of social capability related to the appropriability of returns to innovation also played a part in the inability of British firms to assimilate American improvements. In particular, the distinctively British system of industrial relations, which had emerged during the Industrial Revolution which relied on craft control to police effort levels, was an obstacle to emulating capital and management intensive methods (Lewchuk (1987)). High sunk cost investment in new technologies was vulnerable to workers' opportunistic behavior.

Four reflections might be made arising from this brief survey. First, the advent of endogenous growth theory opens up possibilities of long-run divergences in growth rates not readily contemplated in the early days of new economic history. Interestingly, slower growth may have resulted from factor endowments and scale effects such that the fundamental conclusions of the new economic history regarding "avoidable failure" still apply. Second, there are also reasons to think that British industrial relations may have inhibited the rapid elimination of "ideas gaps" between the US and the UK. If so, it should recognized that reforming these institutional arrangements involved both high switching costs and large externalities. Third, while entrepreneurial failure arguments are probably not re-instated by new growth economics, criticisms (implicit or explicit) of British economic policy might well be strengthened in terms of failure to reform institutions, or to modify industrial and trade policies, or to expand education opportunities more rapidly. Fourth, among the ways of predicting growth rate effects, an R&D-based model seems more suited to the second and third quarters of the twentieth century than to late Victorian times, when a model incorporating strong differences in learning effects may be more helpful. As Nelson and Wright (1992, pp. 1936, 1961) point out, the scope of networks of cumulative technological learning at that time seems to be mostly national rather than international which implies that catching up could be difficult and any tendencies to β-convergence were much weaker.[8]

3.3 British relative economic decline in the Golden Age: beyond proximate explanations?[9]

The early post-war period saw British growth of GDP/person and TFP growth reach all time highs and yet, as tables 2.1 and 2.4 reveal, in terms of international comparisons British performance appears to have been disappointing and this can be seen as a period of relative economic decline. Obviously, this has had a high profile and has provoked a great deal of comment. A useful introduction to this topic by a traditional economic historian is provided by Alford (1988).

Alford's summary, written in innocence of endogenous growth theory, indicates the seriousness of the challenge facing econometric historians: "technical economic analysis has provided much understanding of what we have termed proximate causes of economic performance but not of fundamental causes . . . in our view, of particular importance are the nature and operation of certain institutions" (1988, p. 102). The new growth economics may have the potential to rectify this situation and to identify impacts of industrial relations, capital markets, and political decision-making on growth outcomes – just the kind of explanatory framework that writers like Alford have in mind.

The message of tables 2.1 and 2.4 appears to be as follows. The UK had less scope for catching-up than most countries in 1950 but even so the Golden Age growth rate is disappointing relative to other European countries such as Denmark and Sweden with similar income levels. On a growth accounting basis, a shortfall in "unexplained" TFP growth appears to be a major contributor to the growth shortfall relative to countries like France and West Germany. The economic history literature has long been interested in growth based on catchup – at least since the time of Gerschenkron (1962). A strong emphasis has emerged that catchup is by no means automatic but depends on what Abramovitz (1986) called "social capability." This entails the ability effectively to assimilate the required technical and organizational changes which in turn depends on institutional arrangements and the incentives facing political decision-makers as well as investments in intangible capital. Low "social capability" would tend to imply in the terminology of Romer (1993) that "idea gaps" matter as well as "object gaps" in retarding economic growth.

Prima facie, the UK seems to be a country with a relatively weak social capability which fails to take full advantage of its opportunities in the new post-war economic environment.

Broadly speaking, econometric analysis and further accounting exercises confirm these initial impressions, although they also call for some refinements to this somewhat crude picture. Both Dowrick and Nguyen (1989) and van de Klundert and van Schaik (1996) find in cross-country growth regressions that British growth is well below what might be predicted on the basis of capital accumulation and initial income levels. Crafts (1995c) looks at regional growth in 1950–73 in a conditional convergence framework and finds that a British dummy variable implies growth slower by about 0.5 percent per year. Similarly, comparing the UK with its European peer group on the basis of the cross-section regression results in Levine and Renelt (1992) also indicates an unexplained shortfall of growth over and above that which might be attributed to factor accumulation and scope for catchup (Bean and Crafts (1996, table 4)). This clearly involved inhibitions to productivity growth outside the sphere of R&D.

Denison's detailed growth-accounting exercise led him to conclude that very substantial productivity gaps in 1960 should be attributed to differences in work effort, restrictive labor practices, and management quality amounting to 14.3 percent between the UK and France and 13.2 percent between the UK and West Germany (1968, p. 274). This would certainly correspond to the weight of qualitative evidence in the large number of studies of use of labor listed in Pratten and Atkinson (1976) and the case studies in Prais (1981) which suggest that in many industries difficulties of agreeing reductions in staff numbers slowed down the introduction of new technology.

A later growth accounting exercise for manufacturing in 1979, which paid careful attention to the impact of workers' skills and stocks of R&D, found that German TFP exceeded British TFP by 17.7 percent (O'Mahony and Wagner (1994, p. 24)). O'Mahony and Wagner measured skills by vocational qualifications and show that the UK workers had far less at the intermediate level in 1979 (1994, p. 15). This is not an aspect of human capital formation typically considered in either growth accounting or regression based growth studies which take into account education rather than training. In a companion study, O'Mahony (1992) undertook an econometric analysis of relative productivity in a cross section of British and German industry. Her results suggest that growth accounting may also somewhat underestimate the importance of skill formation – and thus exaggerate TFP differences – by failing to allow for externalities. An upper bound is that about 0.4 percentage points of the unexplained TFP growth difference for 1950–73 in table 2.4 between the UK and Germany might actually be accounted for in this way.

To an unthinking economist steeped in R&D-based endogenous innovation models, it may seem odd to accuse the UK of having a low social capability for growth and surprising that TFP growth was disappointing, given the British record of spending the second largest proportion in the OECD of its GDP on R&D development until the mid 1960s (United Nations (1964)). In fact, these figures are misleading since they include a huge government financed component centered on defence and including economically disastrous programs to support aerospace and nuclear power (Edgerton (1996)). In the years 1967–75 industry-financed R&D actually declined at 0.5 percent per year while in France and Germany this was growing at nearly 6 percent per year (Patel and Pavitt (1989)). The British share of patents granted to non-Americans in the USA fell from 23.4 percent in 1958 to 10.8 percent in 1979 (Pavitt and Soete (1982)) while Verspagen (1996) in an econometric analysis found that, in contrast to France and Germany, British R&D expenditure had virtually no impact on productivity growth.

This review clearly underlines the need for growth economists to devote more time to the construction of data. The inadequacy, at least for comparisons within the OECD, of standardly used proxies for human capital formation and of conventional R&D statistics has been revealed. Nevertheless, it seems there is an innovation and TFP growth failure to be explained in Golden Age Britain, even though there is some doubt about its precise magnitude. There were institutional idiosyncrasies which have attracted considerable attention and which might be encompassed within extensions of the endogenous innovation growth model framework. In particular, British capital markets and industrial relations fall into this category.

An important aspect of the post-war British capital market has been the development of the hostile takeover on a large scale. Jenkinson and Mayer (1992) concluded that the British rules of the game created a unique exposure to this risk and that it normally entails the exit of existing top management. This might be expected to promote short termism and to dampen enthusiasm for long-term investments such as R&D whose payoffs might not result until after the change in ownership (Franks and Mayer (1990)). Mayer (1992) found that large British firms generally felt compelled to maintain dividends at the expense of R&D. In terms of the Grossman–Helpman model, this can be thought of as tantamount to a reduction in market power in reducing the appropriability of profits from discoveries and thus can be expected to have reduced both the allocation of resources to innovation and the long-run growth of TFP.

Crouch has chronicled changes in west European industrial relations systems and has stressed the transformation which occurred in many countries between the 1920s and the early 1950s. Against a background of widespread centralization of bargaining and even adoption of corporatist structures, he saw a case of unusual continuity: "there is in Europe only one case of a powerful, long-established but decentralized unionism – that of Britain" (1993, p. 337). The British system of industrial relations was characterized by multiple unionism, by an absence of legally enforceable contracts and by legal immunities extending to most forms of industrial action. Increasingly bargaining took place with shop stewards rather than union bosses (Batstone (1988)).

Individual firms basically had to accept these rules of the game and it is clear that they impacted adversely on the productivity of foreign multinationals operating in the UK as well as of domestic firms (Lewchuk (1987), Pratten (1976)). Eichengreen (1996) traced out the implications for investment and catchup growth and concluded that they were adverse; in the UK it was harder for the two sides of industry to make commitments to wage moderation in exchange for productivity enhancing investments. In the post-war context these arrangements would be a more serious handicap than hitherto both because workers' bargaining power was enhanced in a situation of full employment in the labor market with weak competition in product markets and also because the enhanced scope for technology transfer meant the forgone productivity growth would be greater.

Grout (1984) showed how bargaining between management and unions can lead to underinvestment in the absence of binding contracts, because *ex post* the workforce can expropriate some of the quasi-rents. When this insight is integrated into an endogenous innovation growth model, the implication is that profits from discoveries are reduced as are the incentive for innovative activity and the growth rate. The disincentives are more severe the more powerful are the workforce and with multiple bargaining. This both increases the inefficiency and, by encouraging free-riding behavior, undermines the possibility of solving the problem via a reputational equilibrium. Bean and Crafts (1996) provide a formal model and econometric estimates of the implication of multiple unionism. Their results, which are set out in appendix 3, indicate that in British manufacturing during 1954–79 the presence of multiple unionism reduced TFP growth by between 0.75 and 1.1 percent per year.

The endogenous innovation approach to growth argues that the growth rate could have been increased by appropriate government interventions.

Yet the historical record suggests that, despite considerable efforts in this direction, supply-side policy was at best ineffective and at worst harmful (Crafts (1991)). There seem to have been three reasons for this. First, there were mistakes due to inexperience or policies which had unintended consequences. The reform of the Companies Act in 1948 which sought to address issues raised by interwar scandals but which led to the development of the hostile takeover is a good example. Second, governments implicitly believed in the wrong growth model and concentrated on subsidizing physical investment rather than facilitating reduction of the ideas gap and TFP growth. An extreme version of this policy error was seen in Northern Ireland (Crafts (1995c)).

Third, and perhaps most fundamental, political decisionmakers saw votes to be lost rather than won through incurring short-term pain from supply-side reform even though the long-term rewards could have been considerable, given that credible promises of compensation to possible losers were not feasible. Price and Sanders (1994) implicitly justify the rationality of this short termism by politicians; in an econometric study they showed that short-term macroeconomic performance had powerful effects on government popularity and that the reforming Thatcher government would have lost office long before seeing any payoff but for the Falklands War. The short-term imperative was to negotiate (tacit or overt) social contracts with the trade unions, especially when substantial macroeconomic problems arose, for example, during post-war reconstruction (Crafts (1993)) or during the oil crisis. These involved in part wage restraint in return for abandoning attempts at reform of industrial relations.

This discussion should be taken to indicate some of the potential of the new growth economics to address the issues which economic historians like Alford (1988) see at the heart of comparative growth performance. Obviously, it is not a balanced or complete account of a complex growth process. Equally clearly, it is the spirit rather than the letter of the well-known models which is applicable. Ultimately, models in which institutions impacting on innovative activity, as well as innovation itself, are endogenous will be required to obtain a deeper understanding of Britain's relative economic decline.

4 THE GOLDEN AGE AND AFTER

The renewal of interest in growth economics has been remarkable for an explosion of regressions seeking to explain cross-country differences in growth rates based on evidence drawn from the post-1960 period for which large samples of purchasing power parity adjusted national income estimates are available. Much of this work is ably reviewed in Levine and

Renelt (1992). A good deal has been learnt from this research program but a longer-run view drawing on findings in economic history helps both to place these results in perspective and also to underline some limitations of this approach. In particular, it is important to note both that the cross-section regressions are generally affected by the special circumstances of the Golden Age and that they say relatively little about the roles that policy and institutions play.

Levine and Renelt (1992) argue that relatively few of the cross-section results will bear much weight but that a basic robust regression relates growth of output per person positively to the share of investment in GDP, and school enrollment rates and negatively to the initial income level which would capture scope for catchup. In Barro and Martin's framework this would be a world of conditional convergence. Such a regression could be used to provide an alternative form of growth accounting to the traditional one of Maddison (1996). In Table 2.7, an illustration of this is reported using a specification which also includes government consumption expenditure, for which there appears to be a robust (negative) relationship in the OECD, if not across the whole world (Dowrick (1992)).

Taken at face value the results in table 2.7 indicate the following. First, the acceleration in growth in the Golden Age is attributed largely to greater investment in both physical and human capital rather than greater scope for catchup in terms of a larger income gap. Second, compared with the traditional growth accounting of table 2.4, this approach attributes more of the acceleration in growth to human capital and less to TFP growth; 1.41 percentage points of the 1.72 increase in growth between 1923–38 and 1950–73 is attributed to broad capital accumulation. Third, the slowdown after 1973 is attributed much more to erosion of catchup opportunities than in the Maddison estimates of table 2.4. Fourth, and by no means least, the speed-up in growth in the Golden Age has a substantial unexplained component (of about a third). It is noticeable that the variables listed in table 2.7 do not capture changes in "social capability"; this may account for at least some of the "unexplained" increase in growth in the "Golden Age."

Recently, more attention has been given to the role of policy choices in growth outcomes. Sachs and Warner (1995) find that openness is a key criterion in facilitating catchup and their openness dummy variable has a 2 percentage point effect on growth in a conditional convergence set up. Taylor (1995) explores this result further and concludes that distortions associated with absence of openness played a significant role in the growth failures of Latin American economies in this period.

Economic historians studying the post-war period against the background of earlier times have argued that for a number of reasons an interval of very rapid TFP growth was possible in Europe; essentially these arguments are similar to those identified, but perhaps not reliably quantified, in the well-known growth accounting studies of Denison (1967) and Maddison (1991). Kindleberger (1967) stressed factors which promoted the redeployment of "surplus labor" from agriculture. Dumke (1990) emphasized the rapid productivity growth accruing from reconstruction of war-damaged economies. Owen (1983) pointed to the strong impact of trade liberalization in promoting cost reductions in the style later envisaged by the Cecchini Report.

In the context of an unprecedented American technological lead, productivity assistance missions strove to speed up imitation of American technology and organization. Attracted by the new economic environment, an American "invasion" of Europe developed. Thus, while in 1930–48 American companies established 93 operations in Britain and 33 in Germany, in 1949–71 the figures were 544 and 330 respectively (Chandler (1990, pp. 158–9)). Nevertheless, success in "technology transfer" varied and seems to have been affected by institutional and policy differences. The bargaining equilibrium between firms and their workers in the context of British industrial relations seems to have limited the productivity gains from exposure to American ideas (Broadberry and Crafts (1996)) while differing national strategies of human capital accumulation seem to have affected the ability to convert information into an effective knowledge base for developing indigenous technological capabilities (von Tunzelmann (1995)). These would not, however, be captured by the enrollment ratios of table 2.7.

Econometric evidence can be found to provide some support for the view that reductions in the ideas gap played a considerable part in the catchup growth of the Golden Age. Verspagen (1996) augmented growth regressions for the OECD to include patenting performance and found that the results imply that post-war patenting had reduced the coefficient of variation of labor productivity in 14 European countries by about 20 percent by 1973. Coe and Helpman (1995) showed in a study for 1971–90 that the TFP growth in European countries has been highly responsive to increases in foreign R&D capital stocks, more strongly so the more open the economy. Ben-David (1993) showed that the coefficient of variation in income levels in European countries was reduced sharply by specific episodes of European economic integration in the post-war period. Chou *et al.* (1995) find econometrically that R&D efforts in OECD countries are substantially boosted by greater international integration.

Two points emerge from this discussion following on that of section 3.3. First, it seems clear that both the detailed attribution of sources of growth by growth accounting and the implicit account of Golden Age growth of the new empirical growth economics are unconvincing. Key areas for further

Table 2.7. *Accounting for changes in European output/head growth using a Levine–Renelt approach (percent per year)*

	1923–38	1950–73	1973–89
Constant	2.01	2.01	2.01
Inital GDP/head	−2.43	−2.49	−3.55
Investment/GDP	1.42	2.22	2.06
Secondary enrollment	0.16	0.68	0.79
Primary enrollment	1.90	1.99	1.79
Government/GDP	−0.62	−0.87	−1.27
Predicted	2.44	3.54	1.83
Actual	2.12	3.84	2.14

Notes: Estimates are for the unweighted average of European countries in Maddison's (1991) database excluding Belgium and Switzerland.
Sources: The estimates are derived using equation (ii) in Levine and Renelt (1992) with population growth and irrelevant dummies ignored. The initial income variable was expressed as a percentage of the US level in each year and was then multiplied by 1960 US income per person. Basic sources of national accounts data were Maddison (1991, 1995a) and OECD, *Economic Outlook* supplement for interwar investment by Maddison (1992) and for interwar government consumption expenditure by den Bakker *et al.* (1990), Feinstein (1972), Hansen (1974), Hjerrpe (1989), Krantz and Nilsson (1975) Rossi *et al.* (1992), Sommariva and Tullio (1986), and Villa (1993).

work would seem to include refinement of measures of human capital formation and continued econometric investigation of the determinants of TFP growth using the pointers provided by economic historians. Second, the historical evidence supports recent suggestions that growth regressions have tended to exaggerate the importance of accumulation relative to innovation and ideas (Romer (1993)) and have obscured the roles of institutions and policy in growth outcomes.[10] Interestingly, recent econometric re-evaluation of the standard international cross-section growth database seems to point to a similar conclusion. Islam (1995) re-estimates standard regressions using a panel data approach which permits the identification of country effects; he concludes both that these are large, that they reflect differences in TFP based on persistent differences in technology levels and institutions, and (tentatively) that human capital may have its effects on growth indirectly through social capability rather than directly through factor accumulation.

In contrast with the recent explosion in empirical research based on recent international cross sections, relatively little effort has been made to examine the implications of endogenous growth theory using time-series data, except insofar as the voluminous literature on unit-roots in GDP tests the general plausibility of these models. A pioneering attempt did, however, note that time-series testing might prove to be an uncomfortable experience for the new growth theory in that it appears that key characteristics of a country's economic activity are much more persistent than are its growth rates across decades (Easterly *et al.* (1993)).

A recent paper by Jones (1995) marks a welcome change by considering OECD, and particularly, American growth over the period since 1900 in the context of predictions that might be drawn from the endogenous growth literature. While his paper makes a good start in exploiting the historical data, a review of its findings suggests quite strongly that historical skills are required to take full advantage of the possibilities.

Jones's main point is that, although investments of the kind regarded as growth promoting by either branch of endogenous growth theory have risen steeply to record highs in the last 40 years or so growth rates of output and TFP are not higher than ever before. He argues that the rejection of the R&D-based endogenous innovation models is particularly strong: "The models posit that the growth rates of per capita output and TFP should be increasing with the level of resources devoted to R&D, which is wildly at odds with empirical evidence" (Jones (1995, p. 519)). Jones finds the basic structure of R&D growth models to be appealing but not the endogenous growth implications.[11]

Clearly Jones's results represent a very strong challenge to R&D-based endogenous growth models. Taking a long-run historical perspective and bearing in mind the work of growth accountants and studies of the impact of R&D on productivity, gives reasons to doubt that his critique is quite so devastating as might appear at first sight. Three points should be considered.

First, as was noted earlier, TFP growth has accrued historically from a wide range of sources including structural change and, given the relatively low fractions of GDP spent on R&D, at least until recent times relatively little TFP growth can be attributed to this source. Equally, reasons for the slowdown in TFP growth in the OECD may lie elsewhere.

Second, direct evidence on the potency of R&D is somewhat mixed and bedevilled by measurement problems. Griliches (1994) reviews the evidence and concludes that on balance it is likely that R&D in the American manufacturing has had as strong an effect on TFP growth in 1978–89 as it had in 1958–73. Furthermore, it may be that our ability accurately to measure TFP growth has declined and that recent official estimates are understated through inadequate treatment of the now much larger services sector in OECD economies.

Third, earlier sections of the chapter have stressed the special and unrepeatable features of the Golden Age in European growth, the need generally to consider phases of economic growth and the role that technological shocks can play in the growth process. Such effects are often felt with a substantial lag – electricity generation was achieved in the 1880s but its major impact on productivity was not felt until the 1920s (David (1991)). If, as some accounts of long-run technological change insist, major changes in "techno-economic paradigm" involve creative destruction and grave adjustment problems, it could be that these initial effects of recent technological improvements show up in slower productivity growth but that the delayed effects are the opposite (Freeman and Perez (1988)).

5 CONCLUDING COMMENTS

The major theme of this chapter has been to consider the potential of endogenous innovation growth models of the genre proposed by Grossman and Helpman (1991) at the interface between economics and economic history and, in particular, to investigate the scope for fruitful interaction in this area. My initial supposition was that there was an excellent opportunity for mutually beneficial trade and the survey tends to support this view.

The central feature of this approach is that productivity growth results from the purposive search for innovations in which the ability to appropriate profits to cover the fixed costs of discovery determines the resources devoted to innovative activity and thus the growth rate. This provides a key point of tangency with economic historians who are always keen to emphasize the role of institutions. These can have crucial effects on the resource allocation process underlying the endogenous growth outcomes. Moreover, for new economic historians, who have always been keen to argue that long-run differences in economic performance are not to be explained in ways which violate the hypotheses of rational expectations and profit maximization by agents who use available information efficiently, the potential attractions of endogenizing productivity growth in this way are apparent.

Each of the case studies set out in section 3 indicated that new insights and better hypotheses could result from employing the new growth economics in conjunction with existing knowledge. At the same time, it is clear that work in economic history will benefit from further work on learning effects in this framework and that sensitivity in using the models is required.

Where, more generally, are the likely gains for economic history from exposure to endogenous innovation growth theory? Three areas seem to be especially worth stressing.

(i) Unlike traditional neoclassical growth economics, the new models can readily allow scope for divergence and for a much richer menu of influences on growth outcomes. The dangers of a Panglossian view of the past and a selective and restrictive search for evidence in evaluating growth performance should be much reduced for the next generation of cliometricians. This branch of growth theory offers improved hypotheses to economic historians unhappy with earlier formal models of induced technological change based on arguments familiar to historical research, these models deserve to be taken seriously in economic history.

(ii) Institutions (and policymaking) can be placed right at the heart of the growth process in a rigorous way. This should help to focus attention on the detailed characteristics of these arrangements and to explain why they really matter. Institutional arrangements will be an intrinsic part of historical accounts of economic growth partly because they exhibit substantial continuity, and windows of opportunity for their reform may well be both narrow and infrequent. There is an opportunity to assimilate key arguments of traditional historians which were previously either excluded by assumption or treated at best discursively.

(iii) There can be strong justification to resume the detailed consideration of the reasons for differences in TFP growth rather than to abandon the idea as old fashioned or simply a reflection of measurement error. Informed by new ideas, better techniques of measuring real output, and imaginative investigation of the notion of "social capability," it may be possible to refine and extend the estimates of the growth accounting pioneers.

Empirical growth economics has relied thus far rather heavily on regression analysis of international cross-sections drawn from the recent past. This has been useful but lacks the perspective that can be gained from a long-run vantage point which takes into account the changing socio-economic environment. So what can growth economics learn from the concerns and research of economic historians? Three points stand out.

(i) Serious exploration of the effects of institutions and policies on economic growth is welcome but to provide adequate understanding of why growth rates differ among first world countries and over time will require much better quantification of key variables impacting on TFP growth and of TFP growth itself than hitherto. Measurement issues are much more serious in this area than growth economists presently seem willing to acknowledge.

(ii) The view of TFP growth embodied in most endogenous innovation models is lopsided. Undue attention is paid to R&D as opposed to learning as a source of productivity improvement and to patents and market size as opposed to other determinants of the profitability of innovation. Similarly, a more explicit focus on the role of international technology transfer in the growth process seems overdue.

(iii) Now that more economists are turning their attention to longer-run growth data it would be timely for modeling exercises to bear in mind other implications of the Schumpeterian vision than those currently stressed by endogenous growth theory, notably that breaks in trend rates of growth may be expected to occur quite often. Failing that, at least the special nature of catchup during the Golden Age must be carefully allowed for both in interpreting results from the Summers–Heston dataset and in thinking about the growth slowdown of the last 20 years.

Finally, one of the most exciting avenues of research for economic historians and economists to pursue together using an endogenous innovation framework is the political economy of growth. This should aim for an understanding both of what the key effects of policy on growth have been and also of how the incentive structures facing politicians and private agents generate growth-retarding or growth-enhancing interventions. This will more likely be successfully achieved through a portfolio of detailed case studies of individual countries than through regressing growth rates against standard political variables.

Notes

Revised draft, December 1995. Paper prepared for the 7th World Congress of the Econometric Society, Tokyo, Japan. I have had very helpful discussions with Stephen Broadberry, Paul David, Alan Green and Leslie Hannah while the paper benefits considerably from joint work with Charles Bean and Terence Mills. Comments from seminar participants at the Institute for Historical Research, London and the University of Loughborough, Reading and Royal Holloway College and the discussant in Tokyo, Professor Tetsuji Okazaki are appreciated. I am, of course, responsible for all errors. A longer version of this chapter including appendices was circulated as Centre for Economic Policy Research Discussion Paper No. 1333. All references to material in appendices refer to the discussion paper.

1 This section draws on Crafts (1995a) which contains a much fuller version of the argument.

2 This point can be reinforced by considering the experience in terms of the robust growth regression in Levine and Renelt (1992) as in Crafts (1995a).

3 Three points might be made about time-series modeling of growth in the nineteenth century. First, we can expect the trend rate of growth to vary even in the absence of traumatic shocks. Second, there are no strong priors concerning break points. Third, the modeling strategy outlined in the text permits rejection of the hypothesis of a unit root in industrial output. More details of the Crafts and Mills (1994) results can be found in appendix 2.

4 Murphy *et al.* (1991) provide an endogenous growth model in which the relative attractions of rent seeking and productive entrepreneurship determine the allocation of talent and thus the rate of technological progress and the growth rate.

5 Issues of this kind are discussed in more depth in the following two subsections. For an endogenous growth model in which bargaining power and structures between firms and their workers affects the growth of TFP see Bean and Crafts (1996). For discussion of this problem and attempts to solve it in a large cotton textiles firm in the early nineteenth century, see Huberman (1991).

6 Although the marginal direct tax rate was lower, indirect tax rates were considerably higher in Britain than in France (Mathias and O'Brien (1976)). In the simplest Grossman–Helpman model the key would be that a lower direct tax rate tends to raise the rate of innovation through its effect on the net rate of return. In the more refined models, which allow for effects from the relative price of human capital, indirect taxes could have an impact – positive or negative – depending on whether human capital (used intensively in innovation) is made cheaper as a result of its imposition and on the use the government makes of the proceeds. See Grossman and Helpman (1991, pp. 66–7 and 267–75).

7 The 0.4 percent gap for 1873–1913 is based on the sources underlying table 2.4. It may be more appropriate to dwell on this longer period despite the attention given to 1899–1913 by some British authors. Time-series analysis does not support the suggestion that there was a significant change in trend growth in this period (Crafts, Leybourne, and Mills (1989) and the TFP growth measure seems to reflect mistakes in investment linked to highly volatile expectations (Crafts and Mills (1992)).

8 Barro and Sala-i-Martin (1991) find that β-convergence is apparent in the states of the United States from 1880, the start of their sample period, onwards. The remarks in the text imply that such a result is more likely to have applied within a country than across the world.

9 This section draws on Bean and Crafts (1996) and on Crafts (1995c) which contain much fuller accounts.

10 Early applications of endogenous growth ideas to policy debates display similar

tendencies. For example, Baldwin's well-known (1989) discussion of the growth effects of the EU's Single Market Programme looks to dynamic effects occurring automatically through Rebelo-style faster capital stock growth whereas the endogenous innovation approach would see the impact of 1992 as much more ambiguous and essentially dependent on the mode of implementation and its effects on rent-seeking, on the appropriability of returns as public procurement practices changes, and on the extent to which the market is widened acting through R&D rather than capital accumulation.

11 Jones (1995) regards the prediction of scale effects as the undesirable feature of the R&D-based growth models. He points out that this can be modified such that growth still arises as a result of profit-maximizing search for innovations but such that the conventional Solow result returns, namely that the long-run growth rate cannot be raised through interventions to subsidize R&D or investment. He shows this as follows using a simplified model.

$$Y = K^{1-\alpha}(AL_y)^{\alpha} \quad (1)$$

$$\dot{A}/A = \delta L_a \quad (2)$$

$$g_y = g_a = \delta s^* L \quad (3)$$

Equations (1)–(3) comprise a conventional endogenous innovation model in which the steady-state growth rate depends on the rate of growth of knowledge (A) which in turn depends on the share of labor(s*) optimally allocated to R&D. Jones suggests the following modifications to (2)

$$\dot{A}/A = \delta(L_a/A^{1-\phi}), \text{ where } \phi < 1 \quad (4)$$

which implies, using (1), that

$$g_y = g_a = n/(1 - \phi) \quad (5)$$

where n is the rate of population growth and (5) is, in effect, a modified concept of the old natural rate of growth.

References

Abramovitz, M. (1986). "Catching-up, forging ahead, and falling behind." *Journal of Economic History*, 36: 385–406.

(1993). "The search for the sources of growth: areas of ignorance, old and new." *Journal of Economic History*, 53: 217–43.

Aghion, P. and Howitt, P. (1995). "Structural aspects of the growth process." Paper presented to Seventh World Congress of the Econometrics Society, Tokyo.

Alford, B. W. E. (1988). *British Economic Performance 1945–1975*. London: Macmillan.

Allen, R. C. (1983). "Collective invention." *Journal of Economic Behavior and Organization*, 1: 1–24.

Bairoch, P. (1991). "The city and technological innovation." In Higonet, P., Landes, D., and Rosovsky, H. (eds.), *Favorites of Fortune*. Cambridge, MA: Harvard University Press.

Baldwin, R. E. (1989). "The growth effects of 1992." *Economic Policy*, 9: 248–81.

Barro, R. J. and Sala-i-Martin, X. (1991). "Convergence across states and regions." *Brookings Papers on Economic Activity*, 1: 107–82.

Batstone, E. (1988). *The Reform of Workplace Industrial Relations*. Oxford: Clarendon Press.

Bean, C. R. and Crafts, N. F. R. (1996). "British economic growth since 1945: relative economic decline . . . and renaissance?" In Crafts, N. F. R. and Toniolo, G. (eds.), *Economic Growth in Europe since 1945*. Cambridge: Cambridge University Press, pp. 131–72.

Ben-David, D. (1993). "Equalizing exchange: trade liberalization and income convergence." *Quarterly Journal of Economics*, 108: 653–79.

Bernard, A. B. and Durlauf, S. N. (1995). "Convergence in international output." *Journal of Applied Econometrics*, 10: 97–108.

Blank, D. M. and Stigler, G. J. (1957). *The Demand and Supply of Scientific Personnel*. New York: NBER.

Boltho, A. (1982). "Economic growth." In Boltho, A. (ed.), *The European Economy: Growth and Crisis*. Oxford: Oxford University Press, pp. 9–37.

Broadberry, S. N. (1994). "Technological leadership and productivity leadership in manufacturing since the Industrial Revolution: implications for the convergence debate." *Economic Journal*, 104: 291–302.

Broadberry, S. N. and Crafts, N. F. R. (1996). "British economic policy and industrial performance in the early postwar period." *Business History*, 38, (forthcoming).

Chandler, A. D. (1990). *Scale and Scope: the Dynamics of Industrial Capitalism*. Cambridge, MA: Harvard University Press.

Chou, C., Kimura, F., and Talmain, G. (1995). "R and D effort, domestic and international scale effects." Paper presented to Seventh World Congress of the Econometrics Society, Tokyo.

Cohen, W. (1995). "Empirical studies of innovation activity." In Stoneman, P. (ed.), *Handbook of the Economics of Innovation and Technological Change*. Oxford: Blackwell, pp. 182–264.

Coe, D. T. and Helpman, E. (1995). "International R & D spillovers." *European Economic Review*, 39: 859–87.

Crafts, N. F. R. (1987). "Economic history." In Eatwell, J., Milgate, M., and Newman, P. (eds.), *The New Palgrave: A Dictionary of Economic Theory and Doctrine*. London: Macmillan, pp. 37–42.

(1989). "Revealed comparative advantage in manufacturing, 1899–1950." *Journal of European Economic History*, 18: 127–37.

(1991). "Reversing relative economic decline? The 1980s in historical perspective." *Oxford Review of Economic Policy*, 7(3): 81–98.

(1993). "Adjusting from war to peace in 1940s Britain." *Economic and Social Review*, 25: 1–20.

(1995a). "Exogenous or endogenous growth? The Industrial Revolution reconsidered." *Journal of Economic History*, 55: 745–72.

(1995b). "Recent research on the national accounts of the UK, 1700–1939." *Scandinavian Economic History Review*, 43: 17–29.

(1995c). "The Golden Age of economic growth in postwar Europe: why did Northern Ireland miss out?" *Irish Economic and Social History*, 22: 5–25.

Crafts, N. F. R. and Harley, C. K. (1992). "Output growth and the British Industrial Revolution: a restatement of the Crafts–Harley view." *Economic History Review*, 45: 703–30.

Crafts. N. F. R., Leybourne, S. J., and Mills, T. C. (1989). "The climacteric in late Victorian Britain and France: a reappraisal of the evidence." *Journal of Applied Econometrics*, 4: 103–17.

Crafts, N. F. R. and Mills, T. C. (1992). "British economic fluctuations, 1851–1913: a perspective based on growth theory." In Broadberry, S. N. and Crafts, N. F. R. (eds.), *Britain in the International Economy, 1870–1939*. Cambridge: Cambridge University Press, pp. 98–134.

(1994). "The Industrial Revolution as a macroeconomic epoch." *Economic History Review*, 47: 769–75.

(1996). "Europe's Golden Age: an econometric investigation of changing trend rates of growth." In van Ark, B. and Crafts, N. F. R. (eds.), *Quantitative Aspects of Postwar European Economic Growth*. Cambridge: Cambridge University Press.

Crafts. N. F. R. and Toniolo, G. (1996). "Postwar growth: an overview." In Crafts, N. F. R. and Toniolo, G. (eds.), *Economic Growth in Europe since 1945*. Cambridge: Cambridge University Press, pp. 1–37.

Crouch, C. (1993). *Industrial Relations and European State Traditions*. Oxford: Clarendon Press.

Cuenca Esteban, J. (1994). "British textile prices, 1770–1831: are British growth rates worth revising once again?" *Economic History Review*, 47: 66–105.

(1995). "Further evidence of falling prices of cotton cloth, 1768–1816." *Economic History Review*, 48: 145–50.

David, P. A. (1975). *Technical Choice, Innovation and Economic Growth*. Cambridge: Cambridge University Press.

(1991). "Computer and dynamo: the modern productivity paradox in a not-too-distant mirror." In *Technology and Productivity*, Paris: OECD, pp. 315–48.

den Bakker, G. P., Huitker, T. A., and van Bochove, C. A. (1990). "The Dutch economy 1921–39: revised macroeconomic data for the interwar period." *Review of Income and Wealth*, 36: 187–206.

Denison, E. F. (1967). *Why Growth Rates Differ*. Washington, DC: Brookings.

(1968). "Economic growth." In Caves, R. E. (ed.), *Britain's Economic Prospects*. Washington, DC: Brookings, pp. 231–78.

Dowrick, S. (1992). "Estimating the impact of government consumption on growth." Australian National University Centre for Economic Policy Research Discussion Paper No. 258.

Dowrick, S. and Nguyen, D-T. (1989). "OECD comparative economic growth

1950–85: catch-up and convergence." *American Economic Review*, 79: 1010–30.

Dumke, R. H. (1990). "Reassessing the Wirtschaftswunder and postwar growth in West Germany in an international context." *Oxford Bulletin of Economics and Statistics*, 52: 451–90.

Dutton, H. I. (1984). *The Patent System and Inventive Activity*. Manchester: Manchester University Press.

Easterly, W., Kremer, M., Prichett, L., and Summers, L. H. (1993). "Good policy or good luck? Country growth performance and temporary shocks." *Journal of Monetary Economics*, 32: 459–83.

Edgerton, D. E. H. (1996). "The 'White Heat' revisited: the British government and technology in the 1960s." *Twentieth Century British History*, forthcoming.

Edgerton, D. E. H. and Horrocks, S. M. (1994). "British industrial research and development before 1945." *Economic History Review*, 47: 213–38.

Eichengreen, B. (1996). "Institutions and economic growth: Europe after World War II." In Crafts, N. F. R. and Toniolo, G. (eds.), *Economic Growth in Europe since 1945*. Cambridge: Cambridge University Press, pp. 38–72.

Feinstein, C. H. (1972). *National Income, Expenditure and Output of the UK, 1855–1965*. Cambridge: Cambridge University Press.

(1988). "National statistics." In Feinstein, C. H. and Pollard, S. (eds.), *Studies in Capital Formation in the United Kingdom, 1750–1920*. Oxford: Clarendon Press, pp. 259–471.

Floud, R. C. and McCloskey, D. N. (eds.) (1994). *The Economic History of Britain Since 1700*, 3 vols. Cambridge: Cambridge University Press.

Franks, J. R. and Mayer, C. (1990). "Capital markets and corporate control: a study of France, Germany and the UK." *Economic Policy*, 10: 191–231.

Freeman, C. and Perez, C. (1988). "Structural crises of adjustment, business cycles and investment behaviour." In Dosi, G., Freeman, C., Nelson, R., Silverberg, G., and Soete, L. (eds.), *Technical Change and Economic Theory*. London: Pinter, pp. 38–66.

Gerschenkron, A. (1962). *Economic Backwardness in Historical Perspective*. Cambridge, MA: Bellknap Press.

Great Britain (1867/8). *Report of the Royal Commission on Education in Schools in England and Wales*. BPP: XXVIII, part 1.

(1895). *Report of the Royal Commission on Secondary Education*. BPP: XLIII.

Griliches, Z. (1994). "Productivity, R and D, and the data constraint." *American Economic Review*, 84: 1–23.

(1995). "R and D and productivity: econometric results and measurement issues." In Stoneman P. (ed.), *Handbook of the Economics of Innovation and Technological Change*. Oxford: Blackwell, pp. 52–89.

Grossman, G. M. and Helpman, E. (1991). *Innovation and Growth in the Global Economy*. Cambridge, MA: MIT Press.

Grout, P. A. (1984). "Investment and wages in the absence of binding contracts: a Nash bargaining approach." *Econometrica*, 52: 449–60.

Hansen, S. A. (1974). *Okonomisk voekst i Danmark*. Copenhagen: Institute of Economic History.

Harris, J. R. (1976). "Skills, coal and British industry in the eighteenth century." *History*, 61: 167–82.

Harley, C. K. and Crafts, N. F. R. (1995). "Cotton textiles and industrial output growth during the Industrial Revolution." *Economic History Review*, 48: 134–44.

Hjerrpe, R. (1989). *The Finnish Economy 1860–1985*. Helsinki: Bank of Finland.

Huberman, M. (1991). "Industrial relations and the Industrial Revolution: evidence from M'Connel and Kennedy, 1810–1840." *Business History Review*, 65: 345–78.

Hyde, C. K. (1977). *Technological Change and the British Iron Industry, 1700–1870*. Princeton: Princeton University Press.

Islam, N. (1995). "Growth empirics: a panel data approach." *Quarterly Journal of Economics*, 110: 1127–70.

Jaffé, A. B. (1988). "Demand and supply influences in R & D intensity and productivity growth." *Review of Economic Statistics*, 70: 431–37.

Jenkinson, T. and Mayer, C. (1992). *Boardroom Battles*. Oxford: Oxford Economic Research Associates.

Jones, C. I. (1995). "Times series tests of endogenous growth models." *Quarterly Journal of Economics*, 110: 495–525.

Kanefsky, J. (1979). "Motive power in British industry and the accuracy of the 1870 Factory Return." *Economic History Review*, 32: 360–75.

Kennedy, W. P. (1987). *Industrial Structure, Capital Markets and the Origins of British Economic Decline*. Cambridge: Cambridge University Press.

Kindleberger, C. P. (1967). *European Postwar Growth: the Role of Labor Supply*. Cambridge, MA: Harvard University Press.

King, R. G. and Levine, R. (1994). "Capital fundamentalism, economic development and economic growth." *Carnegie-Rochester Series on Public Policy*, 40: 259–92.

Krantz, O. and Nilsson, C. A. (1975). *Swedish National Product, 1861–1970*. Lund: CWK Gleerup.

Krugman, P. (1987). "The narrow moving band, the Dutch disease, and the competitive consequences of Mrs Thatcher." *Journal of Development Economics*, 27: 41–55.

Levin, R. C., Klevonick, A. K., Nelson, R. R., and Winter, S. G. (1987). "Appropriating the returns from industrial R and D." *Brookings Papers on Economic Activity*, 3: 783–820.

Levine, R. and Renelt, D. (1992). "A sensitivity analysis of cross-country growth regressions." *American Economic Review*, 82: 942–63.

Lewchuk, W. (1987). *American Technology and the British Vehicle Industry*. Cambridge: Cambridge University Press.

Lucas, R. E. (1988). "On the mechanics of economic development." *Journal of Monetary Economics*, 22: 3–42.

(1993). "Making a miracle." *Econometrica*, 61: 251–72.

McCloskey, D. N. (1970). "Did Victorian Britain fail?" *Economic History Review*, 23: 446–59.

Macleod, C. (1992). "Strategies for innovation: the diffusion of new technology in nineteenth century British industry." *Economic History Review*, 45: 285–307.

Maddison, A. (1991). *Dynamic Forces in Capitalist Development*. Oxford: Oxford University Press.
(1992). "A long-run perspective on saving." *Scandinavian Journal of Economics*, 94: 181–96.
(1995). *Monitoring the World Economy 1820–1992*. Paris: OECD.
(1996). "Macroeconomic accounts for European countries." In van Ark, B. and Crafts, N. F. R. (eds.), *Quantitative Aspects of Postwar European Economic Growth*. Cambridge: Cambridge University Press.
Mankiw, N. G., Romer, D., and Weil, D. (1992). "A contribution to the empirics of economic growth." *Quarterly Journal of Economics*, 107: 407–37.
Mathias, P. and O'Brien, P. K. (1976). "Taxation in Britain and France, 1715–1810: a comparison of the social and economic incidence of taxes collected for central governments." *Journal of European Economic History*, 5: 601–50.
Matthews, R. C. O., Feinstein, C. H., and Odling-Smee, J. C. (1982). *British Economic Growth 1856–1973*. Oxford: Clarendon Press.
Mayer, C. (1992). "The financing of innovation." In Bowen, A. and Ricketts, M. (eds.), *Stimulating Innovation in Industry*. London: Kogan Page, pp. 97–116.
Melman, S. (1956). *Dynamic Factors in Industrial Productivity*. Oxford: Blackwell.
Michie, R. (1988). "The finance of innovation in late Victorian and Edwardian Britain: possibilities and constraints." *Journal of European Economic History*, 17: 491–530.
Mitch, D. (1982). "The spread of literacy in nineteenth century England." Ph.D. Dissertation, University of Chicago.
Mitchell, B. R. (1988). *British Historical Statistics*. Cambridge: Cambridge University Press.
(1993). *International Historical Statistics: The Americas*. London: Macmillan.
Mokyr, J. (1990). *The Lever of Riches*. Oxford: Oxford University Press.
(1993). "Introduction: the new economic history and the Industrial Revolution." In Mokyr, J. (ed.), *The British Industrial Revolution: An Economic Perspective*. Oxford: Westview Press, pp. 1–131.
Mowery, D. C. and Rosenberg, N. (1989). *Technology and the Pursuit of Economic Growth*. Cambridge: Cambridge University Press.
Murphy, K. M., Shleifer, A., and Vishny, R. W. (1991). "The allocation of talent: implications for growth." *Quarterly Journal of Economics*, 106: 503–30.
Nelson, R. R. and Wright, G. (1992). "The rise and fall of American technological leadership." *Journal of Economic Literature*, 30: 1931–64.
North, D. C. and Thomas, R. P. (1973). *The Rise of the Western World*. Cambridge: Cambridge University Press.
O'Mahony, M. (1992). "Productivity and human capital formation in UK and German manufacturing." NIER Discussion Paper No. 28.
O'Mahony, M. and Wagner, K. (1994). *Changing Fortunes: an Industry Study of British and German Productivity Growth over Three Decades*. London: NIESR.
Oulton, N. and O'Mahony, M. (1994). *Productivity and Growth: A Study of British Industry, 1954–1986*. Cambridge: Cambridge University Press.
Owen, N. (1983). *Economies of Scale, Competitiveness and Trade Patterns within the*

European Community. Oxford: Clarendon Press.

Pakes, A. and Schankerman, M. (1984). "An exploration into the determinants of research intensity." In Griliches, Z. (ed.), *R & D, Patents, and Productivity*. Chicago: University of Chicago Press, pp. 209–32.

Patel, P. and Pavitt, K. (1989). "The technological activities of the UK: a fresh look." In Silberston, A. (ed.), *Technology and Economic Progress*. London: Macmillan, pp. 113–54.

(1992). "The innovative performance of the world's largest firms: some new evidence." *Economics of Innovation and New Technology*, 2: 91–102.

Pavitt, K. and Soete, L. (1982). "International differences in economic growth and the international location of innovation." In Giersch, H. (ed.), *Emerging Technologies*. Tubingen: Mohr, pp. 105–33.

Pollard, S. (1989). *Britain's Prime and Britain's Decline*. London: Arnold.

Prais, S. J. (1981). *Productivity and Industrial Structure*. Cambridge: Cambridge University Press.

Pratten, C. F. (1976). *Labour Productivity Differentials Within International Companies*. Cambridge: Cambridge University Press.

Pratten, C. F. and Atkinson, A. G. (1976). "The use of manpower in British industry." *Department of Employment Gazette*, 84: 571–6.

Price, S. and Sanders, D. (1994). "Economic competence, rational expectations and government popularity in postwar Britain." *Manchester School*, 62: 296–312.

Rebelo, S. (1991). "Long-run policy analysis and long-run growth." *Journal of Political Economy*, 99: 500–21.

Reich, L. S. (1985). *The Making of American Industrial Research*. Cambridge: Cambridge University Press.

Romer, P. M. (1993). "Idea gaps and object gaps in economic development." *Journal of Monetary Economics*, 32: 543–73.

Root, H. L. (1991). "The redistributive role of government economic regulation in old regime France and England." *Comparative Studies in Society and History*, 33: 338–69.

Rosenberg, N. (1972). *Technology and American Economic Growth*. New York: Harper and Row.

Rossi, N., Sorgato, A., and Toniolo, G. (1992). "Italian historical statistics, 1880–1990." University of Venice Department of Economics Working Paper No. 92-18.

Routh, G. (1980). *Occupation and Pay in Great Britain, 1906–79*. London: Macmillan.

Rubinstein, W. D. (1983). "The end of 'Old Corruption' in Britain 1780–1860." *Past and Present*, 101: 55–86.

Sachs, J. D. and Warner, A. (1995). "Economic reform and the process of global integration." *Brookings Papers on Economic Activity*, 1: 1–95.

Schofield, R. S. (1973). "Dimensions of illiteracy, 1750–1850." *Explorations in Economic History*, 10: 437–54.

Sommariva, A. and Tullio, G. (1986). *German Macroeconomic History, 1880–1979*. London: Macmillan.

Stoneman, P (1979). "Patenting activity: a re-evaluation of the influence of demand pressures." *Journal of Industrial Economics*, 27: 385–401.

Sullivan, R. J. (1994). "Estimates of the value of patent rights in Great Britain and Ireland, 1852–1876." *Economica*, 61: 37–58.

Szostak, R. (1991). *The Role of Transportation in the Industrial Revolution.* Montreal: McGill-Queen's University Press.

Taylor, A. M. (1995). "On the costs of inward-looking development, price distortions, growth, and divergence in Latin America." Paper presented to Economic History Association Annual Meeting, Chicago.

United Nations (1964). *Some Factors in the Economic Growth of Europe in the 1950s.* Geneva: United Nations.

van de Klundert, T. and van Schaik, A. (1996). "On the historical continuity of the process of economic growth." In van Ark, B. and Crafts, N. F. R. (eds.), *Quantitative Aspects of Postwar European Economic Growth.* Cambridge: Cambridge University Press.

Verspagen, B. (1996). "Technology indicators and economic growth in the European area: some empirical evidence." In van Ark, B. and Crafts, N. F. R. (eds.), *Quantitative Aspects of Postwar European Economic Growth.* Cambridge: Cambridge University Press.

Villa, P. (1993). *Une analyse macroéconomique de la France au XXe siècle.* Paris: CNRS Editions.

von Tunzelmann, G. N. (1978). *Steam Power and British Industrialization to 1860.* Oxford: Clarendon Press.

(1995). *Technology and Industrial Progress.* Aldershot: Edward Elgar.

Williamson, J. G. (1995). "The evolution of global labor markets since 1830: background evidence and hypotheses." *Explorations in Economic History*, 32: 141–96.

Wright, G. (1990). "The origins of American industrial success, 1879–1940." *American Economic Review*, 80: 651–68.

Wrigley, E. A. (1987). *People, Cities and Wealth.* Oxford: Blackwell.

Young, A. (1993). "Invention and bounded learning by doing." *Journal of Political Economy*, 101: 443–72.

CHAPTER 3

Microtheory and recent developments in the study of economic institutions through economic history

Avner Greif

INTRODUCTION

Adam Smith ([1776] 1937) argued that the "propensity to truck, barter, and exchange" is in human nature (p. 13) and proceeded to examine how institutions impact the efficiency implications of this tendency. Arguably, institutions impact efficiency since they influence the allocation of resources to and by economic agents and the set of exchange relations that these agents are willing to assume. The diversity of economic environments and institutions utilized throughout history provides a unique source for examining the nature and implications of institutions.[1] Indeed, a distinctive feature of economic history has always been its concentration on the examination of institutions, their origins, natures, and implications.[2]

This chapter provides a brief survey of the three approaches within economic history – the neoclassical (section 1), the new institutional economic history (section 2), and the historical institutional analysis (section 3) – that utilize microeconomic theory for the study of institutions and their efficiency implications.[3] Each of these complementary approaches focuses on different sets of institutions, utilizes different theoretical frameworks to analyze them, and advances different methodologies to integrate theoretical and historical analyses.

Owing to space limitation this chapter concentrates on highlighting the methodology of and interrelations with microeconomic theory adopted by these approaches, and gives some of their insights with respect the study of economic institutions. Since historical analysis is the most recent development in the study of economic institutions through economic history, most of the survey is devoted to this approach. Furthermore, it briefly describes some historical institutional analysis studies. Finally, owing to space and knowledge limitations this survey is restricted mainly to works focusing on US and European history.[4]

1 THE NEOCLASSICAL APPROACH

In the 1950s, following the cliometric revolution in economic history, economic historians adopted the neoclassical framework and began utilizing econometrics to test hypotheses.[5] The historical study of institutions turned to examine the extent to which a particular institution – the market – governed exchange in the past. Data regarding prices, quantities, and exogenous parameters such as age, gender, and the cyclical nature of various industries were used to evaluate the hypothesis that the relations between these variables are the same as those that resulted if exchange is conducted within a market.

While data availability limits application of this technique, the analysis lends support for the assertion that markets functioned in many historical episodes. For example, labor, capital, and product markets existed in the US from as early as the colonial period; and in the 1890s Michigan's labor market for unskilled workers was so refined that it exhibits compensating wage differential between cyclical and non-cyclical sectors.[6] In Europe, from as early as the fifteenth century the degree of specialization among farmers in the Paris basin indicates the operation of product markets; prices of various securities indicate that international financial markets functioned smoothly among various mercantile states during the eighteenth century.[7]

Markets were found to emerge and integrate following technological changes, particularly improvements in transportation and communication technologies, and following political changes that fostered peace (Hoffman (1996)). The emergence of private capital markets benefited from the need to finance large projects such as railroad systems and, owing to economics of scope, from the existence of markets in government securities (Neal (1990)).

To examine the historical process of market integration prices are used to econometrically evaluate their covariations over time and place. The availability of price data, however, restricts this technique to examining mainly labor and financial markets.[8] Such analysis yields, for example, that there were regional but no national labor markets in the late nineteenth-century US (Rosenbloom (1994)) while London and Amsterdam stock exchanges were well integrated during the eighteenth century (Neal (1990)). To evaluate capital-market integration, Buchinsky and Polak (1993) compared interest rates in London's capital market with the annual registered property transactions in Middlesex and West Yorkshire. Property transactions were not strongly correlated with London's interest rate in the middle of the eighteenth century but were strongly correlated by the end of the century.

Coase's (1937) seminal work influenced the neoclassical approach's view of non-market institutions. Non-market institutions are viewed as contractual relations and patterns of property ownership which are efficient responses to market imperfections or very high prices. Hence, non-market institutions are inversely related to market perfection. Several studies in the neoclassical approach claim to lend support to this conjecture.

For example, McCloskey (1989), claimed that a particular ownership structure that prevailed in pre-modern European villages reflects the absence or high cost of markets for insurance. Each farmer's agricultural land was not concentrated in one field but in many scattered strips within village boundaries. This practice was (technically) inefficient but arguably reduced the probability of total harvest failure for each farmer. Insurance markets did not exist, and alternative means of reducing the probability of starvation, such as grain storage, were more expensive than scattering. The system disappeared in the nineteenth century as economic growth and integration of markets made more efficient means of insurance possible.[9]

Similarly, Galenson (1981) considers the indentured servitude contracts used in the Britain's American colonies during the seventeenth and eighteenth centuries as a response to market imperfection. In the absence of appropriate financial markets, potential immigrants were unable to finance their voyages. Hence, instead of using the financial markets, they used the labor market to finance their voyages using servitude contracts. Servitude declined when financial markets improved and enabled more efficient financing (Grubb (1994)).

Neoclassical economics suggests that markets and the process of market integration foster efficiency and growth. Yet, it has been proved difficult to substantiate this claim based on historical data. For example, Galenson (1989) concluded that the American colonies' economy "benefitted from highly competitive transatlantic markets for . . . labor" (p. 96) but this assertion is based on theoretical arguments rather than on historical information. Similarly, North ([1961] 1996) argued that a main factor behind US growth from 1760 to 1890 was the spread of a market economy that drew resources out of pioneer self-sufficiency. Yet, he was unable to conduct any test or provide direct evidence supporting the claim regarding the relations between growth and market expansion per se. Only recently Sokoloff (1988) provided qualitative support for the assertion that access to larger markets in the US fostered innovations. Using a sample of US patent records from 1790 to 1846 he demonstrated that inventions were positively related to the size of markets. On the other hand, Wright (1987) has claimed that product-market integration in postbellum US hindered the economic development of the South. Industries requiring large initial investment in learning and skills could not emerge in the South. These difficulties in measuring the efficiency implications of institutions are also present in the other two approaches discussed below. I return to this issue in the conclusion.

The neoclassical approach to the study of institutions through economic history established that, contrary to the claims of traditional historians, it is not true that the governance of exchange by markets is a very recent phenomenon. Furthermore, by revealing the economic rationale beyond various contractual relations and patterns of ownerships it lends support to the Coasian view of non-market institutions as substitute for markets. Yet, as North (1977) pointed out, it has not been able to yield much insight regarding non-market institutions and does not indicate why some societies, but not others, developed market economies.

2 NEW INSTITUTIONAL ECONOMIC HISTORY

The New Institutional Economic History (NIEH) attempts to explain "why institutions that produce poor economic (and political) performance can [emerge and] persist" (North (1993, p. 12)).[10] Institutions are identified (North (1981, p. 18)) with "constraints on behavior in the form of rules and regulations" and enforcement procedures. Culture is important to the extent that "moral and ethical behavioral norms reduce enforcement costs."[11] The microeconomic theories NIEH utilizes – transaction cost economics, the theory of property rights, and public choice theory – constrained most of its historical analyses to institutions defined and enforced by the state.[12] This historical analysis is guided by three deductive assertions.[13] First, institutions defined and enforced by the state – property rights, rules, and regulations – determine economic performance through their impact on transaction costs. (Accordingly, in this section, the term institutions will refer to property rights, laws, and regulations specified and enforced by the state.) Second, the economic implications of a given institution change over time owing to technological change, population growth, market integration, and other factors. Hence, economic outcomes depend on efficient institutional change. Furthermore, specialization increases transaction costs (holding institutions constant) implying that institutional change is even more important in advanced economies.[14] Third, institutions are usually inefficient since they reflect interest groups' politics and are influenced by the transaction costs of bargaining, measurement, and enforcement.

Many historical studies indeed substantiated that property rights, laws, and regulations specified and enforced by the state impact efficiency. For example, Haber (1991) examined the relationship between security of property rights, government regulations, and industrial concentration in Brazil, Mexico, and the United States (1830–1930). Poorly defined property rights and cumbersome government regulations in the former two countries resulted in higher concentrations than in the US. Similarly, Rosenthal (1992) demonstrated that various efficient drainage and irrigation projects in Old Regime France were not undertaken. Insecure property rights over the drained area made efficient drainage unprofitable in France while in England, where property rights were secured, efficient drainage was assumed.

The assertion that institutions require adjustment to promote efficiency was examined by Davis and North (1971). They found that in the late nineteenth and early twentieth centuries US, market integration and technological changes initiated institutional change arguably aimed at increasing efficiency. The political process through which institutions are determined was explored, for example, by Libecap (1989). He examined property rights formation in various minerals, range, timberland, fisheries, and crude oil in the US. Distributional issues, asymmetric information, bargaining failure, and the political interests of politicians and bureaucrats crucially impacted the nature, and hence arguably efficiency, of property rights' specification. Similarly, Kantor (1991) examined the closing of Georgia's open range (1872–90). He estimated the efficiency gains from closing the range in various counties and noted that in the political process of enclosure "the potential for efficiency gains [in particular counties] did not guarantee" (p. 884) the closure of their ranges. Alston *et al.* (1994) examined the formation of property rights in land in Brazil and substantiated econometrically that the political importance of a region, rather than its economic needs, determined the extent to which the government secured property rights that fostered land improvements.[15]

3 HISTORICAL INSTITUTIONAL ANALYSIS

The contributions of NIEH for the study of institutions in economic history are beyond doubt. It has drawn attention to the importance of property rights, rules, and regulations defined and enforced by the state, the political process of their formation, and transaction costs. Yet, its reliance on transaction cost economics, the theory of property rights, and public choice theory implies that it can examine only institutions defined and enforced by the state. These theoretical frameworks preclude examining self-enforcing institutions (such as the state itself), non-legal factors influencing the emergence of distinct trajectories of institutional and organizational development, and the influence of non-economic social and cultural factors on institutional selection and path dependence. To exemplify these limitations, consider, for example, North and Thomas's (1973) analysis of the spectacular economic expansion of the late medieval period. Early on feudal lords "fought amongst themselves; but gradually . . . the strife declined". Peace enabled population growth and the realization of gains from "commerce between different parts of Europe" that "had always been potentially of mutual benefit" (p. 11). Hence, their argument asserts that security of property rights provided by the state is a necessary and sufficient condition for economic expansion. Further, this expansion was sufficient to lead to the various institutional innovations that occurred in that period (such as insurance contracts and the bill of lading). The "revival of trade led . . . to a host of institutional arrangements designed to reduce market imperfections" (p. 12).

This deductive analysis fails to address a host of questions regarding the relations between institutions and economic outcomes. For example, what were the institutions that made peace self-enforcing? Was trade expansion only a function of peace and factor endowments, or did institutions influence the time, place, and extent of trade expansion? Why did the European institutional innovations differ from those developed in other (technologically similar) economies in response to trade increases? In addressing such questions the NIEH's methodology was found to be insufficient. As the Historical Institutional Analysis (HIA) papers discussed below in subsections 3.1 and 3.2 indicate, addressing such questions and going beyond the empirical analysis of the state as the fountain of institutions requires a different methodology.

First and foremost, it requires a broader operational concept of institutions. Hence, it views institutions as the non-technologically determined constraints on behavior which are self-enforcing.[16] Game theory provides a natural theoretical framework to examine self-enforcing institutions as it enables us to view an institution as an equilibrium. In a game theoretical framework, two main interrelated institutional components are expectations and organizations. Clearly, to the extent that expectations impact behavior, a player's expectations with respect to other players' behavior is a part of the non-technologically determined constraints that this player faces.[17]

Organizations are non-technologically determined constraints (other than expectations) that impact behavior by introducing a new player (the organization itself), changing the information available to players, or changing payoffs associated with certain actions.[18] The court, the regulator, the credit cooperative, the credit bureau, the firm, and the merchant guild are examples of such organizations. In many cases, it is fruitful for empirical analysis to examine an exogenous introduction of an organization to the original game under consideration. For example, suppose that the essence of the issue under consideration relates to contract enforcement. The players may be unable to establish a court to govern their relations, yet, it may be established by the state and – depending on the expected behavior of the court – drastically alter equilibrium behavior in the modified game. In many cases, however, that consider organizations as exogenous, analysis is insufficient to fully comprehend an economy's institutional structure. In such cases, one has also to examine the broader game in which organizations – such as the court – are the equilibrium outcome.[19] For an organization to be in an equilibrium outcome, the actions required to establish it should be feasible and the players with the ability to take these actions should have the appropriate incentives. In other words, for a particular organization to be selected from the set of possible organizations and to impact behavior, expectations that give this organization (and, if appropriate, its actions) an equilibrium outcome should prevail. The organization should be self-enforcing.

Yet, the use of a game theoretical framework for historical institutional analysis poses a challenge. In many strategic situations there are multiple – efficient and inefficient – equilibria implying that outcomes are not uniquely pre-determined. Furthermore, possible outcomes in strategic models are usually very sensitive to the model's specification. Thus, as further discussed in subsection 3.1, advancing the empirical analysis of institutions in history by viewing institutions as self-enforcing equilibria requires context-specific strategic modeling and an inductive historical analysis. A context-specific model able to capture the details of the historical situation under consideration is required for a constructive game theoretical analysis that can foster an empirical investigation. To construct a context-specific model and to identify the relevant institution there is a need for a microlevel historical study (usually based on primary sources) able to provide the foundations of the model's specification and to facilitate confronting the details of the analysis with the details of historical evidence (at times, even at the level of the individual decisionmaker).

Although HIA relies on equilibrium analysis to identify historical institutions, it goes beyond an empirical analysis of equilibria in games. It aims at empirically examining the processes of institutional selection and institutional path dependence. Namely, it attempts to comprehend the factors, if any, that make institutional development an historical, time-consuming ergodic process. As further discussed in subsection 3.2 below, this empirical analysis requires explicit departure from game theoretical analysis. This departure notwithstanding, it is the development of game theory that indicates the need for, and the promise of, historical inductive analysis of self-enforcing institutions, institutional selection, and institutional path dependence. The multiplicity and indeterminacy of equilibria in strategic situations indicate that the details of the historical context are potentially important in the selection of institutions, the implications of a particular institution, and institutional path dependence.

The game theoretical conceptualization of institutions as equilibria, the use of inductive microlevel historical analysis, and the use of context-specific strategic models enables an empirical analysis that goes beyond the boundaries of NIEH. It enables us to examine self-enforcing institutions (including those that make the state itself self-enforceable) and it enables us to examine institutional selection and path dependence. Particularly, the HIA theoretical framework permits an empirical examination of the relations between cultural and social factors and institutional selection and path dependence.

To elaborate and demonstrate the usefulness of the HIA's theoretical framework the next subsection elaborates on the methodology HIA employs to identify institutions and describes some empirical studies demonstrating the ability of HIA to explore institutions not examined by the NIEH. Particularly, they demonstrate the ability to examine institutions that fostered Smithian growth during the late medieval period without relying on the state and the institutional foundation of the state. Subsection 3.2 demonstrates the usefulness of HIA by discussing findings regarding the relations between the historical – economic, social, cultural, and political – context and institutions, institutional selection, and institutional path dependence.

3.1 Identifying institutions: methodology and some findings

An attempt to identify institutions that were relevant in a particular historical episode can not possibly begin by examining a game devoid of all institutions. Throughout history human interactions were embedded in an institutional context (Field (1981)). Hence, an HIA study begins with a microlevel historical examination aimed at identifying a transaction (Williamson (1995)) or organizational problem (Arrow (1974)) the exact nature of the institution that governs it impacts economic outcomes in that particular historical episode. For example, in economies based on long-distance trade, the institution that governs agency relations among merchants located in distinct trade centers can have significant efficiency and distributional consequences. This may not be an issue in an urban economy. In such an economy, however, the institution mitigating asymmetric information between borrowers and lenders can have important economic implications.

HIA is an inductive approach and does not pre-suppose that an institution with specific attributes (e.g., maximizing efficiency), prevailed. Hence, direct historical evidence, such as explicit statements and empirical regularities, is used to identify exogenous and endogenous institutional features and to form a hypothesis concerning the relevance or irrelevance of a particular institution. For example, historical evidence regarding agency relations in twelfth-century Genoa indicates that less than 16 percent of agency relations were among family members suggesting that agency relations were not governed by family loyalty (Greif (1994a)). Similarly, historical evidence suggests that the notaries of Paris during the eighteenth century, rather than banks, had a role in mitigating asymmetric information problems between borrowers and lenders (Hoffman, Postel-Vinay, and Rosenthal (1994)).

It is usually impossible or impractical to identify the set of all institutions that could have been relevant in a particular situation. Hence, while whenever possible HIA attempts to increase confidence in a hypothesis by rejecting alternative ones, it concentrates on substantiating the hypothesis that a particular institution prevailed rather than proving that all other institutions did not prevail. To refine further and to substantiate the hypothesis that a particular institution prevail, a context specific model is specified through an interactive process of theoretical and historical examination. The model is based on assumptions, the confidence in which can be gained independently from their predictive power. This serves two purposes. The first is ensuring that the analysis does not impose the researcher's perception of a situation on the historical actors. For example, that Edward the First of England noted in 1283 that insufficient protection to alien merchants' property rights deters them from coming to trade enhances the confidence in the relevance of a model of a ruler's problem of committing to alien traders' property rights (Greif, Milgrom, and Weingast (1994)). The second purpose is to sufficiently constrain the set of possible models. In some cases, (e.g., Banerjee, Besley, and Guinnane (1994)) using modeling restrictions identified through the historical analysis was crucial in formulating a useful model.

An equilibrium analysis is usually utilized to refine and facilitate empirical research that enhances confidence in a hypothesis. Although most HIA studies have not been able to formulate econometrically testable models, modeling examines the logic, consistency, and robustness of the argument. It can indicate the exact role of an organization (e.g., Greif, Milgrom, and Weingast (1994)), identify the conditions that have to be fulfilled for the argument to hold (e.g., Baliga and Polak (1995)), and generate – under the assumption that particular strategies prevailed – (comparative statics or other) predictions regarding observables that were not utilized in formulating the model.[20] The attempt is not simply to generate a prediction with respect to *one* observable but to generate predictions with respect to *several* observables.

HIA operationalizes institutional analysis by examining – historically and theoretically – the constraints that reflect technology, organizations, and equilibrium strategies (Greif (1994a)). The rest of this section illustrates the benefit of such examination by presenting two lines of work that, as discussed above, fall outside the scope of NIEH. The first relates to institutions that enable Smithian growth (growth due to trade) by fostering exchange in the absence of a legal system. The second relates to the institutional foundations of the state and how they impact economic efficiency by influencing the use of coercive power. Within each subsection, papers are presented by historical period. (The reader interested only in methodology and broad results can proceed directly to section 3.2.)

3.1.1 Institutions and Smithian growth: institutions that governed exchange in the absence of a centralized legal system

The need to depart from the NIEH's view of the state as the sole fountain of institutions was motivated above by the inability of the NIEH to account for exchange in the absence of the state's legal contract enforcement. What then are the institutional foundations of such exchange? Several HIA studies examined institutions that enabled exchange – and hence arguably enabled Smithian growth – by ensuring the self-enforceability of contractual relations.

During the late medieval commercial revolution in which long-distance trade reemerged in Europe (eleventh to fourteenth centuries) *overseas agents* enabled merchants to reduce the cost of long-distance trade by saving the time and risk of travelling, diversifying sales, and so forth. An overseas agent, however, had control over a merchant's capital abroad and hence could act opportunistically and expropriate it. Thus, unless agents could *ex ante* commit to *ex post* honest behavior, namely, to *ex post* respect the merchants' property rights over their goods, merchants would not have been willing to hire them.

Greif (1989, 1993) examined the institution that governed agency relations among the Maghribi traders who operated in the Muslim Mediterranean during the eleventh century. Owing to information asymmetry in agency relations and the cost and impediments of overseas litigation, the state could not enable agents to commit to respect merchants' property rights. The situation was analyzed through a variant of an efficiency wage model. It assumes, in accordance with historical evidence, that matching of merchants and unemployed agents is not random. A merchant could restrict matching from among the unemployed agents who had taken a particular sequence of actions. Since a merchant sometimes had to cease operating through an agent who had been honest, agency relations could have been governed by a self-enforcing collective punishment.

Specifically, there is an (subgame perfect) equilibrium the strategy which calls for all merchants to refrain from hiring an agent who cheated any of them. (Although the strategy does not call for punishing a merchant who fails to punish.) This off-the-path-of-play collective punishment is profitable to the merchants (and potentially also to the agents) and it is efficiency enhancing since it enables establishment of agency relations when they are not possible under a bilateral reputation mechanism and when only the cheated merchant retaliates. Furthermore, the Maghribis could have mitigated the asymmetric information inherent in agency relations by sharing information about agents' performance while reciprocity with respect to information transmission could make sharing self-enforcing.

Hence, agency relations among the Maghribis could have been governed by an economic institution that can be referred to as a *coalition* – a non-anonymous institution based on a multilateral reputation mechanism and informal information flows. To substantiate that a coalition indeed governed agency relationships among the Maghribis, Greif (1989, 1993) presented direct and indirect evidence. Direct evidence is explicit documentary statements on various aspects of the coalition, such as the operation of the implicit employment contract, the economic nature of the punishment inflicted on cheaters, the linkage between past conduct and future economic rewards, the interest that all coalition members took in the relationship between a specific agent and merchant, and so forth. Indirect evidence is the confirmation of predictions generated under the assumption that a coalition governed agency relations. Such predictions are with respect to, for example, the type of business contracts, accounting procedures, and avoidance of establishing agency relationships with non-Maghribis even when these relationships were considered by them to be – ignoring agency cost – very profitable.

Informal institutions similar to the Maghribis' coalition seem to have governed exchange relations in other historical episodes as well but seem to have been responsive to local conditions. Clay (1994) examined a coalition-like institution among American traders operating in Mexican California. Despite the lack of a formal legal system, these traders provided agency services to each other and sold goods in the local Mexican communities for credit. Since contract enforcement among the Mexican population was based on informal social sanctions the traders could not rely on the legal system to collect debt. To ensure contract enforceability in such credit transactions, a trader had to become part of the local informal contract enforcement mechanism. American retailers settled within the Mexican communities, married locally, raised their children as Catholics, and spoke Spanish at home. This time-consuming sunk investment provided access to the local contract enforcement mechanism and the small size of the Mexican communities implied that only one retailer operated in a particular locality.

Hence, a strategy calling for a permanent and complete boycott of a trader who cheated in agency relations would have barred all traders from operating in the market in which the cheater had the ability to enforce contract. Indeed, there is a punishment strategy that Pareto dominates a complete boycott strategy. It entails a partial boycott for a finite number of periods following the first cheating. The boycott is partial in the sense that it does not preclude transactions requiring the use of the cheater's local enforcement ability. A complete boycott follows only a second act of cheating during a partial boycott. Direct and indirect evidence indicates that such strategy was utilized by the traders. Hence, – as further elaborated in the next section – an environment distinct from that of the Maghribis led to a distinct strategy and institution. In particular, institutions were nested in the sense that the nature of the contract enforcement mechanism among retailers and their customers affected the nature of the institution that governed the relationship among retailers.

Coalitions can provide contract enforcement over time and space among individuals who exchanged frequently in the absence of an effective legal system. But how was contract enforcement achieved among individuals who did not exchange frequently when a state could not provide enforcement? This enforcement problem is particularly acute in exchange relations requiring enforcement through time and space, such as the provision of credit and contracts for future delivery among individuals from different communities. Was such exchange restricted during the late medieval commercial revolution, for example, to those who traded frequently with each other? If not, how was it made possible despite the lack of an effective intercommunity legal system? How could a merchant from one community commit to repay a debt to a merchant from another community at a later date?

Intercommunity exchange during the twelfth and the thirteenth centuries was extensively conducted in the champagne fairs where merchants from different localities entered into contracts that required enforcement through time. Milgrom, North, and Weingast (1990) suggest that in the large merchants' community that frequented the fairs, a reputation mechanism could not surmount the related commitment problem since large communities lacked the social networks required to make past actions known to all. A *Law Merchant* system, however, in which a particular organization – a "court" without a coercive power – supplements a multilateral reputation mechanism can ensure contract enforceability in this case.

Suppose that each pair of traders is matched only once and each trader knows only his own experience. Since the fairs' court lacked the ability to enforce judgment once a trader left the fairs, assume that the court is capable only of verifying past actions and keeping records of traders who cheated in the past. Acquiring information and appealing to the court is costly for each merchant. Despite these costs, there exists an (symmetric sequential) equilibrium in which cheating does not occur and merchants are induced to provide the court with the information required to support cooperation. It is the court's ability to activate the multilateral reputation mechanism by controlling information that provides the appropriate incentives. Evidence that such a system indeed functioned in the champagne fairs, however, is sparse and the paper simply points to the fairs' authorities' control of entry to the fair.

The historical records from as early as the twelfth century, however, indicate the operation of another institution in western and southern Europe that enabled intercommunity exchange. Traders applied a principle of community responsibility that obligated a trader for the conduct of each and every member of his community. Anyone who had the same "community label" as a merchant who cheated was held responsible for the damage incurred by that merchant. If a debtor, for example, failed to show at a particular fair where he was to meet his obligations and his community refused to pay or force him to pay, the lender could have requested any local court to confiscate the goods of any member of the debtor's community present at the fair. The traders whose goods were confiscated could recover their losses from the original debtor. Traders used intra-community enforcement mechanisms to support intercommunity exchange. At the same time, this system fostered asymmetry among otherwise identical economic agents. To an extent, it defined communities and fostered their internal organization. This observation is consistent with North's (1990) claim that "groups of individuals bound by some common purpose to achieve objectives . . . come into existence and . . . evolve [in response to] the institutional framework" (p. 5).

Greif (1994c) used various historical records to document the system and analyze it using a repeated, imperfect monitoring game in which merchants as well as a particular organization, a community (or fair) court, are the players. The analysis highlights the rationale behind various empirical regularities and the interrelations between various organizations and this system. For example, the periodic costly "retaliation phase" in which trade between two communities ceased was not necessarily a reflection of uncivilized rage as historians have claimed. Rather, it reflects, most likely, asymmetric information between local courts regarding a trader's ability or inability to meet his obligations toward another community's member. For cooperation to prevail, there has to be occasional on-the-equilibrium-path breakdown of intercommunity cooperation.

The model also indicates the role of the courts in providing impartial information that enhanced the ability to objectively verify contract fulfillment. This information, and hence these organizations, were crucial in mitigating the divergence of incentives between communities and their members. In the absence of this information under the community responsibility system, a community member could gain from advancing false accusation at the expense to the community. Hence, the model also indicates the rationale behind various regulations aimed at reducing information asymmetry regarding contract fulfillment. The model also indicates the rationale for attempts to increase the personal cost to a lender who was not paid.

These regulations were required since the community responsibility system causes an adverse selection problem. A lender's probability of being paid is not only a function of the trade venture's probability of success but also of the ability to force the borrower's community to pay. Hence, the incentive to verify the borrower's creditworthiness is reduced. Recognition of this adverse selection problem is well reflected in the repercussions of an agreement signed among cities in Tuscany in 1281 in which they contracted not to hold anyone responsible for debt he did not assume. The Florentine authorities warned merchants to pay close attention to personal creditworthiness in intercommunity dealings since now "to whom it is given, from him it will be asked."[21]

The work of Banerjee, Besley, and Guinnane (1994) on nineteenth-century German credit agricultural cooperatives is not directly related to Smithian growth yet it also relates to self-enforcing institutions that promote exchange. Their analysis attempts to differentiate between two possible views of these cooperatives. The first is that they constrained borrowers by their members' ability to sanction each other through their repeated economic and social interactions. The second is that cooperatives constrained borrowers since peer monitoring induced investment only in profitable projects. Under the null that the latter view is valid, they analyzed a model of a credit cooperative's optimal design in terms of the members' liability to default by others, the extent to which one member has to lend to other members, and the interest paid for such lending. Confronting various comparative statics predictions regarding the optimal design with the historical records indicates that indeed the design of German cooperatives changed as predicted by the theory thereby lending support to the null (while this, as they recognized, this does not refute the alternative view).[22]

3.1.2 Institutional foundations of the state

The need to depart from the NIEH view of the state as the fountain of institutions was also motivated above by its inability to account for the institutional foundations of the state itself. For example, during the late medieval period various feudal lords with military ability existed within each single political unit. To what extent did the need to ensure the self-enforceability of the political relations among these lords constrain their ability to cooperate in economic development? Did (self-enforcing) political institutions evolve to relax this constraint?

Greif (1994b, 1995a) addressed these questions with respect to late medieval Genoa. Genoa was established as a republic around 1096 and emerged from obscurity to build a commercial empire that stretched from the Black Sea and beyond to northern Europe. The analysis of its political system indicates that the need to ensure the self-enforceability of the contractual relations among Genoa's noble clans not to militaryily challenge each other constrained Genoa's economic growth for about a century. It was only around 1194 that a severe military threat to Genoa as a whole and accumulated knowledge that motivated and enabled the clans to implement a self-enforcing political organization that relaxed the constraints and fostered political cooperation and economic growth.

To foster the economy of Genoa, its (two main) noble clans had to cooperate militarily and politically in acquiring commercial rights in other political units. Yet, for such cooperation to be forthcoming each clan had to *ex ante* commit not to use its military strength to *ex post* attempt to gain control over Genoa. Greif (1994b, 1995a) analyzed this situation using a repetitive complete information game. Interclan cooperation could not have been supported by the threat of terminating future cooperation since commercial rights yielded rent every period after their acquisition. Hence, additional cooperation required that each clan invest resources in building fortifications and establishing a patronage system to deter the other clan from militaryily challenging it. If investment in military strength is positive at the (economically) efficient level of cooperation, the political cost of deterrence places a wedge between the efficient and the equilibrium level of cooperation.

This implies that Genoa clans' ability to cooperate could have been limited by the extent to which their relations were self-enforcing. If this constraint was binding the model yields various predictions such as the time path of cooperation, investment in military strength, and responses to changes in exogenous factors such as external threats to both clans. Indeed, these predictions are confirmed by the historical records. Furthermore, the model also indicates that when facing a severe external threat both clans may find it optimal to implement a particular political organization. In essence, this organization can foster interclan cooperation by creating a military balance among them. At the same time this organization can be made self-enforcing by providing it with the right incentives not to cooperate with any clan against the other.

Indeed, in 1194 the Genoese clans, facing a severe external threat to Genoa and taking advantage of experiments in political organizations in other Italian city-states, introduced such an organization and altered their political system. They introduced a *podestà* (that is, a "power') to create a military balance among them to foster cooperation. The *podestà* was a non-Genoese hired for a year to be Genoa's military leader, judge, and administrator. In these roles he was supported by non-Genoese soldiers he brought with him. The *podesteria* regulations reflect an explicit attempt to ensure that the *podestà*'s threat to militarily confront any clan that attacked another will indeed be credible and that no clan can collude with him against another. In other words, the introduction of the *podestà* altered the rules of the political and economic game in Genoa in a self-enforcing manner that fostered cooperation. It was under the *podesteria* which formally lasted about 150 years that Genoa reached its political and commercial apex. Yet, the system had its deficiencies. It was based on enhancing interclan mutual deterrence thus making clans a permanent feature in Genoa's political life. Venice – which eventually defeated Genoa militarily – avoided such a fate but the analysis of its political institutions is not sufficiently advanced to clearly indicate how.[23]

Most works on the relations between the institutional foundations of the state and economic efficiency concentrate on the period in which European states were already formed and arguably had substantial coercive power. When a state has such power it can promote efficiency by being able to force individuals to respect others' property rights. But how can a state with such coercive power commit itself to respect individuals' property rights? North (1981, chapter 3) has suggested that a state's ability or inability to provide such commitment is crucial to economic growth.[24] Several HIA studies examined the relations between the nature of the state, institutions that constrained its coercive power, and economic efficiency.

Greif, Milgrom, and Weingast (1994) examined, using an infinitely repeated complete information game, the operation of an organization that enabled late medieval rulers to commit to the property rights of alien merchants. The analysis indicates, theoretically and historically, that commitment could and was enhanced by a particular organization – the merchant guild – that had the ability to coordinate merchants' responses to abuses and force merchants to participate in trade embargoes. Hence, it constrained rulers from abusing property rights at the efficient level of trade by credibly threatening with a trade embargo in response to abuses.

To see why such organization was required consider the extent to which a *bilateral reputation mechanism* (in which a merchant whose rights were abused ceased trading), or an *uncoordinated multilateral reputation mechanism* (in which a subgroup larger than the one that was abused ceased trading) could surmount this commitment problem. Each of these mechanisms can support some level of trade, but neither can support the *efficient level of trade* (independently from the distribution of gains from trade and the ruler's discount factor). The bilateral reputation mechanism fails because, at the efficient level of trade, the value of future trade of the "*marginal*" traders to the ruler is zero, and hence the ruler is tempted to abuse their rights. In a world fraught with information asymmetries, slow communication, and plausible different interpretations of facts, the multilateral reputation mechanism is prone to failure for a similar reason.

Multilateral reputation mechanisms can potentially overcome the commitment problem at the efficient level of trade only when there exists an organization with the ability to coordinate the responses of all merchants to abuses against any merchant. Such an organization implies the existence of a Markov perfect equilibrium at which traders come to trade (at the efficient level) as long as the coordinating organization has never announced a boycott, but none of them comes to trade if a boycott has been announced. The ruler respects merchants' rights as long as a boycott has never been announced, but abuses their rights otherwise.

Although the behavior described forms a perfect equilibrium, the theory in this form remains unconvincing. When a coordinating institution declares an embargo merchants are deterred from disregarding it because they expect the ruler to abuse violators' trading rights. But are these expectations reasonable? Why would a ruler not *encourage* embargo-breakers rather than punish them? This encouragement is potentially credible since during an effective embargo, the volume of trade shrinks and the value of the marginal trader increases; it is then possible for bilateral reputation mechanisms to become effective. This possibility limits the potential severity of an embargo and potentially hinders the ability of any coordinating organization to support efficient trade. The efficient level of trade can be supported when a multilateral reputation mechanism is supplemented by an organization with the ability to coordinate responses *and* to ensure traders' *compliance* with boycott decisions. The traders must have some mechanism that makes the threat of collective action credible.

Direct and indirect historical evidence indicates that during the late medieval commercial revolution an institution with these attributes – the *merchant guild* – emerged and supported trade expansion and market integration. Merchant guilds exhibited a range of administrative forms – from a subdivision of a city administration, such as that of the Italian city-states, to an intercity organization, such as the German Hansa. Yet their functions were the same: to ensure the coordination and internal enforcement required to make the threat of collective action credible.

The merchant guild mitigated a ruler's commitment problem by taking advantage of the territorial limits of his power. Within a ruler's territory, a ruler's commitment problem may be mitigated by endogenously limiting his power in a self-enforcing manner based either on his economic needs or on the appropriate political organizations. The role of the ruler's economic needs in enabling him to commit to his subjects' property rights was explored in several studies. For example, Root (1989) suggested that in Old Regime France, the king's commitment problem to his well-organized financiers was mitigated through his dependency on them. Similarly, Conklin (1994) suggested that the Spanish king's dependency during the sixteenth century on the bureaucratic and military services provided by the Spanish elite enabled him to commit to pay his loans to them.

Rosenthal (1992) has gone further than these studies by examining the broader economic implications of endogenously limiting a ruler's ability to predate. In Old Regime France, the crown relied heavily on borrowing from venal officers who also filled the ranks of the judicial system. Thus, the crown did not reform this system although it was aware that it was undermining economic development. The judicial system undermined development since it was supposed to resolve disputes regarding property rights but the venal officers had no incentive to do so since they were paid by the case and thus were always willing to consider appeals. It could not commit to uphold the property rights it had assigned thus inhibiting efficient investment in land improvement.

North and Weingast (1989) examined the role of political institutions in constraining the English rulers and claimed that the Glorious Revolution (1688) fostered growth since it enhanced the king's commitment to securing private property rights. During the Glorious Revolution the king's prerogatives were curtailed, his legal actions were clearly specified, an independent judiciary was formed, and Parliament assumed a better control over taxation and revenue allocation. These organizational changes limited the king's ability to prey on his subjects and they became self-enforcing by the Parliament's implicit threat to rise in arms against the king if the king abused his subjects' rights. The main support for the view that the Glorious Revolution enhanced property rights security is the rise, during the eighteenth century, in the crown's debt, the reduction in the interest it paid, and the emergence of private capital markets in England.[25]

3.2 The historical – economic, political, cultural, and social – context, institutional selection, and institutional path dependence

As illustrated above, HIA studies utilize equilibrium analysis to identify institutions. They indicate that self-enforcing institutions emerged in various ways: the Maghribi traders coalition (Greif (1993)) evolved spontaneously while the credit cooperative (Guinnane (1994)) was intentionally created. At times organizations created to fulfill one function spontaneously evolved to fulfill another. For example, the Parisian notaries were to enhance legal contract enforcement but ended mitigating asymmetric information (Hoffman, Postel-Vinay, and Rosenthal (1994)). Yet, HIA studies are aimed at, and are able to achieve more than identifying institutions. They are aimed at, and are able to shed light on the process of institutional selection and the factors contributing to institutional path dependence.

Whether spontaneous or intentional, selection over self-enforcing institutions was influenced by the historical – economic, political, cultural, and social – context. That economic environment impacts institutional selection has already been mentioned in the discussion of coalitions. Spot markets for products were well developed around the Mediterranean in the eleventh century but were absent from Mexican California leading to the emergence of distinct types of coalitions to govern agency relations (Greif (1993), Clay (1994)). The impact of political factors on institutional selection is reflected in the analysis of the Merchant Guild (Greif, Milgrom, and Weingast (1994)). It suggests that the political and economic process through which the Italian city-states grew large enabled each of them to function as merchant guilds fostering the expansion of their trade. In Germany, cities emerged through a political process that led to the establishment of relatively small cities. Hence, only after a lengthy organizational development, the German Hansa – an intercity merchant guild – emerged to govern the relations between German merchants and foreign rulers. Finally, the rise of more centralized states in the early modern period led to the decline of local merchant guilds. Similarly, the nature and efficiency of agricultural credit cooperatives and the private-order institutions that governed landlord–tenant relations in Ireland were influenced by the extent to which the state issued bonds and enforced particular laws (Guinnane (1994, 1995)).

Cultural and social factors also impact institutional selection. Distinct cultures provided different focal points while distinct social processes provided different initial networks for information transmission among the Maghribi and the Genoese traders leading to the emergence of distinct institutions in fundamentally the same situation (Greif (1994a, 1995b)). The

Maghribis' cultural heritage made an equilibrium with collective punishment a focal point. The Maghribis assimilated in the Muslim society whose members shared the fundamental duty not only to practice good but also to ensure that others do not practice sin; furthermore, the Maghribis were part of the Jewish community within which it is a prominent idea that "All Israel is responsible for every member." Finally, they began trading around the Mediterranean after immigrating from Iraq to Tunisia. As is common among immigrants, they probably retained social ties that provided them with the information network required to support collective punishment.

In contrast, Christianity during the medieval period placed the individual rather than his social group at the center of its theology and hence the Genoese cultural heritage did not make collectivist punishment a focal point. Furthermore, for political reasons the number of Genoese active in trade rose dramatically toward the end of the twelfth century. At the same time, Genoa experienced a high level of immigration. In the absence of appropriate social networks for information transmission, collectivist punishment was not likely to emerge. Indeed, historical evidence suggests that the Genoese did not practice collective punishment but "individualistic" punishment in which each merchant punished only the agent who had cheated him and Genoa's legal system was used additionally to limit agents' ability to act opportunistically. Distinct social and cultural settings led to distinct institutions in fundamentally the same situation.

Guinnane (1994) in a comparative study of credit cooperatives in Germany and Ireland reached similar conclusions regarding the importance of social and cultural factors in influencing institutional selection. The Raiffeisen agriculture credit cooperatives were a success in nineteenth-century rural Germany and provided a model for the introduction of similar organizations in Ireland in 1894. Yet, the Irish cooperatives were never economically viable. This is partially attributed to the social and cultural differences between the two countries. The success of a cooperative depended on the monitoring and enforcement provided by its own members. Yet, social and cultural factors led to distinct equilibria in Germany and Ireland. The one that prevailed among the German rural people entailed monitoring each other and punishing in case of need but the one that prevailed among the Irish rural population did not entail such behavior.[26]

HIA studies reveal a variety of reasons that lead to institutional change. Institutional changes were generated endogenously due to changes induced by the operation of the institution itself (Greif (1994b, 1994c)). Further, institutional change was due to technological change (Guinnane (1994)), political changes (Rosenthal (1992), Greif, Milgrom, and Weingast (1994)), and observed organizational failure (Greif, Milgrom, and Weingast (1994), Greif (1996)). Institutions also changed due to population increases. For example, Hoffman, Postel-Vinay, and Rosenthal (1994) found that population increases changed the function of the Parisian notaries. The notaries were an organization established to foster legal contract enforceability and this provided them with private information regarding their clients' creditworthiness. Hence, when Paris grew and asymmetric information hindered credit relations the notaries became the intermediaries that mitigated this problem.

As this example illustrates, HIA studies indicate that institutional development exhibits path dependence.[27] Past expectations and organizations influence the process of institutional development. Particularly, institutional path dependence was found to be due to acquired knowledge and information, economies of scale and scope associated with existing organizations, coordination failure, and distributional issues.[28] Yet, perhaps the most intriguing observation with respect to institutional path dependence is that it was found to be related to linkage between games, namely to the nature of responses to exogenous changes in the rules of the game and to the process of organizational innovation through which institutions are endogenously changed.

Classical game theory does not have much to say about linkages among games. The establishment of an organization profitable to those who can bring it about is an action whose benefit would be (in the absence of coordination failure) recognized by the players and hence taken at the outset.[29] More generally, the actions to be taken following an expected change in the rules of the game are a part of the (initial) equilibrium strategy combination. Finally the equilibrium that would be selected following an unexpected change in the rules of the game has no relation with the equilibrium that prevailed prior to the change.

Yet, Greif (1994a, 1996) has found that equilibrium selected following an unexpected change in the rules of the game had predictable relations with the equilibrium that prevailed prior to the change. Furthermore, the equilibrium that prevailed prior to the change was related in a predictable manner to historically subsequent organizational innovations. Particularly, expectations associated with past equilibria were good predictors of the expectations that prevailed following an exogenous change in the rules of the game and of organizational change. In a sense, such expectations became "cultural beliefs," as they transcended the original game in which they had been crystallized and provided the initial conditions for the selection of a strategy in other historically subsequent strategic situations.

Specifically, the rules of the game regarding agency relations that the Maghribis and the Genoese traders faced during the late medieval period changed. Following various military and political events around the Mediterranean, both groups could expand their trade to areas previously inaccessible to them. As far as agency relations are concerned, such expansion could have been done in an "integrative" manner, namely, by hiring agents from the new area or in a "segregative" manner, namely, by having some of them emigrate to the new trade centers and provide agency services. In a game theoretical analysis, the equilibrium that would be selected following such a change in the rules of the game has no relation to the equilibrium that previously prevailed. Game theory does not specify a mapping from an equilibrium in one game to that of another.

The experience of the Maghribis and the Genoese, however, indicates an appropriate mapping. It suggests that the (off-and on-the-path-of-play) expectations associated with the pre-change equilibrium transcended the boundaries of the original game and provided the focal point for the selection of a new equilibrium. In other words, these expectations were not a feature of the game but of individuals. They became a cultural element – cultural beliefs – that provided the initial condition in a dynamic adjustment process through which the new equilibrium is reached.

To consider the possible impact of cultural beliefs, suppose that they provide the initial condition in a dynamic adjustment process through which a new equilibrium is reached following the change in the rules of the game experienced by the traders. From a merchant's point of view, taking the pre-change equilibrium strategies as initial conditions implies that the profitability of establishing intercommunity agency relations depends on the expected responses of the merchants from the agent's community to the agent's actions. Although the merchants from the agent's economy can be expected to respond in various ways, two responses predominate. For any agent's action in intereconomy agency relations, these merchants can regard him either as one who cheated or did not cheat one of them. There is nothing in the pre-change expectations, however, that indicates which of these responses will be selected following an action. Accordingly, assume that in intereconomy agency relations any probability distribution over these two responses can possibly be expected. Considering the pre-change expectations and any such probability distributions as initial conditions provides the mapping required for the examination of a merchant's decision whether to establish intereconomy agency relations (while not imposing any differences between the pre-change economies apart from their expectations).

Given this general mapping, what would the merchants' best response be as a function of their expectations? When the equilibria in two pre-change economies entail collective punishment, the initial expectations specify collective punishment in intra-economy agency relations. Any uncertainty about whether collective punishment also governs intereconomy agency relations increases the wage required to pay the agent in the intercommunity agency relations case relative to the intra-community agency relations case. A decline in the severity of the punishment for cheating must be offset by an increase in the reward for honesty. As the merchants' cost of establishing intereconomy agency relations is higher than the cost of establishing intra-economy agency relations, only the latter will be initiated, and segregation is the end result. If intereconomy agency relations are more efficient, they will be initiated only if the efficiency gains are sufficiently large. This is not the case in the absence of collective punishment as the wage required to keep agents honest is the same in inter and intra-community agency relations. Hence, whenever intercommunity agency relations are more efficient they will be initiated and integration will result.[30]

Hence, theoretical considerations indicate how expectations regarding off-the-path-of-play that constrained on-the-path behavior in one strategic situation, if projected into another strategic situation can direct equilibrium selection, economic efficiency, and social structure. The historical evidence regarding the impact of these cultural beliefs is consistent with theoretical predictions. The Maghribis responded in a segregated manner not only toward non-Jews but also with respect to other Jewish traders even when agency relations with them were (ignoring agency cost) perceived by the Maghribis as very profitable. The Genoese, however, responded in an integrated manner and although the historical sources are biased toward reflecting agency relations among Genoese, they nevertheless clearly indicate the prevalence of agency relations between Genoese and non-Genoese.

The comparative analysis of the Maghribis and Genoese also suggests the sources of uneven development of organizations related to trade in the Italian and the Muslim world during the late medieval period; differences that, as discussed above, could not have been accounted for in the NIEH. HIA, however, link these differences to cultural beliefs that impact the process of organizational innovations. Cultural beliefs provide the initial conditions that influence incentives to introduce various organizations and determine their impact. Hence, they imply path dependence in organizational change while the implications of adopting a particular organization depends on the prevailing cultural beliefs.

Greif (1994a) elaborates on the relations between cultural beliefs and the origin of various organizational differences between the Maghribis and Genoese. Consider, for example, the rise of the family firm among Italian traders (Greif (1996)). When the Maghribi and Genoese merchants first began trading in the Mediterranean, it was common in both groups for a trader's son to start operating as an independent merchant during his father's lifetime. During the thirteenth century, however, the Italian traders adopted the family firm, the essence of which was a permanent partnership with unlimited and joint liability. This organization preserved the family wealth undivided under one management, and a trader's son, reaching the appropriate age, joined his family's firm. It was now the firm, rather then an individual trader, that hired agents. The Maghribi traders, after being active in trade for centuries did not establish similar organizations.

Cultural beliefs provide a consistent explanation for this uneven organizational development when they are assumed to guide expectations with respect to the equilibrium that would be achieved following the organizational change. When agency relations are governed by a reputation mechanism, the lower is the probability of forced separation, namely that agency relations will be terminated despite the agent being honest the lower is the wage required to keep an agent honest. The magnitude of this reduction, however, is a function of the expectations associated with the particular reputation mechanism being used. It is lower under collective punishment since the probability that a cheater will be rehired is lower and the probability that an honest agent will be rehired is higher than otherwise. Collective punishment and reducing the probability of forced separation are substitutes.

Hence, since the Maghribis practiced collective punishment a Maghribi merchant could not gain much, if anything, by introducing an organization that reduces the likelihood of forced separation. Among the Italian traders who did not practice collective punishment, however, merchants were motivated to increase the security of the employment they offered their agents, and the family firm seems to have been the manifestation of this desire. They formed an organization with an infinite life-span and a lower probability of bankruptcy to replace each individual merchant and his relationship with agents.

Once a particular organization is established, it can impact subsequent institutional development, fostering institutional path dependence. Trivially the establishment of the family firm led to the emergence of complementary innovations such as a market in firms' shares and appropriate accounting procedures. Similarly, Guinnane (1994) found that during the nineteenth century, past organizations in Ireland influenced further organizational developments. In Ireland, the state-run post office widely distributed state bonds. The easy access to such bonds in Ireland but not in Germany undermined Irish agricultural credit cooperatives. Similarly, the exact nature of various merchant guilds reflects prior organizational development (Greif, Milgrom, and Weingast (1994)). In England, for example, the king provided local guilds with a monopoly over retail trade and the threat of exclusion from this monopoly was used to ensure the merchants' compliance with boycott decisions. In the Italian cities, however, the legal system was used to insure merchants' compliance with boycott decisions.

Yet, the examination of organizational innovations and path dependence reveals what is, from a (classical) game theoretical perspective, a puzzle. Organizational innovations seem to have taken a long period of time rather than being the instantaneous selection of appropriate actions. The Italians, for example, experimented for over a century at least before they invented double entry bookkeeping, although this invention neither depended on new technology nor involved any strategic interaction.

This puzzle suggests that it may be misleading to view individuals as fully strategic in the sense that they have full knowledge and understanding of all possible actions and their consequences. While this does not contradict the equilibrium analysis conducted above since it focused on actual rather than potential institutions, it indicates the need to examine further the process of institutional innovation. Several interrelated approaches seem promising. Slow institutional development may reflect – similar to the introduction of new technologies – an increase in the stock of knowledge due to intentional pursuit of organizational improvement or the outcome of unintentional experimentation. Slow institutional development may reflect subjective comprehension of reality (North (1990)). Finally, it may reflect bounded rationality or behavioral rules of action. More generally, the observation that strategic analysis was useful for the study of actual institutions, while insufficient to fully comprehend the process of institutional development, indicates, once more, the relevance of Simon's ([1947] 1961) observation that individuals are intentionally "rational, but only limitedly so" (p. xxiv). What seems to be required is to explore the factors that determine the domain of strategic and non-strategic behavior.

One of the broad insights that emerged from HIA analyses relates to the empirical implications of the folk theorem of infinitely repeated games. The folk theorem provides a deductive theory of contract enforcement which is applicable under variety of information structures if the players are sufficiently patient.[31] Hence, it seems to have rendered inductive institutional analysis of contract enforcement – the focus of most HIA studies – obsolete. Yet, some HIA studies reveal the empirical *ir*relevance of the conditions required for the folk theorem to hold (e.g., Milgrom, North, and Weingast (1990), North (1991), Greif (1995b)). But, even when these conditions were likely to hold, the empirical analyses indicate that organizations emerged and affected the equilibrium set while the exact nature of the equilibrium selected effected subsequent organizational and institutional development (e.g., Greif, (1989, 1994a), Greif, Milgrom, and Weingast (1994)).

HIA also indicates the complexity of the interrelations between private-order and state supported institutions that are usually considered as substitutes.[32] For example, the existence of state-issued bonds in nineteenth-century Ireland undermined the operation of the private-order institutions that could have supported the operation of credit cooperatives (Guinnane (1994)). The functioning of the merchant guild required supplementing the reputation-based enforcement in the relations among traders and a ruler with legal enforcement within each merchant community (Greif, Milgrom, and Weingast (1994)). Distinct self-enforcing private-order institutions may imply distinct demand for state-supported institutions. For example, the nature of the private-order institution that governed agency relations among the Genoese traders, but not the Maghribi traders, entailed demand for a specific type of contract enforcement by the state (Greif (1994a, 1995b)). At times, the institutional foundations of the state itself were effected by the nature of the existing private-order institutions. The French kings' ability to alter property rights, for example, was constrained by the self-enforcing organizations they had created (Rosenthal (1992)).

Similarly, HIA studies also indicate the complexity of the interrelations between a society's economic, cultural, social, and economic features. For example, the different institutions that governed agency relations among the Maghribis and Genoese contributed much to their distinct social and cultural characters which, in turn, reinforced their economic institutions. Among the Maghribis, collectivist cultural beliefs and the associated economic self-enforcing collective punishment led to a horizontal social structure (namely, a trader functioned as merchant and agent at the same time), social segregation, and an ingroup social communication network. Among the Genoese, individualist cultural beliefs led to an individualist society with a vertical and integrated social structure and a relatively low level of communication. To the extent that one holds that values evolve over time to justify a pattern of economic and social behavior, these distinct economic and social systems were likely also to lead to distinct values (Greif (1994a, 1995b)).

4 CONCLUDING REMARKS

Three approaches contemporary in economic history utilize microeconomic theory to examine historical institutions. They have in common the objective of examining different aspects of the institutional structures of past societies. The neoclassical approach examines the extent to which the market operated in the past and legally enforceable contractual forms used to mitigate market imperfections. NIEH examines property rights, rules, and regulations defined and enforced by the state and the implications of transaction cost on their efficiency. HIA is an inductive approach that utilizes microlevel historical studies and strategic models to examine self-enforcing institutions.

These approaches build on and supplement each other providing a rich representation of the complexity of economic institutions in past societies. All three approaches still have to resolve various obstacles. As elaborated with respect to the neoclassical approach but equally true with respect to the other two approaches, institutions' (in)efficiency implications are usually argued based on theoretical insights rather than empirical evidence. Neither have developed an appropriate methodology to measure the efficiency implications of an institution. A similar problem exists with respect to the efficiency implications of technological changes. Fogel (1964) proposed to measure a technology's impact by constructing a counterfactual model of the economy assuming that the technology under examination was absent. This methodology, however, remained controversial in economic history and it is even more problematic with respect to institutions since there are usually no prices or costs for the institution's "service" and its alternatives.[33] Similarly, all three approaches have examined the relations between institutions and efficiency but have not found an appropriate manner to explicitly link institutions and growth.

These deficiencies, as well as the need for more empirical studies and better understanding of institutional innovations, notwithstanding, studies of historical economic institutions, have already contributed much to our understanding of institutions and the historical process of institutional development. Particularly, they indicate the need to examine the institutional structure of an economy as a system of interrelated elements in which social, cultural, and political factors – and not only economic efficiency – influence the selection over, and the path dependence of economic institutions. Hence, not only are institutions not necessarily efficient (Greif (1994d)) but the adoption of efficient institutions may be hindered by institutional path dependence. For example, since institutions combine organizations and expectations one society would not be able to adopt an institution of another simply by implementing the associated organization. Unless the appropriate expectations are adopted as well, the same organization would have distinct economic implications. Understanding the failure of societies to adopt the institutions of more economically and political successful ones seems to require better comprehension of their historical process of institutional development.

Notes

The research for this paper was supported by Institutional Reform in the Informal Sector at the University of Maryland at College Park and by National Science Foundation Grants 9009598-01 and 9223974. Masa Aoki, Timothy Guinnane,

Steve Haber, Chiaki Moriguchi, Douglass C. North, Barry Weingast, Gavin Wright, and participants in an All Department Seminar at UC Berkeley contributed valuable comments.

1 This was recognized, for example, by North (1981), Williamson (1982), Olson (1982).

2 For a discussion of the methodological differences between economic history and economics, see, Backhouse (1985, pp. 216–21). For institutional studies during the nineteenth century in the German and English Historical Schools, see, for example, Weber (e.g., [1927] 1987), Cunningham (e.g. 1992).

3 Extensive work in economic history utilizes macro-economic theory to examine organizations and institutions such as central banks and monetary regimes. See, for example, Eichengreen (1994).

4 It also does not discuss papers that do not integrate theory and history.

5 On the cliometric revolution, see Williamson (1994). Hartwell (1973) surveys the methodological developments in economic history. For the many contributions generated by the neoclassical line of research in economic history, see McCloskey (1976).

6 Galenson (1981, 1989), Price (1980), Rothenberg (1992), Hatton and Williamson (1991b).

7 Hoffman (1991, 1996), Neal (1990). For a collection of works on labor markets, see Aerts and Eichengreen (1990).

8 See further, Hatton and Williamson (1991a).

9 Using the mechanism design approach, Townsend (1993) has demonstrated that scattering can be Pareto improving. Fenoaltea (1975) and Allen (1982), however, challenged the theoretical and empirical foundation of McCloskey's analysis.

10 The NIEH is a part of broader movements of institutional analysis in economics and political science known as the New-Institutional Economics (NIE). For surveys, see Eggertsson (1990) (economics), Weingast (1995) (political science).

11 The only empirical work that examines these cultural norms is Levi (1988).

12 Some NIEH works examined contractual relations and voluntary creation of rules and regulations. For recent applications see, for example, Alston and Higgs (1982), Fishback (1992).

13 Davis and North (1971), North and Thomas (1973), North (1981).

14 Wallis and North (1986) provides a time series of transaction costs in the US economy. Cf. Lance (1986).

15 See also Alston and Ferrie (1993), Fishback and Kantor (1995).

16 The definition of institutions as non-technologically determined constraints on economic behavior (Greif, 1994a) is inspired by North (1991): institutions are "rules of the game in a society or, more formally, are the humanly devised constraints that shape human interaction" (p. 3). Definitions similar to his are utilized in the rational choice approach to the study of political institutions (see Weingast (1995)). These definitions, however, do not capture that some rules of the game are technologically determined while expectations also constrain behavior.

17 Most HIA studies limit the set of admissible expectations to those associated with (some refinement of) Nash equilibrium. Yet, other expectations such as those associated with self-confirming equilibrium (Fudenberg and Levine (1991)) or rationalizable equilibrium (Bernheim (1984)) can in principle be used.
18 Clearly, such constraints usually have some technological component to them. The point is that they are not determined by the technology of production or exchange central to the analysis.
19 Reiter and Hughes (1981) is the forerunner of such analysis.
20 E.g., Greif (1993, 1994a, 1996), Banerjee, Besley, and Guinnane (1994).
21 Arias (1901), pp. 166–7.
22 For other recent works on financial systems, see Calomiris (1992), Lamoreaux (1994). For other works regarding institutions and labor relations see Treble (1990), Moselle (1995), Huberman (1996).
23 Although see Greif (1995c).
24 Weingast (1993) went further and argued that antebellum US's political system ensured property rights in slaves thus preventing military confrontation between the North and South. De Long and Shleifer (1992) found that non-absolutist regimes are positively and significantly correlated with cities' growth (as a proxy for economic growth) in Europe, 1000–1800.
25 Carruthers (1990) criticized the claim that limiting the king enabled England to borrow while Clark (1995) cast doubt on the claim that property rights were insecure before 1688. He examined the rate of return on private debt and land, and the price of land from 1540 to 1800 and was unable to detect any impact due to the Glorious Revolution.
26 The paper does not contain an explicit model, making further elaboration on the relations between culture and these two equilibria difficult.
27 On the general theory of path dependence see David (1988, 1992a); on path dependence and institutions, see North (1990) (who emphasizes economics of scale and scope, network externalities, and a subjective view of the world) and David (1994) (who emphasizes conventions, information channels and codes as "sunk" organizational capital, interrelatedness, complementaries, and precedents).
28 Knowledge: Hoffman *et al.* (1994); scale, scope, and coordination: Greif (1994a); distribution: Rosenthal (1992).
29 If there is a coordination failure the organization will never be introduced.
30 Greif (1994a) also analyzes the case when only one economy practiced collective punishment.
31 Fudenberg, Levine, and Maskin (1991), Kandori (1992), Ellison (1993).
32 See Greif (1994d) for elaboration.
33 See, e.g., David (1969).

References

Aerts, Erik and Eichengreen, Barry (eds.) (1990). *Unemployment and Underemployment in Historical Perspective.* Leuven: Leuven University Press.

Allen, Robert (1982). "The efficiency and distributional consequences of eighteenth century enclosures." *Economic Journal*, 92: 937–53.

Alston, J. Lee and Ferrie, Joseph (1993). "Paternalism in agricultrual labor contracts in the US South: implications for the growth of the welfare state." *American Economic Review*, 83(4) (September): 852–76.

Alston, J. Lee and Higgs, Robert (1982). "Contractual mix in southern agriculture since the Civil War: facts, hypotheses, and tests." *Journal of Economic History*, 42 (2) (June): 327–52.

Alston, J. Lee, Libecap, Gary D., and Schneider, Robert (1994). "An analysis of property rights, land rents, and agricultural investment on two frontiers in Brazil." Mimeo, Department of Economics, University of Illinois at Urban Champaign.

Arias, Gino (1901). *I Trattati Commerciali della Repùbblica Fiorentina*. Florence: Successori le Monnier.

Arrow, J. Kenneth (1974). *The Limits of Organization*. New York: Norton.

Backhouse, Roger (1985). *A History of Modern Economic Analysis*. New York: Basil Blackwell.

Baliga, Sandeep and Polak, Ben (1995). "Banks versus bonds: a simple theory of comparative financial institutions." Cowles Foundation Discussion Paper No. 1100, Yale University.

Banerjee, V. Abhijit, Besley, Timothy, and Guinnane, Timothy W. (1994). "Thy neighbor's keeper: the design of a credit cooperative with theory and a test." *Quarterly Journal of Economics*, 109 (May): 491–515.

Bernheim, B. D. (1984). "Rationalizable strategic behavior." *Econometrica*, 52: 1007–28.

Buchinsky, M. and Polak, B. (1993). "The emergence of national capital market in England, 1710–1880." *Journal of Economic History*, 53 (March): 1–24.

Calomiris, Charles (1992). "Regulation, industrial structure, and instability in US banking: an historical perspective." In Klausner, Michael and White, Lawrence J. (eds.), *Structural Change in Banking*. New York: New York University Press.

Carruthers, Bruce E. (1990). "Politics, popery, and property: a comment on North and Weingast." *Journal of Economic History*, 50(3) (September): 693–8.

Clark, Gregory (1995). "The political foundations of modern economic growth: England, 1540–1800." *Journal of Interdisciplinary History*, 26 (Spring): 563–88.

Clay, Karen (1994). "Coalitions and contract enforcement: trade on the California coast, 1830–1846." Working Paper, University of Toronto.

Coase, R. H. (1937). "The nature of the firm." *Economica*, 16(NS): 386–405.

Conklin, James (1994). "Time consistency and commitment: an observation on a mechanism from sixteenth century Spain." Working Paper, Department of Economics. University of Texas, Austin.

Cunningham, William (1882). *The Growth of English Industry and Commerce*. Cambridge: Cambridge University Press.

David, Paul A. (1969). "Transportation innovation and economic growth: Professor Fogel on and off the rails." *Economic History Review*, 22(3) (December): 506–25.

(1988). "Path-dependence: putting the past into the future of economics." Technical Report No. 533, IMSSS, Stanford University, California.

(1992). "Path dependence and the predictability in dynamic systems with local network externalities: a paradigm for historical economics." In Freeman, C. and Foray, D. (eds.), *Technology and the Wealth of Nations.* London: Pinter Publishers.

(1994). "Why are institutions the 'carriers of history'?: path-dependence and the evolution of conventions, organizations and institutions." *Structural Change and Economic Dynamics*, 5(2): 205–20.

Davis, E. Lance and North, Douglas C. (1971). *Institutional Change and American Economic Growth.* Cambridge: Cambridge University Press.

De Long, Bradford J. and Shleifer, Andrei (1992). "Princes and merchants: city growth before the Industrial Revolution." Working Paper, Department of Economics, Harvard University.

Eggertsson, Thrainn (1990). *Economic Behavior and Institutions.* Cambridge: Cambridge University Press.

Eichengreen, Barry (1994). "Institutions and economic growth: Europe after World War II." CEPR Working Paper No. 973.

Ellison, Glenn (1993). "Cooperation in the prisoner's dilemma with anonymous random matching." Working Paper, Harvard University.

Fenoaltea, Stefano (1975). "Authority, efficiency, and agricultural organization in medieval England and beyond." *Journal of Economic History*, 35 (December): 693–718.

Field, Alexander (1981). "The problem with neoclassical institutional economics: a critique with special reference to the North–Thomas model of pre-1500 Europe." *Explorations in Economic History*, 18 (April): 174–98.

Fishback, Price (1992). "The economics of company housing: historical perspectives from the coal fields." *JLEO*, 8(2): 000–00.

Fishback, V. Price and Kantor, Shawn E. (1995). "The adoption of workers' compensation in the United States, 1900–1930." Working Paper, Economics Department, University of Arizona, Tucson.

Fogel, Robert W. (1964). *Railroads and American Economic Growth: Essays in Econometric History.* Baltimore: John Hopkins University Press.

Fudenberg, Drew, Levine, David, and Maskin, Eric (1991). "The folk theorem with imperfect public information." Working Paper, Massachusetts Institute of Technology.

Fudenberg, Drew and Levine, David K. (1991). "Self-confirming equilibrium." Department of Economics Working Paper No. 581. Massachusetts Institute of Technology.

Galenson, David (1981). *White Servitude in Colonial America.* Cambridge: Cambridge University Press.

(1989). "Labor markets in Colonial America." In Galenson, David W. (ed.), *Markets in History.* Cambridge: Cambridge University Press.

Greif, Avner (1989). "Reputation and coalitions in medieval trade: evidence on the Maghribi traders." *Journal of Economic History.*, 49(4) (December): 857–82.

(1992). "Institutions and international trade: lessons from the commerical revolution." *American Economic Review*, 82(2) (May): 128–33.

(1993). "Contract enforceability and economic institutions in early trade: the Maghribi traders' coalition." *American Economic Review*, 83(3) (June): 525–48.

(1994a). "Cultural beliefs and the organization of society: a historical and theoretical reflection on collectivist and individualist societies." *Journal of Political Economy*, 102(5) (October): 912–50.

(1994b). "On the political foundations of the late medieval commercial revolution: Genoa during the twelfth and thirteenth centuries." *Journal of Economic History*, 54(4) (June): 271–87.

(1994c). "Markets and legal systems: the development of markets in late medieval Europe and the transition from community responsibility to an individual responsibility legal doctrine." Manuscript, Department of Economics, Stanford University.

(1994d). "Trading institutions and the commercial revolution in medieval Europe." In Aganbegyan, Abel, Bogomolov, Oleg, and Kaser, Michael (eds.), *Economics in a Changing World*, Vol. I (Proceedings of the Tenth World Congress of the International Economic Association). London: Macmillan, pp. 115–25.

(1995a). "The institutional foundations of Genoa's economic growth: self-enforcing political relations, organizational innovations, and economic growth during the commercial revolution." Manuscript, Stanford University.

(1995b). "Institutional structure and economic development: economic history and the new institutionalism." Forthcoming in Drobak, John N. and Nye, John (eds.), *Frontiers of Institutional Analysis*. Volume in honor of Douglass C. North.

(1995c). "Political organizations, social structure, and institutional success: reflections from Genoa and Venice during the commercial revolution." *Journal of Institutional and Theoretical Economics*, 151 (December): 734–40.

(1996). "On the study of organizations and evolving organizational forms through history: reflection from the late medieval firm." *Industrial and Corporate Change*, 5(2).

Greif, Avner, Milgrom, Paul, and Weingast, Barry (1994). "Coordination, commitment and enforcement: the case of the merchant gild." *Journal of Political Economy*, 102 (4) (August): 912–50.

Grubb, Farley (1994). "The end of European immigrant servitude in the United States: an economic analysis of market collapse, 1772–1835." *Journal of Economic History*, 54(4) (December): 794–824.

Guinnane, Timothy W. (1994). "A failed institutional transplant: Raiffeisen's credit cooperatives in Ireland, 1894–1914." *Explorations in Economic History*, 31(1) (January): 38–61.

Guinnane, Timothy W. and Miller, Roland I. (1996). "Bonds without bondsmen: tenant-right in nineteenth century Ireland." *Journal of Economic History*, 56 (March): 113–42.

Haber, Stephen H. (1991). "Industrial concentration and the capital markets: a comparative study of Brazil, Mexico, and the United States, 1830–1930." *Journal of Economic History*, 51(3) (September): 559–80.

Hartwell, R. M. (1973). "Good old economic history." *Journal of Economic History*, 33(1) (March): 28–40.

Hatton, Timothy and Williamson, Jeffrey G. (1991a). "Integrated and segmented labor markets: thinking in two sectors." *Journal of Economic History*, 51(2) (June): 413–26.

(1991b). "Unemployment, employment contracts, and compensating wage differentials: Michigan in the 1890s." *Journal of Economic History*, 51(3) (September): 605–32.

Hoffman, Philip T. (1991). "Land rents and agricultural productivity: the Paris basin, 1450–1789." *Journal of Economic History*, 51 (December): 771–805.

(1996). *Growth in a Traditional Society: the French Countryside, 1450–1789*. Princeton: Princeton University Press.

Hoffman, Philip T., Postel-Vinay, Gilles, and Rosenthal, Jean-Laurent (1994). "What do notaries do? Overcoming asymmetric information in financial markets: the case of 1751 Paris." Manuscript, Center for Advanced Studies in the Behavioral Sciences, Stanford.

Huberman, Michael (1996). *Escape from the Market: Negotiating Work in Lancashire*. Cambridge: Cambridge University Press.

Kandori, Michihiro (1992). "Social norms and community enforcement." *Review of Economic Studies*, 59: 63–80.

Kantor, Shawn Everett (1991). "Razorback, ticky cows, and the closing of the Georgia open range: the dynamics of institutional change uncovered." *Journal of Economic History*, 51(4) (December): 861–86.

Lamoreaux, Naomi R. (1994). *Insider Lending: Banks, Personal Connections, and Economic Development in Industrial New England, 1784–1912*. Cambridge: Cambridge University Press.

Lance, Davis E. (1986). "Measuring the transaction sector in the American economy, 1870–1970." (Comment on John Joseph Wallis and Douglass C. North. 1986.) In Engerman, Stanley L. and Gallman, Robert E. (eds.), *Long-Term Factors in American Economic Growth*. NBER Studies in Income and Wealth, 51. Chicago: Chicago University Press, pp. 149–61.

Levi, Margaret (1988). *Of Rule and Revenue*. Berkeley: University of California Press.

Libecap, Gary D. (1989). *Contracting for Property Rights*. Cambridge: Cambridge University Press.

McCloskey, Donald N. (1976). "Does the past have useful economics?" *Journal of Economic Literature*, 14 (June): 434–61.

(1989). "The open field of England: rent, risk, and the rate of interest, 1300–1815." In Galenson, David W. (ed.), *Markets in History*. Cambridge: Cambridge University Press.

Milgrom, Paul R., North, Douglass, and Weingast, Barry R. (1990). "The role of institutions in the revival of trade: the medieval law merchant, private judges, and the champagne fairs." *Economics and Politics*, 2 (1) (March): 1–23.

Moselle, Boaz (1995). "Allotments, enclosure and proletarianization in early nineteenth-century southern England." *Economic History Review*, 98 (August): 482–500.

Neal, Larry (1990). *The Rise of Financial Capitalism*. Cambridge: Cambridge University Press.

North, Douglass C. ([1961] 1996). *The Economic Growth of the United States, 1790–1860*. New York: Norton.

(1977). "Non-market forms of economic organization: the challenge of Karl Polanyi." *Journal of European Economic History*, 6 (3) (Winter): 703–16.

(1981). *Structure and Change in Economic History*. New York: Norton.

(1990). *Institutions, Institutional Change and Economic Performance*. Cambridge: Cambridge University Press.

(1991). "Institutions." *Journal of Economic Perspectives*, 5: 97–112.

(1993). "Institutions and credible commitment." *Journal of Institutional and Theoretical Economics*, 149: 11–23.

North, Douglass C. and Thomas, R. (1973). *The Rise of the Western World*. Cambridge: Cambridge University Press.

North, Douglass C. and Weingast, Barry R. (1989). "Constitutions and commitment: evolution of institutions governing public choice." *Journal of Economic History*, 49 (December): 803–32.

Olson, Mancur (1982). *The Rise and Decline of Nations*. New Haven: Yale University Press.

Price, Jacob M. (1980). *Capital and Credit in British Overseas Trade: The View from the Chesapeake*. Cambridge, MA: Harvard University Press.

Reiter, Stanley and Hughes, Jonathan (1981). "A preface on modeling the regulated United States economy." *Hofstra Law Review*, 9 (5) (Summer).

Root, Hilton L. (1989). "Tying the King's hand: credible commitment and royal fiscal policy during the old regime." *Rationality and Society*, 1(2): 240–58.

Rosenbloom, Joshua L. (1994). "Was there a national labor market at the end of the nineteenth century? Intercity and interregional variation in male earnings in manufacturing." Working Paper, Department of Economics, University of Kansas.

Rosenthal, Jean-Laurent (1992). *The Fruits of Revolution*. Cambridge: Cambridge University Press.

Rothenberg, Winifred Barr (1992). *From Market-Places to Market Economy. The Transformation of Rural Massachusetts*. Chicago: Chicago University Press.

Simon, Herbert A. ([1947] 1961). *Administrative Behavior*. 2nd edn. New York: Macmillan.

Smith, Adam ([1776] 1937). *The Wealth of Nations*. New York: The Modern Library.

Sokoloff, Ken (1988). "Inventive activity in early industrial America: evidence from patent records, 1790–1846." *Journal of Economic History*, 48 (4) (December): 813–50.

Townsend, Robert M. (1993). *The Medieval Village Economy*. Princeton, New Jersey: Princeton University Press.

Treble, John (1990). "The pit and the pendulum: arbitration in the British coal industry, 1893–1914." *The Economic Journal*, 100 (December): 1095–108.

Wallis, John Joseph and North, Douglass C. (1986). "Measuring the transaction sector in the American economy, 1870–1970." In Engerman, Stanley L. and Gallman, Robert E. (eds.), *Long-Term Factors in American Economic Growth.* NBER Studies in Income and Wealth, vol. 51. Chicago: Chicago University Press, pp. 95–148.

Weber, Max ([1927] 1987). *General Economic History.* Translated by Frank H. Knight. London: Transaction Books.

Weingast, R. Barry (1993). "The political foundations of antebellum economic growth." Working Paper, The Hoover Institution, Stanford University.

(1995). "Rational choice perspectives on institutions." Working Paper, The Hoover Institution, Stanford.

Williamson, Oliver E. (1982). "Microanalytic business history." *Business and Economic History*, 2nd series, 11: 106–15.

(1985). *The Economic Institutions of Capitalism.* New York: Free Press.

Williamson, Samuel H. (1994). "The history of cliometrics." In *Two Pioneers of Cliometrics*, Miami University, Ohio: The Cliometrics Society.

Wright, Gavin (1987). "The economic revolution in the American South." *Journal of Economic Perspective*, 1(1): 161–78.

CHAPTER 4

Poverty traps

Partha Dasgupta

INTRODUCTION

This chapter is about *poverty traps.* My aims are to explore some of the mechanisms that create and sustain them, and to suggest patterns of public policy for countering them. I will be concerned with certain manifestations of the phenomenon as it occurs in poor countries, such as those in the Indian sub-continent and sub-Saharan Africa. But there may well be other manifestations, even in poor countries, that are not covered here. That there are poverty traps in rich countries is also a claim that is increasingly heard (see section 1.1). Even though the economic mechanisms prevailing there could be expected to be different, the mathematical structures underlying them are likely to be similar. However, I have not been able to demonstrate this in the context of an intertemporal model based on adequate microeconomic foundations. So my approach will be piecemeal. I will look at two models, suitable for an analysis of certain kinds of poverty traps within poor countries. The models are different, focusing as they do on different themes. One studies the biomedical phenomenon of undernourishment and the poverty traps that are allied to it; the other looks at poverty traps associated with high birth rates and deterioration of the local environmental resource base. I apologize for the disparateness, but I have found no simple, overarching model that picks up all the features I want to highlight here.

This said, I do not wish to apologize too much. The themes to be discussed here have not exactly held the high ground in what one may call "official development economics." The nutritional and environmental sciences have been thoroughly neglected in mainstream development economics.[1] Furthermore, someone steeped in development economics would be forgiven for thinking that rapid population growth in today's world poses no serious impediment to the process of economic betterment. Indeed, in recent years, high fertility rates have all too often been dismissed by development economists as being a symptom of poverty, not much else.[2] Since there is scarcely any literature to survey, I am unable to provide a survey here. I will, therefore, present an account of certain fundamental economic problems facing today's poorest countries. In section 1, the links between someone's nutritional status and their physical capacity for work will be discussed. I will argue that the physiological basis for such links gives rise to poverty traps among assetless folk. Population will be taken to be exogenously given in this analysis. So in section 2 I will focus on fertility decisions and suggest that in agrarian populations in poor countries the institutional failures that create links between population growth, poverty, and degradation of the local environmental resource base are also responsible for poverty traps.

Poverty traps are a sharper notion than involuntary unemployment. By extension, they are sharper than the notion of horizontal inequity. To illustrate the differences in the context of nutrition–productivity models, let us consider a stylized example. Later, I will provide flesh to it.

We will denote time by $t(\geq 0)$. Let z_t be a scalar index of a person's health at date t, and $w(z)$ the flow of well being if the index of health is z. Naturally, we will suppose that $w'(z) > 0$. Now let $y(z)$ denote a person's income and $h(z)$ his food requirement (expressed in units of income). Each is taken to be a continuous function of z. We will imagine that a person's health, when viewed as a stock, obeys the deterministic differential equation

$$dz_t/dt = y(z_t) - h(z_t),\ \bar{z} > z_t > \underline{z}, \tag{1}$$

and if $z_{t'} = \bar{z}$ (resp. $\underline{z}$), then $z_t = \bar{z}$ (resp. $\underline{z}$) for all $t \geq t'$.[3]

In figure 4.1, $y(z)$ and $h(z)$ have been so drawn that they intersect once, at $\hat{z}$. Equation (1), therefore, has three equilibria: $\underline{z}$, $\hat{z}$, and $\bar{z}$. Of these, $\hat{z}$ is unstable, while $\underline{z}$ and $\bar{z}$ are stable. Notice also that a person with an initial condition z_0 slightly in excess of $\hat{z}$ enjoys growth in well being, while someone with z_0 slightly less than $\hat{z}$ is trapped in a deteriorating situation. In short, there are people in the neighborhood of z_0 who are similar, but who face widely differing fortunes. Admittedly, if future well being were to be discounted at a positive rate, the integral of the present discounted flow of personal well being ($w(z)$) would be continuous in z_0, even at $z_0 = \hat{z}$. But this merely goes to show that, when life prospects are viewed from a single vantage point of time (e.g., the present), the principle of horizontal equity could be satisfied even in the presence of poverty traps. The example offers a reason why life prospects need to be viewed from all points of time. The reason is that similar people would not remain similar if they were to

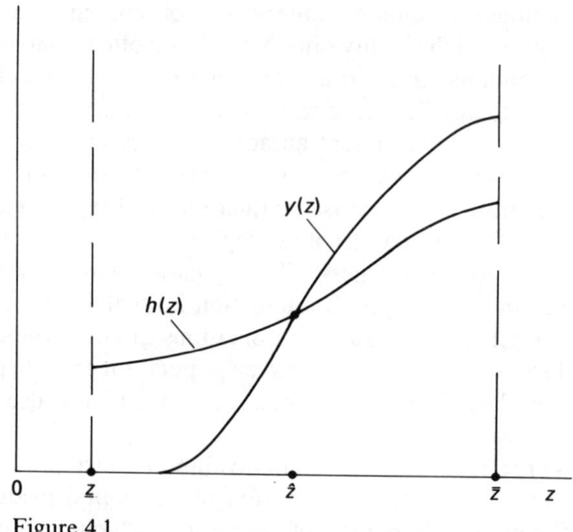

Figure 4.1

experience widely different life histories; which means in turn that the principle of horizontal equity could not be applied to them in later times. This is one reason why the principle, as traditionally formulated, has little ethical bite. It captures egalitarian notions in a minimal way.

One expects that growth in the economy's aggregate wealth, leading, say, to improved capital and insurance markets, would raise the income schedule, $y(z)$. If the entire schedule were to rise sufficiently high, it would not intersect $h(z)$, and $\bar{z}$ would then become the sole equilibrium point of the system described in equation (1). Welfare support and income guarantees would be another set of mechanisms by which $y(z)$ could be lifted. These are among the various pathways by which poverty traps have been eliminated in a number of countries. We will return to matters of public policy in sections 1.8 and 2.4.

1 NUTRITIONAL STATUS, WORK CAPACITY, AND POVERTY TRAPS

1.1 Motivation

Analytical economists, even analytical development economists, have in large measure found it reasonable to assume that the science of nutrition does not exist. At the same time, nutritionists have often ignored economics. Development economists have yet to incorporate into their theoretical models the dynamic effects of nutritional and health-care deprivation on human productivity. Nutritionists, in turn, could better design some of their experiments if they were informed of economic theory. There is a good deal that each group has to say to the other.

The links between the objects of inquiry in the two disciplines should be expected to be both subtle and deep. It is not merely a question of grafting into standard economic models the relationship between *nutritional status* and the *capacity for work*: more is involved.[4] One imagines, for example, that in poor countries the relationship influences not only the way food is allocated among members of households experiencing acute poverty, but also the way labor markets work. More generally, we would expect it to influence the life chances of those who are assetless. As a minimum, the physiological links between nutritional status and work capacity suggest that assetless people are just that: assetless. The only thing they possess is potential labor power, and this is not necessarily an asset.

Why? The reason is that if, over an extended period of time, a person is to convert potential labor power into actual labor power of any specified, physiologically admissible amount, he requires, among other things, nutrition of a corresponding quality and magnitude over that period. But an assetless person with no support would be capable of meeting this requirement in a *laissez-faire* economy only if he were able to obtain appropriate employment. The question arises whether a *laissez-faire* economy can deliver this option to all. One of my purposes in this chapter is to elaborate this question.

The question itself is not new: it has been asked periodically even in recent years, for example, by Leibenstein (1957), Myrdal (1968), Mirrlees (1975), Rodgers (1975), Stiglitz (1976), Bliss and Stern (1978), and Dasgupta and Ray (1986, 1987). For analytical tractability these economists used a timeless – one could say a "reduced-form" – model to capture the links between nutritional status and the capacity for work.[5] One attractive feature of the model is that it explains, through the idea of an "efficiency wage," why involuntary unemployment among unskilled workers is a theoretical possibility in poor countries. Anther is that, in both its assumptions and predictions, the model is sharp.

Paradoxically, this sharpness has been the theory's problem from the outset, in that it has proved easy enough to find evidence that would seem to refute it. So it has been subjected to much empirical criticism in recent years (Bliss and Stern (1982), Rosenzweig (1988), Srinivasan (1994), Strauss and Thomas (1995), see section 1.7). The status of the theory, thus, remains unclear. While no one would wish to assume away bio-medical truths, some of the assumptions and predictions of the model are at variance with evidence, such as they are. Admittedly, the theory is the one route on offer for a study of the causes and consequences of undernourishment and destitution, but it offers it in a halting way. For these reasons the theory resides awkwardly in development thinking.

Here I want to argue, among other things, that empirical criticisms of the nutrition-based efficiency-wage theory have been off the mark because of their dependence on too literal an interpretation of the timeless model.[6] The nutrition-productivity model in a timeless setting is rather like the Solow–Swan growth model with one commodity: and is not unlike models of international trade in which the theory of comparative advantage has traditionally been established: each is designed to point to something real, but neither is meant to be taken literally.[7] I will argue that the timeless nutrition–productivity construct is only a metaphor for something substantive, namely, economic environments that harbor poverty traps, into which some are drawn even when others, who may be similar, are not. This is displayed simply and strikingly in the timeless model, where wage-based labor markets sustain involuntary unemployment if the economy in the aggregate is not wealthy and the distribution of assets is highly unequal (Dasgupta and Ray (1986, 1987)).

Of far greater significance, however, is the timeless model's more general message, which is that in an economy that in the aggregate is not wealthy and in which the distribution of assets is highly unequal, labor-market allocations can violate the principle of horizontal equity, by which I mean that household (or personal) income can be a discontinuous function of household (or personal) characteristics. Dasgupta and Ray (1986) observed that this alone proves the existence of poverty traps, and they concluded that involuntary unemployment is a particular manifestation of horizontal inequity. In subsequent work (Dasgupta (1993)) I used findings in nutrition science to argue that poverty based on the links between nutritional status and productivity can be dynastic: once a household falls into a poverty trap, it can prove especially hard for descendents to emerge out of it, even if the economy in the aggregate were to experience growth in output for a while.

There are, of course, implicit qualifications in all this. I am referring to central tendencies in the nutrition–productivity model. The cycle of poverty I am alluding to is not inevitable: luck can play a role, and even the poorest of households have been known to pull themselves out of the mire. What the timeless model in a deterministic setting does is to explain why growth in aggregate output can be slow to trickle down to the poorest of the poor; it does not assert that growth will *never* trickle down.

The nutrition–productivity link offers one pathway by which people can fall into a poverty trap. We will see below (section 1.6) that the resulting trap is among the worst imaginable, based as it is on ill-health: over time ill-health is both a cause and consequence of someone falling into the poverty trap. However, there are other kinds of poverty traps, and they involve other pathways, ones that are not founded on ill-health. Benabou (1994) and Durlauf (1994), for example, have shown how local externalities associated with the acquisition of human capital, when allied to local school funding, can generate economic stratification. They have shown not only how certain groups get trapped in poverty, but also how the entrapment can persist over generations. And there are other possible pathways; for example, those arising from the fact that the poor are far more constrained then the rich in obtaining credit (Braverman and Stiglitz (1989)).

The standard model of resource allocation (viz. Arrow and Debreu (1954)) respects the principle of horizontal equity: households that are similar in their preferences and initial endowments supply similar amounts of labor services and consume similar bundles of goods. But the standard model is notorious for its neglect of nutrition science (see, e.g., the remarks in Koopmans (1957, pp. 59–63)). One of the attractions of the timeless nutrition–productivity model is that it lays stress on fundamental non-convexities associated with the transformation of energy intake into the capacity for work (sections 1.5–1.6). It has implications that we will study in sections 1.7–1.8.[8]

Modern nutrition science has shown that undernourishment is not necessarily the immediate cause of death. There is much evidence that relatively low mortality rates can coexist with a high incidence of under-nutrition, morbidity, and, thus, low productivity. For this reason, the notion of a subsistence wage receives no mention in the modern literature. Undernutrition is not the same as starvation. So the economics of undernutrition is not the same as the economics of famines. Famines are "disequilibrium" phenomena. They cannot persist, for the reason that their victims do not survive. We do not yet have an economic theory of famines (just as we do not yet have an economic theory of hyper-inflation), because our understanding of the microeconomics of disequilibrium phenomena remains inexpert. The remarks in Koopmans (1957, pp. 59–63) speak to this point. In contrast, even a widespread incidence of undernourishment can persist indefinitely: people are capable of living and breeding in circumstances of extreme poverty. The phenomenon we will be studying here is not a transient one.[9] In view of this, it is necessary to regard the incidence of undernourishment as a characteristic of "equilibrated" resource allocations, although, of course, the equilibria in question are a far cry from the ones realized in the Arrow–Debreu Model.[10]

For reasons of space, I will focus on energy intakes and energy expenditures when reporting the links between nutritional status and physical work capacity. This will mean that, excepting for some brief remarks, I will not consider the contributions of other nutrients (such as proteins, vitamins, and minerals) to human well being. Again, for reasons of space, I will not discuss the effects of disease on nutritional status. This means that issues connected with public health will be neglected here. There are significant omissions, but, given the motivation of the article, it will not matter.[11]

1.2 Nutritional status, hysteresis, and non-convexities

My own attempts at using nutrition science to extend resource allocation theory arose from casual observations. Like many other people, I have observed beggars in poor countries, people so emaciated that they are plainly incapable of doing anything strenuous, like pulling rickshaw or carrying load. The question arise as to how they have come to be in such a state and what options they face. The inevitable next question arises as to what would be required in order that they are able to lift themselves out of this state.

Here I faced a snag. I could find no systematic work that traces the standard of living of persons (or even households) through sufficiently long periods to tell me if people move in and out of dire nutritional states on a regular basis; or whether there are instead "lock-in effects," in the sense that destitutes on average remain destitutes and do not enjoy periodic spells of prosperity, and the well-off on average remain well-off and do not periodically become destitute.[12]

But the scientific literature on undernourishment provided me with hints about hysteresis in the processes that govern nutritional status (section 1.4). I felt that in market economies this could "lock in" emaciated people. Now *stunting* provides an obvious example of hysteresis at work; but it was worth exploring if *wasting* can yield a similar phenomenon. If it can, then one would have an explanation of how even tall adults may fall into a poverty trap. To an economist this is a non-trivial problem, because one may ask why a person who is, say ill and weak and assetless, does not borrow, get well and into shape, find employment, and then pay back the debt. Borrowing, one might thinks, would be a way out of poverty traps.[13]

There are many reasons why credit and insurance markets work badly in rural parts of poor countries (Dasgupta (1993, chapter 9)). But invoking imperfections of such markets would be misleading for the purpose in hand. It would not allow us to see if the links between nutritional status and physical work capacity on their own can provide the required lock-in effect. It they can, then there would be implications for public policy; for example, that improving credit and insurance markets would not on their own be enough. Imperfections of credit and insurance markets, namely those that make credit and insurance harder to come by for the poor, would reinforce the lock-in effect, they would not dampen the effect. Therefore, in this part of the chapter imperfections in the market for credit will be assumed away.

That some among the assetless may become emaciated beggars does not imply that there cannot be assetless people who are able to escape this fate. They may be able to find employment in the formal sector, or perhaps in the informal sector. Indeed, it is possible for some to thrive in the latter. For example, there is not much in the way of a formal labor market among sub-Saharan agricultural farms, while in the Indian sub-continent the agricultural labor market is well established. The institutional background that produces malnourished people in sub-Saharan Africa is different from the one in the Indian sub-continent, and that in turn from the one in Latin America. But *notions* of nutritional status and physical work capacity are not bound by institutional divides. This gives us grounds for thinking that there is an economic theory of undernourishment and destitution to be uncovered; one which encompasses economies that differ in their institutional structures.

No single index of nutritional status suffices for all purposes and occasions. For reasons that will be discussed below, one must, as a minimum, distinguish current from past nutritional status. It would seem reasonable to use height as an index of past nutritional status and weight as an index of current nutritional status. But, for any given adult height, an entire range of body weights and compositions (allied to physical activities) can be consistent with good health. Moreover, weight is no good as an index unless it is normalized for height. So weight-for-height is on occasion used as a measure of current nutritional status, as are skinfold thicknesses and total body haemoglobin. A measure frequently recommended by nutritionists, however, is the body mass index (BMI), which is the ratio of a person's weight (w) to the square of his height (h), or in other words, w/h^2 (James, Ferro-Luzzi, and Waterlow (1988), James *et al.* (1992)). It is also called the Quetelet index. In adults of either sex, BMI has been found to be an index of both the principal stores of energy (i.e., fats) and the active tissue mass (see below). To a reasonable approximation, BMI is independent of height (figures 4.2 and 4.3). This makes it a good measure of adult nutritional status and, more generally, of health. If weight is measured in kilograms and height in metres, the acceptable range for BMI is something like 18.5 to 25, for both men and women. A value in excess of 25 or so is a sign of being overweight. However, being below 18.5 does not imply that a person is wasted. For example, Shetty (1984) found a sample of Indian laborers who performed will in physical fitness tests even though their BMIs were in the range 15–16. This may suggest that we should enlarge the acceptable range to something like 15–25. But to do so on the basis of only a few studies would be to display an obsession with avoiding type-1 errors (calling someone malnourished when he is not). A value less than 15 is an

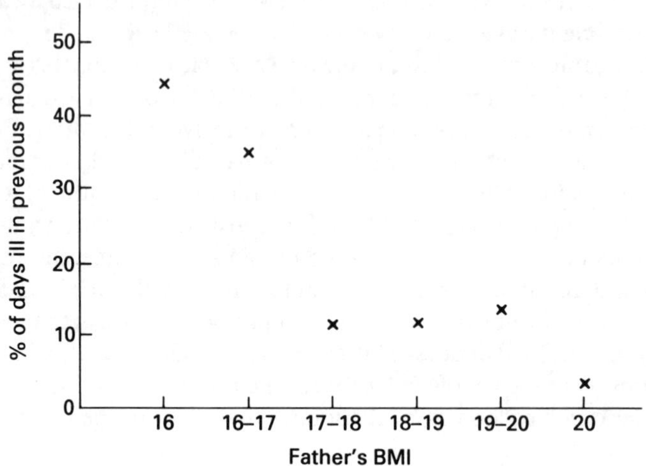

Figure 4.2
Source: Waterlow (1992).

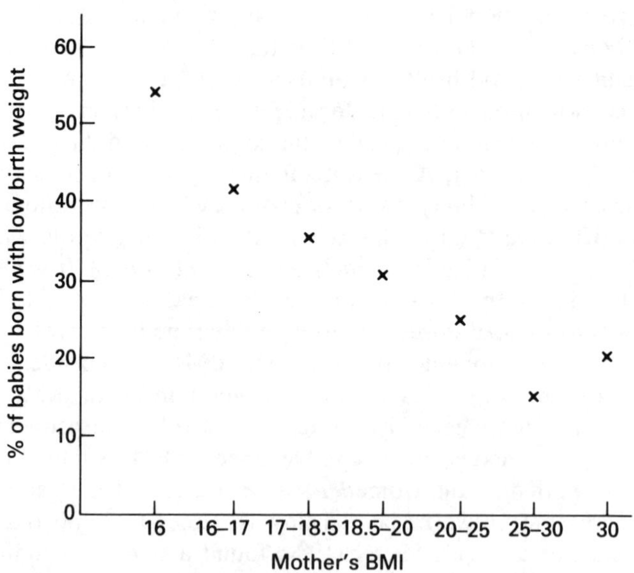

Figure 4.3
Source: Waterlow (1992).

almost sure sign of chronic energy deficiency (the person is wasted), and a value of around 12 is probably the lower limit of survival. But a figure of 15–18.5 or so is an indication that the person is at risk. Indeed below 17 a person should be regarded as frankly undernourished (Waterlow (1986), James, Ferro-Luzzi, and Waterlow (1988)). Figure 4.2 (attributed to J. Pryer) explains one sense in which the body mass index is an indicator of health: with but little exception, the percentage of days in a given month that individuals in a sample of adult males in Bangladesh were ill was found to be a declining function of BMI. Figure 4.3, taken from a study in Hyderabad, India, by A.N. Naidu, J. Neela, and N.P. Rao, is more dramatic. It shows that the chance of a baby being born with low birth weight (under 2.5 kg.) is a declining function of its mother's body mass index. For the undernourished mother low birth weight is a beneficial form of adaptation (it reduces obstetric risks); but not for the baby.

We depict these findings in a stylized form in figure 4.4, which presents the probability (π) of someone *not* experiencing a breakdown in health as a function of the body mass index (m). As I have drawn it, $\pi = 0$ until m reaches the value 12 or thereabouts, it rises slowly until m reaches 15 or so, then rises rapidly until $m \approx 18.5$, and flattens in the interval 18.5–25. The value of π declines beyond $m = 25$, when the dangers of being overweight begin to loom. The analytical point of interest in nutritional economics is that $\pi(m)$ is convex in the interval $0 \leq m \leq 18.5$. This is the (probabilistic) generalization of the fact that there is a large maintenance cost involved in remaining alive, a matter I will come to in section 1.5.

The body mass index reflects current nutritional status. Those that reflect past (or long-term) nutritional status include height; hip, thigh, arm, calf, and waist circumferences; sitting height; breadth of the hip, elbow, knee, and wrist; grip strengths; and daily creatinine excretion (a measure of muscle cell mass). In sections 1.3 and 1.4 we will see that both current and past nutritional status affect an adult's capacity for work.

1.3 Determinants of work capacity and endurance

When nutritionists talk of physical work capacity (Pollitt and Amante (1984), Ferro-Luzzi (1985), and Collins and Roberts (1988)) they mean the maximum power (i.e., maximum work per unit of time) someone is capable of offering. Laboratory methods for estimating this in a person include getting him to run a treadmill, pedal a bicycle ergometer, and so forth. Here we are concerned with indirect measures, those that happen also to be determinants of physical work capacity. In this regard, the most compelling index of a person's physical work capacity is his maximal oxygen uptake, usually denoted by the ungainly formula, $\dot{V}O_2$ max. It is the highest rate of oxygen uptake a person is capable of attaining while engaged in physical work at sea level. The reason maximal oxygen uptake provides us with the measure we need is that it is dependent on the body's capacity for a linked series of oxygen transfers (diffusion through tissues, circulation of haemoglobin, pulmonary ventilation, and so on). $\dot{V}O_2$ max measures (cardiorespiratory) fitness; the higher is its value, the greater is the capacity of the body to convert energy in the tissues into work (Åstrand and Rodahl (1986)). This capacity depends on the (metabolically) active tissue mass, which is very nearly the same as muscle cell mass. The latter is also on occasion called the cell residue. Clinical tests suggest that $\dot{V}O_2$ max per unit of muscle cell mass is approximately constant across well-nourished and marginally undernourished people (Viteri (1971)). Even among undernourished persons the difference is not thought to be great. In one set of studies, over 80 percent of the difference in $\dot{V}O_2$ max between mildly and severely malnourished people have been traced to differences in their muscle cell mass (Barac-Nieto *et al.* (1980)). It is thus useful to have a measure of $\dot{V}O_2$ max per unit of muscle cell mass. A rough approximation to this is provided by the maximal aerobic power, which is $\dot{V}O_2$ max per unit body weight. Moreover, since muscle cell mass and lean body mass are related, we do not lose much in not being particular as to which we identify as the chief determinant of $\dot{V}O_2$ max.[14]

In section 1.2 it was argued that the body mass index is a good indicator of current nutritional status. The matter being discussed here is different; we are trying to identify the determinants of physical work capacity and endurance. It is necessary for one to enjoy good current nutritional status if he is to perform well at strenuous physical work, but it is not sufficient; one can be stunted but healthy. Of two people with the same body mass index, the taller person typically possesses greater muscle cell mass; so his $\dot{V}O_2$ max is higher. Broadly speaking then, taller, heavier, non-obese people have greater physical work capacity. In addition, $\dot{V}O_2$ max depends on the level of habitual physical activity ("training," in sports parlance), but we will ignore the latter's role here.[15] Maximal oxygen uptake depends as well on the concentration of haemoglobin in the blood. We ignore this in what follows.[16] $\dot{V}O_2$ max is usually expressed in litres per minute (ℓ/min). To obtain a sense of orders of magnitude, we may note that the figure 6 ℓ/min is about as high as can be, while the figure 2 ℓ/min and a bit below are the sorts of figures observed among chronically malnourished people (see below).

$\dot{V}O_2$ max measures the maximum volume of oxygen the body is capable of transferring per minute. Excepting for very short bursts this maximum cannot be reached. It transpires that the highest level of oxygen transfer a person is capable of sustaining over an extended period of eight hours or so is of the order of 35–40 percent of his $\dot{V}O_2$ max. More generally, there is a relationship between the rate at which a person works, expressed as a fraction of his $\dot{V}O_2$ max (which is sometimes also called the relative work load), and his endurance in maintaining this rate of work. The negative-exponential function has been found to be a good approximation, even among undernourished subjects (Åstrand and Rodahl (1986)). So, writing endurance time by τ, we have

$$\text{percentage of } \dot{V}O_2 \text{ max} = \exp(-b\tau). \tag{2}$$

In equation (2), $b\,(>0)$ is a constant. Barac-Nieto *et al.* (1980) have found b not to be significantly different among people suffering from degrees of malnourishment ranging from "mild" to "severe." The endurance time for 80 percent of $\dot{V}O_2$ max in their sample was on average 97 minutes, with a coefficient of variation of 12 percent. This means $b \approx 0.0023/\text{min}$. The suggestion is not that this is a human constant. Nor is it claimed that the energy cost of a task does not vary at all with the rate at which it is performed. All it means is that, as a very rough approximation, we may distinguish people's capacity for physical activities by their physical work capacity.

Let P denote physical work capacity, and V the maximal oxygen uptake ($\dot{V}O_2$ max). From equation (2) we conclude that

$$P = KV\exp(-b\tau), \tag{3}$$

where K is a positive constant. The total quantity of work a rested individual is capable of performing is then $P\tau = KV\tau\exp(-b\tau)$, which attains its maximum value at $\tau = 1/b$. I conclude that if it is aggregate work we are interested in (rather than relative work load), the duration of work should be $1/b$. If $b \approx 0.0023/\text{min}$, we have $1/b \approx 7.2$ hours. I do not know if among healthy people in western industrialized countries, a seven-hour day has been arrived at from such a consideration as this.

For strenuous work, those with a low $\dot{V}O_2$ max need to be close to their physical work capacity. This means their hearts must beat at a fast rate. They are then overtaxed, and are incapable of maintaining the pace of work for long. This is reflected in equation (3). Consider as an example the well-known series of studies by G.B. Spurr (1990) and his colleagues on chronically malnourished adult males from Colombia, and on nutritionally normal control subjects among sugarcane cutters, loaders, and agricultural workers (Spurr (1990)). Nutritional status was assessed on the basis of, among other things, weight-for-height, skinfold thicknesses, total body haemoglobin, and daily creatinine excretion. While, roughly speaking, the first three indices reflect current nutritional status, the fourth picks up nutritional history to an extent: *ceteris paribus*, taller people have greater muscle cell mass. A step-wise multiple regression analysis with the data revealed that $\dot{V}O_2$ max is positively related to weight-for-height, total-haemoglobin count and daily creatinine excretion; and it is negatively related to skinfold thicknesses. The chronically undernourished subjects ranged from "mild" to "intermediate" to "severe." Values of their $\dot{V}O_2$ max were in turn, approximately 2.1 ℓ/min, 1.7 ℓ/min, and 1.0 ℓ/min. The average $\dot{V}O_2$ max of the nutritionally normal sugarcane cutters was 2.6 ℓ/min. As evidence in this field goes, this is about as clear as anyone could hope to find for the thesis that undernourished people suffer from depressed levels of $\dot{V}O_2$ max.

Consider an activity whose oxygen is 0.84 ℓ/min. The nutritionally normal group could sustain it at 0.32 of $\dot{V}O_2$ max, whereas the remaining three groups would have to sustain it at 40 percent, 50 percent, and 80 percent, respectively, of their $\dot{V}O_2$ max. At these paces, the nutritionally normal group could work for 8 hours, and the three malnourished groups for 6.5 hours, 5 hours, and 1.5 hours, respectively.

All this bears on physical work capacity and endurance, not physical productivity. One would expect though that they are closely related for unskilled manual work. And they are. For tasks such as sugarcane cutting, loading and unloading, and picking coffee, it is possible to measure physical productivity directly in terms of the amount done. Indeed, payment for such work is often at a piece rate. There is now a wide range of evidence linking nutritional status to productivity in these occupations. In their work on Colombian sugarcane cutters and loaders, Spurr and his colleagues (see Spurr (1990)) found height, weight, and lean body mass (roughly, $\dot{V}O_2$ max) to be significant determinants of productivity, as measured by daily tonnage of sugarcane delivered. Measuring productivity (Φ) in units of tons per day, $\dot{V}O_2$ max (V in the notation below) in litres per minute, height (Ht) in cm., and denoting by F the percentage of body weight in fat, their most-preferred specification was

$$\Phi = 0.81\,\mathrm{V} - 0.14\,\mathrm{F} + 0.03\,\mathrm{Ht} - 1.962. \tag{4}$$

In related work, Immink *et al.* (1984) found the stature (and thus lean body mass and $\dot{V}O_2$ max) of Guatemalan laborers to be positively correlated with the quantity of coffee beans picked per day, the amount of sugarcane cut and loaded, and the time taken to weed a given area.

I turn now to economic investigations. In their study of a sample of both men and women workers in urban Brazil, Thomas and Strauss (1996) report that height has a strong, positive effect on market wages. This is consistent with the findings of Immink *et al.* (1984) and Spurr (1990), since wages would be expected to bear a positive association with productivity. The relationship between height and productivity is a significant finding because, for an adult, height is not a variable; so there is less ambiguity about the direction of causality. However, it has been more usual for investigators to study the links between current nutritional status and productivity. For example, in a sample of factory workers (producing detonator fuses) in India, Satyanarayana *et al.* (1977) found weight-for-height to be the significant determinant of productivity. Strong effects of weight-for-height on both productivity and wages have been found among agricultural workers in south India by Deolalikar (1988). The elasticity of farm output with respect to weight-for-height was estimated as approximately 2, and the elasticity of wages in the region 0.3–0.7; the lower value reflecting the effect in peak seasons, the higher value reflecting the effect in slack seasons, when the tasks are different. In a study of farm workers in Sierra Leone, Strauss (1986) found that energy intake has a positive effect on productivity up to about 5,200 kcal per day. He also found that a worker who consumed 5,200 kcal per day was found to be twice as productive as one who consumed 1,500 kcal per day. Strauss did not report on differences in nutritional status among workers. But if we were to assume that the workers were in energy balance (equation (6) below), we could interpret differences in daily intakes as mirroring a combination of differences in nutritional status and the energy expended in the tasks that were accomplished. In their work on Brazilian laborers, Strauss and Thomas (1996) also found that the body mass index is positively correlated with wages.

There are two weaknesses with applied economic investigations of the link between current nutritional status and productivity. First, none determines causality; for example, it could be that higher wages enable workers to eat more and thereby enjoy greater body mass index. Secondly, and much more importantly, none (including those involving height as a determinant of productivity) explores "non-market" work: the studies are silent on the effects of undernutrition on women's productivity inside the home; and they are silent on the physical disabilities of destitutes (for example, beggars). Even when wages are low, adults employed in the market place are among the more fortunate of people. The sort of poverty trap we are exploring here creates disenfranchised people, but they are not caught in the statistics in applied economic studies mentioned above. However, when their findings are looked at in conjunction with what we know from the nutrition literature, the matter is not opaque. The link between nutritional status, physical work capacity, endurance, and physical productivity is an established fact.

1.4 The imprint of childhood history

The nutrients we depend upon are many and varied. But to an extent they display complementarities among themselves, just as they do with sanitation and personal hygiene. Because of complementarities, the relationship between nutritional status and physical work capacity is at its most vivid when we think of the transformation of energy intake into work. So we will focus on the energy conservation equation for a person. This is the condition which says that over any given period, the energy intake by a person equals his energy expenditure plus energy stored (or minus the amount decumulated).

For simplicity, consider an adult male. His height is given. Let r_t denote his maintenance requirement in period t and e_t the energy he expends in all other activities, such as work and play. The latter would be called discretionary activities.[17] Denote by s_t an index of his stores of energy. These will be mainly adipose tissues, but in crude calculations s_t could stand for body weight. As we noted in section 1.2, if his body weight were low, his health would be at risk (figure 4.4). In a deterministic formulation we cannot talk of risk, so we specify a body weight such that if the person's weight is more than or equal to it, he is in good health, but that if his weight is below it he cannot survive. Denote this critical level as s^*.[18]

We consider time to be continuous. To avoid extraneous matters, I will identify energy intake with metabolizable energy. If x_t represents this at time t, we may write the energy conservation equation as

$$\sigma[ds_t/dt] = x_t - (r_t + e_t), \text{ for } t \geq 0, s_t \geq s^*, \tag{5}$$

where σ (a positive number) is the amount of usable energy that can be converted from a unit of "body mass," which, for simplicity I assume equals the amount of energy required to create a unit of body mass.[19]

Equation (5) itself is in a reduced form, since a person's maintenance requirement is a function of his history, broadly defined. For example, adult height is a summary statistic of past nutrition experience and morbidity, the latter occasioned by, say, infectious diseases during childhood. For a given body mass index, tall people weigh more; their maintenance requirements are more as well. The functional dependence of r on past experiences is one pathway through which nutritional adaptation takes place.[20] This dependence alone shows how a person's physical work capacity is determined by his entire nutritional history. Unless circumstances improve, the first three years of life appear to have a pronounced effect on a person's mature body stature (see Dasgupta (1993) for references). Early nutrition and the extent of freedom from infections leave a deep imprint on one. Why this should be so is not understood well at the physiological level; it is a finding of epidemiological studies (see, e.g., Martorell, Rivera, and Kaplowitz (1990), Bhargava (1994)). Resources permiting, a person may be able to catch up during adolescence if he had suffered from deprivation when young, but the process is slow.

One way a person can economize on his energy expenditure is by

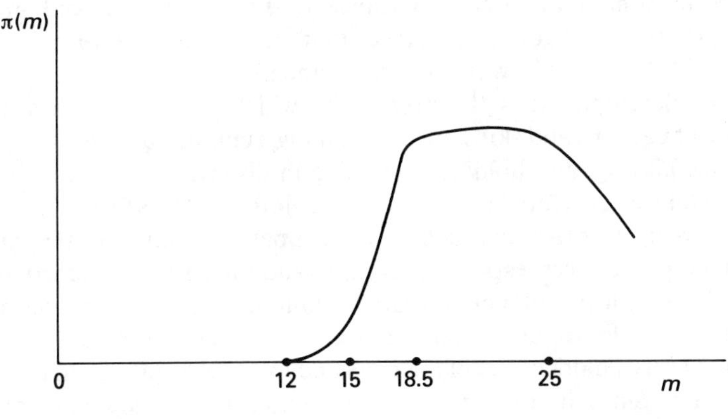

Figure 4.4

reducing physical activities.[21] This is a behavioral pathway through which childhood deprivation leaves an imprint on the capacity for work in adulthood. I turn to this now.

Mild to moderately wasted pre-school children under free-living conditions have been observed to spend more time in sedentary and light activities than their healthy counterparts. They have been found to rest longer and to play more often in a horizontal position. A Jamaican study found stunted children in the age group 12–24 months to be significantly less active than their non-stunted counterparts. The energy thus saved was comparable to the energy cost of growth at that age (see Dasgupta (1993) for references). At the extreme, when we observe little children in poor countries lying expressionless on roadsides and refraining from brushing the flies off their faces, we should infer that it is energy they are conserving. Among pre-school children the first line of defense against low energy intake would appear to be reduced physical activity. Such behavioral modes of adaptation are not deliberately arrived at, we are "wired" to so adapt. Little children by the wayside no more consciously husband their precarious hold on energy than bicyclists solve differential equations in order to maintain balance.

Chavez and Martinez (1984) have reported that among a sample of infants from poor households in rural Mexico, differences in activity levels were marked from about six months of age between those who received nutritional supplements and the control group. Supplemented children made greater contact with the "floor," slept less during the day, spent greater time outdoors, began playing almost six months earlier, and so forth. The thesis here is that low nutrition intake depresses activity and thus isolates the infant (or child) from contact with the environment and from sources of stimuli of vital importance to both cognitive and motor development. It is of significance that the control group in the Chavez–Martinez study was not clearly undernourished.

Motor development is the process by which a child acquires basic movement patterns and skills, such as walking, running, jumping, hopping, throwing, kicking, and holding something in his grip. In normal circumstances children develop these fundamental motor patterns by the age of six or seven years. It is through such movement patterns and skills that many childhood experiences, especially learning and interpersonal experiences, are mediated. During infancy and early childhood, interactions between the mother and child are of critical importance in this development (Malina (1984)). This is a hidden cost of anaemia and low energy intake on the part of mothers. Since housework and production activity are mandatory, reductions in discretionary and child-rearing activities offer the mother a way of maintaining her energy balance. To be sure, societies differ in the way people other than the mother are involved in a child's upbringing. Nevertheless, the mother is an important figure in a child's cognitive and motor development in all societies.

Long-term malnutrition (e.g., stunting) would appear to be particularly associated with mental development; the presence or absence of oedema (i.e., current malnutrition) having a less pronounced effect (Grantham-McGregor *et al.* (1990)). Under conditions of severe undernourishment (e.g., marasmus or marasmic kwashiorkor), retardation of psycho-motor development in young children has physiological reasons as well. Some of the damages are extremely difficult to reverse and may indeed be irreversible. In one study, even after six months of nutritional rehabilitation, a sample of infants hospitalized for severe malnutrition experienced no recovery in their motor development (Chavez and Martinez (1984)).

It may be that severe malnutrition affects development of the brain, which experiences rapid growth starting round ten weeks of pregnancy and continuing in spurts to about three to four year of age. (Fetal iodine deficiency is well known to damage the central nervous system.) However, there is evidence that malnutrition has an effect on brain development only when it coincides with a period of rapid growth and differentiation. Equilibrium reactions (otherwise called "righting reflexes") are functions of the cerebellum and play an important role in the development of motor control. It is, of course, possible that even such anatomical changes as have been observed are retardation rather than permanent injury. But this is not known with any certainty.[22]

Among school children, the matter is somewhat different, in that peer group pressure tends to counter the instinct for reducing physical activities. This is likely to be so especially among boys. To be sure, decreased activity is a line of defense even for them. However, in school-aged children the low energy expenditure associated with nutritional deficiency can be traced to low body weight: their basal metabolic rates are low. The development of lean body mass among undernourished children is retarded. This, as noted in section 1.3, has a detrimental effect on their capacity to work when adults. Among marginally malnourished boys there does not appear to be reduced muscle function; their low capacity for work ($\dot{V}O_2$ max) is due to their lean body mass being low.

On a wider front, malnutrition and infection have been found to have a pronounced detrimental effect among school children on such cognitive processes as attention and concentration. There is abundant evidence of children suffering from nutritional deficiencies and infections performing badly in aptitude tests (Pollitt (1990), Bhargava (1995)). As noted earlier, in extreme cases nutritional deficiencies affect the central nervous system. In less-than-extreme cases the matter is not one of brain function; frequent absence and attrition affect learning as well.

Much international attention has been given to saving lives in times of collective crisis within poor countries. This is as it should be. Attention has also been paid by international agencies toward keeping children alive in normal times through public health measures, such as family-planning counselling, immunization, and oral rehydration. This too is as it should be. That many poor countries fail to do either is not evidence of the problems being especially hard to solve. In fact, they are among the easier social problems: they can be fielded even while no major modification is made to the prevailing resource allocation mechanism. Much the harder problem, in intellectual design, political commitment, and administration, is to ensure that those who remain alive are healthy. It is also a problem whose solution brings no easily visible benefit. But the stunting of both cognitive and motor capacity is a prime hidden cost of energy deficiency and anaemia among children and, at one step removed, among mothers. It affects learning and skill formation and, thereby, future productivity. The price is paid in later years, but it is paid.

These observations bring us back to the point which we began, that a person's current productivity is a function of his nutritional and morbidity history. A reasonable index of a person's productivity over time would be the present-discounted sum of his output of work. This could then be compared with a corresponding index of nutrition intake over time, one which is sensitive to the fact that there are maintenance requirements. The reckoning should start from the earliest stages of the person's life. While this is conceptually not a difficult matter, the detailed mathematics is complicated. But the key insight is straightforward: because a person's maintenance requirements are significant in magnitude, the productivity index is a convex function of the index of nutrition intakes. The reason the timeless nutrition–productivity model is appealing is that it offers this insight with a minimum of fuss. We now turn to it.

1.5 Stationary states

Consider once again an adult male in a deterministic world. Let us envisage a state of affairs where the person's weight is held constant. He is in a stationary state. So equation (5) reduces to the well-known "energy balance" condition

$$x = r + e. \tag{6}$$

In equation (6) I have dropped the time subscript for obvious reasons: we are considering a timeless model. Thus, x should be thought of as habitual consumption and e habitual energy expenditure. r would then be about 60–75 percent of x (WHO (1985)): maintenance expenditure is a substantial fraction of a person's energy requirement. Note also that in a stationary state the person's nutritional status is not a variable; it is a parameter of both r and e. Equation (6) enables us to study the effect of energy intake on the person's productivity in a simple class of situations that I will now describe.

We stipulate a physical activity and relate the level at which it is undertaken to the energy the person expends in undertaking it. The activity could, for example, consist in moving earth and rubble at a construction site. For vividness, I will give it this interpretation and will regard it as a composite task. The thought-experiment I want to consider here has a strong *ceteris paribus* clause: we keep fixed the levels of all his other discretionary activities (e.g., leisure activities) while we vary the number of units of the composite task he is assumed to accomplish. Let β denote the number of units of the composite task he completes in each period (i.e., tons of earth and rubble he moves in each period) and $q(\beta)$ the amount of energy he expends in accomplishing them. (The individual can choose the level of β by choosing the pace at which he undertakes the composite task.) The energy expenditure in all his other discretionary activities is, by assumption, a constant (this is the *ceteris paribus* clause), and we write this as Θ. Thus, $e = \Theta + q(\beta)$ and equation (6) reduces to the form

$$x = r + \Theta + q(\beta). \tag{7}$$

Presumably, the greater is the tonnage of earth and rubble the person moves per period, the more energy he has to expend in accomplishing it. So $q(\beta)$ must be an increasing function of β. In short, $q'(\beta) > 0$. Quite obviously also, $q(0) = 0$. (If the person moves no earth and rubble, he cannot be assumed to expend any energy in moving earth and rubble.) Thus, when the person is in energy balance, his energy expenditure consists of a fixed component (his maintenance requirement, r), and a variable representing external work ($\Theta + q(\beta)$). However, in our example, the energy expenditure, Θ, in all his other discretionary activities has been assumed to be constant. It follows that his fixed requirements amount, not to r, but to $(r + \Theta)$. This is to be contrasted to the energy he expends on the variable, external work, β. So let us define r^* to be $(r + \Theta)$.

The person is in energy balance. So we must have $x \geq r^*$. If follows that equation (7) can be re-expressed as

$$q(\beta) = x - r^*, \text{ for } x \geq r^*. \tag{8}$$

Since $q'(\beta) > 0$, the function q can be inverted. I denote the inverse function of q by the symbol Φ. We may now reassemble the equation as

$$\beta = q^{-1}(x - r^*) \equiv \Phi(x - r^*), \text{ for } x \geq r^*. \tag{9}$$

Φ is measured in units of the composite task (i.e., tonnage of earth and rubble moved). Moreover, since $q'(\beta) > 0$, it follows that $\Phi'(x - r^*) > 0$. Furthermore, $\Phi(0) = 0$ (if no energy is spent on moving earth and rubble, then no earth and rubble will be moved). We have thus obtained a few general properties of Φ. The idea now is to see how Φ could in principle vary with x.

In figure 4.5 I have drawn a proto-type functional form of $\Phi(x - r^*)$. As a matter of convention, I have also set $\Phi = 0$ for $x < r^*$. It bears emphasis that it is merely a convention I am following here, nothing more, and there will be nothing amiss in my doing so. The reason it is only a convention is that the individual, by hypothesis, maintains energy balance (i.e., his body weight remains constant). So we are not entitled to study the region $x < r^*$ in figure 4.5. Were $x < r^*$, the individual would not be in energy balance (even if he were to choose $\beta = 0$) and something would have to give: he would either lose weight or he would have to cut down on some other activity, and we have assumed that he does not experience either sort of loss.

Now it cannot be emphasized strongly enough that figure 4.5 is an idealization. In any event, we are entitled to consider only a limited range of values for x here: between the maintenance requirement plus the fixed expenditure in all other discretionary activities (what we called r^* in equation (8)) and some upper limit. At large levels of daily intake the person's health suffers. As he over-eats relative to his fixed requirements and his maximum capacity for work effort in the composite task (i.e., moving earth and rubble), he is unable to maintain energy balance, and so equation (9) becomes inappropriate. Subject to the restriction that x lies in a

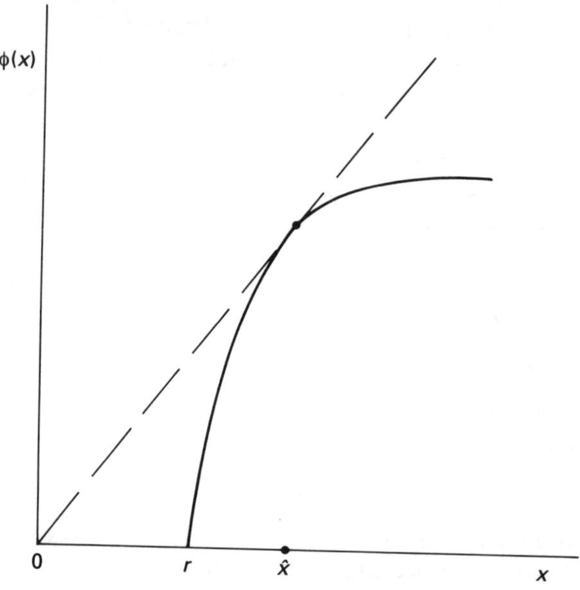

Figure 4.5

limited interval (say, in the region 2,000–5,500 kcal per day for an adult male of average size in the tropics), $\Phi(x)$ can be thought of as the person's *nutrition–productivity* curve.

How does stature (a parameter) affect the curve? It is sometimes argued that there are many economic tasks in which small workers can, and do, specialize; tasks for which such people are more "efficient" than people with high values of, say, $\dot{V}O_2$ max. This is true. On the other hand, incomes that unskilled workers are able to derive from such occupations (hoeing, weeding, and so forth) are typically lower than those from more strenuous occupations, such as ploughing and plantation work. This is often overlooked in debates on these matters.

In any event, "efficiency" is a more subtle concept. We should seek to determine not productivity per se, but productivity per unit nutrition intake. The latter is the appropriate currency for comparing efficiency among persons. To see this, consider two individuals (labeled 1 and 2) differing by way of, say, their stature (or alternatively, lean body mass). We take it that person 2 has the better build. As is well known, his maintenance requirement is typically higher. It follows that at low levels of energy intake he can be out-performed by person 1, in that he cannot manage to accomplish the number of units of the composite task person 1 can. This is

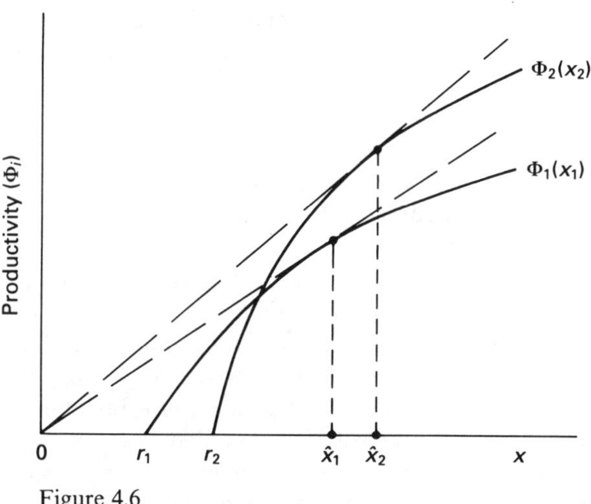

Figure 4.6

shown in figure 4.6, where the nutrition–productivity curves of the two people are depicted as $\Phi_1(x_1)$ and $\Phi_2(x_2)$ respectively.[23] But we should not conclude from this that person 1 is the more efficient worker. The curves have been so drawn that they cross. At higher values of energy intake the ratio of work output to energy intake is higher for person 2. Of greater significance is the fact that, as a worker, person 2 is intrinsically more efficient in that the maximum work output per unit of energy intake person 2 can offer (at consumption level $\hat{x}_2$ in figure 4.6) exceeds the maximum person 1 can offer (at consumption level $\hat{x}_1$). We may call the level of output at which output per unit of energy intake is maximized, the person's *efficient productivity level.*

1.6 Poverty, maintenance costs, and the emergence of inequality

It is important to distinguish critical from inessential assumptions in any model. The matter is particularly delicate when it comes to timeless models. So it is as well to emphasize that the precise shape of the nutrition–productivity curve in figure 4.5 is of no great significance. What are significant are two assumptions that have been incorporated in it: (a) maintenance requirement is a large fraction of total energy expenditure and (b) at levels of energy intake, somewhat in excess of maintenance requirement, there are diminishing gains in productivity from further increases in consumption (i.e., $\Phi''(x) < 0$). As both are incontrovertible (even in an intertemporal setting), we are on firm ground.

In what sense is the first of these two assumptions significant? It is significant in that it offers a reason why, in poor societies, we would expect to see the emergence of inequality among people who may have to begin with been very similar. In short, assumption (a) implies that a society's poverty could in itself be a cause of stark inequality.[24]

Notice the unusual causal direction being identified here. It is a commonplace to say that poverty among households is a reflection (even a consequence) of economic inequality. I am talking of a possible reverse causality: from poverty to inequality.

Perhaps the simplest way of illustrating this possibility would be to consider the allocation problem facing two friends on a life-boat when there is food sufficient for only one's survival. (Survival needs are a draconian form of the first of the two assumptions mentioned above.) Tossing a coin to decide who should eat the food would be a fair procedure, but after the toss there would be inequality in the distribution of food: only one would get to eat. Note also that there would be no need for unequal distribution if there were enough food for both. This stylized example demonstrates also why a poor household cannot afford to treat its members equally.[25]

But a "household" is not the same object as a "market." In the example we have just considered, the two deliberately toss a coin to determine who would be awarded the limited ration of food. The inequality of treatment that is meted out is, therefore, a conscious decision. In contrast, resource allocation in a market economy is not arrived at consciously: it is an unintended consequence of millions of individual decisions. I am thinking here of decentralized resource allocation mechanisms, broadly speaking. The question arises whether the nutrition–productivity link is a reason why, in poor economies, such mechanisms violate the principle of horizontal equity. Of particular interest is the labor "market," where the principle might be expected to be fragile: there is much evidence of involuntary unemployment in poor, agrarian societies.[26] It is simplest to think of wage-based labor markets, and we will do so. Space forbids that I go into this in any detail, but it is possible to given an indication of how the argument works.

Imagine a private-ownership agrarian society containing a large number of assetless people, where by "large" I mean large relative to the aggregate wealth of the economy. Two assumptions are implied in this: (i) the economy is in the aggregate poor and (ii) the distribution of assets is highly unequal.[27] In order to demonstrate that the market mechanism does not sustain resource allocations satisfying the principle of horizontal equity, we will assume that these people are, to begin with, identical in nutritional status. For simplicity of exposition, imagine also that there are markets for unskilled labor and that all markets are competitive. We are thinking of a timeless economy here, but it is as well to stress that the agricultural labor market is to be thought of as one of long-term contracts.[28] Since the economy is poor, the assetless are assumed to spend all their income on food. (I will go further into this issue in section 1.7.) Let us assume for vividness that the only alternative to work in agriculture is to live off local common-property resources (e.g., forest products).[29] Of course, the precise specification of the alternative to agricultural work is of no great importance (begging would do just as well), but it helps to stress the links that I believe exist between the incidence of rural poverty and deteriorations in the local environmental resource base.

In order to illustrate matters in a sharp manner, suppose now that a person either works in agriculture or lives off the commons, but that he cannot do both. Imagine also that the efficient productivity level of a landless agricultural worker is attained at a rate of energy intake ($\hat{x}$ in figure 4.5) that exceeds the food-energy available to him from the commons. We could even imagine that living off the commons (or, alternatively, begging) would involve a steady deterioration in nutritional status. This last assumption would imply that landless people would rather be employed than live off the commons (or, alternatively, survive by begging).

Under these assumptions it is possible to show the agricultural labor market does not clear: there is no wage rate for landless folk at which the demand for labor power can equal its supply. So the labor market in the model imposes rations, and a fraction of the landless find employment in the agricultural sector, while the remaining fraction live off the commons. It transpires that those who are employed receive a wage equal to the energy intake at which efficient productivity is attained (i.e., $\hat{x}$ in figure 4.5). The piece-rate is thus $\hat{x}/\Phi(\hat{x})$. The unemployed would prefer to join the ranks of the employed, but would not be able to match the labor quality the landless employed are able to supply at any wage lower than the one prevailing in the market. In short, any attempt at undercutting the employed would make them less attractive as workers. The model, thus, shows how different classes can emerge from a homogeneous mass of people.[30] Notice that if maintenance requirements were nil, the market I have just described would not disenfranchise a fraction of the landless: the labor market would clear.

The central insight of this model, namely, the emergence of inequality among people who were initially similar, generalizes to include informal markets, even non-market institutions (e.g., the household). This much should be obvious. Of greater subtlety are the consequences of dropping the assumption that there is a single agricultural task. Consider by way of contrast the case where there are a number of possible tasks, each having its own specification. If this number were finite, the argument that there would be rationing among laborers in a poor economy would hold trivially. The market mechanism would slot workers into different tasks, but not all workers would find a slot: a fraction would be disenfranchised. If there were a continuum of tasks, the argument would be more involved, but conditions can be identified under which a fraction of workers would be disenfranchised.

The assumption that, to begin with, people are identical in their nutritional status has only sharpness to commend it: rationing in the labor market is a direct consequence. So let us relax the assumption and imagine that there is a (continuous) distribution of "types," or, in other words, that people differ by way of nutritional status, as in figure 4.6. It is easy to check that the labor market would then not be characterized by rationing (potential laborers are differentiated factors of production in this model), but it would still display horizontal inequity.

This latter feature is made vivid when we introduce time, and thus history. So now introduce a tiny bit of history into our basic model. Suppose the landless are all identical to begin with. Assume too that living on common property resources involves an ever-so-slight deterioration in nutritional status, and therefore in their efficient productivity. In the first period a fraction of the landless would be employed, of whom some would be on long-term contracts. We cannot, of course, tell in advance which particular fraction, because the labor "market" would be rather like a lottery. But in the next period the previously employed would face an ever-so-slight advantage in life because of their better nutritional history. Subsequently many who languished in the first period through bad luck would continue to languish, now no longer through bad luck, but through cumulative causation: having faced different work and nutritional histories, the different classes of people that would emerge would no longer *be* the same, nor would they *look* the same. Emaciated people have no marketable labor quality to offer. No rationing in the labor market would now be required to keep them disenfranchised. From the perspective of the market, they would rightly be seen as unemployable. Equation (1) was a reduced form of such a process.

This account of the emergence of extreme individual poverty has explanatory power. For example, Fogel (1994) has estimated that at about the time of the Industrial Revolution, the poorest 20 percent of the populations of England and France subsisted on diets of such low energy content that they were effectively excluded from the labor force, with many of them lacking the energy even for a few hours of strolling. Fogel uses this fact to explain why beggars constituted as much as a fifth of the populations of *ancien régimes.*

This picture of begging is one of behavioral adaptation with a vengeance. The account tells us that emaciated beggars are not lazy: they have to husband their precarious hold on energy. As we have seen, even the timeless model makes sense of these matters by showing how low energy intake, undernourishment, and behavioral adaptation that takes the form of lethargy, can all be regarded as being endogenously determined. The sketch I have offered also suggests how these variables can feed on one another over time and reduce a person to a state of destitution. Fogel's own piecing together in the form of a narrative of the state of affairs prevailing in England and France some 200 years ago, and of the conquest of high mortality and malnutrition in these countries since then (Fogel (1992), have strong resonance with the implications of the account I have offered here and its extensions.

Emaciated beggars are the economically disenfranchised. I do not know their proportion in today's populations, but we do know that, at a conservative estimate, some 500 million people in Asia, Africa, and Latin America are undernourished (Dasgupta (1993); see also World Bank (1990)). They make for unattractive workers and are unemployable on a regular basis in the formal sector. The nutrition–productivity model I have sketched offers a coherent account of how this could have come about and, more importantly, how it persists.

1.7 Is food all-important for the poor?

A crucial assumption underlying the model in the previous section is that nutrition intake is all-important to the typical landless worker. To put it more broadly, it assumes that his wage is spent on absolute essentials for himself and his family. (Otherwise the unemployed landless person could undercut those who are employed.) In short, it is taken that there is no slack in the household budget; the worker does not indulge in non-essential consumptions.

The empirical grounding of this is ambiguous, in part because the inquiries have not always been faithful to economic theory. However, in extreme situations, such as famines, the answer is clear. Food is of the greatest urgency, and victims act upon it. They travel in search of it, expending their precarious hold on energy in the realization that all other courses of action guarantee starvation.[31] Under "normal" circumstances, however, the matter is unclear. Rough estimates from India indicate that 15–20 percent of the wage of even a casual worker is often sufficient to provide his personal energy requirements. Moreover, the few studies that have attempted to estimate responses in energy intake to increased total cash expenditure by studying cross sections of poor households have arrived at widely disparate conclusions, ranging from negligible to substantial responses, but nearly all have discovered the response to be less than rupee for rupee (see, e.g., Behrman and Deolalikar (1987), Subramanian and

Deaton (1996)). This suggests that even poor households do not place priority on energy intake, and that there is enormous budgetary slack. In view of this, it has been argued that the model I have sketched is not good (Srinivasan (1994), Strauss and Thomas (1995)). However, leaving aside the statistical problems that are inherent in such estimations (their assumption that household expenditure is a linear function of income is almost surely not valid), one should consider that the typical worker has a family to support; so he has to try to provide for their basic food requirements as well. Moreover, housing, clothing, and cooking utensils are basic needs, and the poor are stretched on these fronts as well. Furthermore, a worker cannot ensure that there will be no emergencies (e.g., illness or death in the family). Therefore, it would not do merely to compare the wage rate with a worker's daily energy requirement when employed: the former has to be somewhat larger in order to meet other ends, ends that are even more likely to occur for people engaged in strenuous work. And finally, food energy is not the sole nutrient one needs; an adequate diet also involves vitamins and minerals. So it would seem that, if there remain possibilities for a laborer to further tighten the household belt and so increase his own energy intake, the possibilities are at best small.

Empirical findings that are not inconsistent with this belief have been reported by Bhattacharya *et al.* (1991). These authors studied a sample of 62 poor, rural households in West Bengal, India. They did not find much sign of undernutrition among the households (although they did not test for it), but they did find an extreme paucity of other basic needs, such as clothing, bedding, and kitchen utensils. For example, 50 percent of the adult women in the sample owned only one *saree* for wear, 75 percent did not own a blouse to go with the *saree*, and 30 percent of the adult men owned only one *dhoti* for wear. Some 20 percent of the households used gunny bags on which to lie, while 25 percent used mats. None owned a blanket or quilt for cover in the winter.[32]

The idea of understanding extreme poverty by inquiring into the consumption of easily measurable basic needs, as opposed to estimating income, or expenditure, or calorie intake, has much to commend it. The investigations of Bhattacharya *et al.* (1991) and Chatterjee (1991) are a beginning, and there is a long way to go. Nevertheless, their findings give us reasons for thinking that household budgetary slacks are small among the very poor. If the slack is nil for a household, then the model I have sketched requires no modification. On the other hand, if the slack is positive, then one has to introduce shocks (e.g., illnesses, deaths, civil wars and general political conflicts) into the model to get it to do the work it was designed to do. But it is as well to remark that, if the slack is tiny, only a small shock would be sufficient to tip the household into the mire. Nutritional maintenance requirements would almost surely see to that. This is a central message of the model. Empirically the question of how large is the slack has not been addressed with the care it deserves.

So, although suggestive, the economics literature does not give us a clear answer to the question; but nor does the work of those nutritionists who have studied the matter. In their investigation on caloric supplementation among Guatemalan sugarcane cutters and loaders, Immink and Viteri (1981) found the additional energy to be diffused over a number of activities. Supplemented workers completed their tasks faster, spent less time traveling back home after a day's work, and slept less during their leisure hours. Their productivity at work (as measured by the number of tons of sugar cane delivered) was not significantly greater than that of unsupplemented workers.

But these subjects had not suffered from energy deficiency prior to the introduction of the supplementation program: they were not undernourished people. So the studies cannot tell if workers would have cut down on their leisure activities had nutrition intake among them been reduced, not supplemented. A yet more effective test of the model would be to offer food supplements to seriously undernourished folk to see if they are subsequently able to obtain employment in manual activities they previously were unsuccessful in entering. To the best of my knowledge, this has not been attempted in any systematic way.[33]

1.8 Policy conclusions

In this chapter I have used findings of modern nutritionists to suggest that poverty traps are a reality in those poor societies that harbor extreme inequalities in asset ownership. Nutritional history from the earliest stages of someone's life can have a stranglehold over his life chances. Indeed, even maternal nutritional status can leave a trace; for example, through her infants' birth weights. In the extreme, poverty traps can be dynastic.

In order to eliminate such poverty traps, two kinds of pathways suggest themselves. The first consists in measures that increase the aggregate wealth of an economy: growth in the capital base, *ceteris paribus*, increases the demand for labor power. To illustrate, consider once again the timeless nutrition–productivity model of section 1.6. If the capital base were large enough, the demand for labor power would be so high that the equilibrium piece-rate would exceed $\hat{x}/\Phi(\hat{x})$. The economy would be at an Arrow–Debreu equilibrium: there would be full employment in the organized sector and the nutrition–based poverty trap would not exist.

The second kind of pathway involves various kinds of redistributive measures. The redistribution need not be of the capital base itself (e.g., it need not be land reform), it can be of output (public health services, income guarantees, and so forth). In short, the first set of pathways looks to growth in the capital base, and the second to a redistribution of the capital base. We noted these two contrasting sets of measures in the Introduction. By the "capital base" we mean not only physical and human capital, but also environmental and institutional capital. Of course, it is possible that the economy is so limited in assets that no resource allocation mechanism could ensure adequate food and health-care for all. In this case, the second pathway would not be an option, and only the first would remain. The life-boat problem mentioned in section 1.6 is an example of an economy where no pattern of distribution would enable all to survive.

But if the aggregate asset level of an economy is not *too* low (but not high either), matters are different. Dasgupta and Ray (1987) showed that, in such an economy, certain patterns of egalitarian asset redistribution can lead to a reduction in the incidence of poverty and an increase in aggregate output. The intuition here is that, with guaranteed food income, an assetless person, one who would otherwise not find employment, could work for a wage lower than $\hat{x}$ and still perform adequately as a worker. He would thus be employable in the market. This example demonstrates that the twin goals of poverty eradication and of growth in net national product are not necessarily in conflict with each other.

Writings on the economics of poor countries have alternated between an emphasis on the failure of many such economies to increase sufficiently their aggregate production of goods and services, and on their inability to introduce direct redistributive measures. Thus, if some years ago it was commonly heard (e.g., World Bank (1986)) that the effective policies for alleviating malnutrition and poverty are those that increase growth and the competitiveness of an economy, today it appears to be a commonplace (e.g., UNDP (1994)) that malnutrition and poverty are not a symptom of aggregate poverty but, rather, of distributive (or "entitlement") failures. Economic models based on the links between nutrition and productivity tell us why these two views are both right and wrong. Each is wrong because it makes no sense to seek mono-causal explanation of poverty traps; each is also right because either kind of measure is likely to prove helpful in the elimination of poverty traps. Clearly, then, it would be better if both sets of measures were to be adopted. In Dasgupta (1993) I have tried to identify the package of measures that would suggest themselves if we were to take both sets of means seriously.

Admittedly, these are observations with a broad brush. The institutional arrangements underlying agricultural work in poor countries are so complex and varied and so specific to regions, that no single model can entirely get off the ground. The models have to be partial. We can but nibble at an understanding, and that too only from various ends. To do this it is best to suspend disbelief and capture a few compelling features of the conditions of living among the rural poor in poor countries and see what together they tell us. We should certainly not interpret the models presented here literally, but I have suggested reasons why we should take them seriously.

2 FERTILITY, ENVIRONMENTAL DEGRADATION AND POVERTY TRAPS

2.1 Households, gender and power

In section 1 population was taken to be given; fertility, for example, was not taken to be subject to choice. Since Malthus' writings, however, the endogeneity of population size has been taken to be a possible source of poverty traps. In this section of the chapter I will summarize recent treatments of the issues that relate to population growth and poverty, laying stress on their connection with the degradation of the local environmental resource base in poor countries.

As with politics, we all have widely differing opinions about population. Some point to population growth as the cause of poverty and environmental degradation. Others permute the elements of this causal chain, arguing, for example, that poverty is the cause rather than the consequence of increasing numbers. Yet even when studying the semi-arid regions of sub-Saharan Africa and the Indian sub-continent, economists have usually not regarded population growth, poverty, and the state of the local environmental resource base as interconnected. Inquiry into each factor has in large measure gone along its own narrow route, with discussions of their interactions dominated by popular writings which, while often illuminating (e.g., Ehrlich and Ehrlich (1990)), are in the main descriptive, not analytical.[34]

Over the past several years, though, a few investigators have studied the interactions between the three ingredients more closely. Our approach has been to fuse theoretical modeling with empirical findings drawn from a number of disciplines. The resulting construction regards none of the three factors to be the prior cause of the other two; rather, it sees each as influencing the others and in turn being influenced by them. Focusing on people in small, rural communities in the poorest regions of the world, the work has even identified circumstances in which population growth, poverty, and degradation of the local environmental resource base can fuel one another over extended periods of time.

A decade ago an inquiry was made into the economic consequences of population growth in poor countries (National Research Council (1986)). Drawing on time-series and cross-regional data, the investigators observed, among other things, that population size and its growth can have both positive and negative effects. The investigators recognized that population growth should not be regarded as exogenously given. Nevertheless, for tractability, they treated it as a causal factor in their inquiry, and concluded that, while economic development in most poor countries would be faster with slower rates of population growth, there is no cause for alarm over the high rates being experienced there.[35]

That population growth is best regarded as endogenous is the hallmark of a strand in demographic theory – often called the "new economic demography" (Schultz (1988)) – that had been developed earlier.[36] It contains an elaborate account of the determinants of fertility behavior. One weakness of this literature is that, with but relatively few exceptions, it has focused on decisions made by a single household; it has not studied in detail social mechanisms in which a myriad of individual household decisions lead to outcomes that are a collective failure. In short, the literature has often equated private and social benefits (and costs) of having children. ("The next step is to apply . . . microeconomic models [of household behavior] to understand aggregate developments in a general equilibrium framework. But progress in this field has been slow" – Schultz (1988, p. 418).) The new perspective, in contrast, focuses on various types of externalities that could be associated with fertility decisions. It notes that a number of such externalities can, over time, lead to wide divergences between individual intentions and social realizations (see below). The theory also peers more closely into the character of decision making within rural households and relates fertility behavior to gender issues (see below).[37]

Popular writings on the environment and population growth have also adopted a different slant. They have usually taken a global, futuristic view: the emphasis has been on the deleterious effects that a large population would have on our planet in the future. Although this perspective has its uses, it has drawn attention away from the economic misery that is endemic in large parts of the world today. Disaster is not something the poorest have to wait for; it is occuring to them even now. Moreover, in poor countries decisions on fertility and on allocations concerning education, food, work, health-care, and on the use of the local environmental resource base are in large measure reached and implemented within household. For this reason, the new perspective studies the interface of population growth, poverty, and environmental degradation from a myriad of household, even individual, viewpoints. In contrast to the global, futuristic viewpoint adopted by popular writings, the literature I am concerned with here focuses on a microcosmic, contemporary tone.

The household assumes various guises in different parts of the world. The importance of Becker's work lay in that he worked with an idealized version of the concept to explore how choices made within a household would respond to changes in the outside world, such as employment opportunities, and credit, insurance, health-care, and education facilities.

As mentioned above, one problem with the literature that has been built around Becker's work is that it has for the most part studied households in isolation; it has not investigated the dynamics between interacting households. A second problem is that it has taken an altogether too benign a view of how decisions are reached within households. Control over a family's decisions is, after all, often unequally shared. Who enjoys the greater power can often be identified by the way a household's resources are divided. A number of investigators have discovered that allocations of resources within households are often unequal, even when differences in needs are taken into account. In poor households in the Indian sub-continent, for example, men and boys usually get more sustenance then women and girls, and the elderly less than the young.[38]

It transpires that such inequities prevail over fertility decisions as well. Consider, for example, the cost of child bearing. While it is obvious that women typically bear the larger cost, it is not so obvious how much larger it can be. To get an idea, consider the number of live babies a woman would normally have if she managed to live through her child-bearing years. This number, called the total fertility rate (TFR), is between six to eight in sub-Saharan Africa. Now each successful birth there involves at least a year-and-a-half of pregnancy and breast feeding. So in a society where female life expectancy at birth is 50 years and the TFR is seven, nearly half of a woman's adult life is spent either carrying a child in her womb or breast feeding it; and this does not allow for unsuccessful pregnancies.

Another indicator of the price that women pay is maternal mortality. In most poor countries, death during childbirth is the largest single killer of women in their reproductive years. In some parts of sub-Saharan Africa such mortality rates have been found to be as high as 1 in 50. (The rate in Scandinavia today is about 1 in 10,000.) At a total fertility rate of seven and over, the chances that a woman entering her reproductive years will not live through them is about one in six. The reproductive-cycle thus involves her playing Russian roulette.

Given such a high cost of procreation, one expects that women, given a choice, would opt for fewer children. Thus birth rates should be lower in societies where women have power. Data on the status of women from 79 so-called Third World countries (see table 4.1) display an unmistakable pattern: high fertility, high rates of female illiteracy, low share of paid employment for women, and high percentages of women working at home

Table 4.1. *Fertility rates and women's status*

N	TFR	PE	UE	I
9	>7.0	10.6	46.9	65.7
35	6.1–7.0	16.5	31.7	76.9
10	5.1–6.0	24.5	27.1	46.0
25	<5.0	30.3	18.1	22.6

Notes:
N number of countries.
TFR total fertility rate.
PE women's share of paid employment (%).
UE percentage of women working as unpaid family workers.
I women's illiteracy rate (%).
Source: IIED/WRI (1987, table 2.3).

for no pay . . . they hang together. However, from the data alone, it is difficult to discern which of these measures are causing, and which are merely correlated with, high fertility. Despite this, there are reasons for thinking that lack of paid employment for women reduces their power more directly than does lack of education (Dasgupta (1995c)). Thus the availability of female employment could have an inexorable influence on fertility.

Such an insight has implications for policy. It is all well and good, for example, to urge governments in poor countries to invest in literacy programs. But the results could be disappointing. Many factors militate against poor households taking advantage of subsidized education. If children are needed to work inside and outside the home, for example, then keeping them in school (even a cheap one) is costly for poor households. In patrilineal societies, educated girls can also be perceived as less pliable and harder to marry off. Indeed, the benefits of subsidies to even primary education are captured disproportionately by families that are better off.

In contrast, policies aimed at increasing women's productivity at home and improving their earnings in the marketplace would directly empower women, especially within the household. One would then expect families to have fewer children. Greater earning power would also raise the implicit costs of procreation for adult males in the household, by preventing the woman from earning cash income. This is not at all to say that public investment in primary and secondary education ought not to be increased in poor countries, it is only to say that we should be wary of claims that such investment is a panacea for the population problem.

The new perspective thus identifies gender inequalities as important components of the population problem in poor countries. In this regard, the focal point of the United Nations Conference on Population and Development in Cairo in September 1994, namely, women's reproductive rights and the means by which they could be protected and promoted, is consonant with the new perspective. But the Cairo Conference came very near to treating the problems as identical. This was a mistake. There is more to the population problem than gender inequalities. To see why, it is fruitful to begin by inquiring into the various motives for procreation.

2.2 Motives for procreation

One motive, common to humankind, relates to children as ends in themselves. It ranges from the desire to have children because they are playful and enjoyable, to the desire to obey the dictates of tradition and religion. One such injunction emanates from the cult of the ancestor, which, taking religion to be the act of reproducing the lineage, requires women to bear many children (Caldwell and Caldwell (1990)).

This motivation alone provides several pathways by which reasoned fertility decisions at the level of every household could lead to an unsatisfactory outcome from the perspectives of all households. One such pathway arises from the fact that traditional practice is often perpetuated by imitative behavior. Procreation in closely knit communities is not only a private matter; it is also a social activity, influenced by the cultural milieu. In many societies there are practices encouraging high fertility rates which no household desires unilaterally to break. Such practice may well have had a rationale in the past, but not necessarily any more. It can then be that, so long as all others follow the practice and aim at large family sizes, no household on its own will wish to deviate from the practice; however, if all other households were to restrict their fertility rates, each would desire to restrict its fertility rate as well. In short, there can be multiple, Pareto rankable equilibria. Thus, a society can get stuck in a self-sustaining mode of behavior that is characterized by high fertility, low educational attainment, and low income.

This does not mean that society will be stuck with it for ever. As always, people differ in the extent of their absorption of traditional practice. There are inevitably those who, for one reason or another, experiment, take risks, and refrain from joining the crowd. They are the tradition breakers, and they often lead the way. A concerted social effort (e.g., a massive literacy and employment drive) can help dislodge such a society from the rapacious hold of high fertility rates to a self-sustaining mode of behavior where fertility is low.

There are other motives for procreation: they involve viewing children as productive assets. In a rural economy where avenues for saving are highly restricted, parents value children as a source of security in their old age.[39] Less discussed, at least until recently, is another kind of motivation, explored by Dasgupta and Mäler (1991, 1995) and Nerlove (1991). The motivation stems from the fact that children are valuable to their parents not only in the future, but also as a source of current income.

Poor countries are, for the most part, biomass-based subsistence economies. The rural poor eke out a living from using products gleaned directly from plants and animals. Much labor is needed even for simple tasks. In addition, poor rural households do not have access to modern sources of domestic energy, or water on tap. In semi-arid and arid regions water supply is not even close by. Nor is fuelwood at hand when the forests recede. In addition to cultivation, caring for livestock, cooking food, and producing simple marketable products, a household may have to spend at much as five to six hours a day fetching water and collecting fodder and wood. Children are then needed as workers even when their parents are in their prime. Small households are simply not viable; each household needs many hands. In parts of India, children between 10 and 15 years have been observed to work as much as one-and-a-half times the number of hours that adult males do. By the age of six, children in rural India tend domestic animals and younger siblings, fetch water and collect firewood, dung, and fodder. It can then be that the usefulness of each extra hand increases with declining availability of resources, as measured by, say, the distance to sources of fuel and water.

2.3 Positive feedbacks

The need for many hands can lead to a destructive situation, especially when parents, not having to bear the full costs of rearing their children, find children to be a cheap source of labor, and so produce too many. In recent years, one channel through which parenting costs have declined has been the changing social mores in the use of local environmental resources. Since time immemorial, rural assets, such as village ponds and water holes, threshing grounds, grazing fields, and local forests have been communally owned by households. This form of ownership and control has enabled households in semi-arid regions to pool their risks. A number of investigators (e.g., Howe (1986), Wade (1987), Chopra, Kadekodi, and Murty (1990), Baland and Platteau (1996)) have shown that communities had protected their common-property resources against overexploitation by the inculcation of social norms, the imposition of fines for deviant behavior, and so forth. But the very process of economic development can erode the practice of such traditional methods of control. Increases in urbanization and mobility can be a cause. Social norms are also eroded in the face of civil strife or when the state or a landowner usurps some of the resource, thus altering the structure of power and control. As norms erode, parents pass on some of the costs of child maintenance to their community by overexploiting the commons. They have then an incentive to produce too many children. More children also leads to greater crowding and susceptibility to disease, as well as more pressure on environmental resources. But again, no household, acting on its own, can be expected to take into account the harm if inflicts on others when bringing forth another child.

Parental costs of procreation are also lower than its full cost when the kinship provides a helping hand. While the price of carrying a child is paid by the mother, the cost of rearing the child is often shared among the kinship. In West Africa any figure between 40 and 50 percent of the children have been found *not* to be living in their natal home, but with their kin. However, "fosterage" in the African context is not adoption. It is not intended to, nor does it in fact, break ties between parents and children. Nephews and nieces have the same rights of accommodation and support as biological offspring. The institution affords a form of mutual insurance protection in semi-arid regions. It may also be that, as savings opportunities are few in the low-productivity agricultural regions of sub-Saharan Africa, fosterage enables households to smooth their consumption across time.[40] It is an easy matter to check that the arrangement creates yet another free-rider problem if the parents' share of the benefits from having children exceeds their share of the costs. From the point of view of the parents, taken as a collective, too many children would be produced in these circumstances.[41]

In addition, where conjugal bonds are weak, as they are in sub-Saharan Africa, fathers often do not bear the costs of siring a child. Historical demographers have noted a significant difference between Western Europe in the eighteenth century and modern pre-industrial societies. In the latter, marriage normally meant establishing a new household. This requirement led to late marriages; it also meant that parents bore the cost of rearing their children. Indeed, fertility rates in France dropped before mortality rates registered a decline, before modern family-planning techniques became available, and before women became literate.

Taken together, the perception of low costs and high benefits of procreation induce households to produce too many children, and in certain circumstances a disastrous process can begin. As the community's resources are depleted, more hands are needed to gather fuel and water for a household's daily use. More children are then created, further damaging the local environment and in turn providing the household with an incentive to enlarge. When this happens, fertility and environmental degradation reinforce each other in an escalating spiral. By the time some countervailing set of factors – whether public policy, or falling productivity of additional children – stops the spiral, millions of lives may have suffered through worsening poverty. Recent findings by Cleaver and Schreiber (1994) on sub-Saharan Africa have revealed positive correlations between poverty, fertility, and deterioration of the local environment. Such data cannot reveal causal connections, but they do support the idea of a positive-feedback process such as I have described. Over time the effect of this spiral can be large, as mainfested by battles for resources (Homer-Dixon, Boutwell, and Rathjens (1993)). The worst victims among those who survive are society's outcasts – the migrants and the dispossessed, some of whom in the course of time become the emaciated beggars seen on the streets of large towns and cities in poor countries.

Households with greater access to resources are, however, in a position to limit their size and propel themselves into still higher-income levels. It is my impression that among the urban middle classes in north India, transition to a lower fertility rate has already been achieved. The new perspective shows how extreme poverty can persist amidst a growth in well being in the rest of society. The Matthew Effect ("For unto everyone that hath shall be given, and he shall have abundance; but from him that hath not shall be taken away even that which he hath") works relentlessly in poor countries.

2.4 Policy conclusions

This analysis suggests that the means of reducing fertility is to break the destructive spirals where they occur. Parental demand for children, rather than an unmet need for contraceptives, in great measure explains reproductive behavior in poor countries (Pritchett (1994)). Thus we should try to identify policies that will so change the options that men and women face that their reasoned choice is to lower their fertility.

In this regard, civil liberties, as opposed to coercion, play a particular role. In earlier work, I have argued that even in poor countries, political and civil liberties go hand in hand with improvements in other aspects of life, such as income per head, life expectancy at birth, and the infant survival rate (Dasgupta (1990, 1993)). There are now reasons for thinking that such liberties are not only desirable in themselves, but also have instrumental virtues in empowering people to flourish in the economic sphere. Recently, Przeworski and Limongi (1995) have shown that fertility, as well, is lower in countries where citizens enjoy more civil and political liberties. (China, an exception, is but one of over 100 countries in their sample.)

The most potent solution in semi-arid regions of sub-Saharan Africa and the Indian sub-continent is to deploy a number of policies simultaneously. Family planning services, especially when allied with health services, and measures that empower women, are certainly desirable. As social norms break down and traditional support systems falter, those women who choose to change their behavior become financially and socially more vulnerable. So a literacy and employment drive for women is essential to smooth the transition to lower fertility. But improving social coordination and directly increasing the economic security of the poor are also essential. Providing infrastructural goods such as cheap fuel and potable water will reduce the usefulness of extra hands. When a child becomes perceived as expensive, we may finally have a hope of dislodging the rapacious hold of high fertility rates.

But each of the prescriptions offered by the new perspective is desirable by itself, and not just when we have the population problem in mind. It seems to me that this consonance of means and ends is a most agreeable fact in what is otherwise a depressing field of study.

Notes

This is the text of an invited lecture to the Seventh World Congress of the Econometric Society, held in Tokyo during August 22–29, 1995. It is based on Dasgupta (1995a,b,c). I am most grateful to Mark Armstrong and Paul Seabright, discussions with whom have clarified my understanding of poverty traps.

1 For a more detailed complaint on the neglect of environment concerns in the economics of poor countries, see Dasgupta and Mäler (1995).
2 I have gone into these matters at greater length in Dasgupta (1995c).
3 Thus, $z = \underline{z}$ and $z = \bar{z}$ are absorbing barriers. The constant that preserves dimensionality in equation (1) has been implicitly set equal to unity.
4 If it involved no more, a mere relabeling of models of "human capital" formation would suffice, and in his review of Dasgupta (1993), Nerlove (1995) suggests it would and leaves the matter at that. But as we will see below, such relabeling would not suffice. Recognition that nutritional status is a form of human capital is only the beginning of a thought, not the end.
5 The sense in which their model is in a "reduced form" is this: nutrition intake (a flow) is substituted for nutritional status (a stock) in modeling the links between the latter and work capacity (see below in the text). Guha (1989) and Dasgupta (1993) are exceptions to this rule: they treat nutritional status as a stock in a two-period setting.
6 See Dasgupta and Ray (1987) and Dasgupta (1993, chapters 14–16) for earlier discussion of this point.
7 If taken literally, each would mislead. For example, at a constant savings rate, Harrod's "warranted growth path" does not converge to the "natural" growth path if capital goods are heterogeneous (Hahn (1966)); and the two-factor, two-commodity, two-country example with a constant-returns-to-scale technology with which the theory of comparative advantage is established forecloses the possibility of endogenously determined comparative advantages.

8 The shapes of the curves $y(z)$ and $h(z)$ in figure 1 have been informed by the discussion to be conducted there.
9 For a contrary suggestion, see Srinivasan (1994, p. 1846).
10 Resource allocations sustaining nutrition-based involuntary unemployment are *quasi-equilibria*, in the sense defined in Debreu (1962). On this, see Dasgupta (1993, p. 489).
11 For a remarkable synthesis of what is known about the determinants of nutritional status, see Waterlow (1992). I have gone into these issues in detail in Dasgupta (1993).
12 I am not referring here to periodic hunger, exemplified by seasonal cycles of weight losses. I am talking of destitutes.
13 The potential disasters of short-term illnesses are often avoided by mutual insurance systems in poor countries. Udry (1994) shows that in northern Nigeria credit can have the form of insurance. It is possible to show that "reciprocity" in traditional societies is a form of mutual insurance. It is also possible to show why such social norms have a tendency to break down during the process of economic growth and modernization. See Dasgupta (1993, chapter 8).
14 The mass of muscle tissue and muscles constitutes about 40 percent of body weight, and 50 percent of the lean body mass.
15 Unskilled laborers in poor countries may often be slight and weak, but they are never out of shape; it is sedentary workers who often are.
16 A classic article on iron-deficiency anaemia and its effect on physical work capacity is Basta *et al.* (1979).
17 Maintenance requirement is, roughly speaking, the basal metabolic rate (plus the small, additional energy expended by postural movement) plus dietary thermogenesis. See Dasgupta (1993, chapters 14–15).
18 Given the context, I am ignoring obesity here.
19 The value of σ is specific to the person in question, and in general it is a function of his nutritional status. The reader will have noticed that a number of simplifying moves have implicitly been made in arriving at equation (5). For example, as is well known, the value of σ depends upon the sign of ds_t/dt. I am ignoring all such details here. For an account of such matters where these details are not ignored, see Dasgupta (1993, chapters 14–15).
20 For a time a thesis was aired that there is *metabolic* adaptation to undernourishment (Sukhatme and Margen (1978), Srinivasan (1981), Sukhatme (1989), Edmundson and Sukhatme (1990)). However, there is next-to-no evidence for this. See, for example, the commentaries on Sukhatme (1989) by J.C. Waterlow, W.P.T. James, and M.J.R. Healy in the *European Journal of Clinical Nutrition* (1989, 43: 203–10), Dasgupta (1993, chapter 15), Schultink *et al.* (1993), and Spurr *et al.* (1994). Under severe nutritional stress there is evidence of tissue wastage (e.g., loss in the heart's muscle mass), not so much depressed oxygen utilization of active tissues. Such forms of adaptation are not costless to the adaptor.
21 Equation (5) brings this out sharply, albeit the equation pertains to adult males (no account is taken in it of energy requirements for pregnancy, lactation, or growth during childhood and adolescence).

22 The study of the effect of malnutrition on mental development is fraught with difficulties of interpretation. On this, see the chapter by S.M. Grantham-McGregor in Waterlow (1992).

23 Here, x_1 and x_2 are the nutrition intakes of the two people, respectively.

24 I will not go into the ramifications of assumption (b) here.

25 Mirrlees (1975) is the pioneering article on this point. Unequal food and health-care allocations within households in poor countries have been much studied in the recent development literature. There are additional explanations behind the phenomenon. I go into these matters in Dasgupta (1993, chapters 11–12), and provide extensive references to the literature.

26 Drèze and Mukherjee (1989) and Mazumdar (1989) provide summaries of the evidence.

27 The precise conditions are stated in Dasgupta and Ray (1986, 1987).

28 In an explicit temporal setting of this basic model, Guha (1989) shows that both long- and short-term agricultural labor contracts can prevail. Even if the credit market were to behave perfectly, poverty traps would remain.

29 The importance of the commons for agrarian societies has been much documented in recent years. See Dasgupta (1993, chapter 10) for references.

30 Rudra (1982) offers an account of the process by which labor rationing takes place in a cluster of villages in West Bengal, India (see also Drèze and Mukherjee (1989)). Of course, agricultural workers in Rudra's sample cannot have been identical, so one may argue that what he describes is not a rationing process, but a process in which employers select the best available workers. On this, see immediately below in the text.

31 This was portrayed vividly in Satyajit Ray's 1975 film on the Great Bengal Famine, *Distant Thunder*.

32 Chatterjee (1991) contains a study of a different sample of households. Her findings are similar to those of Bhattacharya *et al.* (1991).

33 The work of G.B. Spurr and his collaborators (e.g., Spurr (1990)) comes close to it, but not close enough: the subjects were not studied under free-living conditions.

Bhargava (1996) has found in a sample of Rwandese households living under free-living conditions that low energy intakes force adults to spend additional time resting and sleeping. But they were not unemployed.

34 Birdsall (1988), Kelley (1988), and Schultz (1988) are authoritative surveys on the subject of population growth in poor countries. None of them focuses on the interactions I am concerned with in this article. Nor does a large literature on poverty (e.g., Drèze and Sen (1990)) address our theme.

35 Kelley (1988) is an excellent review of the findings.

36 Becker (1981) is often regarded as the canonical formulation.

37 Reproductive externalities have not been much studied in the "new economic demography" so far. Surveying the field, Schultz (1988, p. 417) writes: "Consequences of individual fertility decisions that bear on persons outside of the family have proved difficult to quantify, as in many cases social external diseconomies are thought to be important." An interesting recent attempt at

quantifying the magnitude of reproductive externalities in a number of developing countries is Lee and Miller (1991). They find the magnitude to be small; a not-so-surprising finding, given that the potential sources of externalities they study are public expenditures on health, education, and pensions, financed by proportional taxes, each of which is known to be very limited in scale in poor countries. The externalities we are studying in the text are of a different sort altogether.

38 Chen, Huq, and D'Souza (1981) is a pioneering quantitative study. Dasgupta (1993) contains references to what is now an extensive literature on these matters.

39 This aspect has been much studied by Cain (1981, 1983).

40 Renata Serra has developed this latter argument in a graduate thesis at the University of Cambridge.

41 To see that there is no distortion if the shares were the same, suppose c is the cost of rearing a child and N the number of couples within a kinship. For simplicity assume that each child makes available y units of output (this is the norm) to the entire kinship, which is then shared equally among all couples, say in their old age. Suppose also that the cost of rearing each child is shared equally by all couples. Let n^* be the number of children each couple other than the one under study chooses to have. (We will presently endogenize this.) If n were to be the number of children this couple produces, it would incur the resource cost $C = [nc + (N - 1)n^*c]/N$, and eventually the couple would receive an income from the next generation equaling $Y = [ny + (N - 1)n^*y]/N$. Denote the couple's aggregate utility function by the form $U(Y) - K(C)$, where both $U(.)$ and $K(.)$ are increasing and strictly concave functions. Letting n be a continuous variable for simplicity, it is easy to confirm that the couple in question will choose the value of n at which $yU'(Y) = cK'(C)$. The choice sustains a social equilibrium when $n = n^*$. (This is the symmetric non-cooperative Nash equilibrium of the social system.) It is easy to check that this is also the condition which is met in a society where there is not reproductive free-riding. It is a simple matter to confirm that there is free-riding if the parents' share of the benefits from having children exceeds their share of the costs.

References

Arrow, K. J. and Debreu, G. (1954). "Existence of equilibrium for a competitive economy." *Econometrica*, 22: 265–90.

Åstrand, P. O. and Rodahl, K. (1986). *Textbook of Work Physiology*. New York: McGraw-Hill.

Baland, J. -M. and Platteau, J. -P. (1996). *Halting Degradation of Natural Resources: Is There a Role for Rural Communities?* Oxford: Oxford University Press.

Barac-Nieto, M. *et al.* (1980). "Aerobic work capacity and endurance during nutrition repletion of severely undernourished men." *American Journal of Clinical Nutrition*, 33: 2268–75.

Basta, S. S. *et al.* (1979). "Iron deficiency anemia and the productivity of adult males in Indonesia." *American Journal of Clinical Nutrition*, 32: 916–25.

Becker, G. (1981). *A Treatise on the Family*. Cambridge, MA: Harvard University Press.

Behrman, J. and Deolalikar, A. B. (1987). "Will developing country nutrition improve with income? A case study from rural south India." *Journal of Political Economy*, 95: 492–507.

Benabou, R. (1994). "Human capital, inequality and growth: a local perspective." *European Economic Review*, 38: 817–26.

Bhargava, A. (1994). "Modelling the health of Filipino children." *Journal of the Royal Statistical Society*, Series A, 157: 417–32.

(1995). "Econometric analysis of psychometric data: modelling the effects of undernutrition on the health of Kenyan schoolers." Mimeo, Department of Economics, University of Houston.

(1996). "Nutritional status and the allocation of time in Rwandese households." Mimeo, Department of Economics, University of Houston. (Forthcoming in *Journal of Econometrics*.)

Bhattacharya, N. *et al.* (1991). "How do the poor survive?" *Economic and Political Weekly*, 26: 373–81.

Birdsall, N. (1988). "Economic approaches to population growth." In Chenery, H. and Srinivasan, T. N. (eds.), *Handbook of Development Economics*, Vol. I. Amsterdam: North-Holland.

Bliss, C. J. and Stern, N. H. (1978). "Productivity, wages and nutrition: theory and observations." *Journal of Development Economics*, 5: 331–98.

(1982). *Palanpur: The Economy of an Indian Village*. Oxford: Oxford University Press.

Braverman, A. and Stiglitz, J. E. (1989). "Credit rationing, tenancy, productivity, and the dynamics of inequality." In Bardhan, P. (ed.), *The Economic Theory of Agrarian Institutions*. Oxford: Oxford University Press.

Cain, M. (1981). "Risk and insurance: perspectives on fertility and agrarian change in India and Bangladesh." *Population and Development Review*, 7: 435–74.

(1982). "Fertility as an adjustment to risk." *Population and Development Review*, 9: 688–702.

Caldwell, J. C. and Caldwell, P. (1990). "High fertility in sub-Saharan Africa." *Scientific American*, 262: 82–9.

Chatterjee, S. (1991). "*Some aspects of economic inequality in India.*" Ph. D. thesis, Department of Economics, Visva-Bharati University, Santiniketan.

Chavez, A. and Martinez, C. (1984). "Behavioural measurements of activity in children and their relation to food intake in a poor community." In Pollit, E. and Amante, P. (eds.), *Energy Intake and Activity*. New York: Alan R. Liss.

Chen, L. C., Huq, E., and D'Souza, S. (1981). "Sex bias in the family allocation of food and health care in rural Bangladesh." *Population and Development Review*, 7: 55–70.

Chopra, K., Kadekodi, G., and Murty, M. N. (1990). *Participatory Development: People and Common Property Resources*. New Delhi: Sage Publications.

Cleaver, K. M. and Schreiber, G. A. (1994). *Reversing the Spiral: The Population Agriculture, and Environment Nexus in sub-Saharan Africa.* Washington, DC: World Bank.

Collins, K. J. and Roberts, D. F. (1988). *Capacity for Work in the Tropics.* Cambridge: Cambridge University Press.

Dasgupta, P. (1990). "Well-being and the extent of its realization in poor countries." *Economic Journal*, 100 (Supplement): 1–32.

(1993). *An Inquiry into Well-Being and Destitution.* Oxford: Oxford University Press.

(1995a). "Population, poverty and the local environment." *Scientific American*, 272: 40–5.

(1995b). "Nutritional status, the capacity for work, and poverty traps." Mimeo, Faculty of Economics, University of Cambridge. (Forthcoming in *Journal of Econometrics.*)

(1995c). "The population problem: theory and evidence." *Journal of Economic Literature*, 33: 1879–902.

Dasgupta, P. and Mäler, K. G. (1991). "The environment and emerging development issues." *Proceedings of the Annual Bank Conference on Development Economics 1990* (Supplement to the *World Bank Economic Review*): 101–32.

(1995). "Poverty, institutions, and the environmental-resource base." In Behrman, J. and Srinivasan, T. N. (eds.), *Handbook of Development Economics*, Vol. IIIA. Amsterdam: North-Holland.

Dasgupta, P. and Ray, D. (1986). "Inequality as a determinant of malnutrition and unemployment: theory." *Economic Journal*, 96: 1011–34.

(1987). "Inequality as a determinant of malnutrition and unemployment: policy." *Economic Journal*, 97: 177–88.

Debreu, G. (1962). "New concepts and techniques for equilibrium analysis." *International Economic Review*, 3: 257–73.

Deolalikar, A. B. (1988). "Nutrition and labour productivity in agriculture: estimates for rural South India." *Review of Economics and Statistics*, 70: 406–13.

Drèze, J. and Mukherjee, A. (1989). "Labour contracts in rural India: theories and evidence." In Chakravarty, S. (ed.), *The Balance Between Industry and Agriculture in Economic Development*, Vol. III, *Manpower and Transfers.* London: Macmillan.

Drèze, J. and Sen, A. (1990). *Hunger and Public Action.* Oxford: Clarendon Press.

Durlauf, S. N. (1994). "Spillovers, stratification and inequality." *European Economic Review*, 38: 836–45.

Edmundson, W. C. and Sukhatme, P. V. (1990). "Food and work: poverty and hunger?" *Economic Development and Cultural Change*, 38: 263–80.

Ehrlich, P. and Ehrlich, A. (1990). *The Population Explosion.* New York: Simon and Schuster.

Ferro-Luzzi, A. (1985). "Work capacity and productivity in long-term adaptation to low energy intakes." In Blaxter, K. and Waterlow, W. C. (eds.), *Nutritional Adaptation in Man.* London: John Libbey.

Fogel, R. W. (1992). "Second thoughts on the European escape from hunger: famines, chronic malnutrition and mortality." In Osmani, S. (ed.), *Poverty, Undernutrition and Living Standards*. Oxford: Oxford University Press.

(1994). "Economic growth, population theory, and physiology: the bearing of long-term processes on the making of economic policy." *American Economic Review*, 95: 369–95.

Grantham-McGregor, S. M. *et al.* (1990). "The relationship between undernourishment, activity levels and development in young children." In Schurch, B. and Scrimshaw, N. S. (eds.), *Activity, Energy Expenditure and Energy Requirements in Young Children*. Lausanne: Nestlé Foundation.

Guha, A. (1989). "Consumption, efficiency and surplus labour." *Journal of Development Economics*, 31: 1–12.

Hahn, F. H. (1996). "Equilibrium dynamics with heterogeneous capital goods." *Quarterly Journal of Economics*, 80: 633–46.

Homer-Dixon, T., Boutwell, J., and Rathjens, G. (1993). "Environmental change and violent conflict." *Scientific American*, 268: 16–23.

Howe, J. (1986). *The Kuna Gathering: Contemporary Village Politics in Panama*. Austin, TX: University of Texas Press.

IIED/WRI (International Institute for Environment and Development/World Resources Institute) (1987). *World Resources 1987*. New York: Basic Books.

Immink, M. D. C. *et al.* (1984). "Microeconomic consequences in energy deficiency in rural populations in developing countries." In Pollit, E. and Amante, P. (eds.), *Energy Intake and Activity*. New York: Alan R. Liss.

Immink, M. D. C. and Viteri, F. E. (1981). "Energy intake and productivity of Guatemalan sugarcane cutters: an empirical test of the efficiency wage hypothesis, parts I and II." *Journal of Development Economics*, 9: 251–87.

James, W. F. T., Ferro-Luzzi, A., and Waterlow, J. C. (1988). "Definition of chronic energy deficiency in adults." *European Journal of Clinical Nutrition*, 42: 969–82.

James, W. F. T. *et al.* (1992). *Body Mass Index: an Objective Measure of Chronic Energy Deficiency in Adults*. Rome: Food and Agriculture Organization.

Kelley, A. C. (1988). "Economic consequences of population change in the third world." *Journal of Economic Literature*, 26: 1685–728.

Koopmans, T. C. (1957). *Three Essays on the State of Economic Science*. New York: McGraw-Hill.

Lee, R. D. and Miller, T. (1991). "Population growth, externalities to childbearing, and fertility policy in developing countries." *Proceedings of the Annual Bank Conference on Development Economics 1990* (Supplement to the *World Bank Economic Review*): 275–304.

Leibenstein, H. (1957). *Economic Backwardness and Economic Growth: Studies in the Theory of Economic Development*. New York: John Wiley.

Malina, R. M. (1984). "Physical activity and motor development/performance in populations nutritionally at risk." In Pollit, E. and Amante, P. (eds.), *Energy Intake and Activity*. New York: Alan R. Liss.

Martorell, R., Rivera, J., and Kaplowitz, H. (1990). "Consequences of stunting in early childhood for adult body size in rural Guatemalan children." *Annales Nestlé*, 48: 85–92.

Mazumdar, D. (1989). "Microeconomic issues of labour markets in developing countries." EDI Seminar Paper No. 40, World Bank, Washington, DC.

Mirrlees, J. A. (1975). "A pure theory of underdeveloped economies." In Reynolds, L (ed.), *Agriculture in Development Theory*. New Haven, CT: Yale University Press.

Myrdal, G. (1968). *Asian Drama*. London: Allen Lane/Penguin Press.

National Research Council (1986). *Population Growth and Economic Development: Policy Questions*. Washington, DC: US National Academy of Sciences Press.

Nerlove, M. (1991). "Population and the environment: a parable of firewood and other tales." *American Journal of Agricultural Economics*, 73: 1334–57.

(1995). "Review of *An Inquiry into Well-Being and Destitution* by Partha Dasgupta." *Population and Development Review*, 21: 405–14.

Pollitt, E. (1990). *Malnutrition and Infection in the Classroom*. Paris: UNESCO.

Pollitt, E. and Amante, P. (1984). *Energy Intake and Activity*. New York: Alan R. Liss.

Pritchett, L. H. (1994). "Desired fertility and the impact of population policies." *Population and Development Review*, 20: 1–56.

Przeworski, A. and Limongi, F. (1995). "Democracy and development." Working Paper No. 7, Chicago Center on Democracy, University of Chicago.

Rodgers, G. (1975). "Nutritionally based wage determination in the low-income labour market." *Oxford Economic Papers*, 27: 61–81.

Rosenzweig, M. R. (1988). "Labour markets in low-income countries." In Chenery, H. and Srinivasan, T. N. (eds.), *Handbook of Development Economics*. Amsterdam: North-Holland.

Rudra, A. (1982). *Indian Agricultural Economics: Myths and Realities*. New Delhi: Allied Publishers.

Satyanarayana, K. *et al.* (1977). "Body size and work output." *American Journal of Clinical Nutrition*, 30: 322–5.

Schultink, J. W. *et al.* (1993). "Seasonal weight loss and metabolic adaptation in rural Beninese women: the relationship with body mass index." *British Journal of Nutrition*, 70: 689–700.

Schultz, T. Paul (1988). "Economic demography and development." In Ranis, G. and Schultz, T. Paul (eds.), *The State of Development Economics*. Oxford: Basil Blackwell.

Shetty, P. (1984). "Adaptive changes in basal metabolic rate and lean body mass in chronic undernutrition." *Human Nutrition: Clinical Nutrition*, 38C: 443–52.

Spurr, G. B. (1990). "The impact of chronic undernutrition on physical work capacity and daily energy expenditure." In Harrison, G. A. and Waterlow, J. C. (eds.), *Diet and Disease in Traditional and Developing Countries*. Cambridge: Cambridge University Press.

Spurr, G. B. *et al.* (1994). "Variation of the basal metabolic rate and dietary energy intake of Colombian women during 1 year." *American Journal of Clinical Nutrition*, 59: 20–7.

Srinivasan, T. N. (1981). "Malnutrition: some measurement and policy issues." *Journal of Development Economics*, 8: 3–19.

(1994). "Destitution: a discourse." *Journal of Economic Literature*, 32: 1842–55.

Stiglitz, J. E. (1976). "The efficiency-wage hypothesis, surplus labour and the distribution of income in LDCs." *Oxford Economic Papers*, 28: 185–207.

Strauss, J. (1986). "Does better nutrition raise farm productivity?" *Journal of Political Economy*, 94: 297–320.

Strauss, J. and Thomas, D. (1995). "Food, nutrition and economic development." Mimeo, Department of Economics, Michigan State University.

Subramanian, S. and Deaton, A. (1992). "The demand for food and calories: *Journal of Political Economy*, 104: 133–62.

Sukhatme, P. V. (1989). "Nutritional adaptation and variability." *European Journal of Clinical Nutrition*, 43: 75–87.

Sukhatme, P. V. and Margen, S. (1978). "Models of protein deficiency." *American Journal of Clinical Nutrition*, 31: 1237–56.

Thomas, D. and Strauss, J. (1996). "Health and wages: evidence on men and women in urban Brazil." Mimeo, Department of Economics, Michigan State University. (Forthcoming in *Journal of Econometrics*.)

Udry, C. (1994). "Risk and insurance in a rural credit market: an empirical investigation in Northern Nigeria." *Review of Economic Studies*, 61: 495–526.

UNDP (United Nations Development Programme) (1994), *Human Development Report*. New York: Oxford University Press.

Viteri, F. E. (1971). "Considerations on the effects of nutrition on the body composition and physical work capacity of young Guatemalan adults." In Scrimshaw, N. S. and Altshull, A. M. (eds.), *Amino Acid Fortification of Protein Foods*. Cambridge, MA: MIT Press.

Wade, R. (1988). *Village Republics: Economic Conditions for Collective Action in South India*. Cambridge: Cambridge University Press.

Waterlow, J. C. (1986). "Metabolic adaptation to low intakes of energy and protein." *Annual Review of Nutrition*, 6: 495–526.

(1992). *Protein Energy Malnutrition*. Sevenoaks: Edward Arnold.

WHO (1985). *Energy and Protein Requirements*. Geneva: World Health Organization.

World Bank (1986, 1990). *World Development Report*. New York: Oxford University Press.

CHAPTER 5

Microenterprise and macropolicy

Robert M. Townsend

1 SOME BACKGROUND AND MOTIVATION: THREE WELL-KNOWN PROGRAMS

Motivation for this contribution is best provided by describing briefly three relatively recent experiences in the world of banking and finance:

1 The Grameen Bank in Bangladesh was started in 1976 by a Professor of Economics, Muhammad Yunus, Chittagorn University. Bangladesh is a poor country with low levels of average per capita income, high rates of infant mortality, and low levels of literacy especially among women. Believing that economically active but assetless poor households were being excluded from official lending sources and exploited by usurious moneylenders, the Grameen Bank began lending to borrower groups of five people who underwrite each other's loans, promising to pay as a group to the bank in case a member defaults. Currently, the average loan is relatively small, $80.00, and the nominal interest rate is 16.5 percent, with inflation at 10 percent. Again, no collateral is required. Strikingly, the repayment rate of loans is 98 percent, on average, with women constituting the majority of borrowers. This lending system continues to attract donor attention, e.g., the Ford Foundation, and continues to expand dramatically, with the number of borrowers, number of villages, and credit outstanding often doubling from year to year. Grameen-type lending systems have been introduced into Malaysia, Nepal, and, in the United States, into the city of Chicago and rural Arkansas.

2 The Badan Kredit Kecamatan (BKK) began as a provincial development bank in central Java, Indonesia, using government funds to subsidize agricultural credit. Started in the early 1970s, by 1983 the BKK consisted of 483 branches covering most of Java with 1,300 village posts. Then, in 1985,

Indonesia went through a dramatic fiscal stabilization and austerity program, virtually eliminating subsidized credit. There was an accompanying and quite explicit Financial Institutions Development Program, in collaboration with the US Agency of International Development, mobilizing savings though allowing savings to be withdrawn on demand. Government operated BKK-like systems have been adopted in other regions and islands: LPK in west Java, BKPD in west Java, and LPN in west Sumatra, for example. There has been dramatic expansion in the number of participants and amounts saved. Increases in savings of the order of 50 percent per year are typical. Indonesian systems have been influential in the debate on liberalization and financial-sector reform.

3 Accion International operates non-government organizations in 13 countries in Latin America and in the Caribbean, lending to the poor either as individuals or to groups. A specific example is PRODEM in Bolivia, one of Latin America's poorest countries, intent on servicing small-scale business enterprises in the informal sector, particularly those ravaged by inflation prior to stabilization in 1985 and excluded from more formal banks and austere government programs, post stabilization. Charging relatively high real interest rates and promoting savings mobilization, Banco Sol has now emerged from PRODEM as an official, formal bank in Bolivian cities. It is making large profits while retaining its altruistic service orientation. Meanwhile, PRODEM is expanding into relatively remote rural areas. Accion International has expanded its programs to the US, to the cities of New York and Chicago.

2 THE KEY QUESTIONS AND A POLICY ALGORITHM

What do we make of these episodes? How do we evaluate these interventions? Should we recommend similar programs or interventions elsewhere?

Broadly speaking there are three standard responses to these questions. These responses shall be characterized here.

The first response to these episodes and interventions is that we should do nothing in other places. The idea is that the world must be optimal already, the way it is. This is especially so if one takes into account bribes and the difficulty of political action. Apparent inefficiencies may appear from time to time, but any attempts to take action would be thwarted by bureaucracies. Regulatory agencies are captured after all.

This is no place for a long critique of the first view. Suffice it to note that this view undercuts the notion of useful discovery in economics. No researcher can design and help implement a Pareto-improving mechanism.

The second response to these episodes and interventions is also conservative but envisions productive action. Specifically the second response is that the problem is in the regulation. The recommendation is to liberalize financial markets, get the interest rate up to its market level, and separate the operation of credit markets from transfers and subsidies. This is the standard market response, popularized among others by the Ohio State school.

A short critique of the second response might note that the standard supply and demand diagram, with credit on one axis and the interest rate on the other, is a partial equilibrium diagram. The credit market is not embedded into an explicit dynamic general equilibrium context. The commodity point, the credit contract, needs to be spelled out, and the presence or absence of other financial instruments, particularly those for risk-bearing, needs to be made explicit. The applicability of the diagram when there are private information and incentive problems can also be called into question.

The third response to these episodes and interventions is a liberal view, and it extols the virtues of the institutions using the metrics of the institutions themselves. The Grameen Bank in Bangladesh, the BKK in Indonesia, and PRODEM in Bolivia are extolled for profitability, increases in savings, increases in credit, types of borrowers reached, novel lending procedures, and the building of financial infrastructure. The facts may well be accurate; the programs may have an enormous impact by these standards.

The criticism of the third view is obvious. These standards or metrics for success do not come from theory.

All three views lead us to the obvious policy algorithm. Use theory to think about the logic of all the observables. Try to understand what we see, and what happens in an intervention, by describing an economic model, with all the logic made explicit. Indeed, one can go one step further. Theory may suggest an ideal operating system, with standards one can use to judge whether the actual economy is optimal or not. The next step then is to use, or acquire, microeconomic data to see if the theory is correct and if there is some hope for improvement. In practice one iterates from theory to data and back again, as described in more detail in Rashid and Townsend (1994), for example. But the point is that theory and data are being used heavily in crafting responses to the policy question.

3 APPLYING THE ALGORITHM IN THAILAND

This chapter will ask these key policy questions and attempt to get answers via the policy algorithm just described. In this sense this contribution describes a method of analysis, a method which might well be applied to any economy or country. Indeed, the chapter describes research and policy analysis using theory and data from a large variety of contexts. The chapter tries to tie together apparently diverse efforts by showing how they fit into the policy algorithm.

Still, because one is shifting across countries, data sets, and diverse theories, the chapter runs the risk of being poorly focused. So, to tie it all together, repeated references to one country are made. Thailand is featured as a leading example of how the policy algorithm can be applied. Each and every theory is applied and/or interpreted with knowledge of the institutions, the policies of government and non-government organizations, and the characteristics of households in Thailand. The data come from diverse sources, all collected or used by the author. One source is field research conducted in ten villages in northern Thailand (and to a lesser extent in the north-east). A second source is the large Socio-Economic Survey (SES) of the Thailand National Statistics Office (NSO), covering over 12,000 households in each of five years, from 1976 to 1990. A third source is institutional information gathered in 1993 under a preliminary analysis of the Bank for Agriculture and Agricultural Cooperatives (BAAC); the Credit Union League of Thailand (CULT); a temple, Wat Ba, in Chiengmai; and Operation LINK, a Thai-German program linking self-help groups to banks.

Background information on each of these Thai programs is provided in appendix A and appendix B reports on more of the details necessary for program evaluation. Suffice it to note here that the BAAC is a large, quasi-autonomous but government-operated rural development agency, the primary source of credit in rural areas of Thailand. CULT is a more selective, non-government organization promoting village-level and urban credit unions – for saving, borrowing, and some insurance. The Temple Wat Ba is a donor financed religious organization promoting village-level rice banks, buffalo banks, and rotating credit associations. Finally, Operation LINK, linking banks to self-help groups, hopes to connect the BAAC to such groups as Production Credit Groups (PCG's), neglected if not indigenous credit unions promoted earlier by the Community Development Department (CDD) of the Department of the Interior.

More specifically, the chapter proceeds as follows. Section 4 below discusses how Thailand's reasonably high level of growth is accompanied by an increasing degree of income and consumption inequality, a motivating force behind all of the Thai credit programs, all targeting the poor or middle-level households. Such facts on inequality are sometimes taken for granted, but that is not the right way to proceed, not in Thailand nor in any other country. Cross-country evidence is also presented. Section 5 goes on to discuss the logic of the relationship between inequality and growth, and whether there are policy remedies. A tight, theoretical model is presented. The answer to the policy question in these models depends on whether or not there are "artificial" constraints on the allocation of credit. Section 6 critiques empirical work on savings, the permanent income hypothesis, and liquidity constraints as shedding related but as yet insufficient light on this issue. Further work on program evaluation in Thailand is proposed. Note how a macroissue is tied to microdata. Section 7 describes a related, tight theoretical model which makes explicit the link or correlation between measures of financial intermediation and growth. This correlation is sometimes taken for granted, and it does seem to be supported empirically. But section 7 asks whether microdata (testing consumption insurance) supports the tight theoretical intermediation-growth model. Section 8 goes into a more detailed discussion of consumption insurance and market efficiency and of actual and potential tests of the intermediation model, again with program evaluation in mind. Further evaluation along this line is proposed. Section 9 tackles the liberalization issue, asking whether privatization and financial-sector reform is necessarily a good thing and what metrics we might use to judge their success. Most of the metrics mentioned earlier turn out to be misleading. Finally, section 10 takes on the issue of subsidized credit, asking whether a model with imperfect information and incentive constraints would justify comingling altruistically motivated income redistribution with the operation of credit markets. Surprisingly, one such model does. Section 11 concludes with a brief discussion of the relationship between mechanism design models and microdata, how to gather data and test models so that we can evaluate and better design financial systems.

Again, appendixes A and B contain important additional material on the four Thai programs. Much of the material was gathered in the field in 1993 and is not reported elsewhere.

4 INEQUALITY IN THAILAND: MOTIVATION FOR THE THAI PROGRAMS

Figure 5.1 displays the monthly per capita incomes of Thai households sampled five times by the SES from 1975 to 1990. The household income numbers include wages; profits from agriculture, entrepreneurship, and livestock; and income in kind. The consumption numbers reported below include expenditures on food, clothing, shoes, and tobacco. The income numbers are meant to get at pretransfer income, exclusive of taxes, insurance premiums and indemnities, interest earnings, and adjustment to income by the purchase and sale of real and financial assets. These income

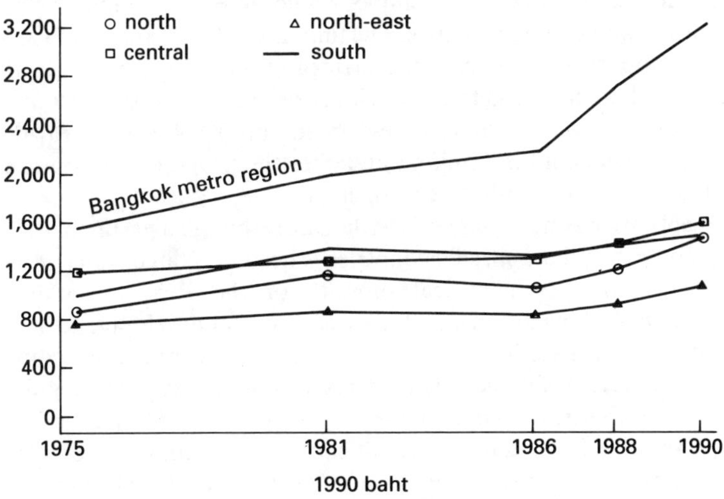

Figure 5.1 Per capita monthly income, 1990

numbers get at underlying income movements, not *ex post* adjustments. The consumption numbers get at necessary items and exclude luxury goods and consumer durables.

As is apparent from figure 5.1, Thailand as a whole experienced relatively high rates of growth of income in the 15-year period, about 4 percent per year on average, with the level of per capita average income in 1990 at $806. Not apparent in the figure, much of this has come in the growth of services and industry, at the expense of agriculture. Further, levels and growth rates are uneven over space. Income and consumption in the north-east were 49 and 63 percent, respectively, of income and consumption in the greater Bangkok area in 1975, and these fell to 33 and 51 percent by 1990. The central, southern, and northern areas of the country display similar patterns relative to Bangkok. Indeed, the growth rate of per capita income of residents in the greater Bangkok area was 6.25 percent, much higher than in other regions.[1] On the other hand, the income and consumption numbers are not adjusted here to account for the increased cost of living in Bangkok, presumably not a small adjustment. Making such adjustments would take us in an important direction, trying to distinguish true welfare, or poverty, in rural and urban areas. But this is not attempted here.

Most of the Thai programs see a link between access to credit and growth of income, envisioning a kind of poverty trap, especially in rural areas. That is, low-income people cannot save much, and, in the absence of credit, cannot invest in productive projects even if the technology is brought to them. The BAAC and the Temple would like to expand credit for agricultural and related activities. The unions of CULT and the PCGs are eager to support as well micro-enterprise programs. All four organizations believe local credit markets do not function well, with usurious money-lenders extracting the profits necessary for investment and growth. As noted, this same kind of thinking underlies the programs of Grameen in Bangladesh and Accion in Latin America.

Perceptions may not be at odds with reality, though measurement in the policy context of these specific countries is needed. Williamson (1991) has argued that there is empirical support for the Kuznets curve, with inequality first rising and then falling with levels of development. There is evidence in a cross section of countries, and evidence for specific countries as well. On the face of it, then, there seems to be some "empirical regularity" which would buttress complaints from policymakers and public interest groups about increasing inequality. It should be noted, however, that the cross-country evidence is weaker at the rising, low end of the Kuznets curve. Latin American countries have experienced more initial inequality than corresponding egalitarian Asians, for example. But this begs again the issue of policy design.

5 INEQUALITY AND GROWTH – IS INTERVENTION DESIRABLE?

The empirical relationship between growth and inequality cannot serve as a springboard for economic policy without further assessment of the logic of the relationship. Is inequality an inevitable product of the growth path? Would a myopic concentration on short-run equality lower all welfare? Does inequality foster accumulation, or would redistribution of wealth lead to higher growth and raise overall welfare? Is equality the right metric for judging the success of interventions?

These questions cannot be answered without coupling explicit theories of these relationships and more detailed measurement. We may take, as an example, the recent model of Lloyd-Ellis and Bernhardt (1993), representative of a larger literature, e.g., Banerjee and Newman (1991). In it, the relatively poor households of rural areas cannot finance newly emerging, highly productive projects in urban areas. Their inheritance or household wealth is too meager. Relatively rich households can finance these projects, with some relatively mediocre or less-talented households among them. Ironically, the large mass of laborers relative to the few initially financed projects keeps wages down and make profits for entrepreneurs yet higher. Inequality between rich and poor thus increases in the short run, with wealth passed along to heirs. Eventually, though, a shortage of labor drives up wages, and savings, accumulated over many generations, slowly reduces constraints on investment and expansion for relatively talented entrepreneurs, independent of wealth. Inequality is ultimately reduced.

Because there are fixed costs to project entry and resources are not unlimited at a point in time, the appropriate government policy in the Lloyd-Ellis–Bernhardt model is redistributive, via inheritance taxes, for example. Still, if the government sets out to maximize national average growth, the goal of redistribution should not be *ex post* equality. Early on, at least, some households should receive relatively large bequests. That is, there should be a constrained-optimal redistribution of wealth based on random assignment, something like a lottery. Induced inequality is necessary to finance yet faster expansion.

Models like that of Lloyd-Ellis and Bernhardt can be made to accommodate a credit market with borrowing linked to wealth. This comes, however, at the cost of some simplification. Piketty (1994) begins with the standard, Solow, capital accumulation model with diverse households. The household of each generation has an investment project which requires its own effort, though this effort is unobserved to outsiders. Each household decides how much to invest in its own project and therefore, given its inheritance, how much to save or to invest. Wealthy households can finance their own projects and save some residual. Moderately wealthy households choose to borrow but exert maximum effort nonetheless. But relatively poor households must borrow more. As a result, their incentive to make effort is low and their likelihood of project success is low. Knowing this the financial system allocates less credit to poor borrowers and does so at a higher rate of interest. Movement to a steady state is associated with increasing average wealth, reduced interest rates, and reduced credit constraints. But the Piketty model seems to allow multiple self-fulfilling steady states. Among these there is an inverse correlation between average wealth, on the one hand, and the level of interest rates, on the other.

Aghion and Bolton (1992) add to this story minimum-sized investment projects, somewhat like a fixed cost. Then, as in Lloyd-Ellis and Bernhardt, many households can be left in a traditional sector for some time. Here, however, these relatively poor households save and thus help to finance more wealthy, borrowing entrepreneurs. There are relatively wealthy, saving entrepreneurs as well. Over time, as aggregate wealth grows, a larger number of investment projects can be financed at lower interest rates. With increased maximum efforts, wealth accumulates all the more. A Kuznets curve is generated.

Though substantial progress is being made in theory, these models do not escape criticism. The technology and preferences seem rather special, at times almost contrived. That is, the stories which are told from the models seem plausible enough, but the models reveal just how special the stories may be. Related, none of these dynamic models does well with economic geography. The relatively recent work of Krugman (1991) spells out an endogenous market structure with industrial concentration, something which a description of growth in Thailand calls to mind. But these spatial models have yet to be made dynamic.

From theory back to data. It is not obvious that this class of well-articulated theoretical models has empirical validity beyond delivering a Kuznets curve. Are households actually constrained in credit markets, in occupational choice, and in financing projects in the sense that the (extended) models predict? These questions can only be addressed by taking such well-articulated models to data.

6 SAVINGS AND LIQUIDITY CONSTRAINTS – A REVIEW OF SOME EMPIRICAL LITERATURE

The model of Lloyd-Ellis and Bernhardt can be used to think about an empirical test of liquidity constraints and a test of production efficiency. If we think of talent or set-up costs for potential entrepreneurs as an unobserved random variable, distributed in the population in a known way, then their model delivers a probabilistic relationship among the variables: the observed levels of bequests, potential inefficiency in production for actual entrepreneurs, and (constrained) occupational choice. Specifically, at relatively high levels of bequests, talented households become entrepreneurs and are unconstrained in production; only the untalented stay in the unproductive sector. At medium levels of bequest some of the relatively talented become entrepreneurs, but many of these are constrained in production, that is, they would hire more labor if they could do so, that is, if they had higher bequests (or access to credit). At relatively low levels of bequests there are talented households who would like to become entrepreneurs but are constrained from this choice. In summary, one could survey households of the model, asking laborers whether they would like to be entrepreneurs and asking the entrepreneurs if they are constrained in production. Similarly, one could choose parameters of technology and preferences to maximize the likelihood of responses in an actual survey.

Remarkably, something close to this exercise has been carried out in the US by Evans and Jovanovic (1989), using the data from the National Longitudinal Survey of Young Men. The wage is presumed to depend on experience and education and on a random iid shock. Entrepreneurial earnings are presumed to depend on a multiplicative talent variable as well as on an iid shock. Talent might also depend exogenously on wealth, a correlation to be estimated in the data along with the cross-sectional distribution of the talent and shock variables. Finally, the model allows entrepreneurs to borrow up to some multiple of their wealth – something similar in spirit to the borrowing levels induced in the model of Aghion and Bolton (1992) and in Piketty (1994). The conclusion is that entrepreneurs are constrained in entry and in the level of operation. Credit constraints bind.

The work of Feder *et al.* (1991) may be seen in a developing country context, namely northern China, as a partial test of the same kind of model. Households who have ample access to credit should not be constrained by initial wealth in deciding which inputs to use, including labor hired on the market. That is, households not constrained by initial wealth should experience a separation between production and consumption decisions. Feder *et al.* confirm that constrained households, among others, those with low previous income or low savings, are influenced in agricultural production by variables such as available household labor.

Benjamin (1992) runs similar tests in Java, but finds households there may not be constrained by the size and composition of the household.

Feder *et al.* (1991) are able to calculate in theory and to estimate in practice the effect of pumping more credit into the economy. The theory allows households to choose among current consumption, future consumption, and investment. The latter is made possible by an exogenous valuation for terminal wealth, something like the bequest motive in the models of growth with inequality reviewed earlier. In theory more credit would increase variable inputs, increase investment, increase consumption, and increase output. In practice these results are confirmed in the Chinese data, but with much of the impact on current consumption.

Households with limited access to credit may also be less efficient in production, not because credit is limited but because they are less talented. That is, a financial institution may limit access to potential credit to a household who is perceived as less than diligent, while lack of diligence would also show up as a negative unobserved fixed effect in a cross-sectional estimate of production functions. To control for this, Feder *et al.* allow correlated errors in the credit selection and production relations. Still, the reduced form equation in Feder *et al.* which determines whether households are liquidity constrained is simply *ad hoc*; it is not derived from theory. Indeed, neither the "supply" nor the "demand" side of that equation is modeled.

The model of Evans and Jovanovic (1989) is explicit in allowing potential entrepreneurs to borrow some multiple of wealth, but one would like to have a model of how banks make decisions. Otherwise, as they note, one is left with an estimate of the impact of liquidity constraints on entrepreneurs and on output without a real suggestion of how to remedy the problem, of how to increase credit. A promising direction would be elaborated versions of the models of Aghion and Bolton (1992), and of Piketty (1994), with the financial structures endogenous, both on the side of savings and on the side of credit. Related, when the decision problem is placed back in the context of the growth model, wages and interest rates move endogenously, no doubt influencing appropriate estimation.

Deaton (1989) has taken up the issue of savings in developing countries, tracking what is known about the relationship of savings and investment to growth. He reminds us again of the financial repression literature, noting however that the effect of increased interest rates on savings is ambiguous both in theory and in practice. He has in mind however a partial equilibrium decision problem, in effect, a partial equilibrium model of growth. But Deaton is skeptical that more or less standard models of growth pick up true motives for household savings. He prefers models in which the interest rate is already below the rate of time preference but models in which risk-averse households save for precautionary reasons.

This brings us naturally to a parallel empirical literature which emphasizes credit constraints but which draws attention to consumption smoothing rather than to investment. Specifically, the permanent income hypothesis supposes that households have free access to credit markets, borrowing and lending at a specified market rate of interest. This delivers a Euler equation in which the marginal utility of present consumption, at date t, is equal to the discounted expected marginal utility of future consumption, at date $t + 1$, times the gross interest rate. Roughly speaking, expected intertemporal marginal rates of substitution across households from dates t to $t + 1$ are equated to a common asset return. This implies a benchmark or standard for consumption smoothing. Specifically, though realized asset returns and incomes at date $t + 1$ can cause deviations from the *ex ante* Euler equality, such error terms should be unrelated to information known and used in forming expectations at date t. In short, after controlling for household-specific demographic changes and for individual, time, and aggregate (e.g., village) fixed effects, a household's consumption growth from t to $t + 1$ should not be related to idiosyncratic shocks at date t, e.g., household-specific income at t.[2]

The Euler equation standard for consumption smoothing has been much used in macroeconomic literature using US data and used in data sets from Third World countries, e.g., Wolpin (1982), and Paxson (1992). Paxson's work is an excellent example, with the added virtue here that it returns us to Thailand (and the SES data). Specifically, Paxson finds that propensities to save out of transitory income due to rainfall shocks are quite high. That is, savings are used to buffer consumption from income shocks. However, propensities to save out of permanent income are also positive, a rejection of the permanent income model.

When Euler equations are shown to be violated, the literature asserts typically that households are liquidity constrained, e.g., Hayashi (1987). Authors Deaton (1989), Zeldes (1989), and other have taken this one step further, supposing households can save at a market rate of interest but cannot borrow. This is as in the Lloyd-Ellis and Bernhardt model, but here there is uncertainty. Then Euler equations continue to apply for those households and time periods when savings (and other liquid assets) are positive. But if savings are driven to zero and the household cannot borrow, then the Euler equation will be satisfied as an inequality. Technically, there is a Lagrange multiplier which is positive when households are liquidity constrained, in this sense, when income and savings are low. Zeldes (1989) applied this test to US households, showing that poor assetless households are constrained.

Morduch (1993) applied this test to data from the International Crops Research Institute for the Semi-Arid Tropics (ICRISAT) showing that poor households in three Indian villages are constrained. More dramatically, constrained households are more likely to diversify *ex ante* into multiple plots and crops, though this may be costly, and less likely to adopt high-yield but risky varieties of seed. We return in this way to models which incorporate production, occupation, and other choices, as at the beginning of this section.

Despite the link between policy and credit constraints as outlined above, relatively little has been done in applied, village-level or program-level analysis. In the context of Thailand, for example, we might sort over households by use or access to local institutions. For example, does a village-level PCG or credit union allow intertemporal consumption smoothing, at least when savings are positive? Are there significant differences in consumption smoothing between villages with one of these institutions and villages without them? Are households in villages without a PCG more vulnerable to fluctuations? Perhaps the latter villages make greater, if costly efforts to diversify income sources. Perhaps the latter villages display more migration. Related, by Euler equation standards, are families and networks of friends and relatives more or less successful in consumption smoothing without policy intervention? Finally, do the formal programs of the BAAC allow this standard of consumption smoothing among its participants across locations?

A second related step is to check on the smoothing devices which households actually use. Own rice storage and livestock are alternative assets, and the associated Euler equations should be satisfied for households who hold positive levels of these assets across periods. Euler equations should be satisfied at an inequality when assets are driven to zero. On the other hand, PCGs may discourage the withdrawal of accumulated savings even in times of stress. We need to understand institutional rules.

A third related step is to link consumption with production. Savings in PCGs may be used as collateral for seasonal production loans, and low savings may limit access to future production credit. This brings us back, of course, to the theoretical model of savings of Lloyd-Ellis and Bernhardt and the econometric credit-constraint model of Feder *et al.* That is, we need to understand better the rules for access and use of existing institutions in savings, in consumption, and in production credit. What are the actual patterns of use across various households? What are the actual patterns across various regions? Can we explain in this way growth with inequality?

7 LINKS OF REAL GROWTH TO FINANCIAL INTERMEDIATION

The BAAC features dramatic increases in savings, in credit, in the number of customers and villages reached, and in continual expansion in spatial access, as measured for example by the number of branches. CULT focuses on improved intermediation at the local, village level, believing its credit unions dominate earlier, indigenous arrangements, if any. Operation Link envisions improved interregional intermediation, with existing or improved local units linked up to a regional or national financial system. (CULT already offers these links to its own unions). Of course the Grameen and Indonesia programs reviewed earlier emphasize dramatic expansion in clients, with a focus on the growth of credit in Grameen and in the growth of savings in Indonesia. Accion is an example of a credit program emphasizing improved intermediation, as with Banco Sol in Bolivia.

Again, it is difficult to know what to make of these expansions in the absence of theory and further measurement. The goals of the programs are explicit, taking the form of targets for expansion, but are these the appropriate metrics for success? What metrics are suggested by a well-articulated model? What does that model predict about the relationship between intermediation and growth?

We shall take up this issue in the context of a model which is explicit about the presence or absence of intermediation while maintaining the standard of Pareto optimality. In the model of Greenwood and Jovanovic (1990), all households have access to two technologies or investment projects: a safe, low yield project and also a higher mean but higher variance project, subject to idiosyncratic and aggregate shocks (this could be extended to allow for multiple industries with common components within an industry). For a fixed cost of entry, and subsequent marginal costs per unit invested, households can join one another in an intermediated system, benefiting from insurance against their idiosyncratic shocks (to smooth consumption) and benefiting from pooled advance information on yields. Both these allow higher average returns, and, with savings a fixed fraction of income, this implies higher growth. On the other hand, each household outside the intermediated sector must choose some combination of the two technologies in isolation and therefore is subjected to consumption which moves up and down with the success and failure of its own projects. There is more risk, a more conservative investment strategy, lower returns, and again, with savings the same fraction of income at low levels of income, lower growth. Initially, there is an unequal distribution of income, and so high-income households are in the financial system and the poor are excluded. Over time, however, more and more of the previously isolated poor save sufficient resources to cover the fixed costs of entry into the intermediated sector. This generates a large rise in measured levels of income and consumption. There is a particularly high rate of increase of growth of intermediation, income, and consumption on the income fringe, so to speak, that is, in expansion areas. Still, at the steady state, the rate of increase of growth slows, but at a higher level of growth than in autarky.

All this is Pareto optimal. It is not economic to finance the fixed entry costs for the poor all at once. Put differently, resources used to finance entry costs would pull others into poverty.

But what do we see in the data? Unfortunately, panel data at the household level are not available in Thailand to carry out the requisite tests of risk sharing and the relationship between risk sharing and growth at the household level. We can, however, make use of the Thai SES survey data by adding up over households in relatively small geographic regions, such as amphoes or, in English, "counties." This gives the average level of consumption and income in counties which were sampled repeatedly. Townsend (1995b) displays the number of households and amphoes which are useable in this way using five years of the SES data.

We can use the county-level income data to decompose income shocks into idiosyncratic and aggregate components. Idiosyncratic shocks are peculiar to a county, something which causes the county-average growth rate of income to diverge from regional- or national-average growth, averaging over all counties in a region or in the kingdom as a whole. As it turns out, income shocks are highly idiosyncratic. Using 193 counties in the north-east from 1988 to 1990, growth rates are dissimilar, with some counties experiencing negative growth or shortfalls of up to 77 percent and with other counties experiencing explosive growth, with growth rates of 111 percent. This is not atypical: a similar pattern emerges across other regions, and across other pairs of years. Moreover, there are relatively few aggregate shocks. That is, there are few common fixed effects in growth rates, effects which are common to a given region and a given pair of years. This is apparent from formal tests reported in table 5.1.

We can sometimes find more common fixed effects by region if we focus attention on specific occupations. Households who report that their principal occupation is farming have more common fixed effects by region and pairs of years, for example. Still, the opposite is true if we restrict attention to rice farmers or to households who report their principal occupation is entrepreneurial (self-employed in industry, trade, and handicrafts). For these groups there are few if any fixed effects – most county-level shocks to their occupation are not shared by other counties in the same region (again, see table 5.1).

Now suppose that all households in a given region (at least all households in an occupational group) were linked up to one another via some common financial system. Then, in principle, idiosyncratic shocks across counties could be pooled. Specifically, under CRRA preferences, county-average consumption growth should track regional-average consumption growth, one to one. Controlling for this common regional shock (fixed effect), county-specific income growth should not influence country-specific consumption growth at all. Indeed, if everyone in the entire kingdom were linked up with one another, then country-average consumption growth should track kingdom-average consumption growth. Even regional shocks would be smoothed.

By this standard, regional- and national-level financial systems in Thailand are imperfect. Formal econometric tests of the risk-sharing hypothesis reject full insurance almost uniformly. Marginal propensities to consume out of idiosyncratic income growth are not zero – coefficients on county-specific income growth are positive and significant, sorting the data by region, pairs of years, and occupation groups. Still, some interesting patterns emerge. Counties in the greater Bangkok area, while experiencing the relatively high levels and growth rates in income and consumption noted earlier, experience as well relatively less insurance. The coefficients on idiosyncratic income growth are relatively high. Similarly, entrepreneurs tend to be less well insured. On the other hand, farmers in the north and the north-east actually pass some tests for full insurance when the 1990 data are excluded from the analysis. Related, please note the common fixed effect in consumption in table 5.1. In regressions the coefficients on idiosyncratic income growth are small and the coefficients on regional-average consumption growth (or a common fixed effect) are high.

These results are directly counter to the prediction of the Greenwood–Jovanovic model on the relationship between insurance and growth. Because growth rates of income and consumption are higher in Bangkok than in other regions, and higher for entrepreneurs than for other occupation groups, one would predict from the model higher levels of insurance, not the other way around. It is possible, of course, that the level of aggregation is leading us astray. Micro, household-level data are needed to sort out whether insurance actually improves (or not) for those entering the financial system. Recall, by way of contrast, that in the model of Lloyd-Ellis and Bernhardt that relatively rich household dynasties experience faster growth through accumulated own savings, not through improved insurance.

In the absence of microdata one can look directly at the major financial institutions of the country and see what provisions for insurance (explicit or implicit) are contained in their operation. Rashid and Townsed (1994) have done this for the Grameen Bank and BRAC in Bangladesh; SEWA and WWF in Ahmnabad and Madras, India; BKK and BRI in Indonesia; and FINCA in Latin America. Appendix B carries out a similar analysis for the BAAC, the Credit Union League, the Temple Wat Ba, and Production Credit Groups (PCGs) of the Community Development Department in Thailand. The interested reader is urged to consult appendix B for details. Suffice it to note here that there are ample possibilities for insurance with the Thai financial organizations.

Other cross-country data would lend support to the Greenwood–Jovanovic hypothesis that there is a link between financial intermediation and growth. Specifically, King and Levine (1993) use various measures of financial intermediation: the ratio of liquidity liabilities of the financial system, M3, to GDP; the ratio of deposits in financial institutions such as banks relative to that plus deposits in the central bank; the proportion of credit allocated to private enterprises excluding credit allocated by government development banks and state-owned enterprise, that is, the ratio of claims on the non-financial private sector to total domestic credit; and the ratio of claims on the non-financial private sector to GDP.

The measures of intermediation that King and Levine use do turn up significant correlations of intermediation with growth in a cross section of 80 countries from 1960 to 1989. In particular, they look at growth of per capita income, growth of capital, levels of investment, and a Solow-like measure of technological progress. Indeed, there is a correlation between lagged financial intermediation and contemporary average growth: "To illustrate the economic size of the coefficient, the results suggest that if in 1970 Zaïre had increased the share of domestic credit allocated by banks as opposed to the central bank from 26 percent to the mean value for developing countries in 1970 (about 57 percent), then Zaïre would have grown 0.9 percent faster each year in the 1970s, and by 1980 real per capita GDP would have been about 9 percent larger than it was."

Table 5.1. *Region, year, and community type patterns in income and consumption growth rates*

		Different occupation groups								Different measures of income and consumption			
	F test for:	All households		All farmers		Rice farmers		Entrepreneurs		All income	No in kind	Wages	Food
		Y	*C*	*Y*	*C*	*Y*	*C*	*Y*	*C*	*Y*	*Y*	*Y*	*C*
1	N: 75–81											*	
2	N: 81–86												
3	N: 86–88						**						
4	N: 88–90									*	**	**	
5	N										**	**	
6	NE: 75–81											**	
7	NE: 81–86												
8	NE: 86–88			**					**		*		*
9	NE: 88–90	**	**	**	**	**	**	**	**	**	*		**
10	NE		**	**	**		**		**			*	**
11	C:75–81												
12	C: 81–86												
13	C: 86–88			**		*	**						
14	C: 88–90			**	**	**							
15	C			**	**	**							
16	S: 75–81												
17	S: 81–86												
18	S: 86–88												

19	S: 88–90	**	**	*		**	
20	S						
21	B: 75–81						
22	B: 81–86						
23	B: 86–88			*			
24	B: 88–90		**	**	**		**
25	B			**			

Notes: This table presents the results of *F*-tests for the joint significance of dummy variables from regressions given by

$$\frac{\overline{\ln y_t^a} - \overline{\ln y_\tau^a}}{t-\tau} - \frac{\overline{\overline{\ln y_t^a}} - \overline{\overline{\ln y_\tau^a}}}{t-\tau} = b_{\tau,\tau}^{r,c}\delta_{t,\tau}^{r,c} + \varepsilon_{t,\tau}^{a,r,c}.$$

The dependent variables are demeaned income (Y) and consumption (C) growth rates. Where the division is by occupation, consumption is equal to expenditures on food, clothing, shoes, and tobacco; and income is equal to wages, profits from farming, entrepreneurial income and income-in-kind. A * indicates that the test is significant at the 10% level, ** indicates significance at the 5% level. N = north, NE = north-east, C = central, S = south, B = Bangkok.

As King and Levine note, however, these illustrative experiments do not consider how to increase the variation in their variable BANK in 1970. Indeed, we are reminded of the model of Greenwood and Jovanovic (1990) which goes further and suggests it is not optimal to increase intermediation precisely because there are costs. So though the empirical results of King and Levine are suggestive of the intermediation results of the Greenwood–Jovanovic model, and roughly support the arguments of BAAC, CULT, PCG, and other Thai program officials that credit (and savings) are a good thing and that program expansion is desirable, the theory and the empirical results offer no real guidance on how fast credit programs should be expanded, and at what costs. Indeed, the Thai SES insurance results suggest that the mechanisms of growth may be unrelated to the insurance components being provided by informal and formal intermediation systems. Of course, this does not mean the logic of insurance theory is wrong. Even if current systems are limited, improved systems of risk sharing may actually increase growth rates and lessen inequality in the distribution of consumption and income.

A related criticism: what measures of financial intermediation should one use? In the Greenwood–Jovanovic model, those in the intermediated sector place all savings in banks while borrowing to finance enterprise activity. So for them the measure of the level of liquid liabilities goes up. However, incomes go up as well. Indeed, the ratio, the savings rate, is exactly the same as for those in the non-intermediated sector, at least for those who do not anticipate to be linked for a long time. Only those about to bear costs of entry save relatively more, suggesting higher savings rates in regions where there is new intermediary activity. However, those outside the intermediated sector save outside the sector, so the presumed increased savings is unmeasured. (Related, the models of Lloyd-Ellis and Bernhardt, and Deaton allow for bequests or savings but are unclear about whether this is done by the individual household alone or through a savings account in a financial institution. In the context of the present discussion, this distinction matters.) Recall also various of the measures assume a distinction between government and non-government savings and finance. These have no analogue in the Greenwood–Jovanovic model.

More generally, the model of Greenwood and Jovanovic allows intermediation and credit-insurance systems at the regional and national levels but contemplates only two extremes. Households in the intermediated sector are not credit-constrained in any way and receive perfect insurance, that is, perfect smoothing with others in the intermediated sector. Households outside the intermediated sector save on their own into their own technologies; there is no intermediation whatsoever, not locally, not even with nearby neighbors. The model of Greenwood and Jovanovic does not allow intermediation to vary, say with good accommodation of local shocks in small groups or in villages, but less accommodation nationally across villages and regions. Related, local systems may be less costly.

8 MICROLEVEL TESTS OF RISK SHARING AND EFFICIENCY

The starting point for an extended analysis of risk sharing and efficiency would be a group of households. The group could be as small as a very local within-village kinship group or a small BAAC joint liability group. Moving up, the group could be all members of a village-level rice bank, a local credit union, or an entire village. Alternatively, the group of households could be a group of cross-village, family-related households or members of the district-level BAAC. Finally, the group could be everyone connected to some national-level organization, or the entire national-level economy itself.

We shall assume in the remainder of this section that markets or an equivalent set of institutions are perfect for any such group, derive implications from this assumption, and discuss how to implement empirical tests with household data. The focus is on the groups, at various levels of aggregation, and how to test for risk-sharing and efficiency.

So imagine a collection of households together for their entire lives. Each household is presumed to try to maximize expected discounted utility from a utility function which is separable over time and has as its arguments consumption and leisure. Each household owns various technologies, that is, has access to livestock, distinguishing types of animals; agriculture, distinguishing crops, soils and location of land; and perhaps to forestry. Each technology is subject to idiosyncratic, household-specific shocks and to aggregate, common shocks, that is, shocks common to the group. There are, as well, shocks to households internally, e.g., sickness, illness, death, and disability. But the group need not be considered in isolation to other groups or markets. Quite possibly, consumption, labor, livestock, and capital goods may be exchanged across groups in these markets. Related, individual households in the group can store grain and money and may be able to borrow or lend, or to give and receive remittances, in external markets, or within individuals and outside institutions.

The presumption, however, is that within-group consumption and leisure allocations are Pareto optimal for the group. This is, within-group credit and insurance markets (or an equivalent set of institutions) function perfectly well, while the smoothing with credit and insurance allowed by outsiders may be limited. Analytically, one can characterize these optimal allocations by maximizing a weighted sum of household utilities subject to a group-wide budget constraint (or resource constraint), that the value of consumption and leisure of the group plus all purchased inputs such as seed and pesticide and all purchased capital inputs such as tractors and livestock of the group should not exceed the value to the group of gross crop output, livestock and assets sold plus income received from outside labor supply plus income from the decumulation of currency and grain stocks plus resources from acquisition of new loans less the paying off of old debts, the giving of remittances and the paying of insurance premia.

The implications of this full-insurance model for any particular group are well known. First, as in the description of risk-sharing in the Greenwood–Jovanovic model, household consumption and leisure should move with group-average consumption and leisure, as if there were common time-varying fixed effects for the group. Household-specific income shocks should have zero residual effects. Further tests along this line are reported momentarily. Second, household consumption and leisure decisions should be separate from production decisions, the standard neoclassical separation hypothesis extended to incorporate risk. Separation has been tested by Benjamin (1992), and also Feder *et al.* (1991) (both noted above), asking whether household labor and other demographic variables have an effect on production beyond time-varying wages or prices facing the group and/or internal shadow prices picked by a group fixed effect. Third, the group's use of currency, livestock, other real and financial assets should all be consistent with one another. Assets dominated in return should be held by no one. We shall come back to the group's smoothing relative to the outside economy in the discussion below.

Much of the existing empirical work has taken the "natural" group to be the village and proceeded with the empirical tests just outlined. Townsend (1994b) conducts extensive tests of villages as risk-sharing groups using data from the International Crops Research Institute of the Semi-Arid Tropics (ICRISAT). Part of the analysis establishes that taken one at a time households fail to take much advantage of diversification possibilities across soil, space, crops, and income sources. With the exception of Kanzara, per capita incomes across households in the village do not co-move much. The second part of the analysis establishes the relatively low influence of present household income on present household consumption: the marginal propensity for a household to consume out of idiosyncratic changes in income was no larger than 0.14 in any of the three villages. Versions of the permanent-income model which permit households to smooth present consumption against income fluctuations by borrowing and lending (as noted above) would make this coefficient close to the village real rate of interest, but reported real rates are much higher than this. However, the income coefficients are statistically positive, thus rejecting the hypothesis of full insurance. The analysis also explores the sensitivity of consumption to other shocks. Neither unemployment nor sickness have a significant impact on a household's consumption.

There are, though, various anomalous patterns in these ICRISAT data and in other data. First, there are variations across households within villages, suggesting at least that the village may not be the "natural" group. Second, there are great variations across villages in apparently similar environments. Third, there may be patterns across relative to integration with the national (growing) economy. We shall take up each of these issues in turn.

First, then, the issue of disparities within villages. In the ICRISAT village of Aurepalle, the poor, landless laborers are significantly less well insured than their village neighbors, the landed farmers (see Townsend (1994b) and Morduch (1991)).

Field research in northern villages in Thailand seems to reinforce the ICRISAT results. An analysis of the village of Yang Pieng in Amphoe Omgoi is illustrative of the analysis. Specifically households in Yang Pieng are found to be producing rice almost exclusively. Yet rice yields vary from farmer to farmer, and good years and bad years are not coincident. Again we have income diversity. The sources of variation are rank ordered by farmers: variable monsoon rains and uneven flow of water within the region are said by virtually all farmers to be the dominant source of fluctuations, but crop diseases and pests are listed as important secondary sources of risk. (Other villages in the survey mention crop disease or pests as the most significant source of variation.) (For more details, see Townsend (1995a).)

Despite this diversity in income fluctuations in Yang Pieng, household consumption and labor supply should co-move. Again, this requires that households be linked to one another either via networks of friends and relatives or via community institutions. But one discovers from village stays and questionnaire responses a group of relatively well-off households who smooth with rice in storage or with the purchase and sale of livestock and who are not linked to others. Such households might pass tests of the permanent income hypothesis, partially smoothing consumption against contemporary shocks, but such asset transactions are not enough to get their consumption to co-move if their incomes do not co-move also. Similarly, village stays and the questionnaires suggest there is a group of relatively poor households who smooth in part with increased labor supply and with borrowing and lending, either from friends and relatives or from a village rice bank. These may be enough to get consumption to co-move for this group. On the other hand, some said increased labor supply was linked to dwindling own storage, and own storage seemed to vary across households experiencing diverse income shocks. Thus labor supply would not co-move. Labor supply linked to asset levels needs to be better documented. Incidentally, some poor households confirm that they use the rice bank first, while others go to friends and relatives. The cost and benefits of quasi-formal institutions versus informal networks needs to be understood, both in theory and practice. We are alerted in particular to the possibility of differential costs.

Another apparent fact from the village stays in Thailand and from the questionnaires is significant variation in arrangements across villages. In amphoe Maajaam, for example, three villages, Mae Wak, Sop Wak, and Maanajohn, all within walking distance to one another, vary considerably in their institutions and risk-response mechanisms.

Mae Wak, for example, has a credit union or PCG fund, a rice bank, a household wife fund, and various input-financing funds. All households in Mae Wak contribute savings to these funds, making them eligible to finance inputs if not year-to-year fluctuations in consumption. Unlike Yang Pieng, all households are linked to one another via these community institutions. No household in Mae Wak reported itself to be credit-constrained, and savings and rice have accumulated in these funds to the extent that the village has become a regional lender. Community measures of financial intermediation would appear to be high.

In contrast, the village of Sop Wak, down the road, was experiencing problems with both its rice bank and its savings funds. Defaults on unpaid loans were said to be a significant problem, and participation in these organizations, and the credit supplied by them, was much more limited than in neighboring Mae Wak. One wonders, of course, if there are local lenders or a broader informal market, as substitutes.

Maanajohn, also nearby, has virtually no community-level institutions. A previously established rice bank was said to have failed with the corruption of a previous headman. Indeed, village stays and the questionnaires turned up poor landless or small landholders responding to bad years with increased labor supply, only. As in Yang Pieng, described above, if incomes after labor supply do not co-move among this group of poor households, and they appear not to do so, then consumption could not co-move. Perhaps a rice bank or other local financial intermediary would prove useful. Yet the only community level "organization" apparent to this researcher was a traditional death benefit system, with all households contributing to a fund for any bereaved family. Nevertheless, the questionnaire did turn up a lively village credit market, both with "traditional" moneylenders and with some kind of network among friends and relatives (though interest is sometimes charged). Loans were frequently said to have provisions for risk. Maanajohn also suffers from land fragmentation. Many households have multiple, spatially separated plots. The adoption of high-yield, high-risk rice varieties was also not in evidence, unlike for its two village neighbors. Perhaps less than adequate risk sharing is leading to costly fragmentation or to low-yield investment strategies, as the work of Morduch (1993) suggests.

In summary, then, there appear to be significant variations across villages even in similar environments. What is the source of this variation? Is it due to more subtle variations in the local ecology after all? Is it due to variations in the ability of the headman or in "human capital" more generally?

A final village of the northern Thai survey is of some interest. Village Ba Pai in amphoe Lee lies along both sides of a major highway to Bangkok and is much more involved in the commercial economy than any other village in this field research. No one was growing rice for subsistence. All were growing cash crops. Like Maanajohn, Ba Pai has no community organizations. More surprisingly, it lacks as well a village credit market. Ba Pai farmers to have access to BAAC loans, and despite diversity in production, few in the survey complained of a shortage of credit. Perhaps income movements are more uniform in this village, as in the ICRISAT village of Kanzara, and internal credit is not needed. Still, the questionnaires also turned up households having suffered loss of income from episodes of serious illness. No one came to their assistance. Indeed, the headman pointed to several "abandoned" elderly in the village, rare for the Thai society. These latter observations from Ba Pai are not inconsistent with the hypothesis that indigenous risk-systems might decline as an economy grows.

More generally, one needs to integrate more reliable facts at the local level or village level with patterns of growth and intermediation at the regional or national level. We need to take the geography seriously, as in the models of Krugman (1991) or Tae Jeong Lee (1994), for example. Specifically, we need to evaluate local, regional, and national financial institutions to see what role they do play or could play in the allocation of credit and risk. Are national systems coping well with the supposed demise of indigenous systems? How do local, informal systems of moneylenders or networks operate and do these resemble the operation of banks as we envision in formal models in Diamond and Dybvig (1983), Krasa and Villamil (1992), or Boyd and Prescott (1986), for example?

9 FINANCIAL SECTOR LIBERALIZATION, INFLATION, AND GROWTH

The BAAC is a rural development bank. It is quasi-autonomous; it does try to cover its costs. While the BAAC's loan rate ceiling is below market rates, the BAAC long resisted (during the 1980s) recurrent political criticism that it does not lend at low enough rates and that its collateral and personal lending criteria are too stiff for the lowest-income (smallest holders, etc.) farmers. The BAAC's response to criticism has been that it must retain its spread between the (concessional) costs of these institutional deposits and the interest rates charged to borrowers in order to cover its loan administration costs and avoid decapitalization. But the BAAC is not completely independent of government fiscal policy. It is still partially funded by transfers from the Department of the Interior, and there are recurrent pressures to engineer transfers to poor regions or those hard hit in areas of distress. This is much in evidence in the recent monsoon flooding of 1995. The work on risk sharing reviewed earlier would suggest that this is not necessarily a bad thing to do.

Still, extrapolating from contemporary policy debates in African and Latin American countries, some policy analysts would surely argue that it would be optimal for the Thai government to reduce or eliminate any threat to the government budget, that the BAAC should be privatized or at least made completely autonomous, and that interest rate controls or subsidized credit be eliminated entirely. Many policy analysts in other countries argue that the elimination of the government's deficits and other macro stabilization programs should come first, before financial-sector liberalization is attempted. If this is done, or so the argument goes, then financial-sector liberalization will increase savings and credit, build financial infrastructure, and ultimately benefit the poor. Indeed, it is implicit in these policy circles that these proximate targets are adequate measures of economic welfare.

Here, however, consistent with the policy algorithm, none of these conclusions is taken for granted. Imagine, for example, a well-articulated model economy that gives rise to both credit and valued currency. In the model economy of Manuelli and Sargent (1994), for example, credit is used among agents in enduring relationships while currency is used among relative strangers, as in Townsend (1980). Specifically, itinerant agents traveling in one direction meet itinerant agents traveling in the opposite direction. At the trading posts where they meet they are paired for two periods, and after this each type resumes its travels to the next post. Because production opportunities change over time, it is worthwhile to enter into two-period loans, but because one of the agent types will enter the next trading post in a period of relatively low income, it is worthwhile to carry currency into that meeting.

This model offers some cautionary tales. First, it is Pareto improving for the government to end any transfers associated with a monetary expansion, but only up to a point. Specifically, one Pareto-optimal allocation is for the government to pay interest on currency and finance this with lump-sum taxes, something akin to Friedman's well-known rule on the optimal quantity of money. But a movement to this equilibrium from a noninterventionist stable money equilibrium is not necessarily Pareto improving. The policy shift is associated with a redistribution which injures certain parties.

Second, suppose interest rates were set so low that credit markets were suppressed. Then financial-sector deregulation, allowing rates to rise to their equilibrium level, would be Pareto improving. But such liberalization can be associated with jumps in the price level (inflation), less real savings, and greater fluctuations in output. Proximate targets in this model economy are terrible indicators of real household welfare.

Unlike the model of Greenwood and Jovanovic described earlier, the model of Manuelli and Sargent envisions good intermediation locally, but not globally. Agents who meet for two periods equate intertemporal marginal rates of substitution, that is, get to some local optimum, but they are then thrown back into the larger national economy where they meet, temporarily, with relative strangers. This is no doubt contrived. We need to build up model economies around observed patterns of local and national exchange, that is, of observed patterns of credit and currency. This cannot be done without taking a good look at household data.

Indeed, the earlier discussion of risk-sharing within and across groups is relevant here. Perhaps the village is a local, stable unit, with an excellent system for sharing inputs and risks, but the village is more isolated in its dealings with outsiders, using currency, for example.

Lim and Townsend (1994) have found only limited evidence for these conclusions in the ICRISAT villages in India. The primary device appears to be crop inventory, consistent with a buffer stock model of the village economy. This is particularly true in the village of Shirapur. But currency changes do play a smoothing role in Kanzara and Aurepalle, spending down accumulated balances during deficits, though the levels are off. Still credit is non-zero, though it plays a somewhat erratic role. These somewhat complicated village-aggregate patterns deserve to be better modeled.

Within-village patterns are of interest as well. Relatively large landholders tend to use crop inventory while relatively small landholders tend to use currency. Again, models of currency and credit need to be built up around measured facts.

Deserving of special attention is the use of currency and national-level credit systems. Again, we imagine some households and some villages are imperfectly integrated into the larger national system, but we do know the facts. Of course one should keep track as well of informal systems, the family and kinship-related households, rather than villages per. se. Rosenzweig (1988) has found that in India households may marry daughters out over space. In that way, remittances can flow among areas, depending on who is suffering a negative shock. In the Côte d'Ivoire, Grimard (1992) sorted the data from the World Bank's Living Standards Measurement Survey by tribe and has argued that networks among tribes allow greater consumption smoothing than is apparent in the non-sorted data. Paulson (1994) has studied remittances from migrants in Thailand and has concluded that these play a role in where to go *ex ante* and what to send home *ex post*. Also, remittances in Thailand are large.

10 SUBSIDIZED CREDIT: INCENTIVE-COMPATIBLE TRANSFER SCHEMES

As noted, it is the goal of the Thai government to help the relatively poor, and it seeks to do this with subsidized credit through the BAAC. Similarly, the Temple Wat Ba does not try to break even; it relies on altruistically motivated transfers of the Thai and international communities. This flies in the face of conventional wisdom that financial organizations should be self-sustaining, that profitability be the sole criterion of ultimate success. Indeed, the conventional wisdom in economics is that altruistically motivated transfers be lump sum, separated if possible from the operation of credit and other markets.

In fact, when information is incomplete, an optimal information-constrained transfer system is not necessarily lump sum. That is, one cannot separate the operation of credit and insurance markets from the transfers of altruistically motivated donors. If follows that the BAAC and the Temple Wat Ba would show losses on their accounts, as more resources are passed through these organizations than are recovered. One needs other metrics to determine if transfer-cum-credit schemes are efficient.

Related, in an optimally designed information-constrained system, certain types of competition are not necessarily a good thing. One must distinguish *ex ante* competition in the right to provide financial contracts from *ex post* competition for customers and the rights of customers to unrestricted access to available markets and institutions.

Because these propositions are hardly self-evident, we explore one particular model economy in somewhat greater detail to illustrate results. Specifically, building on Phelan and Townsend (1991), consider a bank which acquires funds at an outside, competitive rate of interest or funds which are priced at this interest rate even if acquired without cost or obligation from an outside donor, as in the construction of Yaron's (1991) subsidy dependency index. The bank lends then onlends these funds to client borrowers. Each borrower has an investment project which yields profits as a function of the amount of credit-financed input and of individual effort. More effort raises the likelihood of success, but effort is unobserved by the bank. But suppose profits and the use of credit-financed inputs are observed by the bank. Finally, unlike the models of Piketty (1994) and Aghion and Bolton (1992), suppose borrowers are risk averse.

A feasible loan contract is a standard loan contract in which the borrower promises to repay principal and interest no matter what. (Imagine default is simply impossible.) This might make the amount the client is willing to borrow quite small, and risk aversion has a similar effect. The client does not want to face the prospect of paying back a relatively large loan when profits are relatively low; consumption would suffer too much. Indeed, a risk-averse borrower would prefer consumption which is stable in the face of income fluctuations, and if the bank is "risk-neutral" or has a well-diversified portfolio of loans, it can provide this insurance at a price.

If there were full information on labor effort, the bank could provide full insurance. It would be possible in this circumstance to control labor effort and avoid moral hazard problems. Indeed, an altruistic bank, or a bank financed by donors, could raise the welfare of its client borrowers by simply raising the level of promised consumption. In effect the bank's operations would be separated into three components. First, the bank lends credit to client borrowers at the outside, competitive rate of interest, expecting complete repayment. Second, the bank also provides complete insurance to the borrower, covered by *ex ante* premia. Finally, the bank passes a transfer to client borrowers via a lump-sum payment. The financial accounts – for borrowing/lending and insurance at least – would show no losses.

If the effort of the borrower is known only to the borrower, however, then insurance causes an incentive problem. Faced with stable consumption, even when income is low, there is no incentive to work hard, to raise the likelihood of profits. To circumvent this, the bank offers a contract with a carefully tailored blend of credit and insurance. Consumption of the borrower would be higher if profits were higher, and this induces higher effort. But the bank would co-insure with the borrower, in effect taking in a premium when output is high in return for handing out an indemnity when output is low. The borrower does not incur all of the income risk.

Now, imagine in this context that the bank is making positive (or non-negative) profits and an altruistic donor takes over the bank, determined to increase the welfare of client borrowers. This can be done by passing resources through the bank. Now, however, the optimal information-constrained transfer need not be lump sum. At higher levels of wealth or average consumption, the borrower may be less risk averse, making the threat of low consumption when profits are low less effective. This is circumvented by cutting back somewhat on the level of insurance. Though consumption of the borrower is higher than before in states of both high and low profits, the spread, the consumption difference between high and low profits, increases. The ultimate objective is to induce effort by controlling consumption, and lump-sum consumption transfers do not have this property.

If we make this model dynamic, with repeated financing of investment projects by a bank, then a corollary to the story emerges. In a multi-period setting the bank will try to induce high effort not only with high consumption in the event of high profits now, but also higher promised welfare in the future. In effect there is a long-term relationship of the bank with each client borrower, so that high profits and relatively high repayment are rewarded both in the present and in the future, with more favorable loan terms in the next loan cycle on. On the other hand, client borrowers with relatively low profits suffer not only diminished consumption in the present but also less advantageous terms in the future. It is the threat of disadvantageous terms which helps to induce higher effort now.

Still, underlying risk can cause profits to be low when the borrower has been diligent, so some clients experience diminishing welfare. Indeed, the discounted expected utility of these borrowers can fall so low that they would like to tear up the long-term agreement and start over. The bank would be making relatively high profits on these borrowers, and it would be tempting for a new bank to try to coax disgruntled customers away. This kind of *ex post* competition would drive profits to zero, and benefit customers *ex post*, but such competition is not optimal *ex ante*. Ironically, a competitive "safety net" causes banks to lose their ability to induce high effort, and both banks and the client borrower are made worse off *ex ante*.

Again, the above model is presented as an example. The particular scheme which might be optimal *ex ante* depends on the specifics of the environment and the information structure. If household data are available, econometric tests of efficiency are possible.

11 MECHANISM DESIGN AND MICRODATA

Precisely this model was taken to the village-level ICRISAT data by Ethan Ligon (1993). Following the logic of some earlier work by Rogerson (1985), the multi-agent, principal agent model yields a Euler equation or relationship among marginal utilities of present and future consumption. Yet this relationship is not the standard Euler equation of the permanent income literature, and with some (unpleasant) assumptions about aggregate uncertainty, it can be taken to data. Indeed, fixing risk-aversion parameters at a priori reasonable values one discovers that this particular private information model fits the ICRISAT data better than permanent-income or full-insurance alternatives.

By construction the principal in this private-information model acquires full control over all household assets, in order to better control consumption and avoid shirking. Indeed, the above-mentioned Euler equation then implies a peculiar feature: households in the model economy are "saving constrained." They would like to save more but are not allowed to do so. This takes us back, of course, to the earlier liquidity-constrained models reviewed earlier, with the twist here that it is savings, not credit, that is the "problem." But again the allocations here are information-constrained Pareto optimal. One should not let households have full and complete access to savings accounts. Incredibly, even currency accumulation and decumulation should be controlled. There may be savings in the aggregate but again the principal has sole control over this.

One wonders, of course, about the plausibility of the model and auxiliary assumptions which allow the empirical tests. A related literature goes about testing in a different way. Specifically, the private information model under scrutiny allows households to be awarded and penalized based on past histories and contemporary realizations of project yields. This creates diversity in the population of borrowers, a diversity which only increases over the life cycle of borrowers. That is, the variance of the histogram of consumption in the population increases with the age of cohort borrowers. A similar kind of spreading occurs under versions of the permanent income and other private-information models, but quantitatively the mapping from parameters of preferences and technology to the variance of the consumption histograms is different for different models. Phelan (1990) works all of this out and compares his model with the actual spread in US PSID data. Deaton and Paxson (1994) document increasing consumption dispersion in Taiwan, the UK, and other countries.

A related empirical feature which deserves mention here is so-called segmentation of credit markets. As Siamwalla *et al.* (1990), Aleem (1990), and other observers noted, rural credit markets in Thailand and Pakistan have the feature that borrowers often have long-term relationships with one of the several lenders, rarely switching. We have seen above that long-term relationships are *ex ante* optimal under the private-information models under discussion here, and so the literature on segmentation would suggest that information-constrained model economies are good approximations to actual rural economies.

More directly, though, one needs to posit realistic models with information constraints and this can only be done if we measure information sets directly, as in the work of Udry (1990), Townsend (1995a), and Mueller and Townsend (1993).

Now let us turn to the details of credit arrangements with a focus on production. The key driving force in information-constrained optimal arrangements is the inference that the laborer or borrower was diligent or not, the so-called likelihood ratio. If this ratio is in turn influenced by a second credit-financed input, then that input can serve a role as monitor, quite beyond the impact of that input on output directly. Ongoing research (of the author with Ethan Ligon and Andreas Lehnert) has thus produced numerical examples where the principal wants to retain control of this second input, even if its application is fully observed. That is, it is Pareto optimal not to have the principal on-lend credit to the agent-borrower at the outside rate of interest applicable to the principal. The best arrangement is to specify the allocation of credit in advance. A second-best arrangement is to let the borrower choose, but possibly at a "subsidized" interest rate. Either way, the borrower might appear credit constrained, but it is Pareto optimal here that he be so.

A related point brings us at last to endogenous selection and to the distinction between formal and informal credit arrangements. Suppose the principal or local moneylender has access to outside funds, a major cost of doing business, but otherwise offers an information-constrained credit contract with the optimal blend of credit and insurance. Suppose further that competition among potential lenders drives any lender's expected *ex ante* profits to zero, and that at that level there are willing borrowers. In contrast suppose the principal or outside formal lender offers simple credit contracts, obligating the borrower to repay, or forcing bankruptcy. The consequent welfare loss in the second scheme can cause there to be a "missing market." At no welfare level for the borrower can the outside lender sustain positive profits. Ongoing research (mentioned earlier) thus delivers numerical examples of local arrangements separated from more formal markets.

Related, suppose information about project outputs can be acquired at a cost, and that these costs vary with the location of the potential client borrowers. Some villages may be near the bank's branch office, in some district town, and other villages may be quite distant. Then the bank may not make profits on distant villages and it may not select such villages as customers. In effect we have a model of banks which explains limited access. Distant villages may complain of being credit constrained in the sense of Feder *et al.*, but it would be Pareto optimal in the model economy that they be so. These kinds of models seem to have great promise.

A remaining issue in mechanism design has to do with groups and hierarchy in financial systems. Space does not permit an extensive review of the theoretical and applied literature on the subject. Suffice it to note that there are models of group formation based on internal monitoring

(Holmstrom and Milgrom (1990), Itoh (1988), E.S. Prescott and Townsend (1994)); on internal expertise (Varian (1990)); and on screening (Varian (1990)). There are also issues of limited commitment and default, by group members as in Besley (1992), or by bank officials as in Tirole (1985). There are larger enforcement and bargaining issues, as in the work on incomplete contracts in Hart and Moore (1988). There is work more in the "centralized," mechanism design tradition of Banerjee *et al.* (1992) on rotating credit associations, and of Besley, Coate and Loury (1993) on savings funds. There are models of banks based on delegated monitoring, of Boyd and Prescott (1986) and Krasa and Villamil (1992) and the models of bank regulation, of Diamond and Dybvig (1983) and subsequent literature. Some of these models make use of the coalition of the whole, raising the issue of how to define a bank both in theory and in practice.

APPENDIX A
BACKGROUND ON FOUR THAI PROGRAMS

1 The Bank for Agriculture and Agricultural Cooperatives

The Bank for Agriculture and Agricultural Cooperatives (BAAC) is quite explicit about its policy goals, both in its annual report of 1990 and in descriptive documents. The major goals are:

1. The extension of credit to as many farmers as possible, to reduce dependency on informal-sector loans. Specifically: "Experience in Thailand and elsewhere shows that without government intervention, small-scale farmers have very limited access to credit. Left to themselves, commercial banks normally lend very little to agriculture because they consider the administrative costs and risks to be high. Private money lenders are willing to lend, but on terms which severely limit the benefits which farmers may derive from their loans, and which may cause a continuing cycle of indebtedness with no corresponding improvement in technology or productivity" ("Introducing BAAC").
2. Expand field units to District Branches – clients need not travel to towns for dispersement and repayment of loans nor for savings (see map, BAAC Annual Report 1990, figure 5.2).
3. To increase credit opportunities for poor and small-scale farmers. Specifically the relatively new "Whole Village" program lends to all eligible to borrow in selected villages, not just selected, narrowly qualified medium-scale clients. Still, the view persists in the organization that lending to the poor is

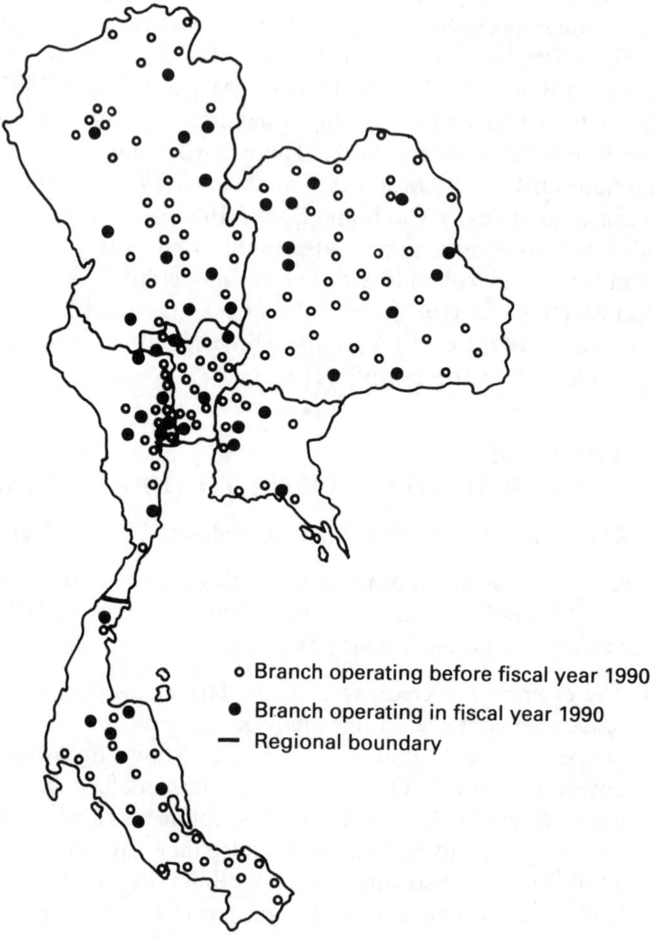

Figure 5.2 BAAC's operating area, 1990

expensive, and thus if lending to the poor had been the original objective of the Bank all along, the Bank would not cover its costs, that it would have failed or would have been taken over by another government agency.

4 Increase cooperative services such as agricultural marketing services to coordinate the purchase of supplies and the sale of products.

5 Promote modern farming techniques, in collaboration with the private sector.
6 Provide special loan facilities for farmers in distress, such as those experiencing tropical storms (IRA) and plant disease (brown plant hoppers).

In fact, the BAAC is a large and growing organization. It opened 50 new branches from 1989 to 1990, many upgraded from field office status but some in previously "remote" areas. The number of branches is now 168. It is reaching 3.1 million farm families, or about 59 percent of all Thai farmers, an increase of 10 percent in 1989–90. This has been accompanied by a large increase in savings (BAAC Annual Report 1990, figure 5.3), reaching 20,000 million baht, and large increases in dispersed loans (BAAC Annual Report 1990, figure 5.4), about an 18 percent increase overall from 1989 to 1990. The bank does this by lending to individual clients, to groups, to cooperatives and to farmer associations (BAAC Annual Report 1990, figure 5.5); and by lending for rice, maize, sugar, soybeans, cassava, livestock and poultry, tree crops and fishery (BAAC Annual Report 1990, figure 5.6); and by an array of short- and long-term loans (BAAC Annual Report 1990, figure 5.7).

Of particular interest here, rates on savings in Thailand, including those of the Bank, are without ceilings, and so the Bank is in competition with private-sector commercial banks for funds, at 8.5 percent at the time of this survey (summer 1989). However, rates on loans to individual client borrowers are still regulated, set at 12.5 percent, and it is from this spread that the Bank is supposed to cover its costs. In fact, the Bank can relend some of its "idle" funds at higher "market" rates. It also receives by law 20 percent of commercial bank deposits, if the banks themselves have not invested in agriculture and agriculture related business, though it pays close to the market rate of interest on these funds. Curiously, commercial banks can lend to farms at 14 percent, though they require collateral, and lend at a prime rate of 16.5 percent to merchants. Commercial banks claim they need 12 percent to cover costs. The Bank's ratio of operating expenses to the average value of loans is only 4.55 percent. It is thus seen that the BAAC is a lean organization intent on minimizing costs. And, in contrast to the world's experience with government development banks, most of the Bank's operating funds are from the public or from commercial banks; there is little dependence on foreign capital or on the Bank of Thailand. Finally, its repayment rates rank among the world's best, with overdue loans at about 8 percent of loans outstanding, and with intensive accounting and monitoring of past due loans (BAAC Annual Report 1990, figure 5.8).

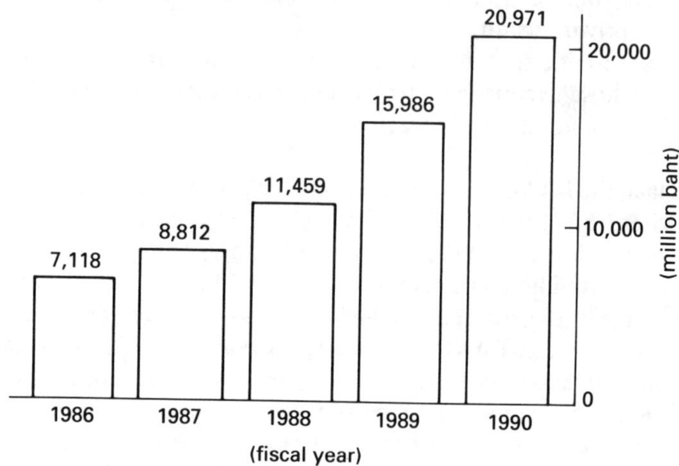

Figure 5.3 Deposit from the general public, fiscal years 1986–1990, BAAC

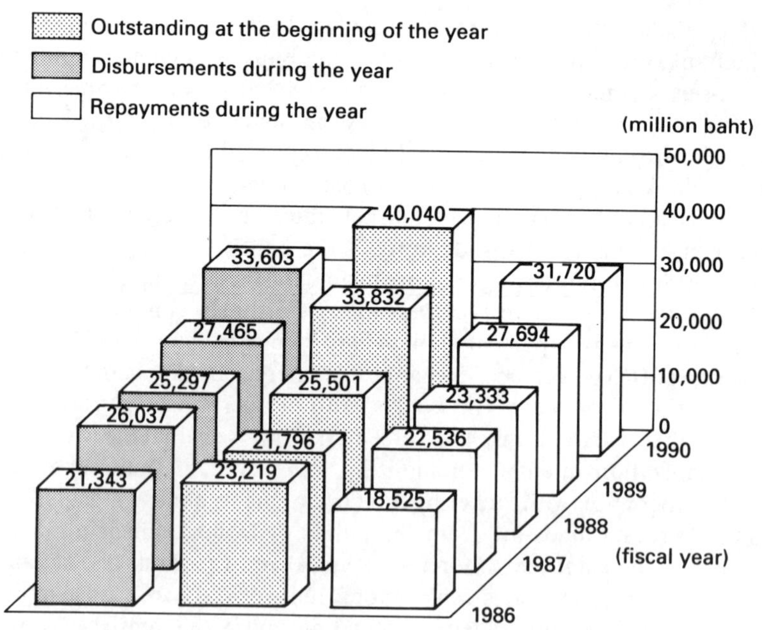

Figure 5.4 Lending operations (all categories), fiscal years 1986–1990, BAAC

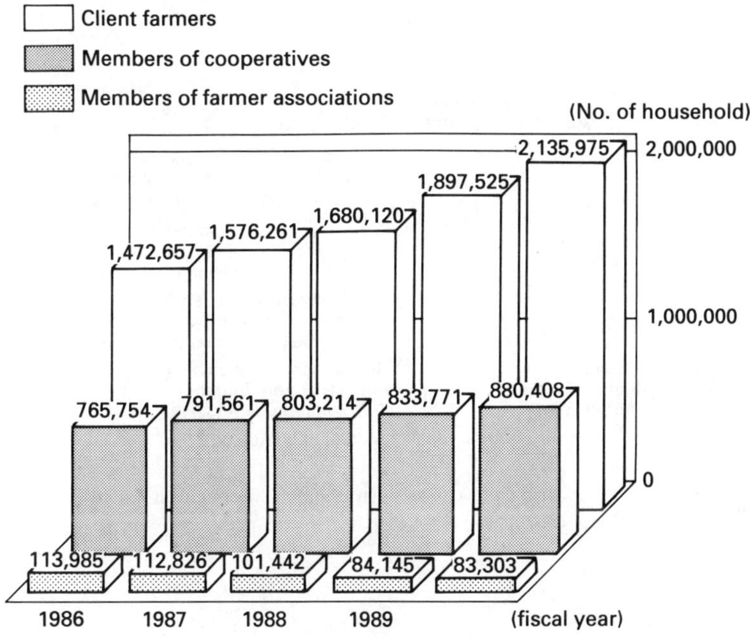

Figure 5.5 Farm households serviced by BAAC, fiscal years 1986–1990

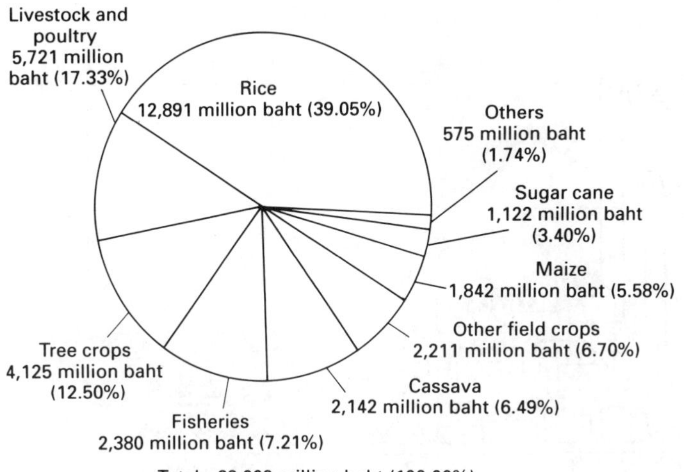

Figure 5.6 Lending operations with client farmers classified by production purpose, fiscal year 1990, BAAC

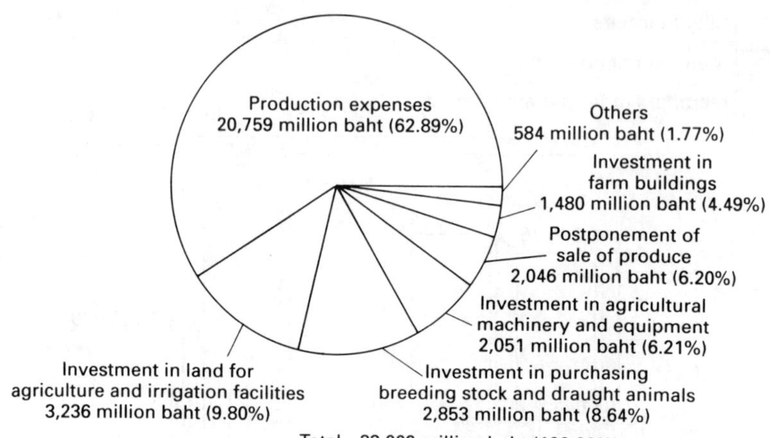

Figure 5.7 Lending operations with client farmers classified by purpose, fiscal year 1990, BAAC

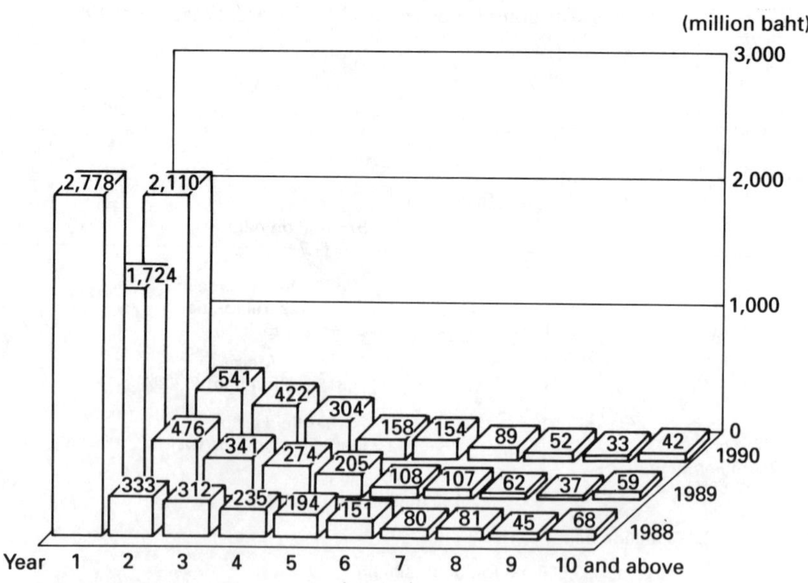

Figure 5.8 Age classification of past due loans (to client farmers), fiscal years 1988–1990, BAAC

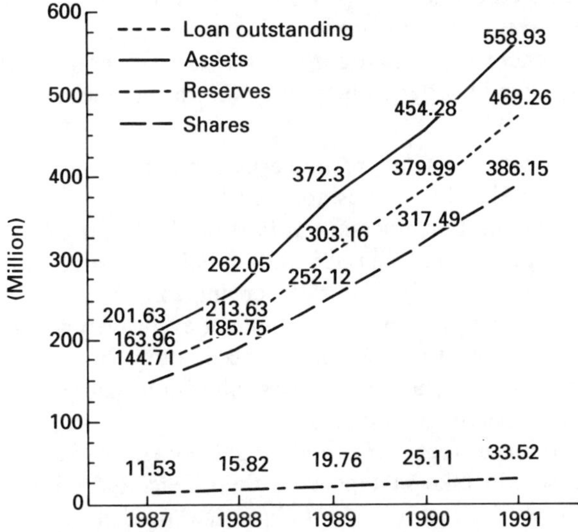

Figure 5.9 Financial growth of credit union

2 The Credit Union League of Thailand

A contrast in goals and size is provided by the Credit Union League of Thailand (CULT), a private, non-government financial organization. Its goals, like credit unions elsewhere in the world, are also explicit. From its literature and interviews with its officers, its goals are:

1. To boost the growth of Thai credit union movement to the extent that it serves at its full capacity the socio-economic uplift of the Thai community. Again, a link among low income, low saving, little investment, and bad technology is envisioned.
2. To strengthen existing credit unions in efficiency and management, to make a strong people's organization. It does this by emphasizing various programs for staff and members in management and accounting, with the goal of administrative autonomy for each union. It aims to reduce dependency on government, emphasizing self-help. Each union has a board of directors, an administrative committee, an education committee, a supervisory committee, and a credit committee. CULT is willing in principle to elicit savings in deposits and shares from the relatively well off in a given local community.

3 To encourage credit unions to become involved in the national cooperative movement, while maintaining autonomy.
4 To encourage members to save for times of distress, household needs, and to save in order to help others in the community.

In fact CULT is a medium-scale but growing organization. Started in the context of a slum in Bangkok, it has now established 482 unions in all major areas of the country, and has a membership in 1991 of 91,885 individuals. Total savings in shares in 1991 reached 386 million baht, and assets and loans have been increasing annually, about 25 percent from 1989 to 1990 (see figure 5.9). The credit union is primarily but not exclusively a rural lender and makes loans not only for investment in occupations, but also for debt release, home improvement, family expenses, education, emergencies, and other smaller categories (see figure 5.10).

Curiously, CULT unions are registered under the Cooperative Security Act of Thailand and so can take savings from the public, and CULT's explicit strategy is to keep this rate at 1 point above the "market," e.g., 9.5 instead of 8.5 percent. There is, in addition, an interbank lending program, and a local union can borrow from Bangkok at 14 percent. Unions in turn lend to their members at about 15–18 percent per year. Still, most funds are raised locally, in shares, paying dividends of about 5–10 percent. Interbank lending stands at 23 million baht, relative to members' own funds at 249 million baht. Initial generation of funds make typical CULT unions different from typical BAAC groups and typical agriculture cooperatives.

One may ask in all of this exactly what the "market rates" on savings and loans are supposed to be, were one to contemplate liberalization. More to the point, there seems to be significant interregional disparities in interest rates, and limits to instantaneous growth.

CULT's delinquency rate is at a low 2.40 percent in August 1993. It accomplishes this with incredibly few staff, for example, 52 overall. Administrative costs, if any, are borne locally. Nationally, the organization is largely self-sustaining, covering 90 percent of its funding; the residual comes from Germany and from the Canadian Cooperative Association (CCA).

3 The Northern Thai Temple Wat Ba – Foundation for Education and Development of Rural Areas

A third program, much different apparently from the first two, is run from the temple grounds of Wat Ba, in district Maa Rim, near Chiengmai. The founder of the Foundation for Education and Development of Rural areas

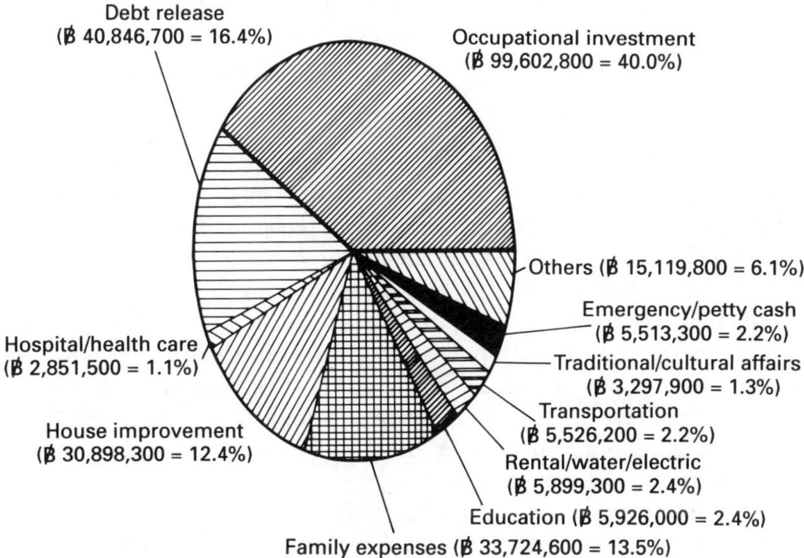

Figure 5.10 Loan granted to overall credit unions

is the well-known monk, Pra Thep Gawee. The goals of the organization are also explicit:

1 To encourage and support agriculture, that is, to develop people in their own occupation. Though people are to learn to solve their own problems, and those of the local area, the Foundation's programs are brought in to coordinate and help where needed.
2 To encourage education. The emphasis is on the acquisition of knowledge and modern technology to support the first goal. But the emphasis is also on practical application. For example, the foundation arranges for teachers and technicians to come in and diagnose local problems and propose appropriate local solutions.
3 To promote Buddhism. The idea is to develop each person's understanding of the reality of the world. Not suffering with delusions of self-importance or permanence, the mind is clearer, and so one can try to solve the larger problems of society and poverty. The specific goals are to promote diligence and hard

work; to strive toward frugality and a sense of spiritual welfare beyond necessary material goals – food, clothing, and shelter; and to practice doing good, that is, promote altruism.

4 To target poor areas, identifying diverse topographical features, peoples, cultures and traditions.

The programs of Wat Ba are on a relatively small scale. Started as a temple school for disadvantaged boys, it was recognized that the educated poor usually do not return to their villages. So from 1975 to 1988 programs were developed and carried into 39 villages, covering three northern states: Chiengmai, Chiengrai, and Lampun. Activities include agriculture promotion and training, improved input use, crop diversification, fish farming, rice growing, pigs, poultry, and fruit trees. Experts are brought in from Mae Jo Agricultural University to find technologies suitable for local conditions. There are continuous training programs, demonstration plots, and a soybean grower's association.

To finance training and the associated investment in new technologies, the Foundation has established various revolving funds. Currently these reach about 1,500 people in 21 villages, at a level of 1,225,000 baht. Loans are given in amounts of up to 1,000 baht per borrower, at about 12 percent per year. Much of the initial funds is brought in from the outside, from the Foundation.

With the idea that the poor lack access to plow animals, or can hire-in only at exorbitant rates, the temple has established buffalo bank programs. These rely on altruism, with a local donor providing an animal or new money to allow the purchase of a buffalo in the local market. This program operates in about 20 villages with 69 initial head plus 191 offspring. Borrowers pay for the animals in rice rentals.

This leads to the third financial program, rice banks. Currently there are about 600 members in 16 villages receiving loans of rice. Rice loans are targeted to the poor falling on especially hard times.

The temple also has day care centers and vocational training programs for women.

The temple makes no pretense that it should be self-supporting. It relies on the altruistic motives of the Thai and international community. It is currently receiving funds from UNICEF, The Asia Foundation, Bread for the World, and the Fredrich Newmann Stifung Foundation.

4 Linking self-help groups with banks – a Thai–German project

The fourth program is a joint venture between the German government, on the one hand, and various branches of the Thai government, on the other.

The program is to link various village-level production credit groups of the Community Development Department with the BAAC. Specifically, the stated goals of the project as of 1993 were:

1 To develop a more integrated national (and formal) financial system, that is, to build the appropriate institutional infrastructure. The program would support interest rate deregulation, but asserts that if the infrastructure is not present, deregulation will not work.
2 To allow funds to be invested in rural areas using existing and strengthened groups. The idea is take advantage of lower costs when groups are used as intermediaries. It is mentioned implicity that the BAAC does not use its own groups effectively.
3 Local savings is to be encouraged first. This will allow the poor access to funds, or access from sources other than unfair moneylenders. The borrower is to be allowed to borrow for more than agriculture.
4 To establish a management information system within the BAAC. For this (re)training of BAAC officers is envisioned.

The German donor is the GTZ, the technical foreign aid branch of the German government. Initial plans called for a survey of existing self-help groups and envisioned corroboration with several of them, including the Credit Union League mentioned earlier and various regional non-government organizations like (but not including) the northern Thai temple. In fact worries about sustainability and cooperation have led to the current choice of the so-called "production credit groups" (PCGs) of the Community Development Department, a branch of the Department of the Interior. In principle, that is on paper, these village level self-help groups are to be linked to banks, that is, to the BAAC, and the program is run out of the research department of the BAAC headquarters in Bangkok.

The program in 1993 was in its pilot stage, with choices of production credit groups in eight states total, two each in the north, north-east, central, and southern regions of the country. In all 184 out of 395 groups have been selected, comprising 51,000 individuals, and rated A, B, C, or D according to whether the group has been long established, whether is has accumulated ample savings, and whether these savings are used locally for lending. As currently measured in an initial survey, the production credit groups have some 125,215,840 baht in savings, of which about 5,477,031 is in accounts with the BAAC. However, Operation Link has been modified.

APPENDIX B RISK SHARING – AN INSTITUTIONAL ANALYSIS OF THE FOUR THAI PROGRAMS

The explicit insurance programs of SEWA, the group savings fund of Grameen, the implicit contingencies in BKK and other Indonesian programs are described in detail in Rashid and Townsed (1994). Similarly, the BAAC has incorporated risk contingencies of various kinds into its standard loan program, as theory and the environment might dictate. Most evident is the procedure for rolling over loans either with a penalty of 3 percent or without any penalty. In particular if a borrower goes bankrupt, uses money for wrongful purposes, intentionally defaults, is in jail, or is no longer a farmer, then a penalty is imposed. But if a borrower suffers from drought, flood, cyclone, pests, fire or theft of produce, difficulties in selling at reasonable prices, or fire or theft of other assets, then no penalty is imposed. All "defaults" are coded with numbers assigned to these events. There has been some discussion in the past in the Bank about whether this system might be expended. The possibilities it offers for explicit insurance, perhaps with high initial fees and greater indemnities, are evident.

Indeed, the Bank does offer low interest rate loans for those affected by natural calamities such as tropical storms (e.g., IRA) and pests (e.g., brown plant hoppers). It may waive interest in the first year altogether and offer "cheap" rehabilitation loans, at 8 percent per annum, for a subsequent year.

The Bank is promoting in various regions an "integrated farm production" plan, which encourages farmers to engage in a range of activities for diversification against price risk and natural calamities.

It offers loans for the postponement of sale produce, up to six months, with the unsold crop held in collateral. But it seems that unlike US farm programs with permanent subsidies, less than 1 percent of the collateral is forfeited.

The bank also offers special medium-term loans for disasters, for death of the borrower, and promotes voluntary death benefit funds, an indigenous Thai risk-sharing institution.

In conjunction with the establishment of village stores or cooperatives the Bank also offers consumption loans, and loan offices understand that a loan up to 60 percent of the gross revenue from cash crops may be used in part for consumption.

Ironically, though, the Bank does not seem to keep track of flows of funds motivated by insurance or consumption stabilization, though it has the records and accounts to do so. Indeed, insurance is not a metric it uses in its evaluation of branch performance. Rather, branches are given explicit beginning-of-the-year goals: number of new clients, number of new small-scale borrowers, designated lending amounts to individuals and to farmer institutions, goals for repayments for loans not yet overdue, repayments already overdue, and savings mobilization. Bank performance is thus scored according to specific weights: to meeting these goals; to efficiency in the administration of credit, that is, to profits per assets, per earnings, and per unit of money received from Bangkok, and to repayments and reduction of past due loans; and to performance according to rules and regulations of the bank, e.g., in credit, accounting, secretaries, assets, and expenses. In fact, it seems most of the variation in scores across branches is in the last two categories, profits and efficiency in administration, not in meeting prespecified goals. Clearly, unusually large outflows or low repayments associated with idiosyncratic or aggregate shocks would lower accounting profits and hence lower a branch's score. Related, perhaps, several loan officers in the branches noted that the system favors "high performing regions," though each can identify counties in their control areas with agroclimatic problems and defaults not attributed to borrower negligence.

The apparent aversion to a formalization of insurance programs, many of which the bank already offers implicitly, is evident in a less-than-successful experiment with a large grain company, CCP. Insurance was offered through this company for BAAC clients, and though initially successful in the first year, there were large losses by the third. From this experiment the view persisted for many years that formal agriculture insurance is not feasible, though this researcher has not yet secured relevant details on the administration program, specifically, how premiums and indemnities were set and how payoffs were determined. The idea of more formal insurance has, however, recently resurfaced.

Ironically, given the appeal in theory and in practice of risk contingencies in loan contracts for poor high-risk borrowers, and given the intent of the Bank to expand its program to the poor farmers, the Bank appears insensitive to the appeal of insurance-like arrangements to potential clients. As noted above, even brief interviews with potential clients quickly reveal that would-be borrowers do not want to brave the risk of paying loans in bad years. This emerged as the reason for not seeking loans in the village of Lao Bao, Jawmtaung, Chiengmai a short 7 km from the main branch office and in a somewhat developed area. (Indeed, it seems hard to find areas not subject to high risk!)

Related, perhaps, is a need to understand better the role of small, joint liability borrowing groups within the BAAC. Surely screening of borrowers and repayments are important. But groups also offer the possibility of internal insurance among their members, even in the context of orthodox loans from the Bank. This could easily take the form of individual members paying off each other's loans, a practice which might be better documented. This researcher found individual members responding readily to questions concerning the practice. Some definitely do it. Related would be the practice of one member borrowing from the BAAC and using the loan proceeds to pay off a second member's loan. More generally, one notes that BAAC borrowers are not supposed to (on)lend funds, certainly not at interest, though charity was said by one loan officer to be fine, nor are BAAC borrowers supposed to be borrowing elsewhere – at least this information is requested in applications for loans. The point again is that the BAAC appears ambivalent about internal insurance, not to mention village-level insurance generally, but theory argues that insurance is a good thing. The village of Lao Bao, for example, was said by its loan officer to have many, many borrowing groups. This researcher quickly uncovered a group of poor who do borrow and lend from each other, at no interest, and who do borrow from a big local lender, who might defer loans if the borrower were sick, but who are not borrowing from the BAAC for fear of risk. Ironically, it was said by these borrowers to be difficult to tell if more credit would be productive because yields are so variable, due to the risk! Still, one can offer the conjecture that BAAC borrowing groups do not automatically form around all "indigenous" groups in villages, groups which in turn may have inadequate risk reduction possibilities or groups which fear that the possibilities they do have may be limited once they join the Bank. One member of a group said that its members definitely do not help each other. These conjectures should be further tested.

A contrast with the BAAC is provided by a more detailed look at the credit program offered by the Credit Union League and its various subsidiary unions. First, credit unions lend explicitly for a variety of occupations, unlike the BAAC which is restricted to agriculture. This would be consistent, of course, with risk diversification. The issue of whether the Bank should expand its lending program beyond agriculture and related activities has come up formally at the BAAC and is favored by many of its program officials. Second, credit unions are explicit about consumption loans, viewed as definitely a good thing. As noted, unions lend for debt release, household improvement, and family expenses among others. Related, unions have special "emergency loan" procedures. In Shompuu, Sarapee, for example, there is a 1,000 baht, 30 day limit, but an emergency loan can be taken almost on demand from the chief clerk and accountant, confirmed quickly by the credit committee. Special blue accounting sheets earmark this as a special category of loan. More formally, the credit union offers life and disability insurance, called loan protection and loan saving insurance. For a relatively inexpensive premium, from 0.58 to 0.65 baht per thousand plus a membership fee of 15 baht per member, individuals in a union take out a policy which would forgive all debts (loan protection) and double all savings (live savings) on the death of the borrower. (It might be noted that formal insurance from well-established companies is far more expensive.) This program is administered and underwritten by the CUNA Mutual Insurance Societies, headquartered in Madison, Wisconsin. Unions are also contemplating hospital insurance and other innovations. Finally, as noted, individual credit unions can participate in explicit intermediation, borrowing (and lending?) to Bangkok. The accounts which denote the flows are easy to read.

Of course what is true on paper is not necessarily true in practice. Unions do vary on the ground, so to speak. In the apparently successful union of Shompuu, Sarapee for example, residents were said to suffer prior to the coming of the union from inflexible moneylenders and relatively little charity. Curiously, some in the village would seem to have access to a local BAAC cooperative, if not the BAAC itself, but only six individuals in total participate in each of these. It was conjectured that collateral was an obstacle, but several members emphasized the strong attraction of the life insurance funds and the funds for emergencies. Current membership stands at 691, with about half the members borrowing, at 18 percent, and all purchasing shares. In principle one can borrow up to three times one's savings in shares. (Still borrowers often limit themselves to amounts which do not exceed their savings, especially the landless.) Two members of the Shompuu union had died last year, and their relatives received death benefit indemnities (oddly enough, there is also an indigenous death benefit fund in the village). Despite all the apparent flexibility, the committee expects timely repayment. In fact several members were in default, including merchants whose business had done poorly.

The village Jede Magluen, Sansai has a three-year-old union, initially established by local school teachers. In fact, its efforts to attract potential farmer members seem mixed, with only about 20 percent of farmers in current membership despite promotional meetings emphasizing the life insurance benefits. Revealing, perhaps, the village has access to a cooperative, and there are BAAC groups, an agricultural credit group, and a potato group.

The third credit insurance program under consideration here, the Temple Wat Ba, has various risk features, noted earlier. Village rice banks stand ready to lend to those running out of rice, though there is perhaps confusion between stabilizing consumption around low levels, versus increasing levels. Revolving funds might similarly provide insurance, but there is mention of sick people in default, with no explicit insurance provision. The temple may be good at identifying inefficiencies in agricultural production and potentially profitable new technologies, but, again, this is not documented.

The fourth and final program under consideration, Operation Link, makes passing reference to increased insurance in its program description, but few details are as yet filled in. The main emphasis is on increased intermediation, presumably with a focus on production efficiency, either with an increase in savings and these used locally, or flows across groups and regions, from high saving areas to areas with high efficient demand for funds. It seems unclear whether these flows are to be accomplished within the BAAC flow-of-funds system or with separate accounts as with credit unions. In any event, flow of funds to facilitate risk sharing would remain a strong possibility, with the pilot areas spanning all four diverse areas of the country. This depends, of course, on implicit or explicit contingencies in the loan contracts.

Surely an attraction of Operation Link is the possibility that it might use existing local groups with indigenous risk-sharing systems to smooth local risks from the standpoint of individual borrowers. Similarly the BAAC might lend to village organizations as groups, just as production credit groups have standing as independent legal entities for savings accounts. The plan seems reasonably straightforward. Identify strong local groups and link them together.

Indeed, the identification of local self-help groups has proceeded with the rating of Production Credit Groups in the Community Development Department. A disadvantage of this plan, however, is the potential to ignore the presence of absence of alternative organizations at the village level. A rather dramatic example of this came to this researcher's attention in talking to production groups of two villages, numbers 5 and 7 in the municipality of Lampun. Both had managed to accumulate some savings, but none was being used for local lending. More to the point, village 7 was relatively disorganized and appeared to have few funds other than its PCG savings funds. (It did have as well various BAAC borrowing groups, with overlapping membership.) But the other second village had a variety of funds, including an *indigenous* group fund which had been used for local lending and for emergencies (at zero interest), and money had accumulated to such an extent that the fund had been twice divided. Obviously, this second village was more successful than the rating of its PCG savings fund might have allowed. Related, this researcher was informed that BAAC borrowing groups in the second village had on occasion used the indigenous village fund to pay off the BAAC loans for individual members.

Notes

Research support from the National Institute for Health and Human Development, the National Science Foundation, and the Institute for Policy Reform are gratefully acknowledged. I would also like to thank the BAAC, and especially Koon Pittayapol Nattaradol and Koon Chamlong Sakdee; the Production Credit Association, the Community Development Department and especially Koon Sombat Sakuntasathien; CULT and especially Koon Anan Chatrapracheewin; and Temple Wa Ba in Maa Rim, and especially Monk Jaokoon Winai for cooperation in carrying out the research. I also thank Anna Paulson and Tae Jeong Lee for discussion, and Dilip Mookherjee for his helpful comments. The chapter has also benefited greatly from ongoing research with Anna Paulson and Tae Jeong Lee.

1 These numbers do not reflect the experience of migrants. When the incomes of migrants are included, the dispersion of growth rates over regions is higher, that is, Bangkok would grow relatively faster with the inclusion. Related, the growth regional gross, domestic product indicates even greater disparities.

2 This allows consumption growth from t to $t + 1$ to be determined by idiosyncratic shocks at $t + 1$, and hence the growth of income from t to $t + 1$, in contrast to a full risk-sharing hypothesis.

References

Aghion, Philippe and Bolton, Patrick (1992). "Distribution and growth in models of imperfect capital markets." *European Economic Review*, 36: 603–11.

Aleem, Irfan (1990). "Imperfect information, screening, and the costs of informal lending: a study of a rural credit market in Pakistan." *World Bank Economic Review*, 9.

BAAC Annual Report (1990). *Introducing BAAC.*

Banerjee, Abhijit, Besley, Timothy, and Guinnane, Timothy (1992). "Thy neighbor's keeper: the design of a credit cooperative, with theory and evidence." Manuscript, Princeton University.

Banerjee, Abhijit and Newman, A. F. (1991). "Risk-bearing and the theory of income distribution." *Review of Economic Studies*, 58: 211–55.

Benjamin, Dwayne (1992). "Household consumption, labor markets and labor demand: testing for separation in agricultural household models." *Econometrica*, 60(2).

Besley, Timothy (1992). "Savings, credit and insurance." Princeton University Working Paper.

Besley, Timothy, Coate, Stephen, and Loury, Glenn (1993). "The economics of rotating savings and credit associations." *American Economic Review*, 83(4): 792–810.

Boyd, John and Prescott, Edward (1986). "Financial intermediary coalitions." *Journal of Economic Theory*, 38 (2).

Deaton, Angus (1989). "Saving in developing countries: theory and review." In *Proceedings of the World Bank Conference on Development Economics.*

Deaton, Angus and Paxson, Christina (1994). "Intertemporal choice and inequality." *Journal of Political Economy*, 102: 437–67.

Diamond, Douglas and Dybvig, Philip (1983). "Bank runs, deposit insurance, and liquidity." *Journal of Political Economy*, 91(3): 401–19.

Evans, D. and Jovanovic, B. (1989). "An estimated model of entrepreneurial choice under liquidity constraints." *Journal of Political Economy* 97 (4) (August).

Feder, Gershon *et al.* (1991). "Credit's effect on productivity in Chinese agriculture." World Bank.

Greenwood, Jeremy and Jovanovic, Boyan (1990). "Financial development, growth and the distribution of Income." *Journal of Political Economy*, 98 (1).

Grimard, Franque (1992). "Consumption smoothing within ethnic groups in Cote d'Ivoire." Typescript, Princeton University.

Hart, Oliver and Moore, John (1988). "Incomplete contracts and renegotiation." *Econometrica*, 56(4): 755–85.

Hayashi, Fumio (1987). "The effect of liquidity constraints on consumption." *Quarterly Journal of Economics*, 100.

Holmstrom, Bengt and Milgrom, Paul (1990). "Regulating trade among agents." *Journal of Institutional and Theoretical Economics*, 146: 85–105.

Itoh, H. (1988). "Essays in the Internal Organization of the Firm." Ph.D. Thesis, Stanford University.

King, Robert G. and Levine, Ross (1993). "Finance and growth: Schumpeter might be right." *Quarterly Journal of Economics*, 108 (August): 717–37.

Krasa, Stefan and Villamil, Anne P. (1992). "Monitoring the monitor: an incentive structure for a financial intermediary." *Journal of Economic Theory* 57 (June).

Krugman, Paul (1991). "Increasing returns and economic geography." *Journal of Political Economy*, 99 (3).

Lee, Tae Jeong (1994). "A spatial pattern of household specialization in the marketing system of peasant economies: evidence from Oaxaca Valley of Mexico and Western Guatemala." Ph.D. Thesis, University of Chicago.

Ligon, Ethan (1993). "Optimal consumption risk sharing: theory and measurement in rural India." Dissertation, University of Chicago.

Lim, Youngjae and Townsend, Robert (1994). "Currency, transaction patterns, and consumption smoothing: theory and measurement in ICRISAT villages." Work Paper.

Lloyd-Ellis, Huw and Bernhardt, Dan (1993). "Enterprise, inequality and economic development." Queen's Insitute for Economic Research Discussion Paper No. 893 (December).

Manuelli, Rodolfo and Sargent, Thomas (1994). "Alternative monetary models in a turnpike economy."

Morduch, Jonathan (1991). "Consumption-Smoothing Across Space: Tests for Village-Level Responses to Risk." Harvard University, draft.

(1993). "Risk, production and saving: theory and evidence from Indian households." Manuscript, Harvard University.

Mueller, Rolf and Townsend, Robert (1993). "Cropping groups in a semi-arid village economy." Manuscript; University of Chicago.

Paulson, Anna (1994). "Insurance motives for migration: evidence from Thailand." Dissertation, University of Chicago.

Paxson, Christina (1992). "Using weather variability to estimate the response of savings to transitory income in Thailand." *American Economic Review*, 82 (1).

Paxson, Christina and Chaudhuri, C. (1994). "Consumption smoothing and income seasonality in rural India." Manuscript, Princeton University.

Phelan, Christopher (1990). "Incentives, insurance and the variability of consumption and leisure." Dissertation, University of Chicago.

Phelan, Christopher and Townsend, Robert (1991). "Computing multiperiod information-constrained optima." *Review of Economic Studies*, 58: 853–81.

Piketty, Thomas (1994). "The dynamics of wealth distribution and the interest rate with credit rationing." Manuscript (October).

Prescott, Edward S. and Townsend, Robert (1994). "Cropping groups as firms: applied mechanism design." Northeastern Development Conference (October).

Rashid, Mansoora and Townsend, Robert (1994). "Targeting credit and insurance: efficiency, mechanism design, and program evaluation." ESP Discussion Paper Series, World Bank.

Rogerson, R. (1985). "Repeated moral hazard." *Econometrica*, 53: 69–76.

Rosenzweig, Mark (1988). "Risk, implicit contracts and the family in rural areas of low-income countries." *Economic Journal*, 98: 1148–70.

Siamwalla, Amar *et al.* (1990). "The Thai rural credit system: public subsidies, private information and segmented markets." *World Bank Economic Review* (September).

Tirole, Jean (1985). "Hierarchies and bureaucracies: on the role of collusion in organizations." *Journal of Law, Economics, and Organization*, 2 (2).

Townsend, Robert (1980). "Models of money with spatially separated agents." In Kareken, John and Wallace, Neil (eds.), *Models of Monetary Economies*. Federal Reserve Bank of Minneapolis, pp. 265–303.

(1994). "Risk and insurance in village India." *Econometrica*, 62(3): 539–91.

(1995a). "Financial systems in northern Thai villages." *Quarterly Journal of Economics* (November): 1011–46.

(1995b). "Consumption insurance: an evaluation of risk-bearing systems in low-income economies." *Journal of Economic Perspectives*, 9(3).

Udry, Christopher (1990). "Credit markets in northern Nigeria: credit as insurance in a rural economy." *World Bank Economic Review*, 4: 251–69.

Varian, H. (1990). "Monitoring agents with other agents." *Journal of Institutional and Theoretical Economics*, 146 (1).

Williamson, Jeffrey (1991). *Inequality, Poverty and History*, Oxford: Basil Blackwell.

Wolpin, Kenneth (1982). "A new test of the permanent income hypothesis: the impact of weather on the income and consumption of farm households in India." *International Economic Review*, 23: 583–94.

Yaron, Jacob (1991). "Development finance institutions: is current assessment of their financial performance adequate?" World Bank (October).

Zeldes, Stephen (1989). "Consumption and liquidity constraints: an empirical investigation." *Journal of Political Economy*, 97(2).

CHAPTER 6

Markets in transition

John McMillan

History's biggest experiment in economics is unfolding in the formerly planned economies of eastern Europe and Asia. Markets are being created from scratch. Novel incentive mechanisms are evolving. Watching the new market institutions grow can teach us much about how markets work. Economics has been used – for good or for ill – as the basis of advice to reforming governments. I shall reverse things and ask what the transition experience says about economics.

The starting point of the transition, the legacy of planning, was an economy with missing markets and unproductive firms. Financial markets were non-existent, product and labor markets rudimentary. Industry was monopolized by the notoriously inefficient state-owned enterprises. Reform means inducing the existing firms to become more productive; creating new firms; and developing financial, labor, and product markets. The catchphrase "getting prices right" – or Arrow–Debreu general equilibrium theory – tells only part of what is needed. Getting prices right requires mechanisms for setting prices. Prices do not encapsulate all the information markets need in order to function, and institutions must emerge for channeling the non-price information.

The market system is a *system*. "Everything is connected to everything else," as Lenin said. Reforms are interlinked. The various incentive mechanisms that constitute a market system can complement or substitute for each other. Incentives are complements if one has a larger effect when the other is already in place (Holmström and Milgrom (1994)). A reform may have little effect if implemented singly. Complementary with the internal restructuring of state-owned firms, for example, is the introduction of a competitive product market, so policies to foster new firms aid the restructuring of the existing firms. Restructuring requires also a managerial labor market to reveal talented managers, as well as a financial market to monitor the managers. On the other hand, incentive devices can also substitute for each other; workable substitutes for familiar institutions can arise. Markets have developed faster than laws in the transition economies, but deals are made, despite the absence of laws of contract and courts able to enforce them. The substitutes for law include reputational incentives and privatized coercion. Also, productivity has been improved in some transition economies by changing how people are paid without relocating the residual control and profit rights, suggesting that contractual incentives can substitute, temporarily, for ownership incentives. These are imperfect substitutes; but in the peculiar situation of the transition economy, they work. The interconnectedness of reforms will be my main theme.

I look at two issues: developing productive firms – improving existing firms and building new firms – and creating functioning markets. Focusing on the microeconomic details of reform, I say little about political economy (on this see the Dewatripont–Roland companion chapter). Macroeconomics also is omitted. Hyperinflation would undercut any attempt to restructure firms or to create markets, so a passably stable macroeconomy is necessary for successful reform. But building a market economy means transforming incentives and property rights, which cannot be achieved by macroeconomic instruments.

1 RESTRUCTURING THE EXISTING FIRMS

Reforming governments have chosen different routes to restructuring state-owned enterprises. Some, like the Czech Republic, privatized state firms at the very start of the reform process. Others procrastinated. China had done little privatization 15 years into its reforms, despite having deeply reformed its economy in other respects. No simple relation exists between privatizing a firm and making it more productive. Privatization does not in itself create an efficient firm. Although privatizing a firm makes it likely it will eventually be restructured, the evidence says privatization is neither necessary nor sufficient for restructuring. In China, Vietnam, and Poland, state firms were restructured while still in state hands, as a result of new incentives imposed by the state and new product-market competition (Jefferson and Rawski (1994), Naughton (1995), Diehl (1995), Belka *et al.* (1994), Pinto (1995)). In the Czech Republic, both privatized and state-owned firms were restructuring themselves by 1994, the privatized firms making the greater restructuring efforts (Zemplinerova, Lastovicka, and Marcincin (1995)). In Russia, by contrast, privatized firms had seen little restructuring by 1994 (mass privatization having begun in late 1992), because the incumbent managers remained entrenched and subsidies continued to flow from the state; the privatized firms appeared to be doing no more restructuring than those firms that were still state-owned (Belyanova and Rozinsky (1995), Earle, Estrin, and Leshchenko (1995)). I leave privatization in the background in what follows[1] and examine the internal restructuring of firms, privatized or not.

What restructuring means is clarified by the Laffont–Tirole (1986) model of the contracting between an agent – the manager – and a principal – either the planner or the firm's owner. The firm's productivity depends on both the manager's ability and his efforts. Generating profits is personally costly for the manager, so there is moral hazard; the cost to the manager of a profit π is $C(\pi, t)$. Here t represents the manager's ability, or *type*, which incorporates not only his inherent abilities and human capital but also any special knowledge he has of the firm's capabilities. The principal does not know the manager's type, which puts the principal at a bargaining disadvantage. This is a reduced-form representation of the manager's decision. The manager can increase productivity by strengthening workers' incentives, using piece rates, bonus payments, and promotion policies, or by firing unproductive workers. He can retrain workers, invest in new equipment, and seek new markets. He can forego his own perquisites. An extreme form of moral hazard is looting the firm. The manager might be able illegitimately to sell parts of the firm for private gain; a cost to him of generating profits is his opportunity of cost of refraining from such activity. The manager's cost function C, then, summarizes his discretionary ability to vary the firm's profit. To induce the manager to make the firm more productive, the principal gives him incentives, making his pay depend on the firm's profit: the offered payment is $s + r\pi$, where the parameters s and r are set by the principal. The manager responds so as to maximize his net return (which is payment minus his own cost, or $s + r\pi - C(\pi, t)$, thus generating profit π such that $C_{\pi}(\pi, \mathrm{t}) = r$. As a result, the firm's efficiency depends on both the manager's ability t and incentive r.

Fully efficient managerial decisions are elicited by a contract with full marginal incentives, or $r = 1$. The principal often, however, sets r less than one, intentionally inducing the firm to operate inefficiently. First, the principal's aims might be at odds with maximizing net revenue (Boycko, Shleifer, and Vishny (1993b, 1995)). Planners overseeing state firms had to meet their own output targets set by their superiors. For political reasons they pursued empire building and technological prestige, maintained excessive employment levels, and redistributed from productive to unproductive enterprises. As a result, the profit incentives they set were muted. Second, even if the principal wants the firm to be efficient, an informational cost of hierarchy – present even in a market economy, but exacerbated by the planned economy's long hierarchies – arises from the separation of ownership from control (Laffont and Tirole (1986)). The manager has bargaining power from knowing more about his own (and the firm's) capabilities than the principal.[2] The principal's rational counter is to distinguish whether the manager has low or high ability by offering a stronger incentive r if he reveals himself to have high ability. Using the marginal payment rate in this way, as a bargaining tool, means setting it at less than 100 percent, inducing inefficiency.

A third possible source of inefficiency is the manager's ability. State planners appointed managers more on political criteria than for their commercial skills. A managerial labor market can be added to the foregoing model (see Laffont and Tirole (1987), McAfee and McMillan (1987)). Competition can reveal who among the potential managers is the most able, so introducing a market-based selection mechanism improves managerial quality. The incentive r and ability t are complements:[3] The principal rationally gives a higher-type manager a higher marginal payment rate. With a better manager receiving steeper incentives, the firm's productivity gets a double boost.

Restructuring, then, consists of giving the existing manager stronger incentives, or shortening the hierarchy, or installing a new and better manager. Each of these changes could be generated by privatizing the firm, for an owner would emphasize productive efficiency more than a planner. Improvements can also come while the firm remains state-owned, through changing the planners' aims to give net revenue more weight.

2 INTERNAL INCENTIVES

The principal can give the manager direct incentives (r in the model) by using a contract that makes pay depend on the firm's performance. China's industrial bureaus began offering state-firm managers such contracts in the mid 1980s; their pay by 1989 was more sensitive to profit than most Western managers' (Groves *et al.* (1995)). In Poland, by contrast, state-firm managers received few monetary incentives. Their basic pay was set by a formula, typically five to seven times an average worker's wage, and their bonuses were not linked to profits (Pinto, Belka, and Krajewski (1993)).

Shortening hierarchies reduces the inefficiencies that come from the separation of ownership and control (McAfee and McMillan (1995)). The Chinese government during the 1980s granted state-firm managers the right to decide output and product mix. Autonomy had significant effects: managers strengthened the workers' incentives, paying more in bonuses and hiring some workers on fixed-term contracts, causing productivity to rise (Groves *et al.* (1994)). As a result of these and other reforms, China's state firms increased their total factor productivity by an average of over 4 percent per year over the decade 1980–9 (Jefferson and Rawski (1994)). In Ukraine, some state firms received autonomy, although unlike in China this was inadvertent. In the Soviet system, some state firms had been controlled from Moscow, others from Kiev. With the break-up of the Soviet Union, the formerly Moscow-run firms lost their overseers, while the Kiev-run firms remained actively state supervised. The newly autonomous firms increased their productivity, while the others did not (Johnson and Ustenko (1994)).

Long-run incentives are needed to supplement the short-run incentives of linking the manager's pay to the firm's profits, otherwise the manager might be tempted to raise current profits at the expense of the firm's future by running down the firm's assets. Long-run incentives therefore complement short-run incentives (Holmström (1982), Roland and Sekkat (1993), Aghion, Blanchard, and Burgess (1994), Gates, Milgrom and Roberts (1996)), although the incentive benefits of giving managers a long time horizon might conflict with the need to be able to remove those managers who are incompetent. In Western firms long-run incentives come from stock options. In a transition economy without a stock market this long-run incentive is not available. In a few of China's state-owned firms, managerial contracts gave long-run incentives by stating that, at the end of the contract, the manager was to be paid a bonus based on the firm's asset value (Gordon and Li (1991)). Also, managers sometimes had to post a personal bond, to be forfeited if the firm failed to meet its profit target. China's state firms in the 1980s reinvested 40 percent of their retained profits (McMillan, Naughton, and Lin (1996)), presumably reflecting the managers' perception that they would eventually be rewarded for rebuilding the firms. In Poland, state-firm managers' motivation was long run: they expected they would acquire shares at low prices when the firm eventually was privatized, and continue to run the firm after privatization. This had beneficial incentive effects, with the managers anticipating eventual reputational and financial rewards from any restructuring they initiated (Pinto, Belka, and Krajewski (1993)).

Granting the managers an ownership stake gives them a direct interest in the firm's profit. Ownership can give long-run incentives as well, eliminating the managers' temptation inefficiently to run down the firm's assets. Offering managers shares does not ensure management improves, however, for the incumbents might become entrenched.

3 PEOPLE VERSUS INCENTIVES

Poor performance of a firm reflects the distorted prices and unstable economy surrounding it, or poor management, or bad luck. Poor management can have two distinct sources: the managers might be incompetent (low t) or undermotivated (low r). Thus an underachieving firm could be improved by giving the incumbent managers stronger incentives, or by replacing them with more capable managers. The inefficiency of state firms in the planned economies had both of these sources, so better managers and stronger incentives are both prescribed. Which of the two is the more effective? Introducing the right incentives for productive effort might convert the most slothful of communist managers into avid profit seekers. Or, bringing in a better managerial team while leaving the structure of the firm unchanged might solve the firm's problems. The principal-agent model sketched above suggests that stronger incentives and better managers are complementary changes. They might be so strongly complementary that neither change would be effective by itself. Some managers might be so inadequate as to be unable to respond to new incentives, no matter how well designed. Good managers might not work well under badly structured incentives. If so, restructuring is effective only if both changes – new managers and new incentives – are introduced together.

Some evidence on people versus incentives comes from Russia's privatized retail shops (Barberis *et al.* (1996)). Restructuring (measured by capital renovation, changing suppliers, and laying off employees) occurred significantly less often when the incumbent managers had acquired an ownership stake then when the owners were entirely new people. Restructuring was not significantly associated with the manager's incentives (measured as the size of the manager's ownership stake). New people in charge with new skills seem to have been needed. Further survey evidence from Russia (Brown (1995)) indicates that the incentives that come from hardening firms' budget constraints are ineffective unless new managers are also installed, as many of the incumbents do not know how to operate in a market environment. Case-study evidence from Poland (Johnson and Loveman (1995)) also suggests that management skills and leadership are crucial, so successful restructuring of state-owned firms often needs a change of managers. In China's state firms in the 1980s, the industrial bureaus imposed managerial turnover and stronger managerial incentives (Groves *et al.* (1995)). When incumbent managers kept their jobs but received a new managerial contract, there followed little improvement in firm performance. But those firms with both a new manager and a new managerial contract did significantly improve. When the manager was replaced, the firm improved more than average if the previous manager had been demoted, and less than average if he had been promoted. Thus, even when a firm initially had a good manager, there was scope for improvement with a new manager and steeper incentives; but this was larger when the firm had a poor manager. Restructuring, then, often seems to require changing managers; stronger incentives are not enough. New incentives and new people are complementary.

The two aspects of restructuring contradict each other, and sometimes a choice must be made between them. Some rewards must be long term, for a manager's restructuring efforts take time to bear fruit. Also, a manager who is about to be fired might be tempted to strip the firm's assets. For incentive purposes, then, a manager must believe his job is secure. But guaranteeing secure employment rules out seeking better managers. If the quality of managerial talent is crucial, then restructuring should be sequenced. First, an attempt should be made to put capable people in managerial positions; then they should be offered some security of tenure. Finding good managers is difficult, however, especially early in the transition when no managerial labor market exists.

4 SELECTING BETTER MANAGERS

Russia's large-scale privatization brought little immediate change in the people running industry. "Most enterprises are still run by the old management teams, which often lack the human capital and interest to initiate significant changes" (Boycko and Shleifer (1994, p.8)). Managers in Russian firms have reported the difficulty of finding new managers who are qualified (Brown (1995)). Most of eastern and central Europe in the early 1990s had no managerial labor market. Management rarely changed either before or after privatization; when a change did occur, the new manager was usually promoted from inside the firm (Carlin, Van Reenan, and Wolfe (1994)). The Czech Republic is an exception: by 1994 many firms, both state-owned and privatized, had new managers (Zemplinerova, Lastovicka, and Marcincin (1995)). China, also, is an exception, in achieving sweeping managerial turnover, even though its firms remained unprivatized and the new managers were installed by the state (Groves *et al.* (1995)). In the first decade of reform, nearly 90 percent of China's state firms acquired a new top manager; by 1989 the average incumbent had held the job for less than six years.

Takeovers of state firms by foreign firms, as in Hungary (Voszka (1993)), can serve as an interim solution before the domestic managerial labor market has had time to develop. Foreign ownership usually results in the incumbent managers being replaced or supplemented by foreigners and, according to Carlin, Van Reenan, and Wolfe (1994), has been the most successful route in central and eastern Europe in the early 1990s to changing the behavior of the formerly state-owned firms. The most extreme case is eastern Germany's mass privatization. Most enterprises were purchased by western German firms, which then usually put their own personnel in charge, resulting in a massive transfer of managers from western to eastern Germany (Dyck (1994)).

Not everyone who ran the state firms was incompetent. Improving management requires identifying talent, both among the existing staff and outside the firm. Finding good people is a harder task in a transition economy than in a stable market economy. The usual source of information on potential managers' ability, and the basis of their being appointed, is their performance over many years in lower-level jobs. But in an economy in as much flux as a transition economy, past performance is hard to evaluate. Someone who has done a good job in a state-planned firm does not necessarily have the skills to run a market-oriented firm. Mechanisms for revealing able managers are needed.

An innovative method for uncovering managerial talent is the auctioning of jobs. In a scheme used occasionally in Poland, potential managers could bid for the right to run a state-owned firm, usually one in financial distress. Bids consisted of business plans for the reorganization of the firm. The privatization ministry awarded the managerial contract to the team it judged to have the best plan. The winning team had to post a bond, around 5 percent of the estimated value of the firm, which it could forfeit if it failed to keep the promises in its bid. The managers would be rewarded for any successful restructuring by receiving shares when the firm eventually became privatized (Slay (1993), Blaszczyk (1995)). China used similar auctions during the 1980s to select new managers in some of its more poorly performing state firms, and there is evidence that the auctions succeeded in installing competent managers (Groves *et al.* (1995)). Management buy-outs with competing bidders, as in the Czech Republic (Charap and Zemplinerova (1993)) can serve a similar purpose in screening managers. By revealing information about the quality of managers, auctions substitute for the usual sources of information about managerial talent which are missing in the transition economy.

Auctions are just one small aspect of finding good managers, and foreign ownership is a limited solution. Ultimately, there must be a functioning managerial labor market, which cannot arise instantaneously.[4] A market for managers is a complex market, subject to adverse-selection failures (Akerlof (1970), Dyck (1994)). Without institutions that transmit information the market might not function, for talented potential managers might be unable to distinguish themselves from their inferiors. Spence (1974) took the market for skilled labor as his leading example of a market in which information is essential but requires subtle mechanisms to transmit. Credentialing mechanisms must arise to enable potential managers credibly to signal their abilities.

5 CAPITAL-MARKET DISCIPLINE

Market-based disciplines reinforce the internal discipline that comes from basing the manager's pay on the firm's profits. As well as the managerial labor market, both the financial market and the product market link the manager's rewards to the firm's performance and give incentives to boost productivity. To the extent that competitive markets are complementary with direct incentives for managers, attempts to reform state firms' internal incentives without liberalizing their external market environment, as in Hungary in the 1960s and 1970s (Kornai (1990)) and North Korea in the 1980s (Lee (1995)), are doomed to be ineffectual.

Financial discipline complements internal incentives in inducing productivity improvements (Aghion, Blanchard, and Burgess (1994)). In Poland's state-owned firms, the combination of the managers' career concerns with hardened budgets caused managers to begin restructuring (Belka *et al.* (1994), Pinto (1995)). In Russia, the managers' ownership stake in privatized firms had little incentive effect by itself, in that the privatized firms appeared to be doing no more restructuring by 1994 than the state-owned firms (Aoki (1995), Barberis *et al.* (1996), Brown (1995), Earle, Estrin, and Leshchenko (1995)). What restructuring was occurring, in either type of firm, seemed to be driven by the installation of new managers and the hardening of budgets.

Financial markets take many years to grow, so capital-market discipline is weak early in transition. The government, as a state firms' owner, in principle could monitor in place of the capital market. In China this has occurred (Naughton (1995)), but in Poland the state has exerted little such oversight (Pinto and van Wijnbergen (1994)). In Russia's privatized firms, shareholders do little monitoring, as managers and workers, owning blocks of shares, prevent the outside shareholders from exercising their rights (Boycko and Shleifer (1994)), moreover, it is not worthwhile for banks to monitor, most bank lending being short-term (Belyanova and Rozinsky (1995)). In Poland and Hungary, bank monitoring has started to emerge, but only slowly, because it requires reliable accounting data (Bauer and Gray (1994)).

Capital allocation was badly distorted in the planned economies. State firms had a soft budget constraint: knowing they could count on being bailed out, they had little incentive to try to prevent losses (Kornai (1979a, 1979b)). Reports of the aggregate indebtedness of state firms can mislead, however, for the situation varied greatly from firm to firm: many received relatively little in subsidies, so the debts were concentrated in a few. In Poland in 1992–3, 90 percent of state-firm output came from firms with almost no debts, while firms producing only 10 percent of output had over a half of total bank debts (Gomulka (1994)). In China, most state firms were profitable most of the time, while a fraction were chronically indebted: through the 1980s, less than one third made losses in more years than they made profits (Morris and Liu (1993)). Privatizing a firm does not in itself eliminate its soft budget constraint. In Russia in the early 1990s, the central bank subsidized privatized firms in financial distress just as it did state firms; a privatized firm was no more allowed to fail than a state firm (Boycko, Shleifer, and Vishny (1993a)).

Budget constraints are soft because credit allocation is centralized, according to the theory of Dewatripont and Maskin (1995), Maskin (1996), and Qian (1994). Competition among banks, in this view, creates the ability to make commitments: a decentralized banking system can commit to abandon any project if it is revealed to be unprofitable, while a monopoly bank cannot. A monopoly bank might have an incentive, once started, to prop up an unprofitable project. If banks are small enough so that it takes more than one to fund a project, on the other hand, then the bank that makes the initial loan has no incentive to persist with the project after it sees it is a money loser, as the benefits from its efforts will accrue to the other lending banks.

The ultimate solution to the soft budget constraint, then, is to develop private, competitive banks. But this happens slowly. Can budget constraints be hardened while banks remain state owned? The logic of the theory just sketched – banks are prevented from perpetually bailing out losing firms by being too small to do so – applies to state owned as well as private banks. This is consistent with evidence from Poland, where the state banks had by 1991 hardened the state firms' budgets: partly because the banks were more strictly monitored by the finance ministry; also because there was now competition among the nine state banks that had been spun off from the National Bank of Poland and commercialized (Pinto, Belka, and Krajewski (1993)). Theory and practice show that enterprise budget constraints can be hardened, even while finance continues to be state controlled, by decentralizing the banks.

6 PRODUCT MARKET DISCIPLINE AND ENTRY

A competitive product market, like a capital market, complements direct managerial incentives, making the firm's internal incentives more effective (Gates *et al.* (1996)). Product-market competition can be initiated in a variety of ways. First, removing price controls, in addition to correcting allocative distortions, forces firms to become more productive, for after the price reform they must compete to sell, instead of having the state buy everything they produce. In China, internal restructuring measures such as installing a new manager and allowing the firm to retain more profits were significantly more effective if in addition the firm was faced with the product-market competition that came with selling on markets (Hong and McMillan (1996)). Second, trade liberalization forces firms to compete with imports. In Poland, import competition was an inducement to restructuring in state-owned and privatized firms (Pinto, Belka, and Krajewski (1993), Belka *et al.* (1994)). Third, antitrust enforcement can in principle put competitive pressure on firms. Antitrust might require more investigative and enforcement capabilities than the state has during the transition, however, and in fact many firms in central and eastern Europe took advantage of their new freedom in the early 1990s to price monopolistically (Boycko, Shleifer, and Vishny (1995), Carlin, Van Reenan, and Wolfe (1994)). The fourth source of product-market competition, and perhaps the most effective, is the entry of new firms.

One of the most striking lessons from the transition economies is the force of entry. China abolished its restrictions on non-state industry in 1979; by 1994 non-state firms were producing, by official estimate, 60 percent of industrial output. In Poland, private firms produced 37 percent of industrial output in 1993, up from 16 percent in 1989. In Bulgaria, the private sector produced somewhere between 24 and 50 percent of GDP in 1993, up from 7 percent in 1988.[5]

The impediments to entry in transition economies are widespread. New firms find it hard to sell their products and to buy inputs, both because of physical problems of distribution – inadequate roads, ill-maintained trucks, etc. – and informational problems of finding potential suppliers and customers (in Vietnam: Ronnås (1992)). The lack of laws of contract makes survival difficult. The absence of a financial market and the state banks' reluctance to lend to private firms means the entrants' initial investments must come from family savings or from informal credit societies at high interest rates (in China: Young (1995); in Vietnam: Ronnås (1992)). Local government officials harass the new firms, using licensing policies to protect their own state firms from new entrants (in Russia: Boycko, Shleifer, and Vishny (1993a)), or extorting bribes in exchange for the licenses without which the firms may not operate (in China: Manion (1994)). State enterprises resist the competitive threat from the new firms: in China, "Their tactics ranged from direct physical assault, to lobbying local officials, to – apparently as a last resort – reforming their own practices in order to cope with the competition economically" (Young (1995, p.48)). Another more subtle entry barrier exists: no one knows which lines of business are going to be profitable, so an early entrant risks investing more than the scale of demand warrants (Rob (1991), Thimann and Thum (1993), Arrow (1995)). Early entrants generate information for later entrants. Once a firm succeeds, others can imitate it; it pays to wait and see. This informational externality could cause entry to be slower than ideal.

In the face of these weighty impediments, the speed of entry in transition economies is remarkable. How is it explained? The initial conditions set by planning created the scope for fast entry. First, most industrial output in the planned economies came from large firms. In market economies, small firms account for much of industrial activity. Numerous niches are best filled by small firms. Those niches being empty in the planned economies, there were usually large rewards for entrepreneurs who arrived first. Second, to raise state firms' profits, the planners set high prices for most manufactured goods, and they kept some goods in short supply. After the state permitted entry, the first entrants reaped large profits from the high-priced and rationed goods.

The new entrants are socially valuable. They produce consumer goods, provide employment, and, by reinvesting their profits, mobilize savings. Their indirect benefits could be still more important. By interacting with the remnants of the planned economy, both state-owned enterprises and bureaucrats, the entrants have systemic effects.

Competition is the main way the entrants cause improvements in the pre-existing state-owned enterprises, but not the only way. They also cooperated productively. In Vietnam and China, many of the new firms became suppliers for state firms, manufacturing components more cheaply than the large state firms could (Ronnås (1992), Byrd and Zhu (1990), Wang and Chen (1991)). These systemic effects of the new firms in China have been quantified. Increasing product-market competition (measured as a falling mark-up of output price over input prices) was correlated with state-firm productivity growth (Li (1994)). The growth of urban non-state firms accounted for an estimated 80 percent of state firms' productivity growth in 1987–91 (Mao (1995)).

The new entrants also constrain the bureaucracy. Entry reduces the central-government bureaucrats' control over the economy, because it means an ever-growing sector is outside their reach. The entrants also have a more subtle effect, changing the way the bureaucrats regulate the state firms (McMillan and Naughton (1992)). The entrants' competition shrinks the state firms' profits; as a result, remittances from the state firms to the government fall. State firms are a major source of government revenue in the transition economy, as in the planned economy. To slow the drop in their revenue, the bureaus spur the state firms to become more profitable, by strengthening their internal incentives. Reform follows a virtuous cycle, reform begetting further reform. An initial reform – new competition for state firms – creates a problem – a squeeze on government revenue – which impels the state to make further reforms – increasingly profit-oriented regulation of the state firms. The dynamics of reform can force the bureaucrats to start to promote productive efficiency.

7 MARKET INFORMATION

The message so far is that the reform of state-owned enterprises is inseparable from the broad development of markets: labor, financial, and product markets. What does it mean to grow a market? A market is not an abstraction in which a demand curve spontaneously intersects a supply curve. A market is an institution, which needs rules and customs in order to operate. Given the disparate goals of the participants and the uneven distribution of information among them, the rules of exchange must be cleverly structured for a market to work smoothly. Institutions and organizations must evolve, to transmit information and to provide appropriate incentives.[6]

Markets need information. In a primitive market with limited information channels, firms are little islands of monopoly, as buyers pay high prices rather than trying to find alternative sellers (as in Diamond (1971)). Search costs generate inefficiencies. The high prices they induce mean losses to consumers. Search costs can cause poor matches, with buyers settling for inappropriate sellers. Search being duplicative, it may be inefficient for buyers to repeat each others' search. Search involves externalities – one buyer's search tends to hold down prices, to the benefit of the others – so individual search decisions generate too little search.

The difficulties caused by inadequate market information are seen in a survey of Vietnam's private firms by Ronnås (1992, 1996). Most firms relied exclusively on local suppliers and sold only to local customers: partly because of transportation problems but also because of the difficulty of identifying distant trading opportunities. Many firms had found their suppliers mainly through personal contacts, though most had undertaken some kind of search as well. In Poland, Hungary, Russia, and the Czech Republic in the early 1990s, state firms trying to reorient their product line to be responsive to market conditions were hindered by the lack of wholesale distribution networks (Carlin, Van Reenan, and Wolfe (1994)). In China in the mid 1980s, newspapers reported (see Solinger (1989, p. 181)) that market information was so inadequate that firms, both state and non-state, often could not find partners to trade with; also, "because of the absence of a regular feedback system, enterprises normally obtain information through personal connections or just by chance."

Market frictions go beyond the problems of finding trading partners to deceptive business practices. If buyers cannot observe quality, sellers might misrepresent it. The buyers' fear of being deceived can cause markets to operate at low levels (Akerlof (1970)). Pervasive under planning, quality problems continued during the transition. In a survey of Russian firms in the early 1990s, many complained of the low quality of the available inputs; they were willing to pay more for quality, but the market was not delivering it (Rubin (1994)). Stories of cheating on quality abound: for example, in China, phony fertilizer was sold under the trademarks of state fertilizer firms (Lyons (1994)).

Information channels grow as markets develop. Intermediaries enter to capture some of the surplus lost to search costs and to internalize the search externalities (Yavas (1994)). Organizations such as chambers of commerce, credit bureaus, and trade associations are set up with information transmission as one of their purposes. Firms making the same product situate themselves close to each other, to reduce buyers' search costs and thereby expand their total market (Dudey (1990)). Buyer–seller networks evolve to economize on search costs (McMillan and Morgan (1988)) and to provide incentives for quality (Klein and Leffler (1981)). Signaling and screening devices arise to assure buyers of product quality (Spence (1974), Rothschild and Stiglitz (1976)).

Devices to reduce search costs have arisen spontaneously, though gradually, during the transition. In China, private traders emerged in the 1980s, locating inputs for both private and state manufacturing firms (Young (1995, p. 75)). In Russia, brokerage houses and wholesale traders emerged to spread information, to match buyers to sellers, and to extend credit. Agricultural wholesale markets originated in 1990, providing private farmers with an outlet for their production, and specialized exchanges in such commodities as oil and aluminum evolved (Wegren (1994), Åslund (1995, p. 264)). The state has helped. In China, the state-run companies that distributed agricultural goods were decentralized and forced to compete with each other. The materials supply bureaus, which used to allocate industrial inputs under the plan, under reform began to manage market information, and new state-sponsored agencies were set up to disseminate economic information (Holton and Sicular (1991), Solinger (1989)). In Vietnam, state agencies sometimes helped private firms to find suppliers (Ronnås (1992, p. 74)).

Warranties and brand names can act as signals, allowing markets to function in the face of quality uncertainty. In Bulgaria, quality problems were prevalent initially, but a few years into the transition some firms were starting to offer warranties and had become willing to replace substandard goods (Koford and Miller (1995)). Russia has attempted to legislate quality, introducing a law on product quality and a national certification body to which manufacturers would voluntarily submit products (Goldberg (1992)). In China, advertising and brand names emerged as the market economy developed (Stross (1990)). In the Chinese countryside, advertisements for feed supply stress that the product comes from a joint venture or uses foreign technology, presumably because these features are seen as assurances of quality.

Ongoing buyer–seller relationships both lower search costs and provide quality incentives. Among Bulgarian firms, suppliers became increasingly willing to guarantee quality and to replace substandard goods as relationships developed (Koford and Miller (1995)). In Poland, Hungary, the Czech Republic, and Russia, some state firms in the course of restructuring spun off plants, which then acted as independent subcontractors to the original enterprise (Carlin, Van Reenan, and Wolfe (1994)). In China, relational contracting is the norm, according to Solinger (1989), who sees interfirm networks as a continuation of practices under planning, when personal connections loosened the rigidities of the planning system. Chinese firms now assure themselves of the quality of their inputs by contracting with firms they know, sometimes cementing the relationship by investing in the supplier.

8 PROPERTY RIGHTS

Our concepts of ownership are stretched by the transition economies. Ownership consists of residual control rights – deciding the use of assets not explicitly assigned by contract – and residual return rights – keeping any funds left after everyone has been paid what they are contractually owed (Grossmand and Hart (1986)). The transition economies, in particular China, show the incentive effects of ownership are not straightforward. Changes in contracted rights but not in ownership have brought big performance gains. And the boundaries between public and private ownership have been blurred.

In China's and Vietnam's farms, the state has vested contractual rights in the people doing the work, without changing ownership. Agricultural communes were abolished in both countries in the early 1980s. Although land ownership remained collectivized, each peasant now worked an individual plot. The peasant delivered a specified amount of grain to the state, retaining anything beyond the quota, so contractually had full marginal incentives. The results were spectacular: within five years output in China rose 67 percent and productivity 50 percent (on China, see McMillan, Whalley, and Zhu (1989), Lin (1992), Rozelle (1996), on Vietnam, Pingali and Xuan (1990)). Initially the contracts were for three years, and the short time horizon induced peasants to overwork the land; but China's reformers quickly recognized this and increased the contracts to 15 years, to balance short-run and long-run incentives. Land is still subject to arbitrary expropriation by the state (Lyons (1994)), so the peasants do not hold residual control rights. But productivity soared with the reassignment of the contractible returns.

A similar contractual reform occurred when China's state firms were granted autonomy: managers could choose outputs, product mix, and technology, instead of following planners' orders. Further, firms received contracts which let them retain a share of their profits. Some contracts simply specified a lump sum to be delivered to the state, with the firm keeping all extra profits (McMillan, Naughton, and Lin (1996)). The advent of competitive product markets following the entry of non-state firms reinforced these internal reforms. Ownership stayed with the state, which retained the right to intervene: it could override a contract; and the contracts were for a fixed duration of three to five years. Nevertheless, productivity increased markedly with the reassignment of the formal profit and control rights (Groves *et al.* (1994)); contractual incentives substituted for ownership incentives.

Ownership need not be all or nothing, state or private. Hybrid ownership forms have emerged and, as transitional devices, are working (Nee (1992)). Informal privatization has put some residual rights in private hands. China's state-owned firms have often partially privatized themselves by setting up subsidiaries which then form joint ventures, often with foreign firms. With multiple subsidiaries, the resulting entities, though still state owned, are relatively free of government control, and residual control rights are in practice held by the firm (Nee and Su (1996), Qian (1995), Qian and Stiglitz (1996)). In Hungary, state-firm managers formed limited-liability companies, with ownership shared by the firm and the manager (Stark (1994), Voszka (1993)). In Russia before privatization, state firms set up internal subsidiaries whose managers were free to act entrepreneurially, keeping a large share of the profits (Johnson and Kroll (1991)).

Much of China's reform-era dynamism has come from its township-and-village enterprises, whose output grew at 30 percent annually in 1979–94, mostly from increasing productivity (Chang and Wang (1994), Che and Qian (1995), Xu (1995), Whiting (1996)). These firms have unusual ownership. While some are private, most are publicly owned, by communities of a few thousand people. They are managed by village government, which holds the residual control rights, not the nominal owners, the villagers. The profits are shared between the villagers and local government by explicit rules. Around 60 percent is reinvested, and the remainder is paid as bonuses to workers or used for local public goods such as education, roads, and irrigation. Managerial discipline in the township-and-village enterprises comes from their hard budgets and their intensely competitive product markets.

While there are huge inefficiencies from public ownership, as the history of the planned economies makes obvious, in the halfway house of the transition economy a firm might receive some benefits from having the state as a partner (Johnson and Kroll (1991), Nee (1992), Solinger (1993), Che and Qian (1995), Li (1995)). Access to state banks and to rationed inputs is eased. The government's stake in the firm can help remedy the lack of laws, protecting against arbitrary expropriation by the state, as well as helping with contract enforcement. Since the state in a transition economy is able to have an impact on a firm, positive or negative, it might be efficient for it to have partial ownership. For this to work, there must be some check on the downside of state ownership, the government's propensity to impose inefficient decisions on the firms or to appropriate the firms' profits. China's local governments, arguably, did not sabotage their township-and-village enterprises because of the combination of the competitiveness of the firms' output markets and the localness of the government control, which meant the government officials could see that if they overtaxed their firms the firms would fail and their own revenue source would be lost.

9 CONTRACTS WITHOUT LAW

Markets cannot function, it is commonly asserted, without laws of contract. The World Bank says: "Reform policies cannot be effective in the absence of a system which translates them into workable rules and makes sure they are complied with." Reform is feasible only with laws, a "system based on abstract *rules* which are actually applied and on functioning *institutions* which ensure the appropriate application of such rules."[7] The view that a functioning legal system is a prerequisite to economic reform is contradicted by the transition economies. Reform has taken place in a legal vacuum. The existing legal system suited central planning, not a market economy. Contracts in the planned economy were insecure, often being overridden by the state. In Vietnam, "Written laws and regulations can only be regarded as general guidelines, establishing the rough ambit of bureaucratic discretion" (Gillespie (1993, p. 143)).

Markets developed faster than laws during the transition. Trade began to occur, even though the contracts it was based on were unenforceable. In China in the early 1990s, "legal institutions remain essentially unreformed and ill-suited to the institutions of a market economy," so "property rights and contract rights are not well defined and reliably enforced" (Clarke (1996)). Writing laws is not all that is needed; the courts must be capable of enforcing them (Clarke (1995)). "Contracts in China have more of a sense of moral obligation than absolute rights. There is no concept that they are binding," said a China-based American lawyer. Nevertheless, deals are made. As a broker in Moscow's new commodities exchange said: "Russian businessmen have gone ahead of the law, but goods have to move."[8] The substitutes for formal legal contract enforcement include repeated games and privatized coercion.

The theory of repeated games shows that concern for the future can induce people to cooperate. With some extrapolation the theory shows how institutions and customs aid cooperation. Repeated games have multiple equilibria, and the players can be stuck in a low-level equilibrium. An institution might serve to select an equilibrium, coordinating people's strategy choices onto a cooperative outcome. Institutions also make cooperation feasible. Cooperation requires that firms that renege are sanctioned; but sanctioning might not be in anyone's interest (Pearce (1992)). An institution can ensure the sanction is applied. If the game is not literally a repeated game but rather a series of interactions between different pairs, a mechanism is needed to provide information linking the transactions, so it is known whether a proposed trading partner has ever reneged on an earlier deal (Kandori (1992)). If firms differ in their trustworthiness, an institution can screen the honest from the fly-by-night firms (Watson (1995)). Bargaining can break down when people have private information about the value of what is being bargained over (Myerson and Satterthwaite (1983)); an institution that moderates bargaining tactics helps to achieve a smooth division of the gains that cooperation achieves.

In Ukraine, banks started lending in the early 1990s despite the lack of a legal framework (Johnson, Kroll, and Horton (1993)). No law on collateral existed, and the ownership of assets suitable as collateral was unclear. Nevertheless, loans were made and repaid. The banks chose carefully to whom they lent: borrowers usually had personal contacts with the bank owners. Loans were short term; the borrower's incentive to repay was that default would preclude future loans. In Bulgaria, firms surveyed by Koford and Miller (1995) said that ongoing relationships with customers and suppliers were needed because of the absence of commercial law. Many firms had been deceived by unscrupulous firms, which appeared in great numbers early in the transition. Firms began carefully evaluating business partners. They tried to find reliable firms who were reliable and then worked with them on a continuing basis. Supplier networks were gradually developed. Most firms eventually acquired a core group of partners with whom they traded frequently, and to whom they offered credit. In Russia in the early 1990s, similarly, personal contacts were essential to support exchange given the lack of laws and the lack of competence of the courts. Firms sometimes merged with their suppliers to ensure a reliable flow of inputs (Rubin (1994), Rubin and Tesche (1995)). In China, trade rests on the trust that comes in ongoing relations (Solinger (1989)). China's highly successful township-and-village enterprises, in particular, often base their transactions on oral agreements rather than written contracts. Long-term relationships are carefully cultivated. Disputes are often settled privately rather than resorting to the courts, so as not to upset the ongoing connections (Xu (1995)). In Vietnam by 1991, private firms acting as suppliers to other private firms or state firms had begun to develop relationships with their customers. While transactions initially were for cash on delivery, gradually credit came to be offered and production done to advance orders (Ronnås (1996)).

For repeated-game sanctions to work in generating cooperative behavior, it helps that any defections become known to other potential trading partners. In China, the lawyers who specialize in debt collection maintain good relations with the local press and threaten debtors with publicity. The absence of enforcement mechanisms means that even the courts sometimes do this. Courts in the province of Heilongjiang threaten newspaper exposure of debtors who fail to pay. This apparently works in the big cities, and with enterprises that are worried about losing a reputation they had spent a lot of advertising money to build. Sanctions are more effective as a deterrent if they are expected to come from many trading partners, not just the trading partner who has been cheated. This can be achieved if a group of firms in the same line of business form an association. If a member is harmed the others are informed and all ostracize the offender. In Russia's commodities brokerages, the sanction against those who renege on payment is exclusion from future deals: a broker said: "There is already a blacklist of people with whom we don't deal anymore" (Greif and Kandel (1995), Rubin and Tesche (1995)).

Sanctions are not always as innocuous as ostracization. Contracting parties often resort to threats of violence, privatizing the state's supposed monopoly on coercion – and causing considerable social damage. Criminal gangs have been used to enforce contracts in Russia, Bulgaria, and elsewhere (Greif and Kandel (1995), Koford and Miller (1995)). In China, the police themselves offer freelance contract enforcement. When a dispute over payment occurs, one firm uses its political connections to get the local police to kidnap the head of the other firm, jailing him on trumped-up charges of fraud or embezzlement and releasing him only after his firm pays the disputed sum.[9] In some cases it might be enough for efficient contracting that only one of the parties be able to enforce an agreement. The party that has powerful friends can pay money in advance, knowing it will be able to prevent the other party from reneging.

A partial move towards state-sanctioned commercial law is the use of official arbitration bodies. In Vietnam dispute resolution is the responsibility of state economic arbitrators, though the avenues for enforcement of awards are limited (Gillespie (1993)). In Russia, arbitration courts started operating in 1992: the application for arbitration must be mutual, and the decision is binding and backed up by the force of the law, but enforcement capabilities are weak (Greif and Kandel (1995)).

"The experience of Asian economies demonstrates that the strict judicial enforcement of property and contract rights is not necessary to economic growth," says Upham (1994, p. 237)), referring to Japan and Taiwan. "What is needed is a recognition of the variety of roads to economic growth in capitalist systems and the variety of roles, including perhaps no role at all, that formal law can play in the process." The transition economies' experience supports this: repeated games can substitute for laws. They are an imperfect substitute, however: self-enforcing contracts have limits. Deals can be made only by people who know each other's reputations. If one party must commit a large sum for a long-delayed return, the deal might not be feasible, for the other party is tempted to renege. If uncertainty is large it is hard for one party to assess whether the other has lived up to the agreement. A fear of arbitrary expropriation by the state inhibits investment. Without laws of contract, therefore, some gainful trades cannot be made. In market economies with sophisticated legal systems, agreements rest on a combination of trust and the law.[10] In the transition economies, relational contracting has developed spontaneously. The formal legal basis for contracting must be implemented by the state.

10 ECONOMIC REFORM AND ECONOMIC THEORY

The new incentive mechanisms in the reforming countries echo the themes of modern economic theory: principal-agent contracting (the incentives facing state-firm managers); auction design (selection of managers); signaling and screening (devices to induce product-quality incentives); search (institutions to uncover trading partners); property rights (firms with mixed public and private ownership); and repeated games (ongoing relationships compensating for absent laws of contract).

Some of what we see happening in the transition economies is mere comforting confirmation of what any economist would have expected. People respond to incentives. Chinese agriculture boomed after the end of the communes, when peasants began working individual plots and keeping the full value of their marginal output. The managers of China's state-owned firms began to improve productivity when they received contracts linking their pay to their firm's profits. State-firm managers in Poland restructured their firms after they saw that they would be likely to keep their jobs long enough to benefit themselves from the success of their restructuring.

Perhaps the most important – and most elementary – lesson from the various countries' transitions is the power of competition. Conspicuously absent in the planned economies, competition is part of most of the reform successes. Competition sets prices right, removing allocative distortions. Competition creates managerial discipline: new firms enter and compete for sales with the old state-run or privatized firms, pressing them to become less inefficient. Competition generates information: in a managerial labor market it reveals skilled managers. Competition permits commitment: decentralized banks overcome the soft budget constraint, giving firms financial discipline.

The evolution of product markets (in Bulgaria, Vietnam, Russia, China, and elsewhere) shows how exchange works under imperfect information. Early in the transition, the new firms trade only with others in their immediate vicinity, because the absence of market information makes it hard to find distant trading partners and because dealing anonymously is risky without a legal basis for contracts. Credit is not offered. Over time these informational frictions ease. As firms become visible players with reputations to maintain, trust develops and transactions become more forward looking. Institutions and organizations – trade associations, credit bureaus, market intermediaries, networks – arise to help identify new trading opportunities and to expose firms that renege on agreements.

Not all the lessons from the transition economies are straightforward. Some of the developments contradict preconceived views on property rights. It would have been a brave economist who in 1980 would have advised China to bet the success of its reforms on firms owned collectively by villagers and run by village governments. Yet the township-and-village enterprises, despite their non-standard ownership, have been the impetus for China's decade-and-a-half of 10 percent annual growth in per capita income. State firms in Poland, Vietnam, and China have significantly improved themselves while remaining in state hands, contradicting the assertion that it would be impossible to reshape them without the incentives that come from private ownership. The amount of successful deal-making in all the transition economies, unsupported by laws of contract, is at odds with the belief that a legal system is needed before markets can function: repeated games work surprisingly well in substituting for formal laws.

The success of unconventional incentives does not constitute an argument against fostering ordinary private firms, or privatizing state firms, or instituting normal property rights and laws of contract. It is an argument against simplistic prescriptions. Not everything has to be set right at once. This conclusion runs counter to official thinking. US Secretary of State Warren Christopher, visiting Vietnam in August 1995, advised his hosts to reform radically. "I would ask you to look at economic reform as a passage over a ravine. You cannot do it by taking several little steps; only one giant leap will get you across."[11] The analogy is inapt. Reforming an economy is not like leaping a ravine, because you don't know where you are going and you don't know how to get there.

The final lesson, then, is modesty. As Robert Solow said, "There is not some glorious theoretical synthesis of capitalism that you can write down in a book and follow. You have to grope your way." Muddling through works better than grand schemes.[12] Although some designing and guiding of the transition is necessary, also needed is spontaneous evolution. The starting point for the transition is misaligned prices, unproductive firms, and unfilled market niches. Such an inefficient economy has large scope for improvement, with a few incentives and some competition. But just what will work is hard to predict. It is necessary to be experimental, living for a while with unconventional solutions, if they work. These solutions might well not be devised in a finance ministry, let alone in the World Bank or a Western university. They are more likely to come from people whose livelihoods are on the line.

Some reforms must come from the state: it must decide, explicitly or implicitly, on the sequence in which to free prices, to privatize enterprises, and to remove trade barriers. Decisions are needed on whether to build a Japanese-style or a US-style financial system, how to implement laws of contract, and what kinds of taxation to impose. Good decisions require knowledge not only of how each of these parts of the system work but also how they fit together. The information needed to plan all of this in advance is unobtainable. Not only is the sheer volume huge, there is yet another incentive obstacle (Hayek (1945), McAfee and McMillan (1995)). Information on the economy, widely dispersed, must be gathered; but the people holding it might distort it for personal gain. If it were possible to plan the transition it would have been possible to plan the economy.

Notes

For their suggestions I thank Donald Clarke, Susan Gates, Charles Gitomer, Takeo Hoshi, Edward Lazear, Paul Milgrom, Barry Naughton, Brian Pinto, Yingyi Qian, James Rauch, Michael Rothschild, Andrei Shleifer, Joel Sobel, Yueting Tong, Christopher Woodruff, and Chenggang Xu; and for support I thank the University of California Pacific Rim Research Program and the project on Institutional Reform and the Informal Sector.

1 For a sampling of the vast literature on the timing and techniques of privatization, see Blanchard (1996), Bolton and Roland (1992), Boycko, Shleifer, and Vishny (1993a, 1995), Dewatripont and Roland (1996), Fischer (1991), Frydman, Rapaczynski, and Earle (1993), Maskin (1992), McMillan and Naughton (1992), Sachs (1993), Sinn and Sinn (1993), and Stiglitz (1994).

2 Agency problems were rife in the Soviet firm: there was "an enormous amount of falsification . . . everywhere there is evasion, false figures, untrue reports." Managers misrepresented their firms' costs to the ministries, exaggerating their needs of labor, materials, and equipment, and omitted to report improvements in techniques (Berliner (1957, pp. 161, 82–91)).

3 More precisely, the complementarity of t and r is a sufficient condition for the first-order conditions to characterize the optimal contract; see McAfee and McMillan (1987).

4 Restructuring also needs an ordinary labor market, to reallocate workers across firms and to adjust wage rates: see Blanchard (1996).

5 Reuters, Beijing, March 4, 1995; Blaszczyk (1995), Pissarides, Singer, and Svejnar (1995).

6 What it takes for a complex market to evolve, in circumstances similar to the transition economies, is seen in Schaede's (1989) account of the origins of a futures market in seventeenth-century Japan.

7 World Bank General Counsel Ibrahim F.I. Shihata, quoted by Upham (1994 pp. 233–4).

8 The quotes are from *Far Eastern Economic Review,* February 11, 1993, p. 42, and *New York Times,* January 17, 1992, p. A1.

9 Police kidnappings of businesspeople in China are reported periodically on the Internet service *HK News.* In Russia (according to the *San Diego Union-Tribune,* September 23, 1995, p. A14), when an electricity company cut off the power supply to a nuclear submarine base because of $4.5 million in unpaid bills, heavily armed sailors forced the duty engineers to switch the power on at gunpoint. In another incident, after power was cut off from an army arsenal, the base commander sent a tank around to the electricity company. The power was turned back on immediately.

10 On informal and reputational incentives supplementing the law in the United States, see Macauley (1963) and Ellickson (1991); and in Japan, see Sako (1992) and Haley (1994).

11 The quote is from *New York Times,* August 9, 1995, p. A3. Managing reform its own way, Vietnam had been growing steadily since the mid 1980s; at the time of Mr Christopher's visit its annual growth rate was 9.5 percent.

12 Several ambitious reform plans, like the 500-Day Plan for the Soviet Union, were promulgated by eastern European or Western academics: see Allison and Yavlinsky (1991), Blanchard *et al.* (1991), Peck and Richardson (1991). (The Solow quote is from *New York Times,* September 29, 1991, p. E1.)

References

Aghion, Philippe, Blanchard, Olivier, and Burgess, Robin (1994). "The behaviour of state firms in eastern Europe, pre-privatisation." *European Economic Review,* 38: 1327–49.

Akerlof, George A. (1970). "The market for 'lemons': quality uncertainty and the market mechanism." *Quarterly Journal of Economics,* 84: 488–500.

Allison, Graham and Yavlinsky, Grigory (1991). *Window of Opportunity: The Grand Bargain for Democracy in the Soviet Union.* New York: Pantheon.

Aoki, Masahiko (1995). "Controlling insider control: issues of corporate governance in transition economies." In Aoki, M. and Kim, H.-K. (eds.), *Corporate Governance in Transitional Economies,* Washington, DC, World Bank.

Arrow, Kenneth J. (1995). "Theoretical considerations on the role of small- and medium-sized enterprises in economic transition." Presented at the Workshop on Policy Studies to Promote Private Sector Development, European Bank for Reconstruction and Development.

Åslund, Anders (1995). *How Russia Became a Market Economy,* Washington, DC: Brookings Institution.

Barberis, Nicholas, Boycko, Maxim, Shleifer, Andrei, and Tsukanova, Natalia (1996). "How does privatization work? Evidence from the Russian shops." *Journal of Political Economy* 104: 764–790.

Bauer, Herbert L. and Gray, Cheryl W. (1994). "Debt as a control device in transitional economies: the experiences of Hungary and Poland." Unpublished, World Bank.

Belka, Marek, Estrin, Saul, Schaffer, Mark E., and Singh, I.J. (1994). "Enterprise adjustment in Poland: evidence from a survey of 200 private, privatized, and state-owned firms." Unpublished, Institute of Economic Sciences, Polish Academy of Sciences.

Belyanova, Elena and Rozinsky, Ivan (1995). "Evolution of commercial banking in Russia and the implications for corporate governance." In Aoki, M. and Kim, H.-K. (eds.), *Corporate Governance in Transitional Economies,* Washington, DC: World Bank.

Berliner, Joseph (1957). *Factory and Manager in the USSR.* Cambridge, MA: Harvard University Press.

Blanchard, Olivier (1996). *The Economics of Transition.* Oxford: Oxford University Press.

Blanchard, Olivier, Dornbusch, Rudiger, Krugman, Paul, Layard, Richard, and Summers, Lawrence (1991). *Reform in Eastern Europe.* Cambridge, MA: MIT Press.

Blaszczyk, Barbara (1995). "Various approaches to privatization in Poland, their implementation and the remaining privatization potential." Unpublished, CASE, Warsaw.

Bolton, Patrick and Roland, Gérard (1992). "Privatization in central and eastern Europe." *Economic Policy,* 15: 276–309.

Boycko, Maxim and Shleifer, Andrei (1994). "What's next? Strategies for enterprise restructuring in Russia." *Transition,* 5: 8–9.

Boycko, Maxim, Shleifer, Andrei, and Vishny, Robert (1993a). "Privatizing Russia." *Brookings Papers on Economic Activity,* 2: 139–92.

(1993b). "A theory of privatization." Unpublished, Harvard University.

(1995). *Privatizing Russia.* Cambridge, MA: MIT Press.

Brown, J. David (1995). "Excess labor and managerial shortage: findings from a survey in St Petersburg." Unpublished, University of Pennsylvania.

Byrd, W.A. and Zhu, N. (1990). "Market interactions and industrial structure." In Byrd, W.A. and Lin, Q. (eds.), *China's Rural Industry*. Oxford: Oxford University Press.

Carlin, Wendy, Van Reenan, John, and Wolfe, Toby (1994). "Enterprise restructuring in the transition: an analytical survey of the case study evidence from central and eastern Europe." Working Paper No. 14, EBRD, London.

Chang, Chun and Wang, Yijiang (1994). "The nature of township-village enterprises." *Journal of Comparative Economics*, 19: 434–52.

Charap, Joshua and Zemplinerova, Alena (1993). "Management buty-outs in the privatisation programme of the Czech Republic." OECD Advisory Group on Privatisation.

Che, Jiahua and Qian, Yingyi (1995). "Boundaries of the firm and governance: understanding China's township-village enterprises." Unpublished, Stanford University.

Clarke, Donald C. (1995). "The execution of civil judgments in China." *China Quarterly*, 141: 65–81.

(1996). "The creation of a legal structure for market institutions in China." In McMillan, John and Naughton, Barry (eds.).

Dewatripont, Mathias and Maskin, Eric (1995). "Credit and efficiency in centralized and decentralized economies." *Review of Economic Studies*, 62: 541–55.

Dewatripont, Mathias and Roland, Gérard (1996). "Transition as a process of large-scale institutional change." In this volume.

Diamond, Peter A. (1971). "A model of price adjustment." *Journal of Economic Theory*, 3: 156–68.

Diehl, Markus (1995). "Enterprise adjustment in the economic transformation process: microeconomic evidence from industrial state enterprises in Northern Vietnam." Working Paper No. 695, Institut für Weltwirtschaft, Kiel.

Dudey, Marc (1990). "Competition by choice: the effect of consumer search on firm location decisions." *American Economic Review*, 80: 1092–104.

Dyck, I.J. Alexander (1994). "Privatization in Eastern Germany: management selection and economic transition." Working Paper 95-030, Harvard Business School.

Earle, John S., Estrin, Saul, and Leschchenko, Larisa L. (1995). "Ownership structures, patterns of control and enterprise behavior in Russia." Unpublished, Central European University, Budapest.

Ellickson, Robert C. (1991). *Order Without Law: How Neighbors Settle Disputes*, Cambridge, MA: Harvard University Press.

Fischer, Stanley (1991). "Privatization in East European transformation." Working Paper No. 578, MIT.

Frydman, Roman, Rapaczynski, Andrzej, and Earle, John S. (eds.) (1993). *The Privatization Process in Central Europe*. Budapest: Central European University Press.

Gates, Susan, Milgrom, Paul, and Roberts, John (1996). "Complementarities in the transition from socialism: a firm-level analysis." In McMillan, John and Naughton, Barry (eds.).

Gillespie, John (1993). "The evolution of private commercial freedoms in Vietnam." In Thayer, C.A. and Marr, D.G. (eds.), *Vietnam and the Rule of Law*. Canberra: Australian National University.

Goldberg, Paul (1992). "Economic reform and product quality improvement efforts in the Soviet Union." *Soviet Studies*, 44: 113–22.

Gomulka, Stanislaw (1994). "The financial situation of enterprises and its impact on monetary and fiscal policies, Poland 1992–3." *Economics of Transition*, 2: 189–208.

Gordon, Roger and Li, Wei (1991). "Chinese enterprise behavior under the reforms." *American Economic Review: Papers and Proceedings*, 81: 202–6.

Greif, Avner and Kandel, Eugene (1995). "Contract enforcement institutions: historical perspective and current status in Russia." In Lazear, E.P. (ed.), *Economic Transition in Eastern Europe and Russia: Realities of Reform*. Stanford: Hoover Institution Press.

Grossman, Sanford J. and Hart, Oliver (1986). "The costs and benefits of ownership: a theory of vertical and lateral integration." *Journal of Political Economy*, 94: 691–719.

Groves, Theodore, Hong, Yongmiao, McMillan, John, and Naughton, Barry (1994). "Autonomy and incentives in Chinese state enterprises." *Quarterly Journal of Economics*, 109: 183–209.

(1995). "China's evolving managerial labor market." *Journal of Political Economy*, 4: 873–92.

Haley, John (1994). *Authority Without Law*. New York: Oxford University Press.

von Hayek, F.A. (1945). "The use of knowledge in society." *American Economic Review*, 35: 519–30.

Holmström, Bengt (1982). "Managerial incentive problems: a dynamic perspective." In *Essays in Economics and Management in Honor of Lars Wahlbeck*. Helsinki: Swedish School of Economics.

Holmström, Bengt and Milgrom, Paul (1994). "The firm as an incentive system." *American Economic Review*, 84: 972–91.

Holton, Richard D. and Sicular, Terry (1991). "Economic reform of the distribution sector in China." *American Economic Review: Papers and Proceedings*, 81: 212–17.

Hong, Yongmiao and McMillan, John (1996). "Restructuring China's state firms." Unpublished, University of California, San Diego.

Jefferson, Gary H. and Rawski, Thomas G. (1994). "Enterprise reform in Chinese industry." *Journal of Economic Perspectives*, 8: 47–70.

Johnson, Simon and Kroll, Heidi (1991). "Managerial strategies for spontaneous privatization." *Soviet Economy*, 7: 281–316.

Johnson, Simon, Kroll, Heidi, and Horton, Mark (1993). "New banks in the former Soviet Union: how do they operate?" In Aslund, A. and Layard, R. (eds.), *Changing the Economic System in Russia*. London: St Martin's Press.

Johnson, Simon and Loveman, Gary W. (1995). *Starting Over in Eastern Europe: Entrepreneurship and Economic Renewal*. Boston: Harvard Business School Press.

Johnson, Simon and Ustenko, Oleg (1994). "Corporate control of enterprises before privatization: the effects of spontaneous privatization." In Siebert, Horst (ed.), *Overcoming the Transformation Crisis: Lessons from Eastern Europe*. Kiel: Kiel Institute of World Economics.

Kandori, Michihiro (1992). "Social norms and community enforcement." *Review of Economic Studies*, 29: 61–80.

Klein, Benjamin and Leffler, Keith B. (1981). "The role of market forces in assuring contractual performance." *Journal of Political Economy*, 89: 615–41.

Koford, Kenneth and Miller, Jeffrey B. (1995). "Contracts in Bulgaria: how firms cope when property rights are incomplete." IRIS Working Paper No. 166.

Kornai, Janos (1979a). "Demand versus resource constrained systems." *Econometrica*, 47: 801–19.

(1979b). *Economics of Shortage*. Amsterdam: North Holland.

(1990). *The Road to a Free Economy*. New York: Norton.

Laffont, Jean-Jacques and Tirole, Jean (1986). "Using cost observation to regulate firms." *Journal of Political Economy*, 94: 614–41.

(1987). "Auctioning incentive contracts." *Journal of Political Economy*, 95: 921–37.

Lee, Doowon (1995). "The North Korean economic system: historical analysis and future prospects." Unpublished, Yonsei University, Seoul.

Li, David D. (1995). "A theory of ambiguous property rights in transitional economies." IRIS Working Paper No. 171.

Li, Wei (1994). "The impact of economic reform on the performance of Chinese state enterprises: 1980–1989." CIBER Working Paper No. 94-001, Duke University.

Lin, Justin Yifu (1992). "Rural reforms and agricultural growth in China." *American Economic Review*, 82: 34–51.

Lyons, Thomas P. (1994). "Economic reform in Fujian: another view from the villages." In Lyons, T.P. and Nee, V. (eds.), *The Economic Transformation of South China*. Ithaca: Cornell University Press.

Macauley, Stewart (1963). "Non-contractual relations in business: a preliminary study." *American Sociological Review*, 28: 55–67.

Manion, Melanie (1994). "Corruption by design: bribery in Chinese enterprise licensing." Unpublished, Department of Political Science, University of Rochester.

Mao, Zhirong (1995). "Economic growth in China, 1978–91." Ph.D. Dissertation, Graduate School of International Relations and Pacific Studies, University of California, San Diego.

Maskin, Eric S. (1992). "Auctions and privatization." In Seibert H. (ed.), *Privatization*. Tübingen: Mohr.

(1996). "Theories of the soft budget constraint." *Japan and the World Economy*, 8: 125–133.

McAfee, R. Preston and McMillan, John (1987). "Competition for agency contracts." *Rand Journal of Economics*, 18: 296–307.

(1995). "Organizational diseconomies of scale." *Journal of Economics and Management Strategy*, 4: 399–426.

McMillan, John and Morgan, Peter B. (1988). "Price dispersion, price flexibility, and repeated purchasing." *Canadian Journal of Economics*, 21: 883–902.

McMillan John and Naughton, Barry (1992). "How to reform a planned economy: lessons from China." *Oxford Review of Economic Policy*, 8: 130–43.

(eds.) (1996). *Reforming Asian Socialism: The Growth of Market Institutions.* Ann Arbor: University of Michigan Press.

McMillan, John, Naughton, Barry, and Lin, Gang (1996). "Contracts between firm and state." In Fureng, D., Lin, C., and Naughton, B. (eds.), *China's State-Owned Enterprise Reforms.* London: Macmillan.

McMillan, John, Whalley, John, and Zhu, Lijing (1989). "The impact of China's economic reforms on agricultural productivity growth." *Journal of Political Economy*, 97: 781–807.

Morris, Derek and Lui, Shaojia Guy (1993). "The soft budget constraint in Chinese industrial enterprises in the 1980s." Unpublished, Oxford University.

Myerson, Roger and Satterthwaite, Mark (1983). "Efficient mechanisms for bilateral trading." *Journal of Economic Theory*, 29: 265–81.

Naughton, Barry (1992). "Implications of the state monopoly over industry and its relaxation." *Modern China*, 18: 14–41.

(1995). *Growing out of the Plan: Chinese Economic Reform 1978–1993.* New York: Cambridge University Press.

Nee, Victor (1992). "Organizational dynamics of market transition: hybrid forms, property rights, and mixed economy in China." *Administrative Science Quarterly*, 37: 1–27.

Nee, Victor and Su, Sijin (1996). "Institutions, social ties, and commitment in China's corporatist transformation." In McMillan, John and Naughton, Barry (eds.).

Pearce, David G. (1992). "Repeated games: cooperation and rationality." In Laffont, J.-J. (ed.), *Advances in Economic Theory: Sixth World Congress*, Vol. 1. New York: Cambridge University Press.

Peck, Martin J. and Richardson, Thomas J. (eds.) (1991). *What Is to Be Done?* New Haven: Yale University Press.

Pingali, Prabhu L. and Xuan, Vo-Tong (1990). "Vietnam: decollectivization and rice productivity growth." Social Science Division Paper 89-16, International Rice Research Institute.

Pinto, Brian (1995). "A primer on enterprise adjustment and governance in transition economies: what Poland has taught us." Unpublished, International Finance Corp.

Pinto, Brian, Belka, Marek, and Krajewski, Stefan (1993). "Transforming state enterprises in Poland: evidence on adjustment by manufacturing firms." *Brookings Papers on Economic Activity*, 1: 213–270.

Pinto, Brian and van Wijnbergen, Sweder (1994). "Ownership and corporate control in Poland: why state firms defied the odds." Unpublished, CEPR, London.

Pissarides, F., Singer, M., and Svejnar, J. (1995). "The formation and growth of small- and medium-sized enterprises: the case of Bulgaria." Unpublished, CERGE-EI, Prague.

Qian, Yingyi (1994). "A theory of shortage in socialist economies based on the 'soft budget constraint'." *American Economic Review*, 84: 145–56.

(1995). "Reforming corporate governance and finance in China." In Aoki, M. and Kim, H.-K. (eds.), *Corporate Governance in Transitional Economies*. Washington, DC: World Bank.

Qian, Yingyi and Stiglitz, Joseph E. (1996). "Institutional innovations and the role of local government in transition economies: the case of Guangdong province of China." In McMillan, John and Naughton, Barry (eds.).

Rob, Rafael (1991). "Learning and capacity expansion under demand uncertainty." *Review of Economic Studies*, 58: 655–75.

Roland, Gérard and Sekkat, Khalid (1993). "Market socialism and the managerial labor market." In Bardhan, P.K. and Roemer, J.E. (eds.), *Market Socialism*. New York: Oxford University Press.

Ronnås, Per (1992). *Employment generation through private entrepreneurship in Vietnam*. Geneva: International Labour Organisation.

(1996). "Private entrepreneurship in the nascent market economy of Vietnam." In McMillan, John and Naughton, Barry (eds.).

Rothschild, Michael and Stiglitz, Joseph E. (1976). "Equilibrium in competitive insurance markets: an essay in the economics of imperfect information." *Quarterly Journal of Economics*, 90: 629–50.

Rozelle, Scott (1996). "Gradual reform and institutional development: the keys to success of China's rural reforms." In McMillan, John and Naughton, Barry (eds.).

Rubin, Paul H. (1994). "Growing a legal system in the post-communist economies." *Cornell Law Journal*, 27: 1–47.

Rubin, Paul H. and Tesche, Jean Ellen (1995). "Private and public enforcement of agreements in Russia." Unpublished, Emory University.

Sachs, Jeffrey (1993). *Poland's Jump to the Market Economy*. Cambridge, MA: MIT Press.

Sako, Mari (1992). *Prices, Quality and Trust*. Cambridge: Cambridge University Press.

Schaede, Ulrike (1989). "Forwards and futures in Tokugawa-period Japan: a new perspective on the Dojima rice market." *Journal of Banking and Finance*, 13: 487–513.

Sinn, Gerlinde and Sinn, Hans-Werner (1993). *Cold Start*. Cambridge, MA: MIT Press.

Slay, Ben (1993). "Poland: the role of managers in privatization." *RFE/RL Research Report*, 2: 52–6.

Solinger, Dorothy J. (1989). "Urban reform and relational contracting in post-Mao China: an interpretation of the transition from plan to market." *Studies in Comparative Communism*, 22: 171–85.

(1993). "Urban entrepreneurs and the state: the merger of state and society." In *China's Transition from Socialism*. New York: M.E. Sharpe.

Spence, A. Michael (1974). *Market Signaling*. Cambridge, MA: Harvard University Press.

Stark, David (1974). "Recombinant property in East European capitalism." IRIS Working Paper No. 133.

Stiglitz, Joseph E. (1994). *Whither Socialism?* Cambridge, MA: MIT Press.

Stross, Randall (1990). "The return of advertising in China: a survey of the ideological reversal." *China Quarterly*, 123: 485–502.

Thimann, Christian and Thum, Marcel (1993). "Investing in the East: waiting and learning." Working Paper No. 33, Center for Economic Studies, University of Munich.

Upham, Frank K. (1994). "Speculations on legal informality: on Winn's 'relational practices and the marginalization of law'." *Law and Society Review*, 28: 233–41.

Voszka, Eva (1993). "Spontaneous privatization in Hungary." In Earle, J.S. *et al.* (eds.), *Privatization in the Transition to a Market Economy*. New York: St Martin's Press.

Wang, Huijong and Chen, Xiaohong (eds.) (1991). *Industrial Organization and Contestable Competition*. Beijing: China Economic Press (in Chinese).

Watson, Joel (1995). "Building a relationship." Unpublished, University of California, San Diego.

Wegren, Stephen K. (1994). "Building market institutions: agricultural commodity exchanges in post-communist Russia." *Communist and Post-Communist Studies*, 27: 195–224.

Whiting, Susan H. (1996). "Contract incentives and market discipline in China's rural industrial sector." In McMillan, John and Naughton, Barry (eds.).

Xu, Chenggang (1995). *A Different Transition Path: Ownership, Performance, and Influence of Chinese Rural Industrial Enterprises*. New York: Garland.

Yavas, Abdullah (1994). "Middlemen in bilateral search markets." *Journal of Labor Economics*, 12: 406–29.

Young, Susan (1995). *Private Business and Economic Reform in China*. Armonk, NY: M.E. Sharpe.

Zemplinerova, Alena, Lastovicka, Radek, and Marcincin, Anton (1995). "Restructuring of Czech manufacturing enterprises." Working Paper 74, CERGE-EI, Prague.

CHAPTER 7

Transition as a process of large-scale institutional change

Mathias Dewatripont and Gérard Roland

INTRODUCTION

In his essay on economic policy and the political process, Avinash Dixit (1994) quotes Alan Blinder's "Murphy's law of economic policy" (1987, p. 1):

> Economists have the least influence on policy where they know the most and most agree; they have the most influence on policy where they know the least and disagree most vehemently.

This statement, its second half at least, seems to be especially valid for the economics of transition. Rarely have economic advisers played such a prominent role in policy debates as has been the case since 1990 in central and eastern European economies. Jeffrey Sachs has attracted worldwide attention for his forceful advocacy of the "big bang" approach to transition. These views were endorsed by one part of the profession and criticized vehemently by another, while many others remained skeptical about what economic theory has to say about the transition from socialism to capitalism. No pre-established theory of transition existed before the fall of the Berlin wall. The ratio to theory to policy papers in transition economics has nevertheless been surprisingly low. The theories with which Western advisers were probably best-equipped were those concerning macroeconomic stabilization. However, most economists will agree that stabilization is only one of the dimensions of transition. Other very important aspects relate to the necessary *large-scale institutional changes*: the creation and development of markets, including financial markets, the institution and enforcement of property rights and other legal and political changes along with enterprise privatization and restructuring. All these complementary changes need to take place without creating too many economic disturbances, as the economy must continue to function and the various needs of the population must continue to be fulfilled. To make things even more complex, because of the magnitude of the changes implied by transition, political support needs to be continuously maintained during the reform process to avoid policy reversals. Theoretical knowledge on how to achieve these changes was scarce before transition. Moreover, the only experience prior to 1989 is that of China, where the political and economic circumstances differ strongly. Not surprisingly, the lack of prior knowledge of the transition process has led to surprises. Economists did not expect the huge output fall observed after price liberalization and stabilization, just as much as they did not expect the political backlash, in the whole region of eastern Europe, with the exception of the Czech Republic so far (where backlash has however taken the form of the break-up of former Czechoslovakia). Future surprises – pleasant or unpleasant – may still be expected.

The goal of theory is to select key features from this complex reality and to analyze their interaction in a tractable framework. Such a selection process, which is never neutral, must be discussed explicitly. From that point of view, it is useful to distinguish *objectives* and *constraints* of transition. Disagreements mainly concern the latter.

In terms of objectives, the following are broadly agreed upon:

1 Improve allocative efficiency by correcting the distortions of socialism through the introduction of flexible relative prices and the creation of a competitive market environment open to the world economy.
2 Stabilize the macroeconomy, which is necessary for a correct functioning of the price system.
3 Provide better incentives to make firms respond to market signals. Privatization on a large scale is an important component of changes in incentives. Corporate governance arrangements are crucial too.
4 Create government institutions "adequate" for a market economy. Economists have different views of what are "adequate" government institutions but there is a relative consensus on (a) the need for political and institutional stability, (b) the need to protect private property rights from encroachment (by government but also by the mafia) and to protect taxpayers from the rent-seeking behavior of pressure groups toward government.

While economists agree on the above, it is also crucial to stress the *constraints* facing the transition process:

1. *Uncertainty* of outcomes, at both the aggregate and the individual levels, is a key feature of transition. Economists sometimes diverge in their appreciation of the importance of uncertainty. Implicit in many policy analyses on transition is the idea of a clearly defined goal, usually the analyst's pet blueprint for an ideal economic system. To be honest, however, one must acknowledge that the model of capitalism toward which transition economies should converge is not necessarily clear. Existing controversies among economists on the role of government in a market economy transpose quite naturally to debates on transition. More importantly, even if there is a clear goal of transition, there is no accepted theory of how to get there. Can our economic theories tell us whether the outcome of the transition in central and east European economies will be closer to the West German miracle or the Weimar republic, not to speak of the recent Yugoslav history? There is thus huge aggregate uncertainty about outcomes, and the experience so far in these countries has not reduced the perception of uncertainty. Moreover, economic agents and policymakers act and take decisions, taking as given this aggregate uncertainty. Because the transition process is the result of decisions made by individuals and policymakers facing important uncertainty of outcomes, a theory of transition must integrate this relative ignorance in modeling the process of transition, as well as the learning process that must take place during transition.
2. Another important constraint is related to the *complementarities* and interactions between reforms. One obtains a wrong picture of transition by focusing on individual reforms. There are for example evident complementarities between privatization and price liberalization. Profit incentives in distorted markets lead to resource misallocation, and free prices alone do not deliver optimal allocative outcomes if firms do not face incentives for value maximization. Macroeconomic stabilization programs also require different instruments if prices are liberalized than if they are not. While economists all tend to agree on these complementarities, we shall see below that, contrary to conventional wisdom, the latter do not necessarily favor big bang reform programs.
3. Finally, *political constraints* are of crucial importance, because transition is an economy-wide process, involving gainers and losers, even if aggregate welfare is enhanced. These political constraints are particularly relevant in the countries of eastern

Europe where political reform – the move to democracy – has preceded economic reform – the move to the market. Political constraints matter *ex ante*, to convince voters to start a (possibly uncertain) reform process and *ex post*, to avoid reversal of this process.

Even though agreement on the ultimate goal of reform exists, important policy disagreements have surfaced concerning the speed and sequencing of reforms. Part of the goal of the chapter is to track down the sources of these disagreements, in terms of the constraints that are stressed and also in terms of the internal logic of the arguments. We will do this, viewing the reform process as one large-scale policy change involving several complementary reforms with uncertain payoffs.

As far as overall content is concerned, an important part of the literature has focused on macrostabilization aspects, relying on previous knowledge of macrostabilization (Lipton and Sachs (1990a), Blanchard *et al.* (1991), McKinnon (1991), and Bruno (1993)). We abstract from those aspects in this survey and focus rather on elements of institutional change. We also chose to abstract largely from the huge quantity of policy papers on transition to concentrate on papers contributing to the theory of transition or to our empirical knowledge of the transition process.

The chapter is organized as follows. In the first two sections, we discuss the theory of transition viewed as a general process of large-scale institutional change. Section 1 discusses the problem of transition under aggregate uncertainty and complementarities, analyzing their effect on the choice of big bang versus more gradualist strategies. This is done in a representative agent framework and we show that many tradeoffs of various transition strategies can already be analyzed in that context. Section 2 extends the analysis to introduce heterogeneity and to analyze the effect of political constraints on reform strategies.

While sections 1 and 2 offer a general perspective on transition processes, sections 3 and 4 focus on the specific incentive and allocative dimensions of the transition from socialism to capitalism. Section 3 discusses incentive changes, analyzing how privatization and enterprise restructuring strategies affect the degree of independence of firms from government. The discussion is organized around the two important and well-known dynamic incentive problems in government–enterprise relationships under socialism: the ratchet effect and the soft budget constraint. Section 4 discusses allocative changes and looks at the speed of reallocation of resources from declining state sectors to the new expanding private sectors.

1 COMPLEMENTARITY OF REFORMS AND AGGREGATE UNCERTAINTY

This section views transition as an uncertain process of interdependent reforms. It leaves aside political economy considerations, as well as more context-specific issues of incentive changes and resource reallocations. However, even in this highly stylized framework, insights can be derived on the optimal *speed* of transition. As we shall see, complementary reforms do not prevent a gradualist strategy from being optimal – contrary to what some authors (Lipton and Sachs (1990a), Murphy, Shleifer, and Vishny (1992)) have argued – but may even be *necessary* for the optimality of gradualism!

1.1 Experimentation and the optimal speed of reform

Let us build on Dewatripont and Roland (1995) and consider the following setup with infinite horizon, discrete time, and discount factor δ less than one. Consider two reforms, $i = 1, 2$, with uncertain outcomes which depend on the respective realized states of nature O_{1j} ($j = 1, 2, \ldots, J$) and O_{2k} ($k = 1, 2, \ldots, K$). When both reforms have been implemented ("full reform"), the net present value payoff for the economy is $F(O_{1j}, O_{2k})$ under realizations O_{1j} and O_{2k}. When only reform i has been implemented ("partial reform"), the net present value payoff for the economy is $P(O_{im})$ under realization O_{im}. Strong complementarity of reforms (see Gates, Milgrom, and Roberts (1993), Murphy, Shleifer, and Vishny (1992)) can be rationalized by having $P(.)$ much smaller than $F(.,.)$.[1] On the other hand, implementing a single reform gives information on $F(.,.)$ through the observation of $P(.)$. Indeed, since $P(O_{im})$ is assumed to be certain *given* O_{im}, observing $P(.)$ means observing a *partition* on the O_{im}'s. This partition can include a single element ($N_i = 1$ or no learning) or up to J or K elements for reforms 1 and 2 respectively ($N_i = J$ or K or full learning of O_{im}). For N_i given, call S_{in} an element of the partition, or "signal" observed when implementing reform i. Let us rank signals in terms of the expected payoff of full reform

$$n > n' \Rightarrow \underset{j,k}{E}(F(O_{1j}, O_{2k}) \mid S_{in}) \geq \underset{j,k}{E}(F(O_{1j}, O_{2k}) \mid S_{in'}).$$

The "default payoff" is normalized to zero, and represents, in reduced form, the evolution of the economy when the reform package under consideration is not enacted (but an alternative one can be). Since $P(.)$ and $F(.,.)$ may be negative, reversing reforms can be optimal. After a reversal of the reform package, the economy is back at its "default payoff." Call ξ_i the cost of reversing reform i when it has been implemented alone. Similarly, ξ is the cost of reversing both reforms. Assume $0 < \max\{\xi_1, \xi_2\} < \xi \leq \xi_1 + \xi_2$, which means that reversing one reform is less costly than reversing both. We will also assume that $P(O_{im})$ is always more negative than $-\xi_i$, so that partial reform is never attractive per se, which reflects the idea of complementarity between reforms.

To illustrate these assumptions, think of the reform package as "insider privatization." Reforms 1 and 2 refer for example to two sectors of the economy, light and heavy industry. Partial privatization is not optimal, because each sector needs the other one to function efficiently. On the other hand, insider privatization may or may not be a success, depending on existing managers' willingness and ability to improve efficiency in their firms. Reversal is costly, because the state has to reclaim control over the assets, in order to try another privatization method, like giving control to a concentrated external investor, or to maintain state ownership. Finally, reversing insider privatization in both sectors is intuitively more costly than reversing it in a single one.

Let us turn to the analysis of this model. Given the reversal option after uncertainty resolution and the assumption that learning takes place in one period, we can define the "big bang" payoff BB obtained when implementing both reforms simultaneously

$$BB = (1-\delta)\underset{j,k}{E}F(O_{1j}, O_{2k}) + \delta \underset{j,k}{E}\max\{-\xi, F(O_{1j}, O_{2k})\}. \tag{1}$$

Outcome $F(O_{1j}, O_{2k})$ is thus experienced for one period, after which one can decide whether or not to abandon the reform package.

What is now the payoff under gradualism? Assume reform 1 has been implemented first and signal S_{1n} has been learned. The continuation payoff $R_2(S_{1n})$ is then

$$R_2(S_{1n}) = (1-\delta)\underset{j,k}{E}(F(O_{1j}, O_{2k}) \mid S_{1n}) + \delta \underset{j,k}{E}\max\{-\xi, F(O_{1j}, O_{2k}) \mid S_{1n}\}.$$

Since the expectation of $F(.,.)$ is increasing in n, define $\tilde{n}$ such that $n \geq \tilde{n}$ if and only if $R_2(S_{1n}) \geq -\xi_1$. That is, reversal takes place only for signals worse than $S_{1\tilde{n}}$. The *ex ante* payoff of a gradualist package starting with reform 1, GR_{12}, is then

$$GR_{12} = (1-\delta)\underset{j}{E}P(O_{1j}) + \delta\,\mathrm{Prob}(n < \tilde{n})(-\xi_1)$$

$$+ \delta \operatorname{Prob}(n \geq \tilde{n}) \underset{n \geq \tilde{n}}{E} (R_2(S_{1n})).$$

Or equivalently

$$GR_{12} = (1 - \delta)\underset{j}{E}P(O_{1j}) + \delta BB + \delta \operatorname{Prob}(n < \tilde{n})(-\xi_1 - \underset{n<\tilde{n}}{E} (R_2(S_{1n}))). \quad (2)$$

The three terms on the right-hand side of (2) tell us that gradualism implies interim suffering (if $EP(.)$ is low because of strong complementarities between reforms) and costly delay in comparison to big bang, but allows for an *option value of early reversal* $(-\xi_1 - E_{n<\tilde{n}}(R_2(S_{1n}))$ being positive. For gradualism to be optimal, the cost of early reversal ξ_1 has to be lower than the cost of full reversal ξ. Moreover, the first reform has to be *informative*: the probability of early reversal ($\operatorname{Prob}(n < \tilde{n})$) has to be smaller than 1 (otherwise the status quo is optimal) and greater than zero (otherwise gradualism is dominated by a big bang strategy). The finer the signals as a partition of states of nature, the higher the chance the first reform will be informative in the above sense.

If early reversal is less costly than full reversal and the first reform is informative, gradualism will be preferable to big bang provided learning is fast enough relative to the interim efficiency loss, that is, provided δ is close enough to one. Otherwise, big bang will be superior. The above discussion suggests that, in the presence of reversal costs and aggregate uncertainty, a key determinant in the choice of big bang or gradualism is less the *outcome* of partial reform than its degree of *informativeness* about future outcomes.

Once a rationale for gradualism has been established, one can address the issue of optimal sequencing of reforms. Dewatripont and Roland (1995) show in the above framework that, *ceteris paribus*, one should first implement reforms which are more popular on average and reforms which are riskier. While the first insight simply results from a positive rate of time preference, the second comes from the fact that the option value of early reversal increases with the variability of the first-period outcome.[2]

This analysis also has interesting implications in terms of the timing of transition programs. Because the option value of early reversal raises the *ex ante* expected payoff of a gradualist program compared with a big bang strategy, it is possible to have $GR_{12} > 0 > BB$. In other words, for a given default payoff, gradualism may be *ex ante* attractive but big bang may not. If one assumes that the default payoff declines over time, this leads to predict that (a) a gradualist program will start earlier; (b) big bang programs will tend to be observed in countries where crisis perceptions are greater (after missed opportunities for gradualism). Both predictions are consistent with the observation that gradualist programs in Hungary and China started earlier than big bang programs in Poland and Russia which started under greater crisis perception.

In the setup of this section, uncertainty over reform outcomes leads to a slowdown in transition. Under alternative assumptions, it can however accelerate it. This is the case with the learning model of Bertocchi and Spagat (1993). They look at the problem facing a government wanting to remove subsidies in the state sector but which fears unnecessarily high induced unemployment. In the absence of uncertainty on the rate of absorption of the unemployed in the private sector, the path of subsidy removal is gradual and in pace with private-sector employment creation. In the presence of uncertainty, a higher initial pace of subsidy removal is optimal in order to learn more about the rate of absorption in the private sector. If this absorption rate turns out to be low, the government may in the next period increase again the level of subsidies in order to reabsorb some of the unemployed in the state sector. The only costs of going fast are thus the temporary unemployment costs associated with learning since there are no reversal costs in the model. Were irreversibility to be introduced so that initial subsidy cuts cannot be undone because of the irreversibility of enterprise closures, then learning effects will be dampened. This points again to the crucial role of reversal costs. If the latter are important for large-scale reform experiments, uncertainty will lead to a slow down in reform. Otherwise uncertainty could lead to an acceleration.

1.2 Complementarity and gradualism

It is interesting to remark that complementarity of reforms does not prevent gradualism from being potentially optimal. Remember that we have assumed a single reform never to be attractive per se, so that it is always followed either by a second reform or by a reversal to the default payoff. In fact, complementarity of reforms is even a *necessary* condition for gradualism to be optimal. To see this, specialize the above framework by assuming $F(O_{1j}, O_{2k}) \equiv O_{1j} + O_{2k}$, and $P(O_{im}) \equiv O_{im} - \gamma$. Until now, we have implicitly assumed γ to be large enough so that $O_{im} - \gamma < -\xi_1$. Assume instead that reforms are *separable* (that is, $\gamma = 0$) as well as statistically independent. In that case, gradualism will *never* be optimal. Each reform can be assessed independently, and will either be tried immediately or never. Instead, in the above framework, we know that gradualism may be optimal. Indeed, even if the second reform looks unattractive *ex ante* ($E_k O_{2k} < 0$), the momentum for further reform can be sustained if there was good news on the first reform (i.e., a high O_{1j}). Because of reform complementarity, implementing the second reform is necessary in order to keep the benefit from the first one, and also to avoid the cost of reversing it. A good example of momentum effects under gradualism is the success of decollectivization in China which created support for complementary reforms such as price liberalization and enterprise reform.

1.3 Decentralization and experimentation: the case of China

The conditions of learning and complementarities of reforms may be crucially affected by the differences in organizational structure of the centrally planned economy itself. This was the case in China compared with eastern Europe as pointed out by Qian and Xu (1993). Planned economies in eastern Europe were organized along the branch principle with sectoral ministries regrouping similar activities. By contrast, China's planned economy was organized along a regional principle, each province being responsible for a whole array of industries. Qian and Xu argue that centrally planned economies of eastern Europe, managed more centrally, were like U-form hierarchies (Williamson (1975), Chandler (1962)) whereas China had a more decentralized structure, very much like an M-form hierarchy.[3] The starting point of their analysis is the observation that China's gradualism yielded spectacular successes compared with Hungary's pre-transition gradualism. One of the disadvantages of the Chinese planning system is that it led to duplication of industries, as provincial authorities were striving to get "their" steel industry, "their" textile industry, etc., whereas, in the east European U-form type of central planning, it was possible to exploit economies of scale and to expand the division of labor in the economy. However, in the context of reform, the Chinese organizational structure gave much more flexibility for experimentation. Indeed, introducing reform in only one region and not in the whole of China still yielded high benefits of learning at substantially lower reversal costs. In east European planned economies, the U-form type hierarchy made regional reform experiments impossible because of the stronger interconnectedness of firms. Any experiment of liberalization at the level of big state-owned enterprises had to take place at the economy-wide level. While differences in organizational structures may explain the "spatial" gradualism observed in Chinese reforms, there has also been an important element of "sectoral" gradualism in this country, with radical reform in agriculture preceding reform in industrial sectors. Even if east European economies did not have the option of spatial gradualism, because of their U-form organization, the argument of Qian and Xu does not preclude the possibility of sectoral gradualism in these economies. The question remains open whether there were not missed opportunities for sectoral gradualism in that region. Reform could for example have been started in the agro-food sector which was well-known for its economic waste and negative value-added activities (see Senik-Leygonie and Hughes (1992) on the Soviet Union; and Hugues and Hare (1991) on eastern Europe). Success of such a reform, in terms of the increased supply of food and shorter queues, could then have increased support for further reforms, possibly avoiding the strong political backlash currently observed in Russia.

2 POLITICAL CONSTRAINTS

We now proceed to a discussion of the role of political constraints on the design of reforms. Political constraints are relevant under any type of political regime, albeit under different forms. They are particularly relevant for transition countries in which the move to democracy preceded the move to the market.

Political constraints were absent in section 1 in that all agents were identical *ex ante* as well as *ex post*. To seriously discuss the effects of political constraints, we must model heterogeneous populations to capture the distributive effects of reform. Section 2.1 extends the model of section 1 to introduce heterogeneity. Section 2.2 looks at how, in the absence of uncertainty, gradualism can be used by an agenda-setting government to implement "divide and rule" tactics to overcome resistance to reform. Section 2.3 analyses the tradeoffs that are present when costly transfers can be made and when, instead of uncertainty, there is asymmetric information about winners and losers from reform. Finally, section 2.4 looks at the effect of the threat of secession on the distributional impact of reform. These various sets of assumptions all shed light in a different way on the effect of political constraints on the speed and sequencing of reforms as well as on the design of privatization and of restructuring programs.

2.1 Option value of early reversal and heterogeneity

In section 1, we concentrated on the role of aggregate uncertainty over reform outcomes. What if we also introduce individual uncertainty? Fernandez and Rodrik (1991) focus solely on this type of uncertainty. They consider a reform where, *ex post*, a proportion q of individuals enjoy a positive gain g, while a proportion $(1 - q)$ suffer a negative net gain l. If the reform is reversible, they show that a *status quo bias* will arise. Assume for simplicity no reversal cost. Assume moreover that majority rule prevails and that all individuals are identical *ex ante*, each having thus a probability q of gaining from the reform. Then, if q is smaller than 0.5, the reform is not worth enacting, because it will be reversed for sure. On the other hand, if q is higher than 0.5, reversal will not occur. The reform will then be undertaken if and only if $qg + (1 - q)l > 0$. This constraint and the condition $q > 0.5$ represent a double hurdle against departing from the status quo.

In the absence of aggregate uncertainty, reversibility of reforms can only induce a status quo bias, since there is no option value of reversal. This was of course different in section 1. We now combine individual and aggregate uncertainty in order to derive more insights on optimal sequencing.

Assume there are two reforms, reform 1 and reform 2, with independent outcomes. For simplicity, assume here *immediate learning*, that is, $\delta = 1$. Each reform has a positive aggregate outcome G occurring with probability p and a negative aggregate outcome L occurring with probability $(1 - p)$. Each individual reform has reversal cost $\xi/2$. Besides these aggregate gains or losses, the two reforms differ in their distributive effects. All individuals are identical *ex ante*. However, *ex post*, reform 1 is assumed to bring an additional positive gain g to two thirds of the population but the other third will be hurt and get $-2g$ on top of the aggregate outcome. Reform 2, on the other hand, benefits a minority *ex post*, yielding $2g$ for one third of the population and $-g$ for two thirds. When both reforms have been implemented, the reversal cost is ξ. These assumptions are such that, after the two reforms have been implemented, the overall distributive effects are neutral for the median voter *ex post* (and for 5/9 of the population).[4] Note also that from the *ex ante* point of view, each reform is distributively neutral. However, each individual reform is not *ex post* distributively neutral. This means that the sequencing of reforms may affect reform reversibility after implementation of a first reform. To see this, compare GR_{12} where reform 1 is implemented first and GR_{21} where reform 2 is implemented first. Assume that $G + L > -\xi > 2L$, so that the full reform package gets reversed *ex post* only in the worst state of nature.

Under GR_{12}, the median voter has to decide whether to go ahead with reform 2 while knowing he is among the relative *winners* of reform 1. If outcome G is realized after the first reform, he will vote for continuation if

$$p(2G + g) + (1 - p)(G + L + g) > -\xi/2.$$

If L is realized, continuation requires instead (given that $\delta = 1$)

$$p(L + G + g) + (1 - p)(-\xi) > -\xi/2.$$

Under GR_{21}, the median voter considers going ahead while knowing he is among the relative *losers* of reform 2. If G is realized, continuation will be voted if

$$p(2G - g) + (1 - p)(G + L - g) > -\xi/2.$$

If L is realized, continuation requires instead

$$p(L + G - g) + (1 - p)(-\xi) > -\xi/2.$$

One immediately sees that continuation is more difficult under GR_{21} than under GR_{12}. In other words, there will be more irreversibility if one starts with reform 1 rather than with reform 2. In particular, there are parameter values such that continuation is decided under GR_{12} if and only if G is realized, while under GR_{21}, reversal can never be avoided. In that case, GR_{12} is optimal and GR_{21} is clearly not. Of course, more irreversibility *ex post* can be a mixed blessing, since it reduces the option value of early reversal. If may be *precisely* because GR_{21} entails more reversibility than GR_{12} or a big bang strategy that it could be *ex ante* more acceptable. This could be the case for parameter values such that GR_{12} would always imply continuation after reform 1 is realized while GR_{21} would yield reversal if and only if L is realized.

In that perspective, one can consider the case of a reformist government trying to maximize the probability of no reversal subject to *ex ante* acceptability. Then, any window of opportunity will be used to get important reform packages through, and big bang strategies will be preferred whenever they are *ex ante* feasible, simply because the option of early reversal disappears. These examples, based on Dewatripont and Roland (1995), thus allow us to understand both the case for big bang (which takes advantage of windows of opportunity to introduce reforms that are costly to reverse) and the case for gradualism (which relaxes *ex ante* political constraints and creates irreversibility through correct sequencing, building constituencies for further reform).

Going beyond this model, the case for big bang or gradualism may also depend on whether the probability of re-election of the incumbent government is *exogenous* or *endogenous*. Models by Persson and Svensson (1989) and Alesina and Tabellini (1990) show the advantages of using political windows of opportunity to take decisions that constrain a potential successor government. In that framework, the occurrence of political backlash and the loss of power by the incumbent government are only the results of exogenous forces. The overriding concern is to constrain one's potential successors by deciding today reforms that will be more difficult to reverse tomorrow. An exogenous probability of re-election would thus tend to favor a big bang approach whenever feasible. If however policymakers face an endogenous probability of re-election, they should strive to build constituencies by starting with more popular reforms. In that framework, political backlash may be the result of wrong sequencing, as in the above examples. Aghion and Bolton (1991) have also developed a model of policy choices where the probability of re-election is endogenous.

In transition economies, political constraints have undoubtedly played an important role in the privatization and restructuring process, in part due to fears of redundancies. Roland and Verdier (1994) show how privatization through giveaways may create political irreversibility by giving the domestic population stakes in the success of privatization, provided the shares distributed to the population cannot be resold. This was certainly an important motive in the design of voucher privatization in Czechoslovakia. The Polish mass privatization program, designed to favor giveaways to the domestic population, was however blocked for several years by coalitions of insiders (Frydman and Rapaczynski (1994)). It is precisely to overcome such potential *ex ante* political constraints that the Russian mass privatization program was designed to favor giveaways to insiders. Boycko, Shleifer, and Vishny (1995) justify the Russian program by arguing that it was the only politically feasible plan and that this consideration outweighed economic considerations, which point to the disadvantages of insider privatization.

2.2 Divide-and-rule tactics

So far, our analysis of the comparison of big bang and gradualism has been made in the context of *aggregate uncertainty*, where gradualism can be used to take advantage of the option value of early reversal. Gradualism may, however, also be desirable in the absence of uncertainty, because it can be used to implement divide-and-rule tactics in a context of dynamic agenda setting.

The analysis below assumes an agenda-setting reformer making proposals to a population subject to majority rule. This agenda-setter can for example be a manager or external investor making restructuring proposals to the firm's workers. Indeed, the analysis may provide an explanation for the ability shown by a great number of managers to impose important layoffs in firms with significant worker control (Pinto, Belka, and Krajewski (1993), Estrin, Schaffer, and Singh (1992), Carlin, Van Reenen, and Wolfe (1994)). While the recent literature on restructuring explores the incentives of managers of state-owned enterprises to downsize output and employment, the question of how managers of worker-controlled firms are able to overcome resistance to layoffs has yet received little attention.

Alternatively, the agenda-setter can be a newly elected reformist government which has to get its reform proposals enacted by Parliament, where the various constituencies are represented. We develop below the interpretation of a liberalization plan of the economy.

The importance of agenda-setting has been stressed by Romer and Rosenthal (1979) in a public finance context. In the field of social choice,

McKelvey (1976) has shown how dynamic agenda-setting can allow governments to exploit Condorcet cycles in the presence of *myopic* voters. Agenda-setting can, however, also be powerful with rational, forward-looking voters. We show this with a model based on Wei (1993).[5] Consider a continuum of voters, with three types of unit mass each, facing the following reform plans:

	Net gain of type 0	*Net gain of type 1*	*Net gain of type 2*
Reform 1	g_1	l_1	g_1
Reform 2	g_2	g_2	l_2

where the above shows per-period deterministic payoffs with $g_i > 0 > l_i$, $i = 1, 2$. Interpret reform i as the liberalization of sector i, and type i to be the workers in that sector who are hurt from its restructuring. Otherwise, everybody gains from liberalization as a consumer, and type 0 represents voters not working in sector 1 or 2.

Under majority rule, two types out of three must vote in favor of the government's proposals to have them enacted. We assume the government can only offer each period either the status quo, or a single reform, or both reforms. Once a reform has been accepted, it is irreversible. While Wei considers a two-period horizon, it is possible to generalize the framework to an infinite horizon.

Assuming the government is unable to pre-commit to future proposals, it is easy to see that, once one reform has been enacted, the second one will go through immediately afterwards, since only the workers in that sector will oppose it. On the other hand, if $l_1 + g_2$ and $l_2 + g_1$ are negative, a big bang strategy proposing both reforms at once will always be opposed. In a stationary infinite-horizon problem, proposals of reform for a single sector will also fail (provided individual voters do not vote for weakly dominated strategies): workers in the other sector know they will be hurt in the next period! Things change dramatically, however, if there are exogenous dates at which the sectors are expected to "disappear." Call these dates t_1 and t_2 and assume, without loss of generality, that t_1 is the earlier date. One can think of t_i as the date at which the sector goes bankrupt because of financial distress or at which workers go into (early) retirement. In that case, divide-and-rule tactics can be very powerful, as the following backward-induction argument shows.

First, at the beginning of period t_1, when sector 1 closes, the government can enlist the support of types 0 and 1 to close sector 2, since workers in sector 1 have just become consumers. Second, since workers in both sectors expect to lose their job at t_1, each group is ready to vote for closing the other sector at $t_1 - 1$. Partial reform is possible at this point, even though full reform is not. Assume, without loss of generality, that the government would rather close sector 1 first. Given the continuation equilibrium, reform 2 is possible at $t_1 - 2$. Indeed, type 1 workers expect to lose their job at $t_1 - 1$ and they gain as consumers to have reform 2 decided at $t_1 - 2$, rather than at t_1! It is interesting to observe that this argument can be repeated, allowing the government to get reform 1 through at $t_1 - 3$, reform 2 at $t_1 - 4, \ldots$! Therefore, the equilibrium involves immediate gradual reform, completed in two periods, with reform 1 enacted in period 1 if t_1 is even, or reform 2 enacted in period 1 if t_1 is odd. This unraveling argument is so powerful as to allow full reform to be completed within two periods, as in the McKelvey setup with myopic voters. This extreme result is, however, only an example, and the analysis should be generalized in future research.

2.3 Transfers

Until now, reforms have been considered without introducing the possibility of explicit transfers from gainers to losers or, equivalently, under the assumption that transfers are prohibitively costly. We can relax this assumption while maintaining a net resource cost of transfers (e.g., because they are financed by distortionary taxation), denoted λ in percentage terms.

We develop two themes in the next subsections. First, we show that under asymmetric information over winners and losers, gradualism can be used to reveal information and thus to reduce the amount of transfers, at the cost of delay in reaching efficiency. Second, secession or the threat of secession can also lead to reductions in transfer payments.

2.3.1 Costly compensation and gradualism

The issue of speed of reform and costs of compensating transfers can best be highlighted by comparing restructuring policies in East Germany and other transition economies. In the former GDR, restructuring has proceeded very fast with massive layoffs at an early stage of transition (Sinn and Sinn (1993)). This policy has, however, been associated with massive transfers from West Germany. In contrast, in central and eastern Europe, where such transfers were not available, redundancies have been more gradual (see Dewatripont and Roland (1992b)). Within the latter groups of countries, "faster" reformers such as Poland, Hungary, or the Czech Republic have been facing higher increases in social security expenditures (unemployment benefits and mainly pensions) due to a higher level of restructuring compared to "slower" reformers who have maintained higher levels of subsidies in ailing industries (Coricelli (1995)). Dewatripont and Roland (1992a and b) provide an analysis which rationalizes this contrast.

Let us concentrate here solely on reforms that must be *unanimously* approved, thus Pareto improving, to be enacted. This allows us to abstract from divide-and-rule tactics. Consider again a continuum of voters with three types of unit mass each. The net present value payoffs of the reform are as follows:

Type 0	$g > 0$
type 1	$\underline{l} < 0$
type 2	$\bar{l} < 0$

with $\underline{l} > \bar{l}$. In a single-period horizon with complete information and minimum, targeted transfers to compensate losers, a Pareto-improving reform will go through if and only if

$$(g + \underline{l} + \bar{l}) + \lambda(\underline{l} + \bar{l}) > 0. \tag{3}$$

Assume the above reform to involve restructuring of the economy with type 0 workers keeping their job in that part of the economy which is in good health and the other types having to suffer transition costs (which are higher for type 2 than for type 1). Transfers can then be interpreted as an exit bonus. If individual types are private information, workers can self-select by choosing to keep their job (which involves a gain for type 0 but a loss for types 1 and 2) or to take the exit bonus. In any case, it is not possible to discriminate between types 1 and 2 if they both leave: they will always take the highest exit bonus available. Enacting the reform in full will thus involve a net payoff of

$$(g + \underline{l} + \bar{l}) + 2\lambda\bar{l} \tag{4}$$

which is smaller than (3). This could induce the government to go for "partial" reform that allows type 2 workers to keep their jobs, so that only type 1 workers suffer transition costs. The idea is that workers with lower transition costs can more easily be induced to exit: they only need a compensation of $\underline{l}$. If such partial reform involves an allocative loss of Δ relative to full reform, its net payoff is

$$(g + \underline{l} + \bar{l} - \Delta) + \lambda\underline{l}. \tag{5}$$

Full reform is efficient under complete information if $\Delta + \lambda\bar{l} > 0$. However, under incomplete information, partial reform allows to reduce the exit bonus of type 1 workers! Partial reform may thus dominate full reform if

$$\Delta + \lambda\bar{l} + \lambda(\bar{l} - \underline{l}) < 0. \tag{6}$$

This tradeoff between allocative efficiency and rent extraction is well known from the adverse selection literature (see, e.g., Caillaud *et al.* (1988)).

As shown by Dewatripont and Roland (1992a and b), it has an interesting dynamic implication: whenever (6) holds, that is, whenever partial reform dominates full reform in a one-period context, gradualism emerges as the optimal time-consistent reform package.

Indeed, without the ability to commit to stick to partial reform, the government will end up compensating type 2 workers with exit bonus $-\bar{l}$ so as to move to full reform one period after the exit of type 1 workers. Anticipating this, type 1 workers will be ready to leave earlier only if given an exit bonus of $-[(1-\delta)\underline{l}+\delta\bar{l}]$ if δ is the discount factor. Otherwise, they would rather remain in the sector for one period and "pretend" to be of type 2. Gradual reform thus gives a payoff of

$$(1-\delta)[g+\underline{l}+\bar{l}-\Delta]+\lambda[(1-\delta)\underline{l}+\delta\bar{l}]+\delta[g+\underline{l}+\bar{l}]+\lambda\delta\bar{l}. \qquad (7)$$

Clearly, (7) is a convex combination of (4) and (5) (with weights δ and $1-\delta$), and gradual reform dominates full reform whenever, in a static context, partial reform dominates full reform. Gradualism, while not as good as maintained partial reform, dominates a big bang strategy and is the time-consistent optimum whenever budget considerations are important enough (i.e., λ is high enough).[6]

2.3.2 *Secession as a way to limit costly transfers*

When transfers are too costly to allow reform to go through, it may lead to the temptation of secession, especially if the gains and losses from reform are expected to be geographically unequally distributed. The analysis below illustrates some of the tensions in transition economies created by the different geographical distributions of pro-reform and anti-reform interests, contributing to the break-up of Czechoslovakia, Yugoslavia, and the USSR. Even though ethnic conflicts have undoubtedly played an important role in these secessions, conflicts on reform strategies and interregional transfers have also played a prominent role after the introduction of democracy in these countries.

Assume as above a reform with net distributive gains of g, $\underline{l}$, and $\bar{l}$ each to one third of the population respectively. In the unified country, a reform-minded agenda-setter can get the reform accepted by a majority provided it is paired with transfers of $-\underline{l}$ to losers. We may assume as above that there is asymmetric information about the losers, though that assumption is not necessary here. Under that reform program, the group of winners will have to be taxed $-(1+\lambda)2\underline{l}$ but assume their net gains are still positive; the median group is made indifferent between reform and status quo whereas those losing most will experience a net loss of $\bar{l}-\underline{l}$ and thus vote against reform.

Against this benchmark case of reform in a unified country, assume now that there are two regions of equal size and that the geographical distribution of gains and losses is as follows: all those having g and one half of those having $\underline{l}$ live in region A, whereas the other half of those with $\underline{l}$ and all those with $\overline{l}$ live in region B. In region A, a majority (including the median voter) gets g whereas in region B a majority gets $\overline{l}$.

Assume now that after a reform proposal is voted in the unified country, a referendum on secession is held in each region. Call s the cost of secession or, equivalently in this simple setup, the cost associated with implementation of reform in one region only. What would be the incentive for each region to secede after a decision in the unified country to adopt the reform with transfers of $-\underline{l}$? One sees immediately that a majority in region A may consider the option of seceding in order to adopt a reform involving no transfers. This would be the case if the cost of secession to the median voter in region A is smaller than the transfers they avoid paying by seceding, i.e., if

$$s < -(1+\lambda)2\underline{l}.$$

However, a majority in region B may also want to secede in order to have no reform adopted. Indeed, after secession, any reform proposal would be rejected in region B since all lose from reform, and thus no group can be taxed to compensate the losers. Secession would take place if the cost of secession to the median voter in region B is smaller than the loss from reform in the unified country, i.e., if

$$s < -(\overline{l} - \underline{l}).$$

The possibility of secession in a region may of course influence the agenda setter's choice of reform proposal. He may indeed want to prevent secession because of the inefficiencies involved. To prevent A from seceding implies an upper bound on the amount of transfers paid to the losers

$$t \leq \frac{s}{2(1+\lambda)}.$$

To prevent B from seceding, however, compensating transfers must satisfy a lower bound

$$t \geq -\overline{l} - s.$$

Putting together these two constraints, one gets

$$\overline{l} - s \leq t \leq \frac{s}{2(1+\lambda)}.$$

If s is small enough, the set of acceptable ts may be empty and secession may be unavoidable because of the contradictory requirements of the pro-reform majority in region A and the anti-reform majority in region B. If s is higher, the possibility of secession may still alter the initial reform proposal compared with the benchmark case without secession. In particular, a reform-minded agenda setter who wants to minimize transfers can set $t = -(\bar{l} - s)$ and get it accepted by a majority. All those in region A will gain: the amount of transfers paid by the winners will be smaller than the secession costs and the minority of those who get $\underline{l}$ will gain compared with secession since they receive some transfers and avoid the costs of secession. On the other hand, since t makes those who get $\underline{l}$ indifferent between secession and reform, those agents will even be better off compared with secession. The possibility of secession allows here to reduce the amount of transfers paid to the losers from reform since it changes the status quo in case of rejection of a reform proposal.

The redrawing of borders inside Europe after the fall of the Berlin wall has renewed the attention of economists to questions of secession and political integration. Bolton and Roland (1994) study the effect of differences in income distribution across regions on the incentives to secede. In the spirit of the example above, it is shown that if the efficiency losses from separation are relatively small, secession may be unavoidable because of contradictory requirements of majorities in the different regions: a majority in a region where pre-tax income distribution is relatively egalitarian may want to secede to reduce the level of redistributive taxation whereas a majority in a less egalitarian region may want to secede in order to increase the level of redistribution. Alesina and Spolaore (1994) study the optimal size of nations as resulting from a tradeoff between economies of scale in the provision of public goods, on the one hand, and a composition of public goods that is closer to the preferences of individuals, on the other hand. Casella and Feinstein (1990) and Wei (1991) similarly look at the tradeoff between the efficiency advantages of trade in a unified country and the costs of having public goods less close to the preferences of individuals and analyze how this tradeoff evolves with economic development.

3 INCENTIVE CHANGES

Central to the transition process from plan to market is the question of adequate incentives facing producers. Usually, in market economies, issues of microeconomic restructuring can be parameterized by variables related to product, labor, and capital markets. The companion chapter by John McMillan discusses these aspects exhaustively. In transition economies, changes in enterprise behavior depend also in a crucial way on the severance of the close government–firm relationships that were a distinctive feature of socialist economies. The discussion in this section will focus on how this problem is solved in transition economies.

The literature on socialist economies has mainly emphasized two crucial problems arising in government–firm relationships: the *ratchet* effect and the *soft budget constraint* problem. The ratchet effect, emphasized in formal work by Freixas, Guésnerie, and Tirole (1985), Laffont and Tirole (1988, 1993), or Litwack (1993), arises when the planner cannot commit not to revise upwards demands on firms that show over time to be efficient. Under central planning, the ratchet effect meant that if managers overfulfilled the production plan by a high enough margin, next year's production plan would be ratcheted up (see Berliner (1952), Keren, Miller, and Thornton (1983), Bain *et al.* (1987), Weitzman (1980)). As a consequence, good managers deliberately avoided exceeding the plan by too large a margin. The soft budget constraint problem, associated with the name of Kornai (1979, 1980), relates to a well-known situation under socialism where the planner could not commit not to bail out loss-making firms. Both the ratchet effect and the soft budget constraint syndrome are general incentive problems that apply beyond the socialist system, but they were particularly present under socialism given the close relationship between firms and the government. As pointed out by Qian and Roland (1995), both problems are intuitively related: the temptation to extract resources from good firms (the ratchet effect) is particularly high when there is an incentive to refinance bad firms (due to the soft budget constraint). Moreover, bad firms have few incentives to respect financial discipline if they know they can rely on cross-subsidization to be bailed out. There is thus a complementarity between these two incentive problems, leading to lower efficiency in both good and bad firms. In this section, we present models that attempt to understand these incentive problems associated with socialist economies[7] and, on that basis, shed some light on the policy solutions in the transition process.[8]

3.1 Soft budget constraints as a time-consistency problem

Kornai's work has focused mainly on the *consequences* of the soft budget constraint, namely the emergence of pervasive shortages under socialism. He primarily attributes the *causes* of the soft budget constraint to political constraints, that is, to the desire of "paternalistic" governments to avoid socially and politically costly layoffs. Dewatripont and Maskin's (1995) analysis of the soft budget constraint stresses instead dynamic commitment problems in the presence of irreversible investment (see also Schaffer (1981) and Qian and Xu (1991)).[9]

They consider the following adverse selection problem. The government faces a population of firms, each needing one unit of funds in initial period 1 in order to start their project. A proportion α of these projects are of the "good, quick" type: after one period, the project is successfully completed, and generates a gross (discounted) financial return $R_g > 1$. Moreover, the manager of the firm (possibly also workers) obtains a positive net (discounted) private benefit E_g. In contrast, there is a proportion $(1 - \alpha)$ of bad and slow projects which generate no financial return after one period. If terminated at that stage, managers obtain a private benefit E_t. Instead, if refinançed, each project generates after two periods a gross (discounted) financial return π_b^* and a net (discounted) private benefit E_b. Initially, α is common knowledge but individual types are private information. A simple result easily follows: if $1 < \pi_b^* < 2$ and $E_b > 0$, refinancing bad projects is sequentially optimal for the government, and bad entrepreneurs who expect to be refinanced apply for initial financing. The government would however be better off if it were able to commit not to refinance bad projects, since it would thereby deter managers with bad projects from applying for initial financing, provided $E_t < 0$.

Termination is here by assumption a discipline device which allows the uninformed investor (creditor) to turn away bad types and only finance good ones.[10] The problem is that termination is not sequentially rational if π_b^* is bigger than one: once the first unit has been sunk into a bad project, its net continuation value is positive so that, in the absence of commitment, the soft budget constraint syndrome arises. In this setup, because irreversibility of investment is such a general economic feature, the challenge for theory is more to explain why hard budget constraints prevail rather than why budget constraints are soft in the first place!

3.2 The ratchet effect as a (connected) time-consistency problem

Take the same setup as in the previous subsection, but assume the government starts with N units of funds in total in the first period, allowing it to finance less than the total number of good projects. Assume moreover that second-period finance has to come solely from first-period returns. Finally, assume that, by exerting "effort" in period 1, good types can, with an additional unit of funds at the beginning of period 2, generate a gross return $\hat{R}_g$ bigger than 1 with a positive net private benefit $\hat{E}_g$ in period 2.

Then, under a hard budget constraint, only good types are financed initially, and they can all get refinancing in period 2. Instead, under a soft budget constraint, total gross financial returns at the end of period 1 only total αR_g. In this case, if π_b^* exceeds $\hat{R}_g$, the government has an incentive to tax away at least part of αR_g in order to finance bad types.

We thus have a ratchet effect connected to the soft budget constraint problem: the government is tough *ex post* with good types *in order* to bail out bad ones! The total needs of bad types equal $(1 - \alpha) N$. The higher this amount relative to αR_g, the smaller the probability that good types get refinanced, and the lower their incentive to exert first-period effort, as in the ratchet models of Freixas, Guésnerie, and Tirole (1985) or Laffont and Tirole (1988).

The above argument is a simplified version of that of Qian and Roland (1995). It provides a useful benchmark to analyze remedies to the incentive problems of socialist economies, to which we now turn.

3.3 Getting around perverse government incentives

Both the ratchet effect and the soft budget constraint problem relate to the absence of credible precommitment of government *vis-à-vis* firms. A key question to solve these problems thus concerns the institutional changes that can endogenously create government commitment.[11]

3.3.1 Privatization

One interpretation of the above problems is to consider that π_b^* internalizes a political bias of socialist governments, for example toward excessive employment. Under this interpretation, a profit-maximizing creditor would *not* refinance bad firms. Moreover, if there were any refinancing, it would be accompanied by different restructuring measures from those that would be chosen if the government were directly in control of the firm.

How can a reformist government constrain the ability of future governments to exercise a political bias in economic activity? Boycko, Shleifer, and Vishny (1992) and Shleifer and Vishny (1994) argue that privatization, namely the allocation of control rights and of profits streams to managers provides the solution. In this case, governments will find it harder and more costly to move firms away from profit-maximizing behavior, since they will have to "bribe" firms instead of simply dictating their behavior. If such bribing is costly for governments, for example because it must be financed through distortionary taxation, one should expect less refinancing of bad firms and fewer deviations from profit-maximizing outcomes. In this story, the ability to bribe managers is reduced if the government is poorer, which then argues for giveaways as opposed to sales as a method of privatization, as advocated by Boycko, Shleifer, and Vishny (1995).

It can indeed be argued that privatization helps solve the ratchet effect. Schmidt (1995) shows that privatization lowers the government's *ability* to extract rents from firms. In this model, this ability is reduced because the information government has for privatized firms is inferior to that for public firms. If the government suffers from a lack of precommitment but is otherwise benevolent, Schmidt shows that privatization distorts *allocative efficiency*, as is usual whenever the firm has market power but, by limiting the ratchet effect, improves *productive efficiency*.

Roland and Sekkat (1992, 1995) have argued that the existence of a private sector in itself helps alleviate the ratchet effect through the development of a managerial labor market in the private sector. The existence of career opportunities outside the state sector helps to alleviate the opportunistic behavior of governments towards managers and creates commitment to incentive schemes. This may also explain why the ratchet effect seems less prevalent in big firms in the West.

Solving the ratchet effect through privatization can also help alleviate the connected soft budget constraint problem by increasing the opportunity cost of refinancing. Note, however, that privatization per se does not necessarily solve soft budget constraint problems inside firms. Indeed, if π_b^* reflects the political bias of government toward excessive unemployment, privatized firms may exploit government's softness in order to get bailed out. Big bailouts such as that of Chrysler or the American Savings and Loan show that the soft budget constraint problem may arise in privatized firms too.[12]

The discussion in this subsection has focused on how privatization helps solve the ratchet effect and the soft budget constraint. Another important debate that has taken place, especially in the early phases of transition, concerns the comparison between various privatization *methods*. Given the size of the total assets to be privatized and the absence of pre-existing private wealth in transition economies, the need arose to introduce new privatization methods. Here the policy debate has mostly opposed partisans of massive giveaways, emphasizing speed (Blanchard *et al.* (1991), Lipton and Sachs (1990b), Frydman and Rapaczynski (1994), Boycko, Shleifer, and Vishny (1995)), to partisans of gradual sales or sales against non-cash bids emphasizing economic efficiency and revenue maximization.[13] (Maskin (1991), Aghion and Burgess (1993), Bolton and Roland (1992), Kornai (1990), Demougin and Sinn (1992) Sinn and Sinn (1993).)

3.3.2 *Decentralization of government decisions*

Qian and Roland (1994) take a similar perspective to that in subsection 3.3.1 above, assuming π_b^* to be too high because of political bias. However, instead of privatization, they investigate *decentralization* as a method to reduce π_b^*. Government remains in control of the financing decisions, and the focus is on altering its incentives by creating competition between local governments through decentralization. Qian and Roland argue that this is one of the main specificities of Chinese reforms so far. Indeed, important improvements in enterprise incentives have taken place in China despite the absence of privatization programs (see the companion chapter by McMillan and the references therein). Most of these improvements have taken place in the township and village enterprises which are not privately owned but started booming after the beginning of the reform process (see, e.g., Weitzman and Xu (1993), Che and Qian (1994), Bolton (1995), and Li (1995)).

Qian and Roland insert the setup of subsection 3.3.1 above in a general equilibrium framework with the following objective function W for the government

$$W = x(K, I) + y + u(z),$$

where K is the level of foreign capital investment into the area and I and z are respectively the levels of public infrastructure investment and public consumption. Moreover, y is the net return of financing and refinancing firms (including managerial private benefits), while $x(.)$ and $u(.)$ are the net returns of the two forms of investment and of public consumption. Assume positive decreasing marginal returns as well as *complementarity* between K and I.

The degree of decentralization of decisions can be seen to influence the budget constraint firms face through the intensity of capital mobility across regions. Maximizing the objective function W implies refinancing bad firms and thus a soft budget constraint if and only if

$$E_b + \pi_b^* - 1 \geq \frac{\partial x(K, I)}{\partial I} + \frac{\partial x(K, I)}{\partial K}\frac{dK}{dI} = u'(z),$$

where the left-hand side $E_b + \pi_b^* - 1$ is the net increase in y when one unit of funds is used to refinance bad firms, while the right-hand side is the net return of infrastructure investment or public consumption ($\tilde{z}$ being the equilibrium level of public consumption). Decentralization can then harden the budget constraint of firms because local governments will compete among each other to attract foreign capital to their region by investing more in infrastructure. In other words, decentralization leads to an increase in dK/dI. Regional governments will thus divert funds toward infrastructure investment and away from public consumption for the purpose of fiscal competition. Simultaneously, refinancing bad firms will have a higher opportunity cost, since $u'(z)$ has increased. Call $\tilde{\tilde{z}}$ the equilibrium level of public consumption with decentralized government. Provided $u'(\tilde{\tilde{z}}) > E_b + \pi_b^* - 1$, only good projects are financed under decentralization, since bad entrepreneurs expect to be terminated.

3.3.3 Decentralization of credit

The setup of subsection 3.3.1 is also compatible with a π_b^* that reflects pure profit-maximization motives. Indeed, in the presence of sunk costs, sequential profit maximization can be inferior to *ex ante* profit maximization. In this case, privatization alone will not solve the soft budget constraint problem unless it is accompanied by other institutional changes. Dewatripont and Maskin (1995) show that the decentralization of credit may be a crucial element in hardening budget constraints. As in the previous subsections, this is achieved through a reduction in π_b^*.

Indeed, assume that the continuation value of bad projects depends on an effort level a to be exerted by the initial creditor. Specifically, assume that the gross (discounted) financial return of a bad project that is refinanced is either 0 or $\bar{R}_b$, and that the probability of $\bar{R}_b$ is a. Finally, assume a to be private information to the initial creditor, who incurs effort cost $\Psi(a)$, assumed to be increasing and convex in a.

In this case, *centralization* of credit means that the initial creditor will also be the one refinancing a bad firm, so that the chosen effort level a^* will fully internalize the benefit of monitoring

$$\pi_b^* = \underset{a}{\text{Max}}\{a\bar{R}_b - \Psi(a)\}, \text{ and } \bar{R}_b = \Psi'(a^*).$$

Under *decentralization* instead the initial creditor is short of money, and refinancing has to be performed by a new creditor who has not observed monitoring effort. Given an expected effort $\hat{a}$ and limited resources for the firm and the initial creditor under perfect competition among new creditors, the refinancing contract will grant $1/\hat{a}$ deducted from $\bar{R}_b$ whenever the bad project ends up being "successful" (since, by assumption, no resources are available if the project is unsuccessful). Given $\hat{a}$, the effort level privately chosen by the first creditor will lead to

$$\pi_b^{**} = \underset{a}{\text{Max}}\left\{a\left(\bar{R}_b - \frac{1}{\hat{a}}\right) - \Psi(a)\right\} + 1.$$

In equilibrium, this effort level a^{**} is equal to $\hat{a}$, and satisfies $\bar{R}_b = \Psi'(a^{**}) + 1/a^{**}$. Consequently, a^{**} is lower than a^*, and the associated continuation value of the project π_b^{**} is lower than π_b^*. If $\pi_b^{**} < 1 < \pi_b^*$, decentralization of credit, as defined above, hardens the budget constraint of the firm.

The general insight behind this result is that decentralized finance may lead to externalities that reduce the attractiveness of refinancing. This suggests that bond or equity finance will typically involve a harder budget constraint than bank finance, a point also stressed by von Thadden (1995). Other models explaining why the multiplicity of creditors can change refinancing outcomes include Bolton and Scharfstein (1995), Berglof and von Thadden (1994), Dewatripont and Tirole (1994), and Hart and Moore (1995).

Note that, in the above setup, if π_b^{**} is bigger than one, decentralization of credit is *worse* than centralization, since refinancing of bad projects is not prevented, but occurs with inefficiently low monitoring. If one allows endogenous creditor size in a market economy, it is, however, possible to show that, in this case, a market economy will simply replicate the centralized financing pattern: in equilibrium creditors will have sufficient resources to perform the refinancing themselves (see Dewatripont and Maskin (1995)). While the market system is thus unambiguously better than exogenous centralization, this is not always true under alternative model specifications, as shown in subsection 3.4.

In transition economies, the creation of a decentralized system of credit and financial intermediation has been at the heart of recent policy debates, the main issue being to harden budget constraints of enterprises. A key issue is related to the stock of bad loans banks inherited from the past. Mitchell (1994) shows that banks tend to be soft with enterprises because initiation of bankruptcy would signal their fragile financial position. Berglof and Roland (1995) show that banks with a higher level of bad loans may find it more profitable to lobby for government bailout subsidies to finance bad firms rather than to impose hard budget constraints. Perotti (1993) shows that potentially profitable firms lacking the necessary funds to restructure may, in a similar way to banks, be led to extend trade credit to insolvent clients and gamble on a collective bailout. Begg and Portes (1993) have argued forcefully for the need of bank recapitalization. One way to improve the financial situation of banks is to put their bad loans in so-called "hospital agencies." Van Wijnbergen (1993) has argued instead in favor of giving banks direct incentives to restructure firms with bad loans by suggesting that bank recapitalization be made conditional on debt–equity swaps in those firms.[14]

3.3.4 Product market demonopolization

The opportunity cost of refinancing a bad project can also be raised by reducing the cost of terminating it. The cost of termination is in turn related to substitution possibilities across projects, as stressed by Segal (1993). While Segal makes the point that the soft budget constraint can at times be seen as the result of underprovision of cost-reduction effort by a monopolist in order to extract subsidies from the government, the argument can also be made in our framework. Indeed, assume that the government can split each project it finances into two halves, at some efficiency cost if there are increasing returns to scale. Assume that the two halves are performed by different entrepreneurs and that, if only one is good, it is optimal for the government to expand its activities instead of refinancing the bad entrepreneur. In that case, there is always an equilibrium where only good entrepreneurs apply for funds, because then a bad entrepreneur knows for sure it will not be refinanced! This equilibrium is moreover unique provided that the probability α of not being refinanced (that is, the probability that the other entrepreneur involved in the same project is good if all entrepreneurs apply) is sufficient to deter bad entrepreneurs from applying for funds in the first place.

3.4 The downside of hard budget constraints

While a hard budget constraint can deter bad entrepreneurs from starting projects, von Thadden (1995) and Dewatripont and Maskin (1995) have pointed out that it can induce short termism among good entrepreneurs. Specifically, introduce into the framework of subsection 3.3.1 the ability for good entrepreneurs to choose between their good quick project that yields R_g and E_g after one period and a good but slow project that yields 0 after one period (and $E_t < 0$ if terminated) but a gross financial return $R_l > 2$ and a positive benefit E_l if refinanced. These projects thus have a positive net present value but, at the end of period 1, they cannot be distinguished from bad projects. This can in fact induce a coordination problem among good entrepreneurs. Indeed, consider the case of subsection 3.3.1 where decentralization of credit is necessary and sufficient for a hard budget constraint, that is, $\pi_b^* > 1 > \pi_b^{**}$. One can then show that:[15] (a) there always exists an equilibrium where credit is decentralized,[16] the budget constraint is hard and all good entrepreneurs choose short-run projects; (b) for R_l sufficiently large, there also exists an equilibrium where credit is centralized, the budget constraint is soft and all good entrepreneurs choose long-run projects; (c) the second equilibrium Pareto dominates the first one.

Intuitively, when $\pi_b^* > 1 > \pi_b^{**}$, decentralized financing is the only way to deter bad projects from being started. Expectations by creditors that all long-term projects are bad are self-fulfilling, since good entrepreneurs expect termination if they do not choose quick projects. Another equilibrium is however possible if financing *all* long-term projects, good and bad, is more profitable than financing solely good, quick projects. In that case, creditors' expectations that all good entrepreneurs choose long-term projects are also self-fulfilling. In this case, the hard budget constraint equilibrium induces "short-termist" behavior which more than offsets the gain from deterring bad long-term projects from being started.

The discussion in this subsection sheds light on the comparison between financial systems. In particular, it rationalizes the idea that a market-oriented system, as in Anglo-Saxon countries, can be short-termist (Corbett (1987)) compared with the Japanese (or German) bank-based system which provides more long-run finance and liquidity to firms (Aoki (1990), Hoshi, Kashyap, and Scharfstein (1992)). On the other hand, the latter system thereby suffers from comparatively soft budget constraints.

4 ALLOCATIVE CHANGES

Socialist economies were not only characterized by a low productivity in the state sector due to the incentive problems discussed above, but they also suffered from severe misallocation of resources because central planning, and the ensuing absence of markets, created a distorted output mix. Transition therefore involves an important *reallocation of resources* across sectors.

In the existing transition literature, this problem has been examined by looking at an economy with two sectors, a state sector with low productivity and a private sector with higher productivity due to higher efficiency and higher demand in the private sector after price liberalization. Sectoral reallocation implies a move of resources away from the declining state sector to the expanding private sector. The transition literature differs from the trade liberalization literature (see Mussa (1978, 1986)) in that reallocation is not necessarily between an import-competing and an export-oriented sector.[17] Instead, the case of a closed economy facing internal resource constraints is considered. External borrowing is generally not allowed, in part because no huge capital flows took place from west to east, and in part because many questions related to foreign borrowing have already been studied in the literature on sovereign debt.

Reallocation of resources across sectors is assumed to be costly, otherwise instantaneous adjustment would be optimal. Existing models therefore raise the question of the *optimal speed of transition viewed as resource reallocation,* in order to shed light on the macroeconomic dynamics of output in transition economies. An important challenge to theory is to explain the double digit output fall observed in central and eastern European economies when transition programs were introduced. Some transition models of resource reallocation deal partly with that question. They analyze the macroeconomic effects of "big bang" policies imposing a fast speed of closure on inefficient state-owned enterprises

(SOEs). A general lesson is that policies trying to accelerate the speed of sectoral reallocation may be counterproductive and actually lead to suboptimally slowing down the process of private job creation, due to their contractionary effect.

For example, Castanheira and Roland (1994) look at a continuous-time model where expansion in the new private sector requires investment. The model is close to the general equilibrium neoclassical Ramsey model of investment. The optimal speed of transition is the solution of the following program

$$\max_{N_G(t)} \int_0^{\infty} U(C(t))e^{-\rho t}dt$$

$$\text{s.t. } \dot{N}_p(t) = Y(N_p(t), N_G(t)) - C(t)$$
$$N_p(t) + N_G(t) \leq N,$$

where national income $Y(t)$ depends on the number of private enterprises $N_p(t)$ and the number of SOE's $N_G(t)$. Y is concave in N_G because of heterogeneous declining productivity in SOEs where: $0 < dY/dN_G < 1$. Productivity is higher in private enterprises: assume for example $dY/dN_P = 1$. Both private and public enterprises each use one unit of labor and the capital–labor ratio in private enterprises is equal to 1. Therefore, aggregate capital accumulation is equivalent to $\dot{N}_p(t)$ and the constraint on labor resources in the economy is equivalent to the constraint on the number of enterprises N. Finally, what is not invested is consumed and generates utility through a time-separable concave function $U(.)$ with discount rate ρ.

To assess the optimal speed of transition in this model, it is best to ask what happens if the government deviates from the optimal rate of closure of SOEs. If the rate of closure is too slow and there is cross-subsidization in the state sector, wages will be too high compared with the optimum. This will reduce the return to new investment and thus reduce aggregate savings and hiring in the private sector. Things are more interesting if the government closes down SOEs too fast. This has two effects: (a) a substitution effect, raising the marginal return on investment since the wage rate is driven down by excess layoffs; (b) an income effect, because a lower state-sector output depresses national income, thus reducing available consumption and savings. The substitution effect tends to accelerate the speed of transition whereas the income effect tends to slow it down.[18] If the excess rate of closure is high enough, the income effect will dominate. The income effect will also tend to be dominant if an excess rate of closures occurs earlier rather than later in the transition process, because the absolute output level is lower at earlier stages of transition. An excess rate of closure of SOEs may thus, through its contractionary effects, lead to slower private job creation.

Using the same model, Castanheira and Roland (1995) show that an adverse productivity shock in the state sector depresses aggregate capital accumulation if it occurs in an early phase of transition but increases investment if it occurs later in transition. Productivity shocks are usually not self-inflicted. Nevertheless, this analysis sheds some light on the output contraction in central and eastern Europe following price and trade liberalization which are recognized to have produced an adverse productivity shock in the state sector. By contrast, in China where the state sector was relatively insulated from early reforms in the countryside, an impressive and sustained process of capital accumulation has occurred and structural shifts are taking place in context of high growth.

Aghion and Blanchard (1994) do not focus on capital accumulation but on the labor market in their analysis of the optimal speed of transition. They focus on the interaction between the public finance aspects of unemployment and labor-market developments. The optimal speed of transition is the solution to the following program

$$\underset{N_G(t)}{\text{Max}} \int_0^{\infty} (N_G(t)y_G + N_p(t)y_p)e^{-\rho t}dt$$

$$\text{s.t. } N_p(t) + N_G(t) + U = 1$$

$$\dot{N}_p(t) = a(1 - (w + z))$$

$$Ub = (1 - U)z$$

$$w = b + c\left(r + \frac{\dot{N}_p(t)}{U}\right),$$

where $y_G < y_p = 1$ are the average productivity levels in the state and private sectors. Private-sector job creation, $N_p(t)$, depends on the wedge between private-sector productivity and private-sector wage costs $(w + z)$, where z denotes contributions to finance unemployment benefits b paid by the $1 - U$ employed workers to finance the unemployed U. Because of the need to balance the budget, for b given, an increase in U implies an increase in z. The private-sector wage level, on the other hand, is deduced from efficiency wage considerations and depends positively on b, on the discount rate ρ and on the ratio of new hires to unemployment $\dot{N}_p(t)/U$. There is then a unique level of unemployment which maximizes the net present value of output. The results are the following: if the unemployment rate is too low, labor-market pressures will increase private-sector wages, thereby slowing down the dynamics of labor demand. If, on the other hand, unemployment is too high, wage costs will be too high because of the need to finance unemployment benefits from wages. This last result, which depends on the specific assumption about how unemployment benefits are financed, shows again that an excessive speed of closure of SOEs may slow down rather than accelerate private job creation.[19]

5 CONCLUDING REMARKS

We have surveyed in this chapter some of the early advances in the theory of transition from socialism to capitalism. The theoretical literature on transition is still at an early stage but we hope to have convinced the reader that it is possible to do serious theoretical work on the complex subject of large-scale institutional change and to analyze transition processes on that basis.

Our survey clearly suggests that the tradeoffs between gradualism and big bang are more numerous and subtle than the impression conveyed by an important part of the policy literature: the main theoretical conclusions from our survey are the following:

> In a world with aggregate uncertainty, reversal costs, and complementarity between reforms, gradualism reduces the costs of experimentation with reform by providing an option of early reversal. It is optimal if learning is fast enough compared with the disturbances caused by partial reform. Otherwise, big bang is optimal.
>
> Complementarities between reform make partial reform costly; while this may seem to favor big bang, it is also a necessary condition for the optimality of gradualism. Otherwise, independent reforms should be tried immediately or not at all.
>
> When gradualism is desirable, optimal sequencing of reforms implies starting first with reforms having the highest expected payoffs and with reforms giving stakes to the median voter to support continuation rather than reversal of the reform process.
>
> There is a tradeoff between the intertemporal budgetary cost of reform and its speed when compensation of losers is necessary to gain political acceptance. Excessive speed of closures can slow down the speed of private job creation due to general equilibrium effects via endogenous savings or fiscal channels. This tradeoff can be improved when a reformist government is in control of the political agenda and can use divide-and-rule strategies. We have also shown how secession threats can affect this tradeoff.

The connected incentive problems of soft budget constraints and the ratchet effect, that were pervasive under socialism, must be addressed by reforms. We showed in turn how privatization, demonopolization and decentralization of government and of credit can contribute to this goal.

We have suggested how these conclusions can help in the understanding of several facts about transition in central and eastern Europe and China. Many aspects of this transition process remain, however, badly understood. This is the case for example with the important output fall associated with liberalization and stabilization policies at an early stage of transition in central and eastern Europe. One of the main challenges, both for theoretical and empirical analysis, will be to better understand the striking differences between the transition process in China and central and eastern Europe. In particular, it is important to assess the relative importance of differences in initial economic conditions, on the one hand, and of policy choices, on the other. This is all the more challenging that, contrary to the study of institutional change by economic history where outcomes are known, the outcome of transition remains uncertain. The jury is still out whether China or Russia will emerge as more prosperous capitalist economies in the twenty-first century. History in the making will show which theories will be rejected and which will not.

Notes

ECARE, Université Libre de Bruxelles. Paper presented at the Seventh World Congress of the Econometric Society, Tokyo, August 1995. The ideas in this chapter owe a lot to joint work with Patrick Bolton, Eric Maskin and Yingyi Qian. We also acknowledge helpful discussions with Philippe Aghion and comments by Howard Rosenthal.

1 Complementarities in price liberalization across sectors are also emphasized by Boycko (1992) and complementarities across time are analyzed by van Wijnbergen (1992). Bennett and Dixon (1995) analyze the complementarities between price liberalization, market structure and macroeconomic equilibrium.

2 Sequencing of reforms is also discussed among others by Hinds (1991), Kornai (1990), Portes (1990, 1991), Tirole (1991), Newbery (1991), McKinnon (1991), Fischer and Gelb (1991), Murrell (1992), Murrell and Wang (1993) and Roland (1991, 1993).

3 On organizational diversity in transition economies, see also Aoki (1995).

4 Given statistical independence, two-ninths of the population have individual gain $3g$, two-ninths have individual loss $3g$, and five-ninths have zero gain or loss.

5 See also Dewatripont and Roland (1992a and b) on divide-and-rule tactics.

6 This result is similar to those in durable good monopoly models (Gul, Sonnen-

schein, and Wilson (1986), Hart and Tirole (1988)) or contract renegotiation models (Dewatripont (1989), Laffont and Tirole (1993)).

7 See also Maskin (1995) for a short survey of soft budget constraint models.

8 There is a huge literature on the incentive schemes used in socialist economies. We will not review them here. References can be found in the books by Bennett (1989) and Kornai (1992).

9 Qian (1994) has shown how this formalization of the soft budget constraint problem may lead to the rational use of shortages by the planner as a way to alleviate this problem.

10 This differs from a static problem à la Stiglitz and Weiss (1981) where creditors can at best finance *all* types, and at worst solely finance bad types (which would be the case here if E_g were negative and if firms with good projects could not keep a sufficient share of R_g).

11 See for example the classical analysis of North and Weingast (1989) on the role of political institutions in England in creating commitment to secure property rights.

12 See Debande and Friebel (1995) for a model where insider privatization may exacerbate this problem relative to state ownership.

13 See also Friebel (1994) on the complementarity between giveaways (used as an informational device) and sales.

14 For a formal analysis of various methods of cleaning banks' balance sheets, see Mitchell (1995) and Berglöf and Roland (1995). For comprehensive empirical surveys of financial reforms and the banking sector, see Dittus (1994) and Anderson and Kegels (1996).

15 See Dewatripont and Maskin (1995) for details.

16 That is, creditor size is such that refinancing of bad projects has to be performed by new creditors.

17 Dehejia (1995) however looks at a trade liberalization model incorporating political constraints to address the question of the optimal speed of transition.

18 The substitution effect would be stronger if, as in Atkeson and Kehoe (1995), one integrates precautionary savings. In their model of transition, there is no investment but costly search of workers from SOEs for a good match in the private sector. When searching, they earn no income, and there is a non-zero probability of not finding a good match. In the absence of social insurance, social welfare is lower but the speed of transition may be higher if there is a precautionary motive for savings. In that case, workers will want to borrow less to consume when searching. Because total consumption in the economy is constrained by national output, this allows more workers to search in equilibrium.

19 Similar arguments involving frictions on the labor market are made by Burda (1993) and Gavin (1993) to make the case for gradualism in the closure of SOEs.

References

Aghion, P. and Blanchard, O. (1994). "On the speed of transition in central Europe." *NBER Macroeconomics Annual*, pp. 283–319.

Aghion, P., Blanchard, O., and Burgess, R. (1994). "The behaviour of state firms in eastern Europe pre-privatization." *European Economic Review*, 38: 1327–49.

Aghion, P. and Bolton, P. (1991). "Government domestic debt and the risk of default: a political economy model of the strategic role of debt." In Dornbusch, R. and Draghi, R. (eds.), *Debt Management: Theory and History*. Cambridge: Cambridge University Press.

Aghion, P. and Burgess, R. (1993). "Financing and development in eastern Europe and the former Soviet Union." In Giovannini, A. (ed.), *Finance and Development: Issues and Experience*. Cambridge: Cambridge University Press.

Alesina, A. and Drazen, A. (1991). "Why are stabilizations delayed?" *American Economic Review*, 81: 1170–88.

Alesina, A. and Spolaore, E. (1994). "On the number and size of nations." NBER Working Paper No. 5050.

Alesina, A. and Tabellini, G. (1990). "A positive theory of fiscal deficits and government debt." *Review of Economic Studies*, 57(3): 403–14.

Anderson, R. and Kegels, C. (1996). *Transition Banking: The Financial Development of Central and Eastern Europe*. Oxford: Oxford University Press.

Aoki, M. (1990). "Towards an economic model of the Japanese firm." *Journal of Economic Literature*, 28(1): 1–27.

(1995). "An evolving diversity of organizational mode and its implications for transitional economies." *Journal of the Japanese and International Economies* (forthcoming).

Atkeson, A. and Kehoe, P.J. (1995). "Social insurance and transition." Mimeo, University of Pennsylvania.

Bain, J. A., Miller, J.B., Thornton, J.R., and Keren, M. (1987). "The ratchet, tautness and managerial behaviour in Soviet-type economies." *European Economic Review*, 31: 1173–202.

Begg, D. and Portes, R. (1993). "Enterprise debt and economic transformation: financial restructuring in central and eastern Europe." In Mayer, C. and Vives, X. (eds.), *Capital Markets and Financial Intermediation*, Cambridge: Cambridge University Press, pp. 230–54.

Bennett, J. (1989). *The Economic Theory of Central Planning*. Oxford: Basil Blackwell.

Bennett, J. and Dixon, H. (1995). "Macroeconomic equilibrium and reform in a transition economy." *European Economic Review*, 39(8): 1465–87.

Berglöf, E. and Roland, G. (1995). "Bank restructuring and soft budget constraints in financial transition." Mimeo, ECARE, Université Libre de Bruxelles.

Berglöf, E. and von Thadden, E.L. (1994). "Short-term versus long-term interests: capital structure with multiple investors." *Quarterly Journal of Economics*, 109: 1055–84.

Berliner, J. (1952). "The informal organization of the Soviet firm." *Quarterly Journal of Economics*, 66: 342–65.

Bertocchi, G. and Spagat, M. (1993). "Structural uncertainty and subsidy removal for economies in transition." Mimeo, Brown University.

Blanchard, O., Dornbusch, R., Krugman, P., Layard, R. and Summers, L. (1991). *Reform in Eastern Europe*. Cambridge, MA: MIT Press.

Blinder, A.S. (1987). *Hard Heads, Soft Hearts.* Reading, MA: Addison-Wesley.

Bolton, P. (1995). "Privatization and the separation of ownership and control: lessons from Chinese enterprise reforms." *Economics of Transition,* 3: 1–12.

Bolton, P. and Roland, G. (1992). "Privatization in central and eastern Europe." *Economic Policy,* 15: 276–309.

(1994). "The breakup of countries: a political economy perspective." Mimeo, ECARE, Université Libre de Bruxelles.

Bolton, P. and Scharfstein, D. (1995). "Optimal debt structure with multiple creditors." *Journal of Political Economy* (forthcoming).

Boycko, M. (1992). "When higher incomes reduce welfare: queues, labor supply, and macroeconomic equilibrium in socialist economies." *Quarterly Journal of Economics,* 107: 907–20.

Boycko, M. Shleifer, A., and Vishny, R. (1992). "Property rights, soft budget constraints and privatization." Mimeo, Harvard University.

(1995). *Privatizing Russia.* Cambridge, MA: MIT Press.

Bruno, M. (1993). "Stabilization and the macroeconomics of transition. How different is eastern Europe?" *Economics of Transition,* 1: 5–19.

Burda, M. (1993). "Unemployment, labour markets and structural change in eastern Europe." *Economic Policy,* 16: 101–38.

Caillaud, B., Guésnerie, R., Rey, P. and Tirole, J. (1988). "Government intervention in production and incentives theory: a review of recent contributions." *Rand Journal of Economics,* 19(1): 1–26.

Carlin, W., Van Reenen, J. and Wolfe, T. (1994). "Enterprise restructuring in the Transition: an analytical survey of the case study evidence from central and eastern Europe." EBRD Working Paper No. 14.

Casella, A. and Feinstein, J.S. (1990). "Public goods in trade: on the formation of markets and political jurisdictions." Mimeo, Hoover Institution.

Castanheira, M. and Roland, G. (1994). "The optimal speed of transition: a general equilibrium analysis." Mimeo, ECARE, Université Libre de Bruxelles.

(1995). "Restructuring and capital accumulation in transition economies: a general equilibrium perspective." Mimeo, ECARE, Université Libre de Bruxelles.

Chandler, A. (1962). *Strategy and Structure.* New York: Doubleday.

Che, J. and Qian, Y. (1994). "Boundaries of the firm and governance: understanding China's township and village enterprises." Mimeo, Stanford University.

Corbett, J. (1987). "International perspectives on financing: evidence from Japan." *Oxford Review of Economic Policy,* 3: 30–55.

Coricelli, F. (1995). "Fiscal constraints, reform strategies and the speed of transition: the case of central-eastern Europe." Mimeo, University of Siena.

Debande, O. and Griebel, G. (1995). "Privatization, employment and managerial decision-taking." Mimeo, ECARE, Université Libre de Bruxelles.

Dehejia, V. (1995). "Will gradualism work when shock therapy doesn't?" Mimeo, Columbia University.

Demougin, D. and Sinn, H.W. (1992). "Risk-taking, privatization and the communist firm." CES Working Paper 16, University of Munich.

Dewatripont, M. (1989). "Renegotiation and information revelation over time: the case of optimal labor contracts." *Quarterly Journal of Economics*, 104: 589–619.

Dewatripont, M. and Maskin, E. (1995). "Credit and efficiency in centralized and decentralized economies." *Review of Economic Studies*, 62: 541–55.

Dewatripont, M. and Roland, G. (1992a). "Economic reform and dynamic political constraints." *Review of Economic Studies*, 59: 703–30.

(1992b). "The virtues of gradualism and legitimacy in the transition to a market economy." *Economic Journal*, 102: 291–300.

(1995). "The design of reform packages under uncertainty." *American Economic Review*, 85: 1207–223.

Dewatripont, M. and Tirole, J. (1994). "A theory of debt and equity: diversity of securities and manager–shareholder congruence." *Quarterly Journal of Economics*, 109(4): 1027–54.

Dittus, P. (1994). "Corporate governance in central Europe: the role of banks." Mimeo, Bank of International Settlements.

Dixit, A. (1994). "Economic policy and the political process." Mimeo, Princeton.

Estrin, S., Schaffer, M., and Singh, I.J. (1992). "Enterprise adjustment in transition economies: Czechoslovakia, Hungary and Poland." World Bank Research Paper No. 27.

Fernandez, R. and Rodrik, D. (1991). "Resistance to reform: status quo bias in the presence of individual-specific uncertainty." *American Economic Review*, 81: 1146–55.

Fischer, S. and Gelb, A. (1991). "The process of economic transformation." *Journal of Economic Perspectives*, 5: 91–106.

Freixas, X., Guésnerie, R., and Tirole, J. (1985). "Planning under incomplete information and the ratchet effect." *Review of Economic Studies*, 52: 173–91.

Friebel, G. (1994). "Privatization and bureaucracies in Russia." Mimeo, ECARE, Université Libre de Bruxelles.

Frydman, R. and Rapaczynski, A. (1994). *Privatization in Eastern Europe: Is the State Withering Away?* London: Central European University Press.

Gates, S., Milgrom, P., and Roberts, J. (1993). "Complementarities in the transition from socialism: a firm-level analysis." Mimeo, Stanford University.

Gavin, M. (1993). "Unemployment, labor markets and structural change in eastern Europe." Mimeo, Columbia University.

Gul, F., Sonnenschein, H., and Wilson, R. (1986). "Foundations of dynamic monopoly and the Coase conjecture." *Journal of Economic Theory*, 39: 155–90.

Hart, O. and Moore, J. (1995). "Debt and seniority: an analysis of the role of hard claims in constraining management." *American Economic Review*, 85: 567–85.

Hart, O. and Tirole, J. (1988). "Contract renegotiation and Coasian dynamics." *Review of Economic Studies*, 55: 509–40.

Hinds, M. (1991). "Issues in the introduction of market forms in eastern European socialist economies." In Commander, S. (ed.), *Managing Inflation in Socialist Economies in Transition*. Washington, DC: World Bank.

Hoshi, T., Kashyap, A., and Scharfstein, D. (1992). "The choice between public and private debt: an examination of post-regulation corporate finance in Japan." Mimeo, University of California San Diego.

Hugues, G. and Hare, P. (1991). "Competitiveness and industrial restructuring in Czechoslovakia, Hungary and Poland." *European Economy*, Special Edition (2): 83–110.

Keren, M., Miller, J.B., and Thornton, J.R. (1983). "The ratchet: a dynamic managerial incentive model of the Soviet enterprise." *Journal of Comparative Economics*, 7: 347–67.

Kornai, J. (1979). "Resource-constrained versus demand-constrained systems." *Ecònometrica*, 47: 801–19.

(1980). *Economics of Shortage*. Amsterdam: North Holland.

(1990). *The Road to a Free Economy*. New York: Norton.

(1992). *The Socialist System: the Political Economy of Communism*. Oxford: Oxford University Press.

Laffont, J.-J. and Tirole, J. (1988). "The dynamics of incentive contracts," *Econometrica*, 51: 1153–75.

(1993). *A Theory of Incentives in Regulation and Procurement*. Cambridge, MA: MIT Press.

Lewis, T.R., Feenstra, R., and Ware, R. (1990). "Eliminating price supports: a political economy perspective." *Journal of Public Economics*, 40: 150–86.

Li, D. (1995). "A theory of ambiguous property rights in transition economies." Mimeo, University of Michigan.

Lipton, D. and Sachs, J. (1990a). "Creating a market economy in eastern Europe: the case of Poland." *Brookings Papers on Economic Activity*, 1: 75–133.

(1990b). "Privatization in eastern Europe: the case of Poland." *Brookings Papers on Economic Activity*, 2: 293–361.

Litwack, J. (1991). "Legality and market reform in Soviet-type economies." *Journal of Economic Perspectives*, 5(4): 77–89.

(1993). "Coordination, incentives and the ratchet effect." *Rand Journal of Economics*, 24(2): 271–85.

Maskin, E. (1991). "Auctions and privatization." Mimeo, Harvard University.

(1995). "Theories of the soft budget constraint." *Japan and the World Economy* (forthcoming).

McKelvey, R.D. (1976). "Intransitivities in multidimensional voting models and some implications for agenda control." *Journal of Economic Theory*, 12: 472–82.

McKinnon, R. (1991). *The Order of Economic Liberalization*. Baltimore: John Hopkins University Press.

McMillan, J. (1996). "Markets in transition," this volume.

McMillan, J. and Naughton, B. (1992). "How to reform a planned economy: lessons from China." *Oxford Review of Economic Policy*, 8: 130–43.

Mitchell, J. (1994). "Strategic creditor passivity in economies in transition." Mimeo, Cornell University.

(1995). "Cancelling, transferring or repaying bad debt: cleaning banks' balance sheets in economies in transition." Mimeo, Cornell University.

Murphy, K., Shleifer, A., and Vishny, R. (1992). "The transition to a market economy: pitfalls of partial reform." *Quarterly Journal of Economics*, 107: 889–906.

Murrell, P. (1992). "Evolution in economics and in the economic reform of the centrally planned economies." In Clague, C. and Raisser, G. (eds.), *The Emergence of Market Economies in Eastern Europe*. Cambridge: Blackwell, pp. 35–53.

Murrell, P. and Wang, Y. (1993). "When privatization should be delayed: the effect of communist legacies on organizational and institutional reforms." *Journal of Comparative Economics*, 17: 385–406.

Mussa, M. (1978). "Dynamic adjustment in the Heckscher–Ohlin–Samuelson model." *Journal of Political Economy*, 86: 775–91.

(1986). "The adjustment process and the timing of trade liberalization." In Chokin, A. and Papageorgiou, D. (eds.), *Economic Reform in Developing Countries*. Oxford: Basil Blackwell, pp. 68–124.

Newbery, D. (1991). "Reform in Hungary: sequencing and privatization." *European Economic Review*, 35: 571–80.

North, D. and Weingast, B. (1989). "Constitutions and commitment: evolutions of institutions governing public choice." *Journal of Economic History*, 49: 803–32.

Perotti, E. (1993). "Collusive trade arrears in the stabilization of transition economies." Mimeo, Boston University.

Persson, T. and Svensson, L. (1989). "Why a stubborn conservative would run a deficit: policy with time-inconsistent preferences." *Quarterly Journal of Economics*, 104: 325–46.

Pinto, B., Belka, M., and Krajewski, S. (1993). "Transforming state enterprises in Poland." *Brookings Papers on Economic Activity*, 1: 213–70.

Portes, R. (1990). "Introduction to economic transformation of Hungary and Poland." *European Economy*, 43: 11–18.

(1991). "The path of reform in central and eastern Europe: an introduction." *European Economy*, Special Issue, 2: 3–15.

Qian, Y. (1994). "A theory of shortage in socialist economies based on the 'Soft Budget Constraint'." *American Economic Review*, 84: 145–56.

Qian, Y. and Roland, G. (1994). "Regional decentralization and the soft budget constraint: the case of China." CEPR Discussion Paper No. 1013.

(1995). "Government paternalism and predation: a theory of enterprise incentives under socialism and transition." Work in progress.

Qian, Y. and Xu, C. (1991). "Innovation and financial constraints in centralized and decentralized economies." Mimeo, London School of Economics.

(1993). "Why China's economic reforms differ: the M-form hierarchy and entry/expansion of the non-state sector." *Economics of Transition*, 1: 135–70.

Roland, G. (1991). "Political economy of sequencing tactics in the transition period." In Csaba, L. (ed.), *Systemic Changes and Stabilization in Eastern Europe*. Aldershot: Dartmouth, pp. 97–64.

(1993). "The political economy of transition in the Soviet Union." *European Economy*, (89) (March): 197–216.

Roland, G. and Sekkat, K. (1992). "Market socialism and the managerial labor market." In Bardhan, P. and Roemer, J. (eds.), *Market Socialism*, Oxford: Oxford University Press, pp. 204–15.

(1995). "Managerial career concerns, privatization and restructuring in transition economies." Mimeo, ECARE, Université Libre de Bruxelles.

Roland, G. and Verdier, T. (1994). "Privatization in eastern Europe: irreversibility and critical mass effects." *Journal of Public Economics*, 54: 161–83.

Romer, T. and Rosenthal, H. (1979). "Bureaucrats versus voters: on the political economy of resource allocation by direct democracy." *Quarterly Journal of Economics*, 93: 563–87.

Sachs (1990). "Eastern Europe's economies: what is to be done?" *The Economist*, January 13, pp. 19–24.

Schaffer, M. (1981). "The credible commitment problem in the center-enterprise relationship." *Journal of Comparative Economics*, 13: 359–82.

Schmidt, K. (1995). "The costs and benefits of privatization: an incomplete contracts approach." Mimeo, University of Bonn.

Segal, I. (1993). "Monopoly and soft budget constraints." Mimeo, Harvard University.

Sénik-Leygonie, C. and Hughes, G. (1992). "Industrial profitability and trade among the former Soviet republics." *Economic Policy*, 15: 353–86.

Shleifer, A. and Vishny, R. (1994). "Politicians and firms." *Quarterly Journal of Economics*, 109: 995–1025.

Sinn, H.-W. and Sinn, G. (1993). *Jumpstart*. Cambridge, MA: MIT Press.

Stiglitz, J. and Weiss, A. (1981). "Credit rationing in markets with imperfect information." *American Economic Review*, 71: 393–410.

Tirole, J. (1991). "Privatization in eastern Europe: incentives and the economics of transition." *NBER Macroeconomics Annual*, pp. 221–59.

van Wijnbergen, S. (1992). "Intertemporal speculation, shortages and the political economy of price reform." *Economic Journal*, 102: 1395–406.

(1993). "On the role of banks in enterprise restructuring: the Polish example." Mimeo, University of Amsterdam.

von Thadden, E.L. (1995). "Bank finance and long term investment." *Review of Economic Studies*, 62: 557–75.

Wei, Shang-Jing (1991). "To divide or to unite: a theory of secessions." Mimeo, Harvard University.

(1993). "Gradualism versus big bang: speed and sustainability of reforms." Mimeo, Harvard University.

Weitzman, M. (1980). "The 'ratchet principle' and performance incentives." *Bell Journal of Economics*, 11: 302–8.

Wietzman, M. and Xu, C. (1993). "Chinese township and village enterprises as vaguely defined cooperatives." *Journal of Comparative Economics*, 18: 121–45.

Williamson, O. (1975). *Markets and Hierarchies*. New York: Free Press.

CHAPTER 8

A Schumpeterian perspective on growth and competition

Philippe Aghion and Peter Howitt

INTRODUCTION

The revival of growth theory in the 1980s was originally stimulated by "technical progress within economics" – by the development of new tools for handling old ideas. The neoclassical models of the 1960s had already shown that growth in per capita income was sustainable only through the continual growth of technological knowledge. Also it had long been understood that technological knowledge, like capital, grows only because people find it profitable to make it grow; research, development, study, experimentation, and learning by doing all employ resources with alternative uses. The neoclassical model of Solow and Swan ignored these activities and treated technological growth as exogenous, not on grounds of realism but because there were no available techniques for incorporating them into standard economic analysis.

The main difficulty arose from increasing returns. Developing a technology requires a lumpy set-up cost, which does not have to be incurred again as the technology is implemented. Dealing with this in a dynamic general equilibrium framework required the gradual accumulation of knowledge in various subdisciplines of economics, especially international trade theory and industrial organization theory. Macroeconomists have taken these techniques and adapted them to the study of economic growth. As a result we now have an array of relatively simple models with which to study the economic determinants of economic growth.

Some of the more aggregative models in the endogenous growth literature deal with knowledge-generating activities in an abstract way and treat knowledge as little more than another capital good. By contrast, the Schumpeterian models[1] that focus on research and development (R&D) as the engine of growth treat technological change more directly and explicitly by positing particular forms in which new knowledge is created and used; they show how innovations impinge on individual markets, and work out the consequences of the gains and losses generated by Schumpeter's process of creative destruction.

Schumpeterian models allow one to study detailed structural aspects of the growth process, making use of the particularities of technological change. One can see in some detail how regulation, taxation, intellectual property regimes, and various non-economic factors affect the incentive to perform the innovative activities driving growth. One can also examine the role of strategic interactions between innovative firms in the growth process, and see how the intensity of competition affects the rate of growth. Organizational aspects of R&D can be introduced, and interaction between different sorts of innovations and different sources of technological knowledge can be studied.

These models have now taken endogenous growth theory beyond the point of pure technique, and are shedding new light on several structural aspects of the growth process. For example, the interaction between fundamental and secondary research (research versus development, basic versus applied research, etc.) and the implications of this interaction for growth are being explored by various authors, with often surprising results. Jovanovic and Nyarko (1994) show that if people have developed an existing fundamental technology beyond a certain point they may rationally choose not to adopt newer technologies, and hence the economy will not grow, even though under other initial conditions positive growth would be sustained in the long run. Aghion and Howitt (1996) find that this distinction alters the usual Schumpeterian tradeoff between competition and growth, as illustrated below.

A second structural aspect being explored in the literature is the two-way relationship between business cycles and economic growth. Stadler (1990) shows how recessions can have permanent hysteretic effects on the long-run growth path because they retard R&D and learning by doing. Stiglitz (1993) points out another effect in the same direction that arises because cyclical downturns threaten the survival of the small new firms that tend to introduce radically new technologies, but that are rationed relatively tightly in credit markets during recessions. On the other hand, Galí and Hammour (1991) show how recessions can stimulate growth by their "cleansing effect," that is, during downturns the opportunity cost of switching technologies is reduced, as is the ability to survive of weak non-adaptive firms. As for effects of growth on cycles, many Schumpeterian models have the property that innovations underlying long-run growth tend to come in cycles, because of technology spillovers or network externalities of various sorts (Shleifer

(1986)) or because there are multiple dynamic equilibria (Aghion and Howitt (1992)).

A related structural aspect of growth is introduced by considering what Bresnahan and Trajtenberg (1995) call General Purpose Technologies, like steam power, electric motors, or computers, that affect the whole economy. The analyses of Atkeson and Kehoe (1993) and Helpman and Trajtenberg (1994) show that the introduction of radical technological change will typically proceed not smoothly but through an irregular wave of innovations. Unlike the productivity shocks of real business cycle analysis, however, the initial effect of such a wave will be not to raise the levels of output and employment but to reduce them, as people take time to learn the new technology, and as they must devote resources to developing secondary innovations and components in order to make use of the new technology.

The interrelationship between growth and unemployment is another structural phenomenon on which Schumpeterian models are beginning to shed light. As Aghion and Howitt (1994) show, a faster growing economy is not necessarily one with a lower long-run rate of unemployment, because each individual innovation hits a particular subset of the economy and will tend to require a reallocation of resources between sunrise and sunset sectors, between firms with new and old technological capacities, and between occupations that are favored and not favored by the innovation. Opposing these forces of creative destruction is a capitalization effect whereby faster growth tends to encourage the creation of job vacancies to take advantage of more rapidly growing markets. Aghion and Howitt show that creative destruction tends to dominate at low rates of growth and capitalization at high rates, so that unemployment is maximized at intermediate rates of growth.

As the reader will have seen by now, Schumpeterian theory bears on too many structural aspects of growth for us to explain them all in detail in a single chapter. Instead, we have chosen in what follows to focus on what we consider one of the most interesting, namely the relationship between growth and competition. The first Schumpeterian models implied a tradeoff between growth and competition. In a more competitive economy, where innovators could not anticipate as high a level of monopoly profits from their innovations, or for as long a time, innovation would be discouraged and hence growth would be reduced. However, this inverse relationship between growth and competition has not found much empirical support, either from historians (see chatper 2 by Crafts in the current volume) or from econometricians (Nickell (1994), Blundell *et al.* (1995)), who find on the contrary a positive effect of competition on growth.

These findings might seem to contradict the basic Schumpeterian approach. What we argue in the following, however, is that, on the contrary, once one begins to add some obviously needed structural detail to the stark preliminary models of Schumpeterian growth theory, one finds a large variety of possible explanations for the apparently positive effect of competition on growth. Thus in what follows we will first develop a basic general Schumpeterian model, based on Aghion and Howitt (1992) and then show how relaxing the strict assumptions of the model in different directions can produce four separate Schumpeterian explanations for why a more competitive market structure might be conducive to a higher rate of growth.

1 THE SCHUMPETERIAN APPROACH: BASIC FRAMEWORK

1.1 A basic setup

The earliest example of the Schumpeterian approach to endogenous growth was that of Segerstrom *et al.* (1990), who modeled sustained growth as arising from a succession of product improvements in a fixed number of sectors, but with no uncertainty in the innovation process. Aghion and Howitt (1992) constructed an endogenous growth model with both product improvements and uncertainty, which we now proceed to sketch.

The basic model abstracts from capital accumulation completely.[2] The economy is populated by a continuous mass L of individuals with linear intertemporal preferences: $u(y) = \int_0^\infty y_\tau e^{-r\tau} \cdot d\tau$. Each individual is endowed with one unit of labor, so L is also equal to the aggregate flow of labor supply. Output of the consumption good depends upon the input of an intermediate good, x, according to

$$y = AF(x), \tag{1}$$

where the production function F is increasing and concave. Innovations consist of the invention of a new variety of intermediate good that replaces the old one, and whose use raises the technology parameter, A, by the constant factor, $\gamma > 1$.

Society's fixed stock of labor has two competing uses. It can produce intermediate goods, one for one, and it can be used in research. When the amount n is used in research, innovations arrive randomly with a Poisson arrival rate $\lambda \cdot \phi(n)$, where $\lambda > 0$ is a parameter indicating the productivity of the research technology, and $\phi' > 0, \phi'' \leq 0$. The firm that succeeds in innovating can monopolize the intermediate sector until replaced by the next innovator.

As in most endogenous growth models, there are positive spillovers from the activities that generate growth in A, in two senses. The monopoly rents that the innovator can capture are generally less than the consumer surplus created by the intermediate good, and more importantly the invention makes it possible for other researchers to begin working on the next innovation. However, there is a negative spillover in the form of a "business-stealing effect," whereby the successful innovator destroys the surplus attributable to the previous generation of intermediate goods by making it obsolete.

The research sector is portrayed as in the patent race literature that has been surveyed by Tirole (1988) and Reinganum (1989). The amount of labor devoted to research is determined by the arbitrage condition

$$w_t = \lambda \cdot \phi'(n_t) \cdot V_{t+1}, \tag{2}$$

where t is not time but the number of innovations that have occurred, w_t the wage, and V_{t+1} the discounted expected payoff to the $(t+1)^{\text{th}}$ innovator. The latter is just[3]

$$V_{t+1} = \pi_{t+1}/(r + \lambda \cdot \phi(n_{t+1})), \tag{3}$$

where n_{t+1} is the amount of labor devoted to R&D after the $(t+1)^{\text{th}}$ innovation has occurred; and $\pi_{t+1} = A_{t+1} \cdot \tilde{\pi}\left(\frac{w_{t+1}}{A_{t+1}}\right)$, $\tilde{\pi}' < 0$, is the flow of profit attainable by the $(t+1)^{\text{th}}$ intermediate good monopolist.[4]

The denominator of (3), which can be interpreted as the obsolescence-adjusted interest rate, shows the effects of creative destruction. The more research people expect following the next innovation, the shorter the likely duration of the monopoly profits that will be enjoyed by the creator of the next innovation, and hence the smaller the payoff.

Letting $\omega_t = \frac{w_t}{A_t}$ denote the growth-adjusted wage rate after the tth innovation, dividing both sides of equation (2) by A_t, and using (3), we obtain the following *arbitrage equation* which reflects the fact that labor can be freely allocated between *manufacturing* and *research*

(A)

$$\omega_t = \lambda \phi'(n_t) \cdot \frac{\gamma \tilde{\pi}(\omega_{t+1})}{r + \lambda \phi(n_{t+1})}.$$

The model is then fully characterized by (A) and by a *labor market clearing equation* which reflects the frictionless nature of the labor market, and determines the growth-adjusted wage rate ω_t as a function of the residual supply of manufacturing labor $L - n_t$

(L)

$$L = n_t + \tilde{x}(\omega_t),$$

where the demand for manufacturing labor $\tilde{x}$ is a decreasing function of the growth-adjusted wage rate ω_t.[5]

In a steady state the above two equations become

($\hat{A}$)

$$\omega = \lambda\phi'(n)\cdot\frac{\gamma\tilde{\pi}(\omega)}{r + \lambda\phi(n)}$$

($\hat{L}$)

$$n + \tilde{x}(\omega) = L.$$

Positive results Since the two curves corresponding to ($\hat{A}$) and ($\hat{L}$) in the (n, ω) space are respectively downward and upward sloping, the steady state equilibrium $(\hat{n}, \hat{\omega})$ is unique. Using figure 8.1 it is easy to see that the equilibrium level of research $\hat{n}$ – and therefore the average growth rate $\hat{g} = \lambda\phi(\hat{n})\ln\gamma$[6] – will be raised by a lower interest rate r, a larger labor market L, a higher productivity of R&D λ, or a larger size of innovations γ.

In order to analyze the effects of competition on growth, consider the Cobb–Douglas case where $F(x) = x^{\alpha}(0 < \alpha < 1)$. Here the parameter α is a measure of the degree of competition, since the derived demand curve faced by an intermediate monopolist (i.e., the marginal product schedule) has an elasticity equal to $1/(1 - \alpha)$ which is increasing in α. Accordingly, profits will constitute the fraction $(1 - \alpha)$ of value added in the intermediate sector, the rest consisting of labor income

$$\pi = \frac{1-\alpha}{\alpha}\omega x \equiv \frac{1-\alpha}{\alpha}\omega(L - n).$$

Substituting this expression into ($\hat{A}$) yields the modified research-arbitrage equation

($\hat{A}^c$)

$$1 = \lambda\phi'(\hat{n})\frac{\gamma\cdot\frac{1-\alpha}{\alpha}\cdot(L - \hat{n})}{r + \lambda\phi(\hat{n})}$$

which defines $\hat{n}$ as a decreasing function of α. In other words, product-market competition is unambiguously bad for growth: it reduces the size of monopoly rents that can be appropriated by successful innovators, and therefore diminishes the incentive to innovate. This unambiguous – but also somewhat simplistic – prediction of the basic Schumpeterian model will be discussed in section 2 below.

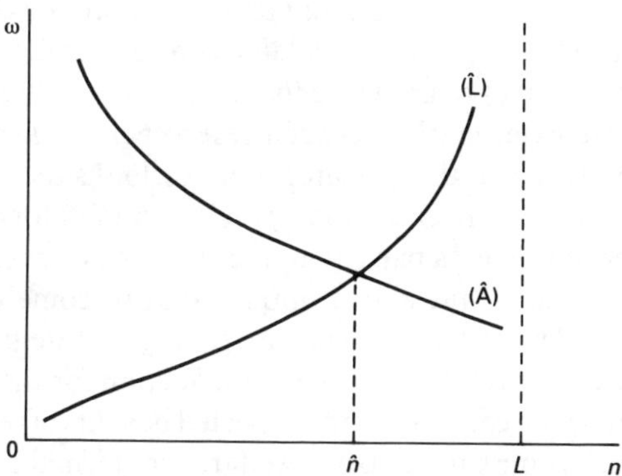

Figure 8.1

Note: The equilibrium level of research $\hat{n}$ is determined by the intersection of a downward-sloping research-arbitrage equation with an upward-sloping labor-market equilibrium curve.

Growth in the economy is *stochastic*, reflecting the uncertainty of the innovation process. In particular in the steady state where $n_t \equiv \hat{n}$ and $\omega_t = \omega$, the log of output follows a random walk with drift, in accordance with recent empirical studies emphasizing the random nature of the economic trend (e.g., Campbell and Mankiw (1987)). The Schumpeterian paradigm thus departs from a long-standing tradition of looking at productivity growth and business fluctuations *separately*. It implies, rather that both growth and fluctuations arise from the same source, namely R&D activity.

That the basic Schumpeterian model outlined above can generate cyclical growth becomes even more transparent once we notice that the above system (A)–(L) yields a *continuum* of Perfect Foresight Equilibria including *non-stationary periodic* trajectories in *n*.[7] In these periodic solutions, the amount of labor devoted to research oscillates regularly between a high and a low level, thereby generating a *cyclical* growth pattern.

However, the following considerations qualify the above conclusion. As shown in Grossman and Helpman (1991), aggregate growth in the steady state ceases to be random if innovations apply to a continuum of uncorrelated sectors. Of course, aggregate fluctuations will persist if productivity growth in a positive mass of sectors hinges on the *same fundamental innovation*. But then an important aspect of innovation-drive cycles is the *diffusion* process of fundamental innovations throughout the economy. The above framework is too simple in this respect: it assumes *instantaneous* diffusion of new discoveries to all firms and sectors.

Normative results A general presumption that emerges from non-Schumpeterian endogenous growth models is that a laissez-faire equilibrium will tend to allocate too few resources to growth-enhancing activities because of the prevalence of positive externalities between researchers or firms that accumulate knowledge. However, this presumption overlooks the *negative* externality that current innovators exert upon previous innovators whose technologies they render obsolete. In particular, the creative destruction (or *business-stealing*) effect pointed out above implies that in some cases a free-market economy will devote *too many* resources to growth-enhancing research, because private research firms make no deduction for the loss of surplus to the incumbent when calculating the expected benefits of research, whereas someone trying to maximize social welfare would make such a deduction by considering only the incremental gain from a prospective innovation.

The overall comparison between the laissez-faire growth rate $\hat{g} = \lambda\phi(\hat{n})\ln\gamma$ and the optimal growth rate $g^* = \lambda\phi(n^*)\ln\gamma$[8] is ambiguous. Growth under laissez-faire will be excessive when the size of innovations γ is close to 1 and the degree of monopoly power is large (α close to 0); and it will be insufficient when the size of innovations is large and/or monopoly rents are small (α close to 1) so that the private benefits from innovating (RHS of (3)) are far below the social benefits.

1.2 Multi-sectors

Consider the following multi-sector extension – inspired by Caballero and Jaffé (1993) – of the basic model outlined above. Final output is now produced by continuum of intermediate goods indexed on the unit interval, according to the production function

$$y = \int_0^1 A_i \cdot F(x_i)di, \tag{4}$$

where x_i is the flow of output of intermediate good i, F is again a production function with positive and diminishing marginal product, and A_i is a productivity parameter attached to the latest version of intermediate good i. Each intermediate input is still produced from manufacturing labor, according to a one-for-one technology.

Let $A = \max_i A_i$ denote the leading-edge productivity parameter. Growth in the leading edge occurs from innovations, at rate

$$\dot{A}/A = \lambda\phi(n)\ln\gamma, \tag{5}$$

where n is the aggregate flow of research labor.[9]

We shall again restrict attention to steady-state equilibria in which final output, consumption, the wage rate, and the leading edge all grow at the same constant rate g, and the distribution of relative productivities $a_i = \frac{A_i}{A}$ is constant over time. It follows from (4) and (5) that the growth rate g must equal $\lambda\phi(n)\ln\gamma$.

Let ω denote the (stationary) growth-adjusted wage rate, w_t/A_t. Since individuals are free to choose whether to be employed in manufacturing or in research, then as before the following arbitrage condition must hold in equilibrium

$$\omega = \lambda\phi'(n)\cdot V, \tag{6}$$

where V is the (growth-adjusted) net present value of a new patent. $\left(V = \frac{V_t}{A_t}\right)$.

The value V_t of discovering technology A_t is again equal to the expected present value of the rents that will accrue until the intermediate producer is replaced. The time until replacement is distributed exponentially with parameter $\lambda\phi(n)$. Therefore

$$V_t = \int_t^{\infty} e^{-(r+\lambda\varphi(n))(s-t)}\cdot\pi_{s,t}ds, \tag{7}$$

where $\pi_{s,t}$ is the flow of monopoly rents earned by a producer with technology A_t at date $s > t$ if the producer has not yet been replaced at that date; that is

$$\begin{aligned}\pi_{s,t} &= \max_x\{A_t\cdot F'(x)x - w_s\cdot x\} \\ &= A_t\cdot\tilde{\pi}(\omega\cdot e^{g(s-t)}) \text{ where } \tilde{\pi}' < 0.\end{aligned} \tag{8}$$

Substituting for $\pi_{s,t}$ in (7) and for $V = \frac{V_t}{A_t}$ in (6), we obtain the following arbitrage equation

(A′)

$$\omega = \lambda\cdot\phi'(n)\int_0^{\infty} e^{-(r+\lambda\varphi(n))s}\cdot\tilde{\pi}(\omega e^{gs})ds.$$

To complete the specification of this multi-sector model, we have to derive the new labor-market clearing condition. Let

$$\tilde{x}\left(\frac{w_s}{A_t}\right) = \tilde{x}\left(\frac{\omega}{a_{t,s}}\right)$$

denote the solution to the above maximization program (8), where $a_{t,s} = \frac{A_t}{A_s}$.
The labor-market clearing condition becomes

(L′)

$$n + \int_0^1 \tilde{x}(\omega/a)\cdot h(a)\cdot da = L,$$

where (see appendix 1) the unique invariant density function $h(a)$ is given by

(D)

$$h(a) = a\frac{1}{\ln\gamma} - 1/\ln\gamma.$$

As before, the (A′) curve is downward sloping in (n, ω) whereas the (L′) curve is upward sloping. So again there exists a unique steady-state equilibrium to which we can apply the same comparative statics experiments as in the previous section, with some new effects. Consider first an increase in the R&D productivity parameter λ. Since λ does not enter the labor equation (L′), we can treat the adjusted wage rate ω as a constant and focus on the arbitrage equation (A′). As in the basic model, increasing λ will increase the arrival rate $\lambda\phi'(n)$, which is good for research and growth, and will also increase the rate of creative destruction $\lambda\phi(n)$, which is bad for growth. But now, a higher λ will also increase the rate at which a producer's profits will fall over time as a result of competing for manufacturing labor with the leading edge. This additional obsolescence effect which reinforces the above creative destruction effect, is captured by the term $\tilde{\pi}(\omega e^{gs}) = \tilde{\pi}(\omega e^{\lambda\varphi(n)\ln\gamma s})$ in the RHS of (A′).

In the Cobb–Douglas case where $F(x) = 0 < \alpha < 1$, as before we have

$$\tilde{\pi}(\omega/a) = \frac{1-a}{\alpha}\cdot(\omega/a)\cdot\tilde{x}(w/a) = \frac{1-\alpha}{\alpha}\cdot\omega\cdot\tilde{x}(\omega)\cdot a^{\frac{\alpha}{1-\alpha}},$$

so that $(\hat{A}^c)$ becomes

$$1 = \lambda\phi'(n)\frac{\frac{1-\alpha}{\alpha}\cdot x(\omega)}{\underbrace{r + \lambda\phi(n)}_{\textit{creative destruction}} \qquad \underbrace{+\,\lambda\phi(n)\tfrac{\alpha}{1-\alpha}\ln\gamma}_{\textit{new obsolescence effect}}}. \tag{9}$$

Equation (9) shows that in spite of the obsolescence effect reinforcing the creative destruction effect the overall effect of an increase in λ on research and growth in the steady state remains positive in the Cobb–Douglas case.

Next, consider the effect of an increased innovation size γ. Recall first that the right-hand side of the research arbitrage equations ($\hat{A}$ or $\hat{A}^c$) in the one-sector model includes a factor γ, indicating a "productivity effect." That is, because an innovation would raise all incomes by γ, the expected productivity of research is correspondingly higher relative to the productivity of the alternative activity, manufacturing. It turns out that the multi-sector model also has a productivity effect, but of a more subtle nature. Specifically, a single innovation will no longer have a measurable effect on income levels at the leading edge; but an increase in γ will nevertheless increase the expected productivity of research, which always takes place on the leading edge, relative to the average productivity of manufacturing across all sectors. That is, an increase γ will tilt the steady-state distribution $h(a)$ of relative productivities toward less-efficient manufacturing firms.

To see this modified productivity effect more clearly, notice that, from (L′) and (D) above

$$\tilde{x}(\omega) = \left[1 + \frac{\ln\gamma}{1-\alpha}\right] \cdot [L - n].$$

That is, the demand for labor in leading-edge firms will exceed the average demand in manufacturing by the factor $\left[1 + \frac{\ln\gamma}{1-\alpha}\right]$. Substituting this demand into (9) yields the reduced form research-arbitrage equation

$$(\hat{A}^{cm}) \qquad 1 = \lambda\phi'(n) \frac{\frac{1-\alpha}{\alpha} \overbrace{\left[1 + \frac{\ln\gamma}{1-\alpha}\right]}^{\text{modified productivity effect}} \cdot [L - n]}{r + \lambda\phi(n) + \frac{\alpha}{1-\alpha}\lambda\phi(n)\ln\gamma}$$

which differs from the one-sector version ($\hat{A}^c$) not only because of the "new obsolescence effect" but also because of the "modified productivity effect."

Thus in the multi-sectoral model an increase in the size of innovations will still have a positive productivity effect on research and growth, but this will now be mitigated by a negative obsolescence effect similar to that discussed above in connection with a change in λ. It is straightforward, however, to show that the overall effect will still be positive; larger innovations still produce more research and hence generate faster growth.

These two new effects also modify somewhat our analysis of the effects of competition on growth, but without changing the end result. That is, as can be seen directly in ($\hat{A}^{cm}$), an increase in the "competitiveness" parameter α

will continue to have same negative "appropriability" effect on research as before, working through the term $\frac{1-\alpha}{\alpha}$ in the numerator of ($\hat{A}^{cm}$). This will now be reinforced by the new obsolescence effect. That is, more competition means that growth in the leading edge will have a more detrimental effect on existing rents. But these two negative effects will now be mitigated by a positive productivity effect. That is, a firm that innovates to put itself on the leading edge will be better able to exploit its productivity gain when it can compete more freely. It is easily seen, however, that the appropriability effect always dominates the productivity effect, so that more competition will still have an unambiguously negative effect on research and on growth.

1.3 Introducing physical capital

The endogenous growth models described above assume that technological innovations are not embodied in any *durable* good (i.e., physical capital or machinery) that would typically depreciate as the corresponding technology becomes obsolete. On the other hand, recent empirical studies (e.g., DeLong and Summers (1991)) have pointed toward a positive relationship between physical capital accumulation and growth. Without entering the debate as to whether investments in machinery should be seen as fundamental or subsidiary[10] to the growth process, we shall simply look for the most straightforward implications of introducing capital goods into the Schumpeterian framework.

Going back to the multi-sector model of section 1.2, let us now assume that each intermediate good i is produced according to the production function

$$x_i = G(K_i^p/A_i, N_i), \tag{10}$$

where K_i^p and N_i are the inputs of capital and labor into production in sector i, and G is a regular constant-returns production function.[11] We divide K_i^p by A_i in (10) to indicate that successive vintages of the intermediate good are produced by increasingly capital-intensive techniques.

When an intermediate monopolist is replaced, we assume that his capital has no second-hand value (in the language of traditional growth theory we assume putty-clay capital). Hence his cost of capital is

$$\bar{r} = r + \delta_k + \lambda\phi(n), \tag{11}$$

where δ_k is the proportional rate of capital depreciation and the last term is the expected rate of (endogenous) obsolescence[12] resulting from being replaced by a new entrant.

Given (10), (11), and the fact that the intermediate firm's production function exhibits constant returns to scale, the unit cost $c_{s,t}$ can be written as

$$c_{s,t} = A_t\Gamma(\bar{r}, \omega e^{g(s-t)});\ \Gamma_1 > 0, \Gamma_2 > 0$$

so that the firms' profit flow and manufacturing employment can be expressed respectively as

$$\pi_{s,t} = A_t\hat{\pi}(\bar{r}, \omega e^{g(s-t)});\ \hat{\pi}_1 < 0, \hat{\pi}_2 < 0$$

and

$$N_i = \tilde{x}\left(\bar{r}, \frac{\omega}{a_i}\right);\ \tilde{x}_1 < 0;\ \tilde{x}_2 < 0.$$

The *arbitrage* and *labor-market clearing* equations (A′) and (L′) thus become

(A′)

$$\omega = \lambda\phi'(n)\int_0^\infty e^{-(r+\lambda\varphi(n))s}\cdot\tilde{\pi}(r + \delta_k + \lambda\phi(n), \omega e^{gs})ds$$

and

(L′)

$$L = n + \int_0^1 \tilde{x}\left(r + \delta_k + \lambda\phi(n), \frac{\omega}{a}\right)h(a)da.$$

Consider now an increase in the R&D productivity parameter λ: in addition to the various effects pointed out in 1.1, *this will increase the cost of capital* $\bar{r}$ with two opposite effects on research and growth. On the one hand, given ω, it will reduce the rents from innovating ($\hat{\pi}_1 < 0$) and thus discourage research and growth.[13] On the other hand, the increased capital cost will also reduce the demand for manufacturing labor ($\tilde{x}_i < 0$), thereby reducing the adjusted wage ω. This latter wage effect, in turn, will tend to mitigate the former *capital obsolescence* effect.[14] As shown by Cannon (1995), the *capital obsolescence effect* may sometimes be so strong that growth will actually *slow down* as a result of increasing R&D productivity.

2 MARKET STRUCTURE

2.1 Introduction

Is market competition good or bad for growth? The Schumpeterian answer to this question, as described in section 1.1 above, appeared to be one-sided: to the extent that monopoly rents are the inducement to innovation, and are therefore the mainspring of growth, product market competition can only be detrimental to growth. By the same token, more intense imitation activities will discourage innovations and growth. Hence the importance of preserving Intellectual Property Rights through an adequate system of (international) patent protection (see Grossman and Helpman (1991)).

On the other hand, recent empirical work (e.g., by Nickell (1994) or Blundell *et al.* (1995)) suggests a *positive* correlation between *product market competition* (as measured either by the number of competitors in the same industry or by the inverse of a market share or profitability index) and *productivity growth*, within a firm or industry. This evidence, in turn, appears to be more consistent with the view that competition is good for growth.

How can we reconcile the view supported by Nickell and others with the Schumpeterian paradigm developed above? Several tentative answers to this question will be explored in this section. A first approach, developed in section 2.2, is to introduce barriers to entry into research. It is then easy to show that reducing these barriers to competition will raise the growth rate. A second approach, developed in section 2.3, is to introduce *agency considerations* into the decision-making process of innovating firms, and then investigate the idea that by reducing "slack" (i.e., the amount of free-cash available to managers), product-market competition combined with the threat of liquidation can act as a disciplinary device which fosters technology adoption and thus growth. A third approach, developed in section 2.4, is to introduce the idea of "tacit knowledge." If firms must engage in R&D to acquire the non-codifiable knowledge embodied in a rival's innovation, then the implicit assumption made earlier that incumbent innovators are automatically leapfrogged by their rivals must be replaced by a more *gradualist* (*"step-by-step"*) technological progress assumption. Finally, a fourth approach, developed in section 2.5 below, will be to decompose R&D activities into *research* (leading to the discovery of new fundamental paradigms or product lines) and *development* (aimed at exploiting the new paradigms and filling up the new product lines).

2.2 Barriers to entry in research

Schumpeter's notion of creative destruction projects a view of the "competitive struggle" somewhat at odds with the standard textbook version, one in which the main instrument of competition is innovation rather than price. Clearly, "more competition" in this Schumpeterian sense means not a higher price-elasticity of demand faced by a monopolist, but an increased freedom of entry into the competitive innovation sector by potentially rent-stealing rivals. It is relatively straightforward to show that more competition in this sense will lead to higher growth.

2.2.1 *The Arrow effect*

Going back to the basic Schumpeterian model of section 1.1, where the research sector was implicitly assumed to be competitive (with any individual being free to engage in research activities), what would happen to innovations and growth in the steady state if the research sector was instead monopolistic? The main difference between the two cases is that, in the latter, research would be done by the incumbent innovator. More formally, the above equation (2) would become

$$w_t = \lambda\phi'(n_t)\cdot(V_{t+1} - V_t), \tag{12}$$

where

$$rV_t = \pi_t + \lambda\phi(n_t)\cdot(V_{t+1} - V_t). \tag{13}$$

The RHS of (12) expresses the fact that the incumbent innovator internalizes the business-stealing effect or his/her new innovation: the difference between (2) and (12) reflects the well-known *replacement effect* of Arrow. The RHS of (13), in turn, expresses the fact that the incumbent innovator internalizes the positive (intertemporal spillover) externality of current innovation on future research activities. In other words, a monopolist researcher will essentially[15] behave like a social planner. The comparison between research (and growth) respectively in the benchmark model with competitive research and in the monopolistic research case will thus boil down to a reinterpretation of the welfare analysis of the benchmark model. Whether or not demonopolizing the research sector will create more growth depends upon whether the business-stealing (Arrow) effect exceeds the intertemporal spillover effect.

This apparent ambiguity of the effect of demonopolizing research is, however, an artifact of the simplifying assumption that there is only one sector. In the multi-sector extension of section 1.2 above the ambiguity disappears, because even if each sector is monopolized, no sector is large enough to internalize the intertemporal spillovers, which benefit all the other local monopolists, not just the monopolist generating the spillovers. In this case only the Arrow effect remains, and competition is unambiguously favorable to growth.

2.2.2 *The case of U-shaped individual R&D cost functions*

The same result can be demonstrated in the basic (one-sector) model when there exists initially more than one research firm. To show this we must relax the assumption implicitly invoked up to now that there are constant returns to scale in research activities.[16] Instead assume that each individual firm faces a Poisson probability equal to $\lambda{\cdot}\theta(z-\phi)$, where the unit cost function corresponding to θ is U-shaped, and where ϕ is an entry fee (expressed in labor units) to be paid by individual firms to the government. (Thus, if z denotes the research firm's total labor investment, only the fraction $(z-\phi)$ will be directly available for research activities.)

By the usual reasoning, free entry into research implies that the average and marginal costs of innovations must be equal, which in turn implies:

(C)

$$\frac{\theta(z-\phi)}{z} = \theta'(z-\phi).$$

Let N denote the number of research firms in equilibrium. Since the aggregate arrival rate of new innovations is equal to $\lambda N{\cdot}\theta(z-\theta)$, the steady-state *arbitrage equation* becomes

(A)

$$\omega = \lambda{\cdot}\theta'(z-\phi)\gamma\frac{\tilde{\pi}(\omega)}{r+\lambda N\theta(z-\phi)},$$

where z is defined by (C).

The steady-state equilibrium $(\hat{\omega}, \hat{z}, \hat{N})$ is then fully determined by (C), (A), and the labor-*market clearing equation*

(L)

$$N{\cdot}z + \tilde{x}(\omega) = L.$$

How does the steady-state growth rate $g = \lambda\hat{N}{\cdot}\theta(\hat{z}-\phi){\cdot}\ln\gamma$ respond to a reduction in the entry fee ϕ, that is to making the research sector become more competitive? The answer turns out to be straightforward: consider the change of variables

$$\tilde{\lambda} = \lambda\frac{\theta(z-\phi)}{z} \text{ and } \tilde{n} = N{\cdot}z.$$

Using (C), we can re-express the above equations (A) and (L) respectively as

(A)

$$\omega = \tilde{\lambda}{\cdot}\gamma\frac{\tilde{\pi}(\omega)}{r+\tilde{\lambda}{\cdot}\tilde{n}}$$

and

(L)

$$L = \tilde{n} + \tilde{x}(\omega),$$

which turn out to be identical to (A) and (L) in the basic model, except that λ and n have been replaced by $\tilde{\lambda}$ and $\tilde{n}$ respectively.

A reduction in the entry fee ϕ amounts to increasing $\tilde{\lambda}$ (which is nothing but the arrival rate of innovation per unit of labor spent by a research firm). Now, we know from our comparative statics analysis of the basic model in section 1.1 that $\frac{d\tilde{n}}{d\tilde{\lambda}} > 0$. Therefore the steady-state growth rate, which is equal to $\lambda \cdot \tilde{n} \cdot \ln\gamma$, will also increase as a result of a lower entry fee. This, in turn, vindicates the Schumpeterian claim that more competition in research activities is growth enhancing.

2.3 Introducing agency considerations[17]

The next three sections all deal with competition in output markets. First, we relax the assumption that innovating firms are profit maximizing. Instead, we assume that managers are mainly concerned with preserving their private benefits of control while at the same time minimizing (innovation) costs, an assumption commonly made in the corporate finance literature. (Innovation costs here refer to the *private* managerial costs – training costs or the non-monetary cost of reorganizing the firm – of switching to a new technology.) Intensifying product-market competition may then become growth enhancing by forcing managers to *speed up* the adoption of new technologies in order to avoid bankruptcy and the resulting loss of control rights. This Darwinian argument is consistent with the view that Porter (1990) presents of the role of competition in fostering growth.

More formally, consider the multi-sector model of 1.2, with the final good being produced using a continuum of intermediate inputs of different technological vintages according to the production function

$$y = \int_i A_i \cdot x_i^{\alpha} di,$$

where A_i is the productivity parameter in sector i.

Intermediate firms are now involved in two kinds of decisions:

(a) Production decisions (for a given technology)

As before, an intermediate firm with technological vintage A_τ will choose its current output flow $x = x_{t,\tau}$ so as to

$$\max_x\{p_\tau(x)x - w_t x\},$$

where

$$p_\tau(x) = A_\tau \cdot \alpha x^{\alpha - 1}.$$

In the steady-state, we have $w_t = A_t \cdot \omega$, where A_t is the leading edge; and $A_t = A_0 \cdot e^{gt}$, where g is the steady-state growth rate. Therefore the output flow of a firm of vintage τ at date t (also the flow demand for labor by that firm) is

$$x_{t,\tau} = \left(\frac{\omega}{\alpha^2}\right)^{1/\alpha - 1} \cdot e^{-\frac{g(t-\tau)}{1-\alpha}},$$

that is, it decreases exponentially with the age of the firm's vintage $(t - \tau)$.

Assume that intermediate firms must incur a fixed operating cost (also in terms of labor) equal to $k_{t,\tau} = w_t \cdot k e^{\rho(t-\tau)}$ with $\rho \geq r$. Then the firms' *net* profit flow is given by

$$\begin{aligned}\pi_{t,\tau} &= \left[\pi(\omega)e^{-\frac{g(t-\tau)}{1-\alpha}} - \omega k e^{\rho(t-\tau)}\right]e^{gt} \\ &= \psi(\pi, u)\cdot e^{gt},\end{aligned}$$

where $u = t - \tau$ is the age of the firm's vintage and $\pi = \pi(\alpha, \omega) = s(\alpha)\cdot\omega^{\alpha/\alpha - 1}$ is a profit parameter.

The growth-adjusted profit flow, ψ, is thus positive for $u = 0$ but decreasing in age and negative for u sufficiently large. This, in turn, will play a key role in the Darwinian argument developed below.

(b) Technological adoption

Departing from the previous sections, let us suppose that new technological vintages result from *sunk adoption* decisions directly made by intermediate firms (rather than from a continuous *flow* of research investments).

Let f denote the sunk cost (in labor units) of adopting the leading-edge technology.[18] Measured in units of final output, the adoption cost at date τ is, $f_\tau = f \cdot w_\tau = f \cdot \omega e^{g\tau}$. In a steady state each intermediate firm adopts the leading-edge technology every T units of time, and the age distribution of firms remains uniform on $[0, T]$. Thus the aggregate flow of new adoptions per unit of time is $1/T$, and the aggregate flow of research labor is $n = f/T$. As in the multi-sector model of section 1.2, assume that adoptions lead incrementally to growth on the leading edge, at the rate $\ln\gamma$ per unit of innovation. Then as before, the steady-state growth rate is

(G)
$$g = \dot{A}/A = \ln\gamma/T.$$

(c) Labor-market equilibrium

In addition to the flow f/T of research labor there is an aggregate flow $\int_0^T (1/T)\tilde{x}(\omega e^{gu})du = \tilde{x}(\omega)\int_0^T (1/T)e^{-gu/(1-\alpha)}du$ of manufacturing labor and a flow $\int_0^T (1/T)ke^{\rho u}du$ of "overhead" labor. Evaluating these integrals using (G) leads to the labor-market clearing condition

(L)
$$\frac{e^{\rho T}-1}{\rho T}\cdot k + \frac{f}{T} + \tilde{x}(\omega)\left[\frac{1-e^{-\ln\gamma/(1-\alpha)}}{\ln\gamma/(1-\alpha)}\right] = L.$$

For future reference, note that the term in square brackets in (L) represents another "productivity effect," whereby an increase in γ reduces the aggregate demand for labor relative to the leading-edge demand $x(\omega)$, as in the multi-sector model of 1.2.

(i) Profit-maximizing firms

First consider an intermediate firm born at date 0 that does *not* face agency problems. Such a firm will, in a steady state, choose to switch to the leading edge at times $T_1, T_1 + T_2, \ldots, T_1 + \ldots + T_k$, etc., where (T_k) is a solution of the maximization program

$$\to \max_{(T_k)}\Bigg[W - f\omega + \int_0^{T_1} \psi(\pi,u)e^{-(r-g)u}du$$
$$+ e^{-(r-g)T_1}\left[-f\omega + \int_0^{T_2} \psi(\pi,u)e^{-(r-g)u}du\right]$$
$$+ e^{-(r-g)(T_1+T_2)}\left[-f\omega + \int_0^{T_3} \psi(\pi,u)e^{-(r-g)u}du\right]$$
$$+ \ldots\Bigg],$$

where W is the firm's initial endowment at date 0.

One can easily see that the optimal adoption policy is stationary ($T_k \equiv \hat{T}$ for $k \geq 1$), where

(A^p)

$$\hat{T} = \arg\max_T \frac{\left[-f\cdot\omega + \int_0^T \psi(\pi, u)e^{-(r-g)u}du\right]}{1 - e^{-(r-g)T}}.$$

This equation will replace the arbitrage equation (A) of the previous sections.

It turns out (see Aghion, Dewatripont and Rey (1995)) that the equilibrium adoption policy $\hat{T}$ defined by (A^p) and (L) satisfies

$$\frac{d\hat{T}}{d\alpha} > 0$$

This is again the appropriability effect pointed out in the basic Schumpeterian model: more product-market competition (i.e., a lower π) will discourage technological adoptions ($\hat{T} \nearrow$) and thereby reduce growth.

(*ii*) *Non-profit-maximizing firms*
A common assumption in the corporate finance literature is that the managers of large companies are mainly concerned with preserving their private benefits of control over the company while at the same time minimizing "effort." To model this, we assume the following utility function for intermediate firms' managers

$$U_0 = \int_0^\infty B_t\cdot e^{-\delta t}dt - \sum_{j\geq 1} C\cdot e^{-\delta(T_1 + \ldots + T_j)},$$

where C is the *private cost for the manager to switch* to a new technological vintage (training cost for example); B_t is the *current private benefit of control* at date t, equal to $B > 0$ if the firm has financially survived up to time t and equal to zero otherwise; and δ is the subjective rate at which managers discount future private costs and benefits.

For B and δ sufficiently large, one can show that the above objective function is observationally equivalent to a lexicographic preference ordering whereby the manager always seeks to delay as much as possible the next innovation subject to keeping the firm afloat, that is with a positive net financial wealth. Consider now an intermediate firm where the manager obeys such a lexicographic preference ordering, and suppose that this firm has entered the market with wealth ωf and innovated at date $t = 0$.

If the firm has not innovated thereafter, its accumulated profits at date $t = T$ (evaluated as of date zero) are equal to

$$\int_0^T \psi(\pi, u)e^{-(r-g)u}\cdot du.$$

Given that $\psi(\pi, 0) > 0, \psi(\pi, u) < 0$ for u large and $\rho \geq r$, these cumulative profits will be inverted-U shaped with respect to T, being initially increasing and positive for T small and then decreasing and eventually negative for T sufficiently large. This implies that the intermediate firm will necessarily become insolvent (and therefore go bankrupt) if it never innovates after date 0. More precisely, there exists a maximum date $\tilde{T}$ at which the firm's cumulative profits just cover the adoption cost $f{\cdot}e^{-(r-g)\tilde{T}}$ at that date (evaluated as of date zero), where $\tilde{T}$ is defined by

$$\omega f e^{-(r-g)T} = \int_0^T [\pi(\omega) e^{\frac{-gu}{1-\alpha}} - \omega k e^{\rho u}] e^{-(r-g)u} du. \tag{14}$$

Intuitively, an increase in competition, by reducing the flow of variable profits $\pi(\omega)$ will hasten the day when a firm's wealth (the RHS) is exhausted by the rising overhead costs $\omega k e^{\rho u}$, thus forcing it to adopt sooner while it still has enough wealth remaining to do so.

To see this effect more clearly, we again use the fact that, in this Cobb–Douglas world, $\pi = \dfrac{1-\alpha}{\alpha}\omega x$, along with the labor-market clearing condition (L) and the growth equation (G) to derive from (14) the reduced-form arbitrage equation

(A^F)

$$fe^{-rT+\ln\gamma} = \int_0^T \left\{ \overbrace{\frac{1-\alpha}{\alpha}}^{\text{appropriability}} \cdot \left[\frac{\overbrace{\ln\gamma/(1-\alpha)}^{\text{productivity}}}{1-e^{-\ln\gamma/(1-\tau)}} \right] \left[L - \frac{f}{T} - \frac{e^{\rho T}-1}{\rho T} k \right] \overbrace{e^{\frac{-\ln\gamma u}{T(1-\alpha)}}}^{\text{obselescence}} - ke^{\rho u} \right\} e^{-(r-\ln\gamma/T)u} du.$$

The two sides of (A^F), adoption cost and wealth, are described in figure 8.2 below. Wealth is less than cost for $T = 0$ and again as $T \rightarrow \infty$. So the equilibrium, which is the *maximal* delay possible, occurs at a point like E where wealth is falling faster than cost. Thus an increase in the competitiveness parameter α will reduce T, and hence raise growth, if it shifts the wealth curve down.

As indicated in (A^F), the same three effects of α will be at work on wealth as we saw at work on the right-hand side of the arbitrage equation ($\hat{A}^{cm}$) in the multi-sector model. Again, the appropriability and obsolescence effects are negative and the productivity effect is positive, but the appropriability effect dominates the productivity effect. Thus the overall effect of increased competition, as before, is to reduce wealth, but in this case the result is to increase research rather than decrease it, because in this case firms have

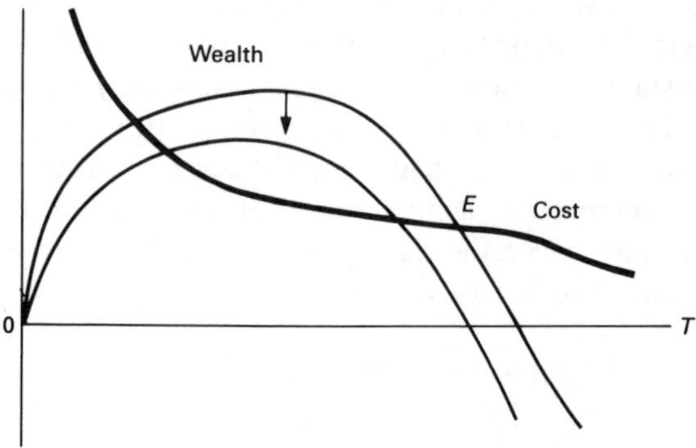

Figure 8.2

Note: An increase in competitiveness, by reducing wealth, forces firms to adopt sooner, thus raising the rate of growth.

waited so long that their profits are increasing with respect to the level of research, whereas in the models in section 1 the right-hand side of the arbitrage equation was always decreasing in the economy-wide level of research, mainly because of the negative creative-destruction externality.

Remark Contrary to the basic Schumpeterian model where a higher productivity of R&D has an unambiguously boosting effect on growth, a lower adoption cost f may *slow down* adoptions and growth: indeed for given wage ω, a lower f increases the financial slack of intermediate firms, thereby allowing managers to delay the next technological adoption while keeping their firm solvent.

2.4 From leap-frogging to step-by-step technological progress[19]

An alternative approach for reconciling the Schumpeterian paradigm with recent empirical evidence on productivity growth and product-market competition, is to replace the *leap frogging* assumption of the basic Schumpeterian model (with incumbent innovators being systemically overtaken by outside researchers) by a less radical *step-by-step* assumption. That is, a firm that is currently m steps behind the technological leader in its industry must successively go through all m steps and catch up with the leader before becoming a leader itself. This step-by-step assumption can be rationalized by supposing that an innovator acquires tacit knowledge that cannot be duplicated by a rival without engaging in its own R&D to catch up. Once it has caught up we suppose that no patent protects the former leader from Bertrand competition.

This change leads to a richer analysis of the interplay between product-market competition, innovation, and growth, by allowing firms in an industry to be *neck-to-neck*. A higher degree of product-market competition, by making life more difficult for neck-to-neck firms, will encourage them to innovate in order to acquire a significant lead over their rivals.

More formally suppose that final output is produced at any time t using input services from a continuum of intermediate sectors, according to the production function

$$\ln y_t = \int_0^1 \ln Q_i(t) di.$$

As shown in Grossman and Helpman (1991), this logarithmic technology implies that the same amount $E(t)$ will be spent at any time t by the final-good sector on *all* intermediate industries. Choosing current aggregate spending as the numeraire, we then have: $E(t) \equiv 1$.

Each sector i is assumed to be *duopolistic* with respect to both production and research activities, with firms A and B, and

$$Q_i = v(q_{Ai}, q_{Bi}),$$

where v is homogenous of degree one and symmetric in its two arguments.[20]

Let k denote the technology level of a duopoly firm in a given industry. That is, in order to produce one unit of an intermediate good, this firm needs to employ γ^{-k} units of labor, where $\gamma > 1$. An industry is thus fully characterized by a pair of integers (l, m), where l is the leader's technology and m is the technological gap between the leader and the follower.

Let π_m(resp. π_{-m}) denote the equilibrium profit flow of a firm m steps ahead of (resp. behind) its rival.[21] For expositional simplicity, we assume that knowledge spillovers between leaders and followers in an industry are such that the maximum sustainable gap is $m = 1$. That is, if a firm one step ahead innovates, the follower will automatically learn to copy the leader's previous technology and will then remain only one step behind.

We now come to the basic feature of the model, namely the *step-by-step* technological assumption. We denote by $\psi(x) = \frac{1}{2}x^2$ the R&D cost (in units of labor) of a firm innovating with Poisson hazard rate x.

Then, if V_m denotes the steady-state growth-adjusted value of being currently a leader (or a follower if m is negative) in an industry with technological gap m, we have the following Bellman equations:[22]

$$rV_1 = \pi_1 + x_{-1}(V_0 - V_1) \tag{15}$$

$$rV_0 = \pi_0 + \bar{x}_0(V_{-1} - V_0) + x_0(V_1 - V_0) - wx_0^2/2 \tag{16}$$

$$rV_{-1} = \pi_{-1} + x_{-1}(V_0 - V_{-1}) - wx_{-1}^2/2. \tag{17}$$

Note that $x_1 = 0$, since our assumption of automatic catchup means a leader cannot get any further advantage by innovating. In equations (16) and (17), respectively, x_0 and x_{-1} are chosen to maximize the RHS. Thus we have the first-order conditions

$$w{\cdot}x_i = V_{i+1} - V_i;\ i = -1, 0. \tag{18}$$

Equation (15) ~ (18) together with the symmetric-equilibrium condition $x_0 = \bar{x}_0$ yield the reduced-form research equations.

$$(w/2)x_0^2 + rw{\cdot}x_0 - (\pi_1 - \pi_0) = 0 \tag{19}$$

$$(w/2)x_{-1}^2 + (r + x_0)wx_{-1} - (\pi_0 - \pi_{-1}) - (w/2)x_0^2 = 0. \tag{20}$$

Given any wage w, these equations solve for unique non-negative values of x_0 and x_{-1}.

We represent an increase in competition as an increase in the elasticity of substitution between the products A and B in each sector in a neighborhood of the 45° line, which translates into a reduction in the profit level π_0 earned by a firm that is neck and neck with its rival.[23] It is then straightforward to show that x_0 will rise while x_{-1} falls. The latter effect is the basic Schumpeterian effect that results from reducing the rents that can be captured by a follower who succeeds in catching up with his rival by innovating. The former is the new effect introduced by tacit knowledge; competition reduces the rents in the neck-and-neck status quo, and thus encourages innovation among firms that are even with their rivals, by raising the incremental value of getting ahead.

The model is then closed by a labor-market clearing equation which determines ω as a function of the xs and the πs.[24] We shall ignore that equation and take the wage rate ω as given in our analysis below. It now remains to express the steady-state average growth rate of the economy.

Let μ_1 denote the steady-state fraction of industries with technological gap $m = 1$, and $\mu_0 = 1 - \mu_1$. During time interval dt, in $\mu_1 x_{-1}{\cdot}dt$ sectors the follower catches up with the leader; in $2\mu_0 x_0 dt$ sectors one firm acquires a lead. Since the distribution of sectors (the μ_ms) remains stationary over time, we have

$$\underbrace{\mu_1 x_{-1}}_{\substack{\text{flow of sectors that}\\ \text{become } \textit{leveled}}} = \underbrace{2\mu_0 x_0}_{\substack{\text{flow of sectors that}\\ \text{become } \textit{unleveled}}} \tag{21}$$

Each industry follows a strict two-stage cycle, alternating between $m = 0$ and $m = 1$. The log of its output rises by γ with each completed cycle. The frequency of completed cycles is the fraction μ_1 of time spent in stage 2, times the frequency x_{-1} of innovations in stage 2. Hence the average

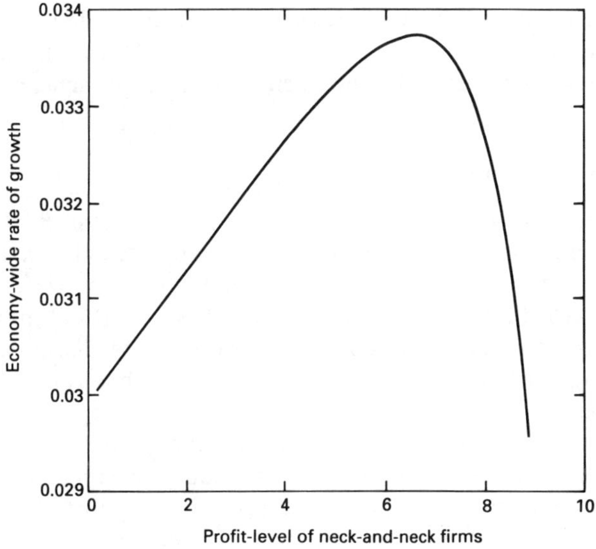

Figure 8.3

Note: As competition decreases, the equilibrium profit level π_0 of neck-and-neck firms increases, resulting eventually in a fall in the economy-wide rate of growth.

growth rate of each industry is $\mu_1 x_{-1} \ln\gamma$. From (21) it follows that the fraction of industries with a leader is $\mu_1 = \frac{2x_0}{2x_0 + x_{-1}}$. Hence we have the following expression for the average growth rate of final output

(G)

$$g = \mu_1 x_{-1} \ln\gamma = \frac{2x_0 x_{-1}}{2x_0 + x_{-1}} \cdot \ln\gamma.$$

From (G) it is clear that increased competition can either raise growth or lower it, depending upon which effect is stronger: the rise in x_0 which raises g, or the fall in x_{-1}, which lowers g. Just as clearly, however, the effect on x_0 will be the dominant one if π_0 is close enough to π_1, because in the limit, as π_0 approaches π_1, x_0 will fall to zero,[25] and hence, according to (G), the growth rate will also fall to zero. Intuitively, if $\pi_1 - \pi_0$ is small, then firms that are behind will have an incentive to catch up, but once even they will have little incentive to get ahead. Hence most firms in a steady state will be neck and neck, doing little R&D. That is, most firms will be in sectors in which R&D will be stimulated by an increase in competition. Figure 8.3 shows a numerical example in which $r = 0.04, \pi_{-1} = 0, \pi_1 = 10, w = 1$, and $\gamma = 1.02$. As π_0 rises, growth rises at first, but then falls as π_0 approaches π_1.

2.5 Research and development

All the endogenous growth models surveyed above represent R&D activities as homogeneous, performed by only one kind of researcher, and generating just one kind of innovation and/or one kind of knowledge. However, whether growth will be enhanced by a subsidy to R&D may depend not only upon the *size* of the subsidy but also upon its *allocation*, e.g., to *basic versus applied* research or to *independent* research labs versus integrated industries.

In this section we distinguish between two kinds of innovative activity, research and development. Research opens up new windows of opportunity by inventing new product lines. Development realizes those opportunities by inventing concrete plans that allow the products to be produced. We show that the level of research, and therefore the growth rate, are increased if developers become more *adaptable*; that is, if the rate at which they are able to switch from developing old lines to developing new ones increases. This result supports Lucas's (1993) claim to the effect that the key to success of some newly industrialized countries is their ability to move skilled workers quickly from sectors where learning is beginning to slow down to those where new ideas can more fruitfully be developed. When we endogenize this adaptability parameter we also find that the same result implies a *positive effect of competition on growth.* That is, an increase in the substitutability between new and old product lines, which implies an increase in competitiveness between them, will induce developers to leave old lines more rapidly, with the effect of inducing a higher level of research and growth. Contrary to the basic Schumpeterian model of section 1 this implies that *increased competition may again lead to faster growth.*

We consider a variant of the multi-sector model above, in which the sectors are distinguished by the age u of their fundamental technology. In this variant an innovation creates a new sector, without destroying an old one. Aggregate output at date t in a steady state is

$$y_t = A_t \int_0^\infty e^{-gu} F(x_u) \cdot S_u du,$$

where S_u is the number of products from lines of age u and x_u the amount of labor allocated to producing each of them.

To focus on the relationship between research and development we suppose that there are two kinds of workers; L unskilled workers can produce goods and H skilled workers can engage in innovative activity – either research or development. At each date, labor will be allocated across vintages so as to satisfy the equilibrium conditions

$$e^{-gu}\{F'(x_u) + x_u F''(x_u)\} = \omega \text{ for all } u \tag{22}$$

$$\int_0^\infty x_u \cdot S_u du = L,$$

where the left-hand side of (22) is the marginal revenue product of labor in sector u and ω is the economy-wide wage, divided by the leading edge A_t.

The intermediate goods in sector u embody the technology A_{t-u} that was on the leading edge at $t - u$. But they were almost all invented after $t - u$. Instead, each one comes from a "product line" that was invented at $t - u$. Product lines are the result of research, and arrive continually at the flow rate $\lambda^r H^r$, where H^r is the amount of skilled labor allocated to research and λ^r the Poisson arrival rate per researcher. New goods on any product line arise from the discoveries by developers who attach themselves to that line.

For expository purposes we suppose initially that developers attach themselves only to a line of the most recent vintage, but that once attached they remain so until they are "freed" to go into research, or to go into developing a newer line, by an exogenous event with a constant Poisson arrival rate σ to each worker. The "relocation rate" σ will play a major role in what follows, and will eventually be endogenized.

We suppose that the Poisson arrival rate of secondary innovations to any developer depends upon the number η_u of developers on the same line, according to $\lambda^d \eta_u^{-\nu} (0 < \nu < 1)$. Let h^d be the flow of skilled workers into developing new lines per period. Since there are $\lambda^r H^r$ new lines per period, $\eta_u = (h^d / \lambda^r H^r) e^{-\sigma u}$ and[26]

$$S_u = (\lambda^r H^r)^\nu \lambda^d (h^d)^{1-\nu} (1 - e^{-\sigma(1-\nu) \cdot u}) / \sigma \cdot (1 - \nu). \tag{23}$$

The leading edge A_t embodies the general knowledge available to all. Every one takes it as exogenous. Its growth rate will become the economy's growth rate g in a steady state. We assume that general knowledge is created only by research.[27] Thus we have the growth equation

(G)

$$g = \lambda^r H^r.$$

Since the stock of developers changes over time according to the relocation equation $\dot{H}_t^d = h_t^d - \sigma H_t^d = h_t^d - \sigma(H - H_t^r)$, in a steady state the flow of skilled workers into developing new lines will be constant and equal to

(R)

$$h^d = \sigma(H - H^r).$$

Figure 8.4 shows the structure of output in the economy at any given date t. Nothing can be produced on lines that have not yet been invented, therefore, $Y_{t,\tau} = 0$ for all $\tau \geq t$. Because older vintages are less efficient, output of very old lines will be very low. Hence the profile will tend to have the wave form depicted by figure 8.4. Over time, the profile will shift to the right, as research opens up new product lines. Near the leading edge the profile will be shifting up, as development creates new goods. But far back from the leading edge the profile will be shifting down, as the rise in real wages associated with growth draws labor from old product lines, and the reallocation of old developers into new lines reduces the rate at which new goods are being introduced on old lines. However, there will always be some development taking place no matter how old the line.[28]

For both kinds of innovative activity to coexist in a steady state, skilled workers who have just been upgraded must be indifferent between research and development on a new line. To specify the arbitrage equation that reflects this indifference we must describe how each kind of innovative activity is compensated. Each plan (to produce a new intermediate good) on a line is implemented by a company formed by the researcher who discovered the line and the developer who found the plan. When the developer first begins work on the line it is agreed that a certain fraction κ of each company's profits will go to the researcher, with $1 - \kappa$ going to the developer. At each date t there will be $\lambda^r H^r$ researchers with new lines of vintage t competing for developers, using κ as their strategic variable. As we show in the appendix, this competition defines a unique equilibrium value of κ, namely $\kappa = \nu$. That is, as in any model of perfect competition, the developers' share of rents will be the Cobb–Douglas exponent of development in producing rents on a line, since the arrival rate of new products on a line with η developers is proportional to $\eta^{1-\nu}$.[29]

Let $V_t^r = V^r e^{gt}$ denote the expected present value of the income that a researcher will receive until his alternative choice as a developer is upgraded to a new line. That is, V_t^r is the value of a claim to all the researcher's rents from fundamental innovations made over the time period (of stochastic length) during which he could have been developing a line of vintage t. Let $V_t^d = V^d \cdot e^{gt}$ denote the value of the income the researcher would have received in development over the same period. Since a newly upgraded skilled worker can freely choose either activity, a steady state with both research and development requires

$$V^r = V^d.$$

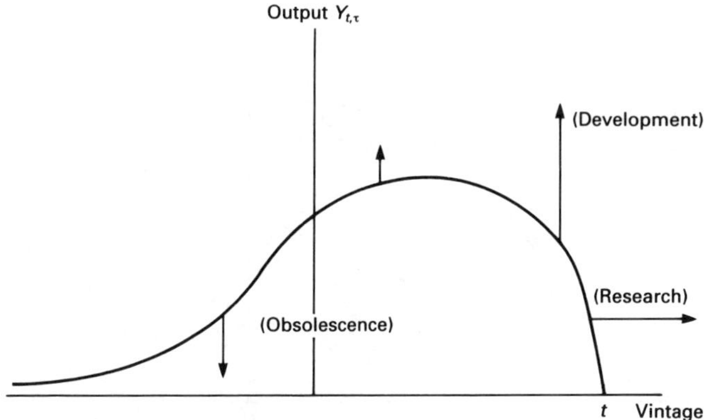

Figure 8.4

Note: The profile of output across lines of different vintages, at date t.

In a steady state the value V_t^r grows at rate g and capitalizes flow payoffs (per unit of time) equal to the flow probability of discovering a new line λ^r times the researcher's share of a new product line κW_t (where W_t denotes the capitalized value of rents generated by the intermediate plans on each product line opened up at date t). Since upgrading occurs at Poisson rate σ, the Bellman equation defining the steady-state value of V^r is

$$r \cdot V^r = \lambda^r \cdot \kappa \cdot W - \sigma \cdot V^r + g \cdot V^r.$$

Since each developer receives the fraction $1/\eta$ of $(1 - k) \cdot W$, we have

$$V^d = (\lambda^r \cdot H^r / h^d) \cdot (1 - k) \cdot W.$$

The previous three equations, together with the steady-state condition (R) and the fact that $\kappa = \nu$ yield the arbitrage equation

(A)

$$r + \sigma - g = \frac{\nu}{1 - \nu} \sigma \frac{(H - H^r)}{H^r}.$$

According to (A) an increase in the growth rate will result in a larger equilibrium level of research. This positive effect of growth on research is clearly a reflection of the more forward-looking nature of research as compared with development.

The steady-state values of g and H^r are jointly determined by the arbitrage equation (A) and the growth equation (G), shown in figure 8.5. As

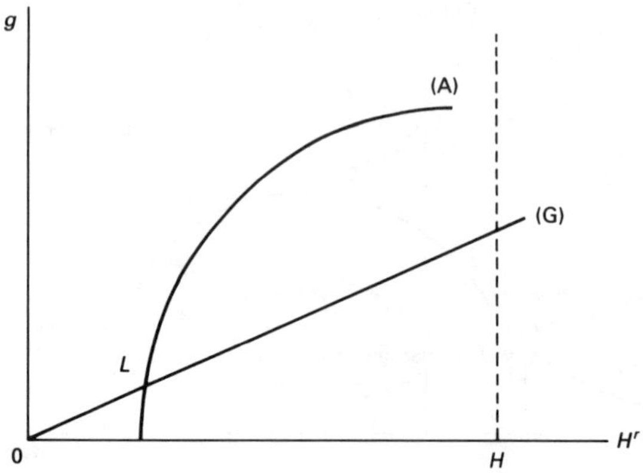

Figure 8.5

we have seen, both are upward sloping. An increase in the relocation rate σ will increase both the amount of research H^r and the growth rate g, by shifting the (A) curve to the right.

The positive effect of the upgrading rate σ on research and growth can be explained as follows: holding the total supply of skilled workers H constant, an increase in σ implies an increase in the initial flow of developers into newly discovered lines. It also increases the speed at which current lines are being depleted of their developers, but time-discounting implies that the former effect dominates the latter; that is, a higher σ increases the value of being a researcher relative to that of being a developer. Hence the positive effect of the upgrading rate σ on research and thus on growth by equation (G). This is the "*Lucas effect*" referred to above, whereby adaptability increases growth. (Although, contrary to Lucas (1993), a higher mobility of developers across lines enhances growth not so much because it increases aggregate learning by doing but rather because it increases the steady-state mass of researchers.) As we show below, the same effect translates into a positive effect of competition on growth when we endogenize σ.

Remark The above analysis may convey the wrong impression that the positive effect of σ on g is essentially driven by our extreme assumption about the growth equation (G), namely that only fundamental innovations (i.e., ultimately research) generate new general knowledge. However, we can show (see Aghion and Howitt (1996)) that the above comparative statics results carry over to the general case where *both* fundamental *and* secondary innovations contribute to the growth of general knowledge. The main reason is that, because of its more forward-looking nature relative to development, research has a larger marginal product than development in generating *either* kind of innovations, fundamental *or* applied.[30]

Suppose now that developers are free at each instant to engage in research or to do development on any line. To keep the model tractable we restrict attention to the Cobb–Douglas case, where $F(x) = x^{\alpha}(0 < \alpha < 1)$. It turns out that an analogous arbitrage equation results, because developers will again relocate at a constant rate in the steady-state equilibrium, except that the rate of upgrading is now endogenous. The positive results are identical to those obtained under an exogenous σ, except that the Cobb–Douglas parameter α now matters for positive results, because it affects the endogenous upgrading rate.

Let $W_{t,\tau}$ denote the value at date t of a plan of vintage τ: $\int_t^{\infty} e^{-r(s-t)}\pi_{s,\tau}ds$, where $\pi_{s,\tau}$ is the flow of profits to the producer of an intermediate good of vintage τ. In the Cobb–Douglas case it is easily shown that $\pi_{s,\tau} = \delta A_{\tau}^{1/(1-\alpha)} w_s^{\alpha/(\alpha-1)}$, where δ is a positive constant. Since A_{τ} grows at the constant rate g in a steady state, therefore

$$W_{t,\tau} = W_{t,t}e^{-g(t-\tau)/(1-\alpha)}.$$

Since all skilled workers are mobile across all innovative activities, they must all earn the same expected income x_t at date t. In particular, a researcher who has a line of vintage τ at date t will have to pay x_t to each developer he employs at that date. Thus he will choose $\eta_{t,\tau}$ so as to maximize his flow of new development royalties

$$\text{Max}\{\lambda^d \eta_{t,\tau}^{1-v} W_{t,t}e^{-g(t-\tau)/(1-\alpha)} - x_t\eta_{t,\tau}\}.$$

(Recall that each developer's arrival rate is $\lambda^d \eta_{t,\tau}^{-v}$.) The solution to this maximization problem is

$$\eta_{t,\tau} = [x_t/(1-v)\lambda^d W_{t,t}e^{-g(t-\tau)/(1-\alpha)}]^{-1/v} = \eta_{t,t}e^{-g(t-\tau)/v(1-\alpha)}.$$

This shows that the unique candidate for an endogenous steady-state relocation rate is $\sigma = \dfrac{g}{v(1-\alpha)}$.

It turns out that the economy must satisfy the same arbitrage equation (A) as before,[31] but with σ being replaced by the endogenous relocation rate

$$\frac{g}{v(1-\alpha)},$$

that is

(A′)

$$r + [g/v(1-\alpha)] - g = \frac{v}{1-v}[g/v(1-\alpha)]\frac{(H-H^r)}{H^r}.$$

A steady-rate equilibrium occurs when the growth equation (G) and the modified arbitrage equation (A′) are both satisfied. It is straightforward to verify that the curve representing (A′) in figure 8.5 would be upward sloping and would be affected by parameter changes in exactly the same direction as is the curve representing (A), except that now the Cobb–Douglas parameter α will shift it to the right because it has a direct effect on the endogenous upgrading rate $[g/v(1-\alpha)]$, whereas neither α nor any parameter of the general production function F had an effect when the upgrading rate was exogenous.

Thus an increase in competition, as measured by α, will increase the equilibrium levels of research and growth.[32] We have thus obtained a fourth "explanation" for the observed positive correlation between product market competition and productivity growth, which again relies upon extending the basic Schumpeterian model of section 1.

3 CONCLUSION

We began this chapter by claiming that Schumpeterian models of endogenous growth are shedding new substantive light on structural aspects of growth, because of their specificity concerning the details of the innovation process. We then went on to illustrate this claim by showing how these models can help to explain the apparent fact that competition and growth are positively correlated, even though this fact contradicts the most elementary Schumpeterian models, which embody only the appropriability effect of competition.

We end by observing that the various Schumpeterian explanations of this apparent fact provide a number of empirical hypotheses that are worth pursuing, and which suggest a potential empirical test of the Schumpeterian approach. First, the argument of section 2.2 suggests that competition in research, as opposed to product-market competition, is almost always likely to be favorable to growth. As for product-market competition, the various explanations presented above suggest that the correlation between competition and growth is more likely to be positive in subgroups of the economy where the various factors introduced in each of the explanations is prevalent to a large enough extent that the positive effects derived from them might outweigh the negative appropriability effect that is always present.

Thus, for example, if industries were classified into two subgroups characterized respectively by strong and weak control of managers by shareholders, one ought to find a stronger positive effect of competition on growth within the latter group than within the former, since the agency problems at the heart of our Darwinian argument of 2.3 above are more likely to prevail in the latter group. Likewise, there should be a stronger positive effect of competition on growth between sectors where tacit knowledge is the limiting barrier to imitation relative to the effect between sectors where patent protection is the limiting barrier, since patent protection reduces the scope for the neck-and-neck competition shown in 2.4 above to be favorable to growth. By the same token, the positive effect of competition on growth should show up more strongly within a group of sectors or countries where developers are mobile across product lines than where heavy technology-specific fixed investments limits their ability to move in response to increased competition, since it is this response which gives rise to the positive effect shown in 2.5 above. Our hope is that empirical work aimed at testing these various propositions will allow econometricians not only to confront Schumpeterian growth theory with evidence, but also to sharpen our understanding of how competition affects growth.

APPENDIX 1

This appendix derives (D) of section 1.2. Let $F_A(\cdot, t)$ denote the cumulative distribution of the absolute productivity parameters A across sectors in a steady state at date t. Pick $\bar{A} > 0$ and define $\Phi(t) \equiv F_A(\bar{A}, t), t_0 \equiv \ln\bar{A}/g$. Then

$$\Phi(t_0) = 1, \text{ and}$$
$$\dot{\Phi}(t) = -\lambda\cdot\phi(n)\cdot\Phi(t) \text{ for all } t \geq t_0.$$

That is, $\bar{A}$ is by construction the leading edge at t_0, and after t_0 the fraction of sectors behind $\bar{A}$ falls at the aggregate rate of innovations, each of which leaves the innovating sector ahead of $\bar{A}$, times the fraction of innovations occurring in sectors behind $\bar{A}$ at the time. Thus

$$\Phi(t) = e^{-\lambda\varphi(n)\cdot(t-t_0)} \text{ for all } t \geq t_0.$$

Since $t \equiv \ln A_t/g, t_0 \equiv \ln\bar{A}/g$ and $g = \ln\gamma\cdot\lambda\cdot\phi(n)$

$$F_A(\bar{A}, t) \equiv \Phi(t) = (\bar{A}/A_t)^{1/\ln\gamma}.$$

By definition the cumulative distribution of relative productivities a is

$$F_a(a) \equiv F_A(aA_t, t).$$

Hence

$$F_a(a) = a^{1/\ln\gamma}.$$

The density h is the derivative of F_a, which the above equation shows is given by (D) in the text.

APPENDIX 2

This appendix shows that $\kappa = \nu$ as asserted in section 2.5. Let W_t denote the capitalized value of the anticipated rents generated by each product line of vintage t, at date t. Since there are $\lambda^r H^r$ product lines of each vintage and S_u goods across all lines of age u, in a steady state $W_t = e^{gt} \cdot W$, where

$$W = \int_0^\infty e^{-ru} S_u \tilde{\pi}(we^{gu}) du / \lambda^r H^r.$$

This equation, equation (23) and the definition $\eta \equiv h^d/\lambda^r H^r$ together yield

$$W = \eta^{1-\nu} \cdot \lambda^d \int_0^\infty e^{-ru} \tilde{\pi}(\omega e^{gu})(1 - e^{-\sigma(1-\nu)u}) du / \sigma(1-\nu)$$

$$= \eta^{1-\nu} \times \text{constant}.$$

Perfect competition implies each developer is paid his marginal contribution to W

$$V^d = \partial W / \partial \eta = (1 - \nu) W / \eta.$$

Thus the fraction $1 - \kappa$ of W going to developers is $\eta V^d / W = 1 - \nu$; that is, $\kappa = \nu$.

Notes

1 For example, Segerstrom, Anant and Dinopoulos (1990), Aghion and Howitt (1992), Corriveau (1991), Romer (1990), Grossman and Helpman (1991), and Young (1993a and b).

2 Some implications of introducing physical capital accumulation are discussed in section 1.3 below.

3 This follows from the following asset equation for the annuity value of innovation $(t+1)$

$$rV_{t+1} = \pi_{t+1} - \lambda \cdot \phi(n_{t+1}) \cdot V_{t+1}$$

(with probability $\lambda \cdot \phi(n_{t+1})$ the $(t+1)^{\text{th}}$ innovator will be replaced by the following innovation, therefore the second term on the RHS is the annual expected loss for the $(t+1)^{\text{th}}$ innovator).

4 More precisely, we have

$$\pi_t = \max_x [A_t \cdot F'(x) - w_t]x,$$

where $A_t F'(x) = P_t$ is the inverse demand curve facing the tth innovator and w_t is the wage. We assume that innovations are big enough that the monopolist need not worry about competition from the previous generation of intermediate goods, i.e., that innovations are "drastic." No significant differences arise in the "non-drastic" case – see Aghion and Howitt (1992).

When the production function $F(x)$ is such that the marginal revenue function is downward sloping, then it can be immediately seen that π_t and the solution x_t to the above program are decreasing functions of the growth-adjusted wage rate, $\omega_t = w_t/A_t$ with $x_t = \tilde{x}(\omega_t)$ and $\pi_t = A_t \cdot \tilde{\pi}(\omega_t)$.

5 See note 4 above.

6 In a steady state the flow of final (consumption) output produced during the time interval between the tth and the $(t+1)^{\text{th}}$ innovation is: $y_t = A_t F(\hat{x}) = A_t F(L - \hat{n})$. Thus $\ln y_{t+1} = \ln y_t + \ln \gamma$. In real time, we then have: $\ln y(\tau + 1) = \ln y(\tau) + (\ln \gamma)\varepsilon(\tau)$, where $\varepsilon(\tau)$ is the number of innovations between τ and $\tau + 1$. Given that $\varepsilon(\tau)$ is Poisson distributed with parameter $\lambda\phi(\hat{n})$ we have $E(\ln y(\tau + 1) - \ln y(\tau)) = \lambda\phi(\hat{n})\ln\gamma$, where the LHS is nothing but the average growth rate.

7 To see this, notice that if we substitute for ω_t and ω_{t+1} using (L) (or equivalently: $\omega_t = \tilde{x}^{-1}(L - n_t)$), the arbitrage equation (A) becomes

$$n_t = \psi(n_{t+1}), \psi' < 0.$$

In addition to the steady state $\hat{n} = \Psi(\hat{n})$, this difference equation can also have periodic solutions of order two.

8 The optimal labor allocation between research and manufacturing activities is determined as the solution to the program

$$\max_{x,n} \int_0^\infty e^{-r\tau} \sum_{t=0}^{\infty} \pi(t,\tau) \cdot A_t \cdot F(x) d\tau$$

$$\text{s.t.: } x + n = L,$$

where $\pi(t, \tau) = (\lambda n \tau)^t \cdot e^{-\lambda n \tau}/t!$ is the Poisson probability that t innovations occur during the time interval $[0, \tau]$.

9 A natural interpretation for this growth equation is that there is an infinite list of techniques, each embodying a productivity parameter whose log equals that technique's number on the list multiplied by $\ln\gamma$, and that R&D consists in discovering these techniques one at a time. Each discovery is implementable only in the chosen sector of the innovator, but its discovery allows the next innovator to discover a slightly better technique in another sector.

10 See Grossman and Helpman (1991, chapter 5) for another extension of the basic Schumpeterian model in 1.1, where physical capital enters as an additional input for producing final output but otherwise does not interact at all with the innovation process and therefore with long-run growth.

11 We were previously assuming $G(K_i^p/A_i, N_i) \equiv N_i$.
12 See also Redding (1993).
13 This effect has first been pointed out by Cannon (1995).
14 Note that the same two opposite effects on research and growth will follow from an increase in the exogenous rate of depreciation δ_k.
15 Except for the fact that a monopolist maximizes profits whereas a social planner will seek to maximize intertemporal consumption.
16 That is we have implicitly assumed that individual firms have Poisson innovation rates of the form: $\lambda\psi(z, k)$, where z is the firm's R&D effort, k is a complementary input into research (e.g., capital), and ψ is homogeneous of degree one in z and k. We have implicitly taken k as fixed.
17 See Aghion, Dewatripont, and Rey (1995) from which this section is drawn.
18 We thus posit a deterministic innovation process at the firm level, which in turn can be interpreted as assuming either that each intermediate firm hires a large number (continuum) of researchers subject to uncorrelated Poisson processes or simply that a firm adopts existing new inventions.
19 See Aghion, Harris, and Vickers (1995).
20 A particular case is when $Q_i = q_A + q_B$, that is when the two intermediate inputs produced in industry i are perfect substitutes.
21 The above logarithmic final good technology, together with the linear production cost structure $c(q) = q{\cdot}\gamma^{-k}$, imply indeed that the equilibrium profit flows of the leader and the follower in an industry depend only upon the technological gap m in that industry.
22 Where r still denotes the individual rate of time preference. The π and Vs in this and the following equations are obviously expressed in units of numeraire, where the numeraire is current total expenditures.

In words, the annuity value of being a technological leader in an industry with technological gap m is equal to the current profit flow π_m, plus the expected capital gain if the leader makes a further innovation and thereby increases the gap from m to $m + 1$, minus the expected capital loss if the follower makes an innovation and thereby reduces the gap from m to $(m - 1)$, minus the R&D cost.
23 For simplicity we assume that π_1 and π_{-1} are unaffected by a change in competitiveness, although the analysis goes through essentially unmodified if π_1 is increased and/or π_{-1} is reduced.
24 See Aghion, Harris, and Vickers (1995).
25 From (19), $x_0 = \sqrt{r^2 + 2{\cdot}(\pi_1 - \pi_0)/w} - r$.
26 That is, S_u is the number of lines times the integral of the flow of secondary innovations per line: $S_u = \lambda^r H^r \int_0^u \lambda^d{\cdot}(h^d e^{-\sigma\alpha}/\lambda^r H^r)^{1-v} d\alpha$.
27 In Aghion and Howitt (1996) we derive the same result as below assuming that both research *and* development contribute to the growth of general knowledge.
28 Hence the model exhibits at least part of what economic historians sometimes call the "sailing-ship effect," whereby development continues even on obsolescent lines.
29 In particular if $v = 0$, that is if there are constant returns to development on a

product line, Bertrand competition for developers among the researchers who discovered the newest lines will drive the equilibrium share κ of the researchers down to zero. In other words, this is a case where no research will ever take place in steady-state equilibrium, and thus where the growth process, if any, will be driven entirely by horizontal product development on the initial lines. This is why in order for both research and development to coexist in a steady state, we must assume $v > 0$.

30 The difference in marginal products of research and development in the production function for secondary innovations in proportional to

$$\frac{v}{H^r} - \frac{1-v}{H-H^r},$$

whereas the arbitrage equation (A) can be rewritten as

$$r - g = \sigma \cdot \left[\frac{H-H^r}{1-v}\right] \cdot \left[\frac{v}{H^r} - \frac{1-v}{H-H^r}\right].$$

Thus research has a larger marginal product than development in generating secondary innovations. Research also has a larger marginal product than development in producing fundamental innovations since the marginal product of development is simply equal to zero.

31 See Aghion and Howitt (1996) for a detailed proof.

32 Of course it there were a variable sum of research and development then we would expect to find both our effect and the traditional Schumpeterian effect at work.

References

Aghion, Philippe, Dewatripont, Mathias, and Rey, Patrick (1995). "Competition, financial discipline and growth." Unpublished, April. Nuffield College, Oxford.

Aghion, Philippe, Harris, Christopher, and Vickers, John (1995). "Competition and growth with step-by-step technological progress." Unpublished, January. Nuffield College, Oxford.

Aghion, Philippe and Howitt, Peter (1992). "A model of growth through creative destruction." *Econometrica*, 60 (March): 323–51.

(1994). "Growth and unemployment." *Review of Economic Studies*, 61: 477–94.

(1996). "Research and development in the growth process." *Journal of Economic Growth*, 1 (March): 49–73.

Atkeson, Andrew and Kehoe, Pat (1993). "Industry evolution and transition: the role of information capital." Unpublished, University of Pennsylvania.

Blundell, R., Griffith, R., and Van Reenen, J. (1995). "Dynamic count data models of technological innovation." *Economic Journal*, 105 (March): 333–44.

Bresnahan, Timothy F. and Trajtenberg, Manuel (1995). "General purpose technologies: 'engines of growth'?" *Journal of Econometrics*, 65: 83–108.

Caballero, Ricardo J. and Jaffé, Adam B. (1993). "How high are the giants' shoulders: an empirical assessment of knowledge spillovers and creative destruction in a model of economic growth." In *NBER Macroeconomics Annual*. Cambridge, MA: MIT Press.

Campbell, John Y. and Mankiw, N. Gregory (1987). "Are output fluctuations transitory?" *Quarterly Journal of Economics*, 102 (November): 857–80.

Cannon, Edmund (1995). "Endogenous growth and depreciation of physical capital." Mimeo, Nuffield College, Oxford.

Corriveau, L. (1991). "Entrepreneurs, growth, and cycles." Ph.D. Dissertation, University of Western Ontario.

Crafts, N. (1997). "Endogenous growth: lessons for and from economic history." In Kreps, David and Wallis, Ken (eds.), *Advances in Economics and Econometrics: Theory and Applications*. Cambridge: Cambridge University Press (this volume).

De Long, J. Bradford and Summers, Lawrence H. (1991). "Equipment investment and economic growth." *Quarterly Journal of Economics*, 106 (May): 445–502.

Galí, Jordi and Hammour, M. (1991). "Long-run effects of business cycles." Unpublished, Columbia University.

Grossman, G.M. and Helpman, E. (1991). *Innovation and Growth in the Global Economy*. Cambridge, MA: MIT Press.

Helpman, E. and Trajtenberg, M. (1994). "A time to sow and a time to reap: growth based on general purpose technologies." CIAR Working Paper No. 32, August.

Jovanovic, Boyan and Nyarko, Yaw (1994). "The Bayesian foundations of learning by doing." Unpublished, NYU, April.

Lucas, Robert E. Jr. (1993). "Making a miracle." *Econometrica*, 60 (March): 251–72.

Nickell, S.J. (1994). "Competition and corporate performance." IES, Oxford (March).

Porter, Michael (1990). *The Competition Advantage of Nations*. New York: Free Press.

Redding, Stephen (1993). "Invention, innovation and technical progress." M.Phil Thesis, Oxford University.

Reinganum, Jennifer (1989). "The timing of innovation: research, development and diffusion." In Schmalensee, R. and Willig, R. (eds.), *Handbook of Industrial Organization*, Vol. I. Amsterdam: North-Holland.

Romer, Paul M. (1990). "Endogenous technological change." *Journal of Political Economy*, 98: S71–S102.

Segerstrom, Paul S., Anant, T.C.A., and Dinopoulos, E. (1990). "A Schumpeterian model of the product life cycle." *American Economic Review*, 80: 1077–91.

Shleifer, Andrei (1986). "Implementation cycles." *Journal of Political Economy*, 94 (December): 1163–90.

Stadler, George (1990). "Business cycle models with endogenous technology." *American Economic Review*, 80 (September): 763–78.

Stiglitz, Joseph (1993). "Endogenous growth and cycles." NBER Working Paper No. 4286 (March).

Tirole, Jean (1988). *The Theory of Industrial Organization*. Cambridge, MA: MIT Press.

Young, Alwyn (1993a). "Invention and bounded learning by doing." *Journal of Political Economy*, 101 (June): 443–72.

(1993b). "Substitution and complementarity in endogenous innovation." *Quarterly Journal of Economics*, 108 (August): 775–807.

CHAPTER 9

Learning and growth

Boyan Jovanovic

1 INTRODUCTION

In this survey, I discuss four sources of growth of knowledge: research, schooling, learning by doing, and training. In trying to disentangle what is important; I emphasize the following facts: (1) even the most advanced countries spend far more on adoption of existing technologies than on inventing new ones, and (2) countries frequently adopt "dominated" technologies. These facts provide a useful background for evaluating the different theories. They will also sharpen the point that it is important to distinguish between technology and human capital.

The conclusion is two fold: First, for world growth, research outlays surely are essential. But for most agents in most countries, productivity growth is the result of their adopting existing technologies. This point deserves more emphasis than it has so far been given. Second, in the field of growth, theory is not much disciplined by fact – the handful of models that I survey contains a bewildering array of diverse engines of growth, few of which are based on any firm evidence.

I find that it helps to use the following terminology: Define *technologies* to be laws of physics that are relevant to a particular way of producing something. These laws are described in blueprints. A blueprint, however, is an incomplete description of what it is useful to know about the technology at hand. For example, even a thick manual – say a computer manual – does not guarantee that its reader will be able to use the technology effectively right away. *Human capital* is the knowledge of how to work the blueprints. The blueprint's incompleteness creates a role for training and learning by doing as ways of building up the technology-specific human capital. Features of technologies that can be clearly explained in manuals will not call for training or experience. Other features of the optimal decision are specific to the situation at hand, to the nature of the factors of production, the raw materials, the location, the workspace, the specifications of the output, and so on. These, the workers will have to be taught, or they will have to infer them through trail and error.

One class of models does *not* distinguish technology from human capital. I will refer to this class as *hybrid* models. In contrast to models in this class, one can distinguish technology from human capital, and one can assume that there are different types of technology, and/or different types of human capital. When a new technology appears on society's menu, unless the discovery was accidental, society pays an *invention* cost. Then there is the *adoption* cost. I shall focus on that component of the adoption cost to do with creating the human capital specific to the new technology. Essentially, this is the cost of training people – in school or on the job – to use the technology. Some of these costs are direct, others are in the form of forgone output. If there is no duplication in research, an invention cost needs to be incurred only once per new technology, whereas an adoption cost must be paid once per user. After this, there are just user costs.

When there are many types of technology, and many types of human capital, each somewhat specific to a technology, then it is not always optimal to pay the adoption costs in order to adopt the best technology. The class of models in which this is true, I shall call *adoption* models. There are three reasons why adoption models help us understand growth:

(i) Most countries grow not by inventing, but by adopting inventions of others. Evenson (1984) finds that developing countries issue few patents. Even in developed countries, most technical change derives from transferred technology (see Baumol (1993, chapter 8)).

(ii) Even in advanced countries, most of the costs of productivity growth are adoption costs: I will produce a rough estimate saying that in the US adoption costs outweigh invention costs by 20 or 30 to 1! To use a new invention, I must first learn that it exists, what it means, how to make it useful, where to acquire all the complementary goods, and so on. Schooling and on-the-job training, as well as applied research, are all ways to prepare me for using *any* technology – old or new.

(iii) Adoption models can magnify the effects of any institutional feature that affects the incentive to adopt: small changes in adoption costs seem to have a big effect on growth for much the same reasons as tax rates on saving do in "*Ak*" models. These models say that growth is explained by adoption incentives, which we know vary widely among countries.

I divide models into those that have scale effects, and "other models." The latter are divided into hybrid models and adoption models. I cover *some* of the models that I think are state of the art, and I apologize for omitting so many others. The plan of the body of the chapter is as follows. After introducing some notation in section 2, section 3 describes two models with scale effects: Arrow (1962), Jones (1995b), and Romer (1990), followed by a discussion of the relevant evidence on scale effects that seem invariably to accompany models of this type. I then end the section by showing how the introduction of adoption costs can act as a limit to scale effects – essentially a restatement of an argument made by Radner and Van Zandt (1992).

Section 4 takes up the description of *hybrid models*. These include Lucas (1988), Prescott and Boyd (1987), and Parente and Prescott (1994). It concludes with a discussion of the evidence bearing on these models – this is the class of models that has been subjected to most scrutiny.

Section 5 describes two adoption models: Parente (1994) and Lucas (1993), and concludes with a discussion of the evidence that bears on these models. This is the class of models where a lot remains to be done. Section 6 concludes.

2 NOTATION

I shall try to use consistent notation throughout. This will make it easier to compare and contrast the engines of growth. I shall use the term *agent* to denote the decision unit which may be an individual, a plant, or a firm. The agent's growth of knowledge can be written as

$$\frac{ds(t)}{dt} = F[s(t), a(t), S(t), A(t)]. \tag{1}$$

Here s is the agent's *state* this period – which may include things other than knowledge, a is that agent's action, and S and A denote the "population" state and action, sometimes denominated as a population average and sometimes denominated as a population total.

3 MODELS WITH SCALE EFFECTS

By a *scale*, I mean the number of agents in the economy and their endowments. A *scale effect* is a change in some per capita variables – productivity level or productivity growth – that comes about if we increase the economy's scale, while assuming that the *distribution agents' actions and endowments are unchanged*. So, a scale effect is a feature of the technology, not necessarily a property of equilibrium, as Young (1995) has recently emphasized. The two models I shall discuss in this section assume an exogenous and fixed labor quality, so in a sense they have no human capital. They do have different types of technologies – an ascending ladder. As formulated, they both have scale effects.

3.1 Learning by doing in the capital-goods sector

In *Arrow* (1962), the engine is learning by doing in the capital-goods industry. Each producer is negligible, and learning is purely external in that the efficiency of each producer depends on the cumulative aggregate output of capital goods. There are no invention costs: the menu of technologies expands as a joint product with the supply of capital goods. Each new capital good is of superior quality to the previous ones. There are no adoption costs either, so that only the latest vintages of capital goods are ever purchased.

Let s be the efficiency of a capital-goods producer, and a his output of capital goods. Aggregate output, A, of capital goods is, by definition, the economy-wide gross investment in the capital-using industries. Specifically, let $s(t)$ be the reciprocal of Arrow's labor requirement of a vintage t capital good. Then Arrow's equation (8) – his engine of growth – reads $s(t) = \delta(\int^{t} A(\tau)d\tau)^{\theta}$. To make this expression the equivalent of (1), we take the time derivative and obtain

$$\frac{ds}{dt} = \delta^{1/\theta}\theta s(t)^{1-1/\theta}A(t), \tag{2}$$

where $\theta > 0$. At any time, capital goods of different ages are in use in production, but all capital goods producers are equally efficient, so that $s = S$.

Arrow's model has a scale effect in the levels: in a bigger economy, A would be bigger; doubling the level of A at all dates raises the level of $s(t)$ by a factor 2^{θ}. There is *no* scale effect in the growth rate

$$\frac{1}{s(t)}\frac{ds(t)}{dt} = \theta\frac{A(t)}{\int^{t} A(\tau)d\tau}.$$

That is, doubling A at all dates leaves the growth rate unchanged.

The learning effects of A are like a public good – management learning perhaps, produced collectively by all the capital goods firms jointly with their output of capital goods. One could remove the scale effect in the levels by letting A be output *per worker* in the capital-goods sector. This changes the interpretation of A entirely, and it makes learning internal to the capital-goods producers, changing their optimal decisions. This is more or less how Parente (1994) and Lucas (1993) model learning by doing.

3.2 Learning though research

In *Jones* (1995b) and *Romer* (1990), and several other similar models like Aghion and Howitt (1992, 1995), Grossman and Helpman (1991), and Kremer (1993b), the engine is research. There are invention costs, but no adoption costs. The output of research is designs. Designs are sold by inventors to intermediate-goods producers. In equilibrium, per capita income grows at the same rate as the aggregate number of designs, S.

Let s be the cumulative number of designs invented by a researcher, and a the labor input that the researcher hires in his research firm. Then S is the cumulative number of designs invented by *all* researchers, and (1) can be written as

$$\frac{ds(t)}{dt} = \delta S(t)^{\gamma} a(t). \tag{3}$$

Romer assumes $\gamma = 1$.

Let $n(t)$ denote the number of researchers. If the population is fixed, so is the equilibrium number of researchers, so that $n(t) = n$. Then $dS/dt = nds/dt$. The growth rate of s (and therefore also of S) becomes

$$\frac{1}{s(t)} \frac{ds(t)}{dt} = \delta \text{nas}^{\gamma - 1}. \tag{4}$$

So long as population is fixed and $\gamma < 1$, the rate of growth goes to zero. If we once and for all double the population, and hence n too, we raise the growth rate at each date by a factor of 2.

Now assume that population, and hence presumably n grow at a constant rate g_n, the steady-state growth rate of s is equal to $g_n/(1 - \gamma)$ when $\gamma < 1$. There remains a scale effect in the levels, but there is no scale effect on the long-run growth rate.

3.3 Evidence

Arrow, Romer, and Jones identify capital goods as the conduit of higher productivity, and in support of this assumption, recent series (e.g., Gordon 1990) show capital goods falling in price relative to consumption goods. But these authors simply *assume* that capital goods have the greater technological opportunity for improved efficiency, and an open question is *why* capital goods should enjoy faster progress. Cooley *et al.* (1995) say that this is because capital goods are more human capital intensive, but Klenow (1995) finds that sectors that enjoy faster TFP growth do not hire a disproportionate number of non-production workers. If non-production workers are a good proxy for research intensity (which is by no means obvious), this finding constitutes evidence against Cooley *et al.*'s claim.

The secular decline in the relative price of capital is one reason why I have not highlighted the contribution by Rebelo (1991), in which the capital-goods sector is also the engine of growth. In that model, capital can reproduce itself with constant returns (the "Ak" feature) and there is (contrary to evidence) no technical change in that sector. The Ak structure is more appealing when one thinks of k as including physical *and* human capital (as Black (1995) does), but it still does not exhibit technical change, unless there are external effects (so that instead of Ak, one assumes $A(k)k$).)

The research model certainly gets support from cross-sectional firm data – firms that do R&D issue more patents, and their productivity is higher. And basic research – which is where the bulk of the inventions presumably come from – does seem to be associated with high rates of productivity growth at the firm level (Griliches (1986)).

What about the side implication of research-based models that there are *scale effects* (at least in levels)? They get modest support in time series and cross-section data.

Time-series evidence As Jones (1995a and b) notes, the world's productivity growth has not risen over this century. On the other hand, Kremer (1993a, section 4B) argues that the scale effect in (4) helps explain some long-run historical patterns. In particular, the growth rate of the world's per capita incomes is higher now than in earlier times when the world was more sparsely populated. A nice case study by Sokoloff (1988) shows that when effective market size grew in some US regions because of an expansion of the canal system, this was followed by a rise in patenting activity in these areas.

Cross-section evidence If we measure n and s at the economy-wide level, we would resoundingly reject (4), because big economies do not grow faster than little ones. Nor are bigger economies wealthier per capita – Backus *et al.* (1992) fail to find even *level* effects of economy size (although they find some effects of level effects of the size of countries' manufacturing sectors). At any rate, such tests are not the correct way to look for scale effects, because they ignore the obvious fact that technologies cross borders. In terms of (1), we know that S must include some measure of foreign knowledge, and A must include something about foreign actions – e.g., do they trade with us? This is precisely how Coe *et al.* (1995) and Keller (1995) proceed, extending the methodology Griliches (1979) proposed for analyzing the productivity growth of firms. They assume that research capital stocks are distributed lags of *total* research outlays, not of *per capita* spending, and so these capital stocks have the dimensions of *na* in (4). So, augmented in this way, the research engine seems to fit the facts at the country level reasonably well.

We should expect to see some scale effects, since research, as expressed in (3) or (4), is surely essential in generating at least some of the outward movement of the *world*'s knowledge frontier. And even when the world's knowledge frontier moves outward because of accidental discovery (which absorbs no resources) we expect a scale effect of the sort contained in (3). But, as Baumol (1993) argues persuasively, and as I will argue below, the lion's share the costs that the world incurs to raise its technological efficiency seems to be in the form of adoption costs, so that any scale effects that derive from invention should be small. Certainly this is so for the LDCs, and for all but a few developed countries.

How big a scale effect must we have in a research-based model? Young (1995) has emphasized that as the economy grows, we may see more duplication in research, and that this is one limit on scale effects. Here, I want to emphasize a different limit on scale effects of research – the adoption cost. This is what I do in the next subsection.

3.4 Adoption costs as a limit to research-based scale effects

One way to minimize scale effects is to assume that there is an adoption cost for each new technology, proportional to the number of workers that use it. What I am about to present is really a caricature of an argument made by Radner and Van Zandt (1992) who point out that more information can actually be harmful because the assimilation costs can outweigh the benefits! They argue that the costs of processing information acts to limit the size of organizations and the span of control.

To simplify, assume no physical capital, and that ideas are not embodied in machines. Let Y denote the output of final goods and A the number of ideas. The model is static, and production of A and Y is instantaneous and given by the production functions

$$Y = AL_Y, \text{ and } A = \eta L_A,$$

where $L_Y + L_A = L$.

The scale of the economy is measured by L. The only decision is how much labor to allocate to the research and the final-goods sector. Let these allocations be given by

$$L_A = \theta L \text{ and } L_Y = (1 - \theta)L.$$

We are interested in what happens to per capita income if we keep the distribution of decisions fixed (which here means a constant θ) and let the scale of the economy increase. If there are no adoption costs, this model clearly has a scale effect on the level of per capita income because

$$\frac{Y}{L} = \eta\theta(1-\theta)L.$$

So, if we double the scale of the economy, we double per capita income.

Let us now show how the presence of adoption costs can remove the scale effect entirely. Assume that workers must learn how to use the ideas. Suppose that each worker must familiarize himself with a fraction m of the ideas, and that the time it takes a worker to familiarize himself with an idea is τ. Since there are L_Y workers in the manufacturing sector, the total time cost of learning the ideas is

$$m\tau AL_Y = m\tau\eta\theta(1-\theta)L^2.$$

This means that the effective time allocation in manufacturing is

$$L_Y(1 - m\tau A) = (1 - m\tau\eta\theta L)(1-\theta)L$$

so that now, per capita output is

$$\frac{Y}{L} = (1 - m\tau\eta\theta L)(1-\theta)\eta\theta L.$$

Output cannot be positive unless $\eta\theta\mathrm{L} < 1/m\tau$, from which we find that

$$\frac{Y}{L} \leq \frac{1-\theta}{m\tau}.$$

There is therefore an absolute upper bound to the *level* benefits of scale.

4 HYBRID MODELS

In this section we turn to models that do not distinguish technology from human capital. Moreover, they do not distinguish types of knowledge, and so there is no distinction between invention and adoption. But since there are no scale effects in these models, they make sense only if adoption costs are the primary expense concerning the growth of knowledge.

1 In *Lucas* (1988), knowledge grows because time is taken from other uses and put into the accumulation of knowledge. Unlike Arrow's model there is no jointness in production; s is a worker's knowledge, a is the fraction of the worker's time spent learning, and (1) reads

$$\frac{ds(t)}{dt} = \delta a(t)s(t). \tag{5}$$

This formulation, first proposed by Ben-Porath (1967), can be termed "learning *or* doing," because only a fraction $1 - a$ of time can be devoted to production. For later purposes, note that the costs of growth of s are *convex* in the consumption good: because of diminishing marginal productivity of labor in the consumption-goods sector, raising a is more and more costly.

In equation (2.5) of Lucas (1993), (5) is modified to allow for spillovers

$$\frac{ds(t)}{dt} = \delta a(t)s(t)^{1-\theta}S(t)^{\theta}, \tag{6}$$

where S is average knowledge. (Note that (6) is *not* part of Lucas's adoption model described in section 5 of this chapter.)

2 *Prescott and Boyd* (1987) replace the infinite-lived agent by overlapping generations. A worker is trained by the firm. The inputs are the knowledge *per older worker* S, and time forgone, which, unlike Lucas (1988), Prescott and Boyd express in units of forgone output, which depends on the time allocation of young and old workers, respectively a and A, and on the knowledge per older worker, S. This is necessarily a discrete time setup, in which we write s' for the knowledge bestowed to the young workers. Then (1) can be written as

$$s' = Sf(a, A). \tag{7}$$

The growth factor, $f(a, A)$, depends on the actions of the old and young members of the firm. The formulation has constant returns to scale, so that small firms train and produce as easily as large firms. Implicitly, therefore, the costs of productivity improvement are proportional to the number of workers, and implicity, therefore these are *adoption*-type costs – such as training learning by doing at the level of the worker. The knowledge is entirely firm specific; there are no spillovers from other firms. (Related models are Chari and Hopenhayn (1991) and Kremer and Thomson (1994).)

3 *Parente and Prescott* (1994) interpret s as the efficiency of a firm, and a as that firm's cost-reduction spending, and so expertise can be thought of as "business capital." But, since the number of workers per firm is exogenous, one can think of the workers as the users, and of the adoption cost as a training expense in firm-specific skills; these skills cannot be used in any other firm. Knowledge spills over from abroad. Thus S stands for *world* knowledge, the time path of which is exogenously given. They write (1) as

$$\frac{ds(t)}{dt} = \delta\left(\frac{S}{s}\right)^{\alpha} a. \tag{8}$$

Since $\alpha > 0$, the returns to a are higher for a backward economy. In contrast to Parente (1994), the cost to adjusting a technology is convex: to close the gap between a country's technology and the frontier by one half is more than twice as cheap as closing it fully. This convexity implies a convergence to the frontier productivity level. Presumably α depends on a country's degree of openness. But further microfoundations are needed for both δ and α.

4 *Evidence on hybrid models* The hybrid model is the only one that has been confronted with evidence in anything like a systematic way, and this is a point in its favor. However, I will focus here on a couple of ways that the model fails: (a) marginal products of capital are implied to be too high in developing countries relative to developed ones, and (b) there is evidence that the assumption that we can add up efficiency units of labor is not a good one.

At the outset, one should note that we still do not have reliable estimates even of how workers learn on the job as a function of training, learning, and so on. There are two reasons for this. First, on-the-job training is not observed, and is often inferred by assuming that it is chosen optimally. And second, vintage effects are hard to control for because observations of a worker are not, typically, well matched with the vintage or quality of the technology that he works on. In this line of the literature, the state of the art still seems to be Brown (1976), Haley (1976), and Heckman (1976). But it is hard to draw lessons these studies – the production functions they specify differ, as do their parameter estimates and conclusions.

On to evidence form aggregate data. Lucas (1990), in asking why inequality among countries persists in the face of apparent mobility of physical capital, argues that labor quality in poor countries is low – so low, that the marginal product of capital in the rich and poor countries is the same. Lucas used some old estimates of Anne Kruger's to pin down the human capital level in India relative to that of the US. For his argument to work, there has to be a sizeable externality in labor quality – i.e., in knowledge per head. The evidence, however, is not as favorable as Lucas's estimates suggest. He overestimates spillovers of knowledge when he attributes *all* the growth of the Solow residual to the growth of *domestic* knowledge. This is because, presumably, foreign knowledge matters as well. For example, in a somewhat different structure, Eaton and Kortum come up with the findings summarized in table 9.1.

Foreign knowledge can matter in two ways. First, it can enter the production equation. Let the production function for output be

Table 9.1. *Eaton and Kortum's spillover estimates*

Fraction of productivity growth in	Due to research performed in:				
	Germany	France	UK	Japan	US
Germany	0.38	0.06	0.09	0.31	0.16
France	0.23	0.22	0.09	0.31	0.16
UK	0.24	0.05	0.30	0.29	0.12
Japan	0.16	0.03	0.06	0.65	0.09
US	0.14	0.03	0.06	0.19	0.58

Source: Eaton and Kortum (1995, table 5), Growth Decomposition.

$Y = K^{\beta}H^{1-\beta}s^{\gamma}S^{\sigma}$. Here s and S mean the same thing as in (7). Then let $y = Y/H$, and $x = K/H$. Then

$$y = x^{\beta}s^{\gamma}S^{\sigma}, \tag{9}$$

and the residual is $s^{\gamma}S^{\sigma}$, and Lucas fits it to s alone. So his estimate of γ is really an estimate of $\gamma + \sigma[d\log(S)/d\log(s)]$. Since s and S are highly correlated over long periods of time, $d\log(S)/d\log(s)$ is close to unity, and so he is really estimating $\gamma + \sigma$.

Keller (1995) and Coe *et al.* (1995) offer indirect evidence on γ and σ. Indirect, because they construct scale-based measures of s and S. Note that scale effects are not necessary for there to be asymmetries related to countries' scale: the US and Luxembourg are similarly developed, yet one can be sure that the average Luxembourg resident learns more from the US than an American learns from Luxembourg. This could be due to two separate factors:

(i) The US does more *total* R&D than Luxembourg, so that there is more knowledge in the US – a scale effect.

(ii) The share of Luxembourg's imports that come from the US is far greater than the share of the US's imports that come from Luxembourg – an accounting relation, *not* a scale effect. In principle, both (i) and (ii) could work to create an asymmetry in the coefficients as calculated by Keller and by Coe *et al.*, and for this reason, one cannot interpret their estimates as direct evidence of the Lucas model.

Still, the evidence is suggestive. According to Keller, the point estimates of $\gamma = 0.18$, and $\sigma = 0.12$ are the most reasonable. (And his more recent work suggests that γ is actually less than σ.) The true γ is therefore possibly much less than Lucas's estimated 0.36, and the implied cross-country disparity in the marginal product of capital much bigger – see Lucas (1990, equation (4)). When γ is small, the model does pretty badly in terms of equalizing the marginal product of capital over countries, and the incentives for labor to migrate to rich countries go away. (Of course, just because a model fails to explain *all* of migration should not be a serious shortcoming *per se*. There are things besides human capital externalities that could lead to pressure for migration: (a) better infrastructure, (b) better schools, (c) more specialized services, and (d) more political freedom. (a) and (b) are public goods financed by the higher-average income in rich countries, and (a) and (c) would mean immigrants would earn more in the US than in their country of origin.)

The second possibility is that: S may enter the accumulation equation for s, as in (6) or (8) (Benhabib and Spiegel (1995, table 5, esp. column 5)), in a hybrid model, find evidence for such a formation. In this case Anne Kruger's procedure for calculating human capital stocks is not appropriate because it ignores the spillover. In fact, if, say, (6) were true, her procedure exaggerates cross-country differentials in proportion to θ (and the Keller estimate suggests that $\theta \approx 0.4$) and this again reduces the power of Lucas's explanation (in which we would now be forced to set $\sigma = 0$ in (9)).

A further difficulty with hybrid models that add up efficiency units of labor is the following: from the work of Bartel and Lichtenberg (1987), Mincer and Higuchi (1988), and others it is by now clear that more educated and more skilled workers have a comparative advantage in the implementing new technology. A hybrid model that adds up efficiency units of labor is incapable of variations in the earnings of skilled workers relative to unskilled that seem to accompany variations in the growth rate. In contrast, Parente's adoption model easily explains the correlation between the growth rate and skill differentials.

5 ADOPTION MODELS

These models (a) distinguish human capital from technology, and (b) distinguish different types of each. To the old Johansen–Salter vintage capital model, they add vintage-specific training and labor experience. This creates tension (absent in, say, Arrow (1962) where every investor wants to buy the latest vintage capital equipment) in choosing between a familiar method and switching to a better, but untried one. The adoption cost is in part implicit – it is the output forgone because of the productivity drop following a switch. I will not discuss the excellent Chari and Hopenhayn (1991) model as it has exogenous growth.

1 In *Parente* (1994), $s(t) = [n(t), h(t)]$, where $n(t)$ is an index of the currently

used technological blueprint (the "status quo" grade), and $h \in [0,1]$ is the level of expertise on that grade. Output equals $n(t)h(t)$. The action $a(t) \geq 1$ is the size of the firm's technological upgrade. Then

$$n(t + dt) = a(t)n(t). \tag{10}$$

If $a(t) = 1$, the firm does not upgrade. In this case, it accumulates grade-specific human capital (i.e., $h' > h$). But upgrading ($a > 1$) leads to a loss of expertise. The exact relation is

$$h(t + dt) = \begin{cases} h(t) + (\lambda[1 - h(t)])dt & \text{if } a(t) = 1 \\ h(t) - \kappa - \delta a(t) & \text{if } a(t) > 1, \end{cases} \tag{11}$$

where $\lambda > 0$ measures the speed of learning for a given technological grade $n, \kappa > 0$ is a fixed cost of upgrading (its presence ensures that upgrading will not happen continuously), and δ is a cost proportional to the size of the upgrade. When there is an upgrade, total adoption costs are $\kappa + \delta a(t)$.. Of course, these costs do not matter as λ gets large: any drop in human capital (resulting from an upgrade) is quickly restored, and h would revert to 1 almost immediately. So, for λ large enough, the optimal thing to do is upgrade as fast as possible. The same holds true as κ and δ go to zero.

2 *Lucas*'s (1993) is much the same, except that $h(t)$ can be any positive number, and the firm's output is $n(t)h(t)^{\alpha}$. Lucas has (10) as well, but instead of (11), he has (see his equations 4.2 and 4.7)

$$h(t + dt) = \begin{cases} h(t) + h(t)^{\alpha}dt & \text{if } a = 1 \\ \displaystyle\int_{-\infty}^{n(t+dt)} w[n(t + dt) - x]h(x)dx & \text{if } a > 1, \end{cases} \tag{12}$$

where $w(.)$ is a weighting function, and $h(x)$ is the firm's productivity on technological grade $x \leq n'$, with $h(x) = 0$ for $x \in (n, n']$. This formulation is consistent with there being no knowledge spillovers among firms.

Lucas has a more general distributed lag for how nearby technologies are related in terms of human capital requirements, but Parente actually carries out an equilibrium analysis of the problem. Stokey (1991) and Young (1993) analyze similar structures. Parente and Lucas conclude that highlighting the adoption choice can produce large growth-rate differentials. This is most firmly established in Parente's figures 4–8, in which there are small changes in tastes and especially in the adoption cost parameters λ, and κ, and δ. Parente's unpublished results show that the big effects on growth remain when instead of the unrealistically low value $\lambda = 0.025$ assumed in the published version, the simulations are done using the value $\lambda = 0.3$. In Lucas (1993), the parameter ξ (which is the one most likely to depend on national policies and institutions) seems to have a big effect on the long-run rate of growth as determined implicitly in (4.10). Also relevant is Lucas's (1993) exposition of the hybrid model and its *inability* to generate miracles and disasters for realistic parameters and policies.

Why do small changes in adoption incentives matter so much for growth? My intuition says that, just as in the Rebelo-type "*Ak*" model, costs of growth are linear in the growth rate, and not convex as they are in the hybrid models that we discussed. Consider (6); if we want s to grow at the rate g, say, we must give up $\delta^{-1}g$ units of effort in each period. But, because of diminishing returns for effort in the output equation, each additional unit of effort costs more – costs of growth are convex, and so the response of growth is less to external stimuli in the hybrid models. Now consider (11), in which $a = 1 + g$, where g is the growth rate of the blueprint quality. Suppose we constrain switches to be one per unit of time. Then the costs of growth are $(\kappa + \delta) + \delta g$, and they are *linear* in g.

But, if this intuition is roughly correct, then it is clear that the size of the growth response to external stimuli does not *have* to be bigger in an adoption model than in a hybrid model. One can write down hybrid models in which costs of growth are linear, and Mulligan and Sala-i-Martin (1993) have done so. One can also write down adoption models in which the costs of growth are convex (one would, in (11), simply change δa to $\delta(a)$ and assume that the function $\delta(.)$ is convex), and Cooley *et al.* (1995) have done so, with the result that the effects on the growth rate of changing the investment tax credit (their analog of Parente's κ) is much smaller than in Parente's model. So, as always, we need to look at microdata for information on what restrictions are, in each class of models, reasonable.

As descriptions of world growth, or the growth of the world's technological leaders, the Parente and Lucas adoption models would need to be extended to treat the growth of the frontiers of knowledge – the size of the technological menu. In Lucas's model, any upgrading speed is feasible. Parente restricts $h(t + dt)$ in (11) to be non-negative, which restricts the feasible growth factors $a(t)$ to those satisfying $a(t) \leq [h(t) - \kappa]/\delta$.

3 *Evidence on adoption models* There are three types of evidence in favor of the adoption model. The first two deal with the importance of adoption costs – evidence that λ is small, or that κ and δ are large. The last says that adoption costs have tended to vary a lot over time and space.

Adoption costs swamp invention costs The fraction of US resources spent on invention are tiny compared with resources spent on adoption. Money spent on inventing new things should be listed under "basic research." So let us suppose that all of basic research is invention. In the US, R&D spending is less than 3 percent. Of this, less than one-fifth is spending on basic research, and so about one half of 1 percent of US output goes on invention.

Now learning-based adoption costs. These include the cost of injecting the labor force with the skills necessary to work with the methods that have been invented. Such skills are learned in school and on the job. Mincer (1994) estimates that schooling costs are over 10 percent of GNP, and the bulk of what goes on in school is probably designed to inform us about the technologies that are on the menu of available options. Let us say that at least half of what goes on in school prepares us for work. (And, while some of the schooling teaches us to invent things too, since only 1 or 2 percent of people end up doing research, this number is negligible [$\approx (0.10) \times (0.02) = 0.002$ of GNP]). Mincer also estimates that on-the-job training and learning costs are about 3 percent – an underestimate in my opinion. To this, we add applied R&D spending, which is another 2 percent of output. So, total adoption costs are at least 10–15 percent of US output. This rough calculation says that adoption costs outweigh invention costs roughly 20 or 30 to 1. In LDCs the ratio must be astronomical.

Micro evidence that adoption costs are large

(a) Teece (1977) and Mansfield *et al.* (1981) produce firm-level evidence that, for many processes, the adoption costs of a single user (sometimes referred to as imitation costs) can be almost as large as the costs of invention. More generally, diffusion lags for new technologies are long, suggesting that some sort of sizable adoption cost is at work.

(b) Plant-level data show evidence of periodic, lumpy re-tooling (Power, 1993).

(c) Dwyer (1994) shows that faster growing sectors show greater interplant dispersion of productivity, just what one would expect in Parente's model when the upgrading decision is not perfectly synchronized.

(d) Entry of new plants and firms is common to all manufacturing industries. This is true of firms at the two digit level (Dunne *et al.* (1988)) and is true of plants at the four digit level in textile industries in Dwyer's data. Some of these are declining industries. This entry probably represents the adoption of new technologies of plants, reflecting, probably a high upgrading cost on the part of existing plants.

(e) Bakh and Gort (1993) produce plant-level evidence that productivity continues to rise significantly, years after a plant has been built, and this suggests large forgone output costs to switching technologies. In Parente's terms, λ is small, certainly less than 0.5.

(f) Klenow (1993) discusses evidence that technological upgrading is accompanied by sizable drops in productivity, which supports the vintage human capital model in general, and shows that κ or δ or both are significant.
(g) The management science literature has hundreds of examples of sizable learning-by doing gains – see Yelle (1979) for a survey.

People invest in dominated technologies Such investment are common. Let us say that technology A *dominates* technology B if, given equal experience with A and B, a firm would prefer A to B at all input and output prices. And let us say that A dominates B *conditional* on some price being given, if A is preferred to B no matter what the other prices happen to be. In this subsection I shall claim that, in a wide variety of instances, people invest in (conditionally) dominated technologies because of accumulated vintage-specific human capital.

Here are some examples: (a) The *steam engine* continued to be sold in substantial numbers by some US railroads, long after the Diesel engine (which conditionally dominated at the then prevailing prices of steam and oil) was introduced in the US in the early 1920s (Interstate Commerce Commission (1950, tables A-4, A-5)). (b) New *agricultural seeds*, arguably a dominant technology, took a long time to replace older ones (Griliches (1957)). The effectiveness of extension services in inducing the switch strongly suggests that ignorance about how to manage the new seeds was a key deterrent to adoption. (c) The *FORTRAN* programming language has been superseded, but programs continue to be written, and people continue to be trained in it. (d) By 1890, the steam ship had become more cost effective on long and short routes (Harley (1971, p. 227)), and yet *sailing ships* continued to be built well into the twentieth century. (e) As the *Boeing* 707 airplane was being phased out of commercial use in the US in the early 1980s, the largest market for it was foreign airlines, even though the 707 was dominated: at the then price of fuel in the US, it was inferior on grounds of fuel efficiency, noise, and baggage room. Some (but not an overwhelming proportion) of the 707s were sold to OPEC countries for whom their fuel inefficiency did not matter (see Goolsbee (1995)).

There are dozens of other examples. It is well documented that, in the US, most new technologies take years to spread to the majority of firms – see Mansfield (1968, chapter 8). And, since these firms invest more or less continuously, by implication their investment often flows into old technologies.

The existence of adoption delays and investments in old technology does not *per se* prove that the barrier is technology-specific human capital (as

Lucas and Parente emphasize). For that, we need stronger evidence. But we must note that the vintage *physical* capital model without adoption costs (Johansen (1959), Salter (1960)) does *not* explain why someone would invest in even a *conditionally* dominated technology. Having old equipment on hand will cause a firm to delay replacing it, but when it finally does so, the firm should invest in an undominated technology. Now if we add adoption costs in the form of sunk costs or gestation lags associated with the new technology, as Benhabib and Rusticchini (1991) do, the physical capital vintage model starts to look a lot like the Parente and Lucas models, since the sunk cost and gestation lags play the same role that training costs and learning periods do.

While vintage physical capital cannot explain dominated investment, we should note that, aside from vintage human capital, there are other explanations: (a) cheap labor induces poor countries to acquire old, labor intensive equipment that is not unconditionally dominated, (b) trade restrictions, as Romer (1994) has emphasized, prevent the adoption of foreign equipment, (c) finance constraints may preclude investment in bulky and expensive new equipment, (d) coordination problems to do with compatibility of machinery are severe in poor countries. It is worth elaborating on this last point: Frankel (1955, section 5), and Salter (1960, p. 85) discuss the issue in railways, in weaving, in iron and steel manufacture, and elsewhere. When such "network externalities" are important, reliable maintenance and availability of spare parts can greatly affect productivity, as Pack (1987, p. 119) notes. Let output Q depend on intermediates X_i as follows: $Q = \min_i(X_1, X_2, \ldots, X_n)$, where $X_i = 1$ with probability $1 - \varepsilon$, and 0 with probability ε. So ε measures "unreliability." Then $E(Q) = (1 - \varepsilon)^n$. So the effects of unreliability accumulate geometrically (see Matsuyama (1995) for more on this issue).

Adoption costs vary among countries and over time In most places, new technology is imported from abroad, restrictions on the operation of multinationals or joint ventures with a foreign partner will be quite important. Other legal and illegal historical instances of the suppressing of innovations, and other writings by economic historians are discussed at length by Baumol (1993). In Parente's terms, such activities raise κ and δ, with large predicted consequences for growth.

In some countries, skilled labor is scarce. Looking across countries, Benhabib and Spiegel (1994) find that the *level* of education is a stimulus to growth. This fits in with the hypothesis that educated workers have a comparative advantage in implementing new technology. Parente's model naturally explains the phenomenon: if skilled people have a higher λ, they optimally upgrade faster.

In some countries social mobility is restricted, and background is important for how talent is allocated to occupations. Galor and Tsiddon (1995) show that, if able people have a comparative advantage in new technologies, a system that overemphasizes background and restricts mobility across occupations will reduce long-run growth. Since countries differ a lot in the latitude they allow to social mobility, this may be an important explanation of differential growth experience.

6 CONCLUSION

The adoption models that I have described highlight the adoption margin as the critical one for growth, and in a specification like Parente's distorting this margin can greatly change the rate of growth. Why would adoption incentives differ among countries and over time? As it stands, the model can only answer this by focusing on initial conditions – the existing profile of past investments.

Of course there is more to it than this – tradition, institutions, politics, culture – all of these influence not only adoption incentives in particular, but attitudes to work and interest in material rewards more generally. The adoption model says that to understand the way tradition and institutions affect growth, we must analyze how they affect the incentives, and the sheer ability to adopt and implement technology from abroad.

I have not mentioned exogenous growth models, which usually are the starting point of any survey of growth theory. The debate about the usefulness of the exogenous growth model will go on. Here I will mention two points that relate the exogenous growth model to the points that I have emphasized above. First and foremost, these models assume that technological adoption costs are zero – two countries with the same level of education and the same level of physical capital will produce the same amount of output. There is no cost to accessing the world's frontier, no cost to adopting new technologies. This seems patently false – with all the computerization and high-speed communication that we now have, the process of *gathering* of information is becoming instantaneous and costless, but its processing and *effective* access certainly is not.

Second, the exogenous growth models imply that if countries have identical tastes and technologies, they should converge to the same level. But the evidence against unconditional convergence is overwhelming. Instead, there is a large empirical literature, summarized recently in Evans (1995), showing that one can find relatively rapid convergence to very different (and permanently different) steady states. Different steady states can be represented by country-specific "fixed effects," or by including some endogenous proxies for investment in human and physical capital, development of political and financial institutions, and so forth, on the right-hand side of a growth regression. Of course, fixed effects are unattractive if one is attempting to implement a complete theoretical model empirically. In practice, however, theoretical models abstract from all but the most crucial features of the environment that they seek to understand, and, moreover, attaching explicit names to some of the sources of cross-country heterogeneity is not hard; e.g., climate, topography, war, etc.

In the models that I do survey in this chapter, there is, of course, room for fixed effects to represent unmodeled differences among countries.

More to the point, cross-country regressions generally fail to recognize technological and factor-market dependence adequately. Most economies are not closed, there is factor mobility between most countries, and in most places people can access the technological frontier at a cost. Every business must choose from the menu of technologies. Anybody can buy a pentium, and yet, not everyone owns one. The point is that the option to transfer frontier technology, though generally available, is rejected in most places. Models that ignore this point miss what to me seems the key element in the process of growth and development.

Notes

I thank Will Baumol, Jess Benhabib, Fischer Black, Robin Cowan, Doug Dwyer, Paul Evans, Mark Gertler, Jeremy Greenwood, Jordi Gali, Chad Jones, Wolfgang Keller, Pete Klenow, Yaw Nyarko, Sergio Rebelo, and Noriyuki Yanagawa for comments, and the CV Starr Center of Applied Economics at New York University for technical assistance.

References

Aghion, Philippe and Howitt, Peter (1992). "A model of growth through creative destruction." *Econometrica*, 60(2): 323–51.

(1995). "Structural aspects of the growth process." Nuffield College, Oxford University.

Arrow, Kenneth (1962). "The economic implications of learning by doing." *Review of Economic Studies*, 29: 155–74.

Backus, David, Kehoe, Patrick, and Kehoe, Timothy (1992). "In search of scale effects in trade and growth." *Journal of Economic Theory*, 58: 377–409.

Black, Fischer (1995). *Exploring General Equilibrium.* Cambridge, MA: MIT Press.

Bakh, Byong-Hyong and Gort, Michael (1993). "Decomposing learning by doing in new plants." *Journal of Political Economy*, 101(4): 561–83.

Bartel, Anne and Lichtenberg, Frank (1987). "The comparative advantage of educated workers in implementing new technology." *Review of Economics and Statistics*, 69: 1–11.

Baumol, William (1993). *Entrepreneurship, Management, and the Structure of Payoffs*. Cambridge, MA: MIT Press.

Benhabib, Jess and Rusticchini, Aldo (1991). "Vintage capital, investment, and growth." *Journal of Economic Theory*, 55: 323–39.

Benhabib, Jess and Spiegel, Mark (1994). "The role of human capital in economic development: evidence from aggregate cross country data." *Journal of Monetary Economics*, 34: 143–73.

Ben-Porath, Yoram (1967). "The production of human capital, and the life cycle of earnings." *Journal of Political Economy*, 75(4, 1): 352–61.

Brown, Charles (1976). "A model of optimal human-capital accumulation and the wages of young high school graduates." *Journal of Political Economy*, 84(2): 299–316.

Chari, V.V. and Hopenhayn, Hugo (1991). "Vintage human capital." *Journal of Political Economy*, 99(6): 1142–65.

Coe, David, Helpman, Elhanan, and Hoffmeister, Alexander (1995). "North–South R&D spillovers." NBER Working Paper No. 5048.

Cooley, Thomas, Greenwood, Jeremy, and Yorukoglu, Mehmet (1995). "The replacement problem." Unpublished, University of Rochester.

Dunne, Timothy, Roberts, Mark, and Samuelson, Larry (1988). "Patterns of firm entry and exit in the US manufacturing industries." *Rand Journal of Economics*, 19(4): 495–515.

Dwyer, Douglas (1994). "Technology locks, creative destruction, and non-convergence in productivity levels." Unpublished Paper, Columbia University.

Eaton, Johnathan and Kortum, Samuel (1995). "International patenting and technology diffusion." Boston University.

Evans, Paul (1995). "How to estimate growth regressions consistently." Ohio State University.

Evenson, Robert (1984). "International invention: implications for technology market analysis." In Griliches, Zvi (ed.), *R&D, Patents and Productivity*. Chicago: University of Chicago Press.

Frankel, Marvin (1955). "Obsolescence and technical change." *American Economic Review*, 35(3): 296–319.

Galor, Oded and Tsiddon, Daniel (1995). "Technological progress, mobility, and economic growth." Working Paper No. 95-32, Brown University.

Goolsbee, Austan (1995). "Factor prices and the retirement of capital goods." Unpublished, Graduate School of Business, University of Chicago.

Gordon, Robert (1990). *The Measurement of Durable Goods Prices*. NBER, Chicago, IL: University of Chicago Press.

Griliches, Zvi (1957). "Hybrid corn: an exploration in the economics of technological change." *Econometrica*, 25(4): 501–22.

(1979). "Issues in assessing the contribution of research and development to productivity growth." *Bell Journal of Economics*, 10: 92–116.

(1986). "Productivity, R&D, and basic research at the firm level in the 1970s." *American Economic Review*, 76(1): 141–54.

Grossman, Gene and Helpman, Elhanan (1991). "Quality ladders and product cycles." *Quarterly Journal of Economics*, 106: 557–86.

Haley, William (1976). "Estimation of the earnings profile from optimal human capital accumulation." *Econometrica*, 44(6): 1223–38.

Harley, Charles (1971). "The shift from sailing ships to steamships 1850–1890: a study in technological change and its diffusion." *Essays on a Mature Economy: Britain After 1840*, Princeton, NJ: Princeton University Press.

Heckman, James (1976). "Estimates of a human capital production function embedded in a life-cycle model of labor supply." In *Household Production and Consumption*. Conference on Income and Wealth, Vol. CXXXIX, New York: Columbia University Press, pp. 227–58.

Interstate Commerce Commission (1950). "Bureau of transport economics and statistics." *Study of Railroad Motive Power*. Washington, DC: Interstate Commerce Comm.

Johansen, Leif (1959). "Substitution versus fixed production coefficients in the theory of economic growth." *Econometrica*, 27(2): 157–76.

Jones, Charles (1995a). "Time series tests of endogenous growth models." *Quarterly Journal of Economics:* 495–525.

(1995b). "R&D-based models of economic growth." *Journal of Political Economy*, 103(4).

Keller, Wolfgang (1995). "International R&D spillover and interesectoral trade flows: do they match?" Unpublished Paper, Yale University.

Klenow, Peter (1993). "Learning curves and the cyclical behavior of manufacturing industries." Unpublished Paper, Graduate School of Business, University of Chicago.

(1995). "Human capital vs. ideas: industry evidence on growth models." Unpublished Paper, Graduate School of Business, University of Chicago.

Kremer, Michael (1993a). "The O-ring theory of economic development." *Quarterly Journal of Economics*, 108: 551–75.

(1993b). "Population growth and technological change: one million B.C. to 1990." *Quarterly Journal of Economics*, 109: 681–716.

Kremer, Michael and Thomson, Jim (1994). "Young workers, old workers, and convergence." NBER Working Paper No. 4827.

Lucas, Robert E. (1988). "On the mechanics of economic development." *Journal of Monetary Economics*, 22: 3–42.

(1990). "Why doesn't capital flow from rich to poor countries?" *American Economic Review*, 80(2) (Papers and Proceedings): 92–6.

(1993). "Making a miracle." *Econometrica*, 61(2): 251–72.

Mansfield, Edwin, Schwartz, Mark, and Wagner, Samuel (1981). "Imitation costs and patents: an empirical study." *Economic Journal*, 41: 907–18.

Matsuyama, Kimonoir (1995). "Economic development as coordination problems." Discussion Paper No. 1123, Northwestern University.

Mincer, Jacob (1994). "Investment in US education and training." NBER Working Paper No. 4844.

Mincer, Jacob and Higuchi, Yoshio (1988). "Wage structures and labor turnover in the US and Japan." *Journal of the Japanese and International Economies*, 2: 97–133.

Mulligan, Casey, and Sala-i-Martin, Xavier (1993). "Transitional dynamics in two-sector models of endogenous growth." *Quarterly Journal of Economics*, 108(3): 739–74.

Pack, Howard (1987). *Productivity, Technology, and Industrial Development: A Case Study in Textiles.* New York: Oxford University Press.

Parente, Stephen (1994). "Technology adoption, learning-by-doing, and economic growth." *Journal of Economic Theory*, 63(2): 346–69.

Parente, Stephen and Prescott, Edward (1994). "Barriers to technology adoption and development." *Journal of Political Economy*, 102(2): 298–321.

Power, Laura (1993). "Causes and consequences of investment spikes in US manufacturing plants." Unpublished Manuscript, University of Maryland.

Prescott, Edward and Boyd, John (1987). "Dynamic coalitions, engines of growth." *American Economic Review, Papers and Proceedings*, 77: 63–7.

Radner, Roy and Van Zandt, Tim (1992). "Information processing in firms and returns to scale." *Annales d'Economie et de Statistique 25/26:* 265–98.

Rebelo, Sergio (1991). "Long-run policy analysis and long run growth." *Journal of Political Economy*, 99(3): 500–21.

Romer, Paul (1990). "Endogenous technological change." *Journal of Political Economy*, 48(5, 2): S71–S102.

(1994). "New goods, old theory, and the welfare costs of trade restrictions." *Journal of Development Economics*, 43: 5–38.

Salter, W.E.G. (1960). *Productivity and Technical Change.* New York: Cambridge University Press.

Schmitz, James (1993). "Early progress on the 'problem of economic development'." *Federal Reserve Bank of Minneapolis Quarterly Review* (Spring): 17–35.

Sokoloff, Kenneth L. (1988). "Inventive activity in early industrial America: evidence from patent records, 1790–1846." *Journal of Economic History*, 48: 813–50.

Stokey, Nancy (1991). "Human capital, product quality, and growth." *Quarterly Journal of Economics*, 106: 587–616.

Symposium on the New Growth Theory, *Journal of Economic Perspectives*, 8(1) (Winter): 3–72.

Teece, David (1977). "Technology transfer by multinational firms: the resource cost of transferring technological knowhow." *Economic Journal*, 87: 242–61.

Yelle, Louis (1979). "The learning curve: historical review and comprehensive survey." *Decision Sciences*, 10: 302–28.

Young, Alwyn (1993). "Invention and bounded learning by doing." *Journal of Political Economy*, 101(3): 443–72.

(1995). "Growth without scale effects." NBER Working Paper No. 5211.

Index